THE INCARCERATED MODERN

Stanford Studies in Middle Eastern and
Islamic Societies and Cultures

THE INCARCERATED MODERN

Prisons and Public Life in Iran

Golnar Nikpour

STANFORD UNIVERSITY PRESS
Stanford, California

Stanford University Press
Stanford, California

© 2024 by Golnar Nikpour. All rights reserved.

No part of this book may be reproduced or transmitted in any form or by any means, electronic or mechanical, including photocopying and recording, or in any information storage or retrieval system, without the prior written permission of Stanford University Press.

Printed in the United States of America on acid-free, archival-quality paper

ISBN 9781503636699 (cloth)
ISBN 9781503637634 (paper)
ISBN 9781503637641 (ebook)

Library of Congress Control Number 2023020708

CIP data available upon request.

Cover design: Michel Vranna

"We are prisoners entangled in fear and hope but still
In this fear and hope my heart is elsewhere
In this tumultuous city full of turmoil I am happy
For in this sorrowful camp I have another refuge."

MEHDI AKHAVAN-SALES
From "Me, This Autumn in Prison"
Written in Qasr Prison, Tehran, 1966

Contents

	Acknowledgments	ix
Introduction	On the Significance of the Iranian Prison	1
One	Lawlessness and Order	34
	The Qajar Roots of Modern Prisons in Iran	
Two	The Criminal Is the Patient, the Prison Will Be the Cure	61
	Building the Carceral Imagination in Pahlavi Iran	
Three	Like a Fertile Storm	95
	Prisons and Revolutionary Worldmaking in the Iranian Guerrilla Era	
Four	The Iranian Prison Goes Global	129
	Iranian Revolutionaries and the International Human Rights Movement	
Five	Making an Example	166
	Carceral Utopianism and Prison Expansion in Revolutionary Iran	
Six	Carcerality beyond Prisons?	191
	The Politics of Punishment in the Contemporary Islamic Republic	
Conclusion	Politics and Prisons beyond Reform	218
	Notes	225
	Bibliography	287
	Index	319

Acknowledgments

Writing this book has been a project spanning over a decade that took me to multiple cities for research, elicited I-don't-know-how-many sleepless nights, and required the boundless love, friendship, and material support of far too many people for me to easily name.

This book would not exist without the people at Stanford University Press. Kate Wahl has been a dream editor, making the writing and thinking in this book much sharper. Laleh Khalili probably deserves to be thanked three or four times for the different hats she's worn through this process—series editor, manuscript reader, supportive mentor. Cat Ng Pavel answered my anxious emails and took care of details with care and grace. Adriana Smith copyedited the manuscript as lovingly and as brilliantly as I could have ever dreamed. Tiffany Mok and the entire production team made the final part of making this book a joyful one.

At Columbia University, I had the opportunity to work with wonderful mentors whose work shaped my thinking and whose support kept me grounded. As my graduate advisor, Hamid Dabashi pushed me to challenge conventional wisdom and stay true to my moral compass. Anupama Rao was singularly important to shaping my intellectual interests, providing a model of engaged scholarship I have tried to follow ever since we first met. Firoozeh Kashani-Sabet took me under her wing and helped me better understand the historian's craft. Sudipta Kaviraj, Joseph Massad, and Timothy Mitchell provided invaluable scholarly guidance.

I was extraordinarily fortunate to be a fellow at the Center for the Humanities at the University of Wisconsin–Madison. The intellectual communities fostered by Sara Guyer at the center and Susan Stanford-Friedman at the Institute for Research in the Humanities were models of feminist humanistic inquiry. Megan Massino is among the most caring and supportive colleagues I have ever had, Florence Bernault provided precious mentorship, Giuliana Chamedes was a treasured colleague and friend, and Daniel Elam kept me sane over many drinks and much conversation, scholarly and otherwise.

As a postdoctoral fellow at the Crown Center for Middle East Studies at Brandeis University, I was part of an intellectual community that engaged with my work deeply and made it much better in the process. Pascal Menoret and Naghmeh Sohrabi were key in this regard, reading several versions of multiple chapters and providing sage advice, mentorship, and camaraderie. Naghmeh went the extra mile both while I was at Brandeis and after, helping me navigate the complex terrain of our shared field.

The Department of History at Dartmouth College has been a fantastic scholarly home, and my departmental colleagues have been nothing short of amazing. I owe extra thanks to Cecilia Gaposchkin, Udi Greenberg, Rashauna Johnson, Jorell Meléndez-Badillo, Ed Miller, Jennie Miller, Bethany Moreton, Annelise Orleck, Naaborko Sackeyfio-Lenoch, and Pamela Voekel for going above and beyond. Others at Dartmouth also have also provided much-needed community and friendship: Becky Clark, Kelly Chung, Yui Hashimoto, Mingwei Huang, Summer Kim Lee, Aaron Kovalchik, Laura McTighe, Eman Morsi, Lakshmi Padmanabhan, Emily Raymundo, and Aurora Santiago-Ortiz.

Numerous other brilliant colleagues, mentors, and friends across the academy have read parts of the book, talked to me about its ideas, and invited me to present my work in various forums, enriching it immensely in the process: Ervand Abrahamian, Ziad Abu-Rish, Stephanie Cronin, Noura Erekat, Bassam Haddad, Monica Kim, Afshin Matin-Asgari, Karen Miller, Sam Moyn, Babak Rahimi, Siavush Randjbar-Daemi, Kamran Rastegar, Cyrus Schayegh, Nazanin Shahrokni, Shahla Talebi, and Anand Yang. I am very thankful for the time and care afforded to my work by all of them.

I am particularly grateful to Arang Keshavarzian and Ali Mirsepassi for inviting me to be part of the *Global 1979* edited volume, which helped shape the thinking in this book. I am also thankful to the scholars who participated in that project for their generous and learned feedback.

Behrooz Ghamari-Tabrizi and Naomi Paik provided me with truly exhaustive feedback on my manuscript, giving me far more time, energy, and brilliance than I had any right to request of them. I am forever indebted to both of them.

There is no way I would have been able to do this work without the indefatigable librarians and archivists at the International Institute of Social History in Amsterdam, the Library of Congress, the British Library, the British National Archives, the National Library of Iran, and numerous university libraries and private archives across three continents. I am grateful that the best of the bunch, Wendel Cox, is at my home institution of Dartmouth.

I was able to conduct research for this book as a result of the generous support of the Social Science Research Council and the Whiting Foundation. I spent several months conducting research in London, and while I was there, I was generously taken in and shown around by Bryony Beynon, Paco Mus, and Ben Fordree. In Iran, I was housed by and supported by several other friends and loved ones, to whom I owe my heartfelt gratitude.

There are numerous people who spoke to me about their prison or political experiences or shared private archival materials with me, and although many of them prefer to go unnamed, they deserve the most profound of my thanks. Those are conversations that I will always deeply cherish. I have tried sincerely to honor the knowledge, experiences, and solidarity they've shared with me throughout this book.

In the last two years of writing this book, Joe Logan, George Pitsakis, and my teammates at Juniper Muay Thai in Philadelphia provided a caring community, not to mention a place to kick and punch things. In New Hampshire, I similarly relied on the friendship of Adrian Aguirre, Maria Kritikos, and Lindsay Tepfer at Baan Muay Thai. My record store people, especially Mike Catalano, Cory Feierman, and Evan Woodward, provided support, fun, and bonzers.

It's genuinely hard to say who I would be without *Maximum Rocknroll*. My experiences at *Maximum* shaped not only the course of life but also my aesthetic sensibility, my moral compass, and my ability to meet a deadline. The people with whom I collaborated while there—in particular, Grace Ambrose (who also helped edit this book), Arwen Curry, Layla Gibbon, Chris Hubbard, Clara Jeffers, and Martin Sorrondeguy—are some of the best friends I've ever had.

I'd like to extend my most loving and sincere thanks to my family: The Nikpours/Heravis (plus): Benjamin, Charlotte, Gelareh (my genetic half sister), Kamyar, Noushi, Irene. The Samiis/Eskandaris/Deals: Ryan, Hannah, Goli, Dariush, Layli, Haleh.

And then there are my ride-or-dies, many of whom have read, listened to, and edited my work, but all of whom have nurtured me in ways I cannot adequately describe in a simple acknowledgments section: Nimmy Abianka, Sarah Ahn, Nathan Albert, Althea Baird, Spencer Bastedo, Bidi Choudhury, Talya Cooper, Arash Davari, Sam Dolbee, Tina Dulani, Kim Garcia, Livia Huang, Naveed Mansoori, Manijeh Moradian, Mimi Nguyen, Ben Parker, Jessica Rosenberg, Eskandar Sadeghi-Boroujerdi, Solmaz Sharif, Courtney Szper, Lindsay Thomas, and Thera Webb (who also helped me with finding rare materials). Oh, and I would be remiss not to mention Hannah the Cat, whose cuddles and headbutts I miss deeply and who kept me company for the writing of most of this book.

Yumi Lee is the smartest person I've ever known and the most loving friend I've ever had. She's read every word of this book maybe eight times by now, and of course she's enriched every page, but much more importantly, she's reminded me at my lowest points that she would be by my side even if I ever just wanted to rip it all up and start again. She makes my life the sweetest in the world. Saranghae, Yumi.

My mom and dad, Floria Samii-Nikpour and Mahyar Nikpour, are the foundation of absolutely everything I do in my life and in my work. I truly cannot thank them enough for sharing their love of learning, for trusting me with their stories, and for encouraging me to make my own path even when none of us were sure just where that path was leading. This book is dedicated, with all my love, to them.

Introduction

ON THE SIGNIFICANCE OF THE IRANIAN PRISON

"Prison? Who understands what this word really means? For most people, this word is a mute concept. But you must look just one time behind the iron bars to dried and cracked lips, to bruised noses and bony faces, to begin to guess or at least try to guess what this word really signifies."

BOZORG ALAVI
Scrap Papers from Prison

PRISONS IN IRAN HAVE AN UNHAPPY GLOBAL REPUTATION. EVEN those onlookers with only cursory knowledge of Iranian politics or history have heard troubling accounts of arbitrary arrests and torture in today's Islamic Republic. In recent years, international news has been rife with stories of the hunger strikes of imprisoned human rights lawyer Nasrin Sotoudeh,[1] the opaque judicial processes endured by British national Nazanin Zaghari-Ratcliffe,[2] the arrest and execution of dissident pro wrestler Navid Afkari,[3] and numerous other high-profile cases of Iranians who have run afoul of their government and found themselves incarcerated or even executed for their political views or actions. Most recently, amid a mass uprising that began in September 2022, headlines have announced the arrests of tens of thousands of protesters. This grim knowledge of incarceration in Iran is underscored by the widespread circulation of popular English-language texts with titles like *My Prison, My Home* and *Prisoner of Tehran* that explicitly use the metaphor of the prison to describe life in the Islamic Republic[4] and by the work of global human rights organizations, which routinely remind us that in Iran "torture and other ill-treatment of detainees ... [is] committed with impunity."[5] From the first months after the 1979 revolution in Iran, exiled opposition groups have been among the most forceful in their condemnations of Islamic Republic prisons, describing these sites as places "where human dignity and animal savagery come face to face."[6] For their part, Iranian expatriates—with sometimes-competing political worldviews, agendas, and funding streams—have worked to publicize the carceral violence of the Iranian government around the world, publishing prison memoirs,[7] producing scholarship,[8] engaging in letter-writing campaigns,[9] and founding organizations in defense of incarcerated Iranian activists. Unsurprisingly, a vast network of sometimes strange bedfellows—including international human rights organizations and activists, scholars and journalists, Iranian diaspora organizations and parties, international politicians of differing political stripes, artists and celebrities, and a hostile US government—have focused on Iran's carceral record to name and shame the Iranian government, push for the release of detained Iranians, and, in many cases, advocate against the Islamic Republic's continued existence altogether.

Given this blood-soaked reputation, it might surprise some to learn that the Islamic Republic of Iran—that is, Iran's post-1979 government—has also long used Iran's prisons as proof of its moral and political legitimacy. Of course, the story that Iran's contemporary government promotes regarding Iranian prisons is different from the one told by its myriad critics. For the Islamic Republic, the 1979 revolution represented an unequivocal break with the brutality of the Pahlavi monarchy led by Mohammad Reza Pahlavi, and particularly with the violence and cruelty of the former shah's prisons and interrogation centers. Reminding Iranians of the spectacular violence of Iran's prerevolutionary prisons has long been a cottage industry for the post-1979 Iranian state and high-ranking officials in the government, just as downplaying the Islamic Republic's own record of carceral violence is those same officials' modus operandi. Institutions affiliated with the cultural wing of the Islamic Republic have sponsored numerous publications on the prisons and interrogation centers of the fallen monarchy, focusing the narrative on the incarceration and torture of clerical and Islamist prisoners. Major state-sponsored research institutes and initiatives, including those affiliated with the Organization for Islamic Propaganda (Sazman-e tabliqat-e eslami), publish regularly on the topic of torture in monarchic Iran, as well as on torture and political imprisonment in countries toward which the Islamic Republic is politically hostile, such as Israel.[10] Members of the Islamic Republic elite who spent time in the prisons of the prerevolutionary Pahlavi monarchy continue to routinely trade in tales of their prerevolutionary detention and torture. The carceral misdeeds of the erstwhile monarchy are so important to the narrative that the Islamic Republic tells about its own moral legitimacy that Leader Ali Khamenei himself devotes significant space on his official website to recounting his experiences of torture in the shah's prisons.[11] And, in what is perhaps the most physically conspicuous example of this pattern, the Islamic Republic has also turned some notorious prisons and interrogation centers first opened during the prerevolutionary era into museums, repurposing institutional spaces built by the fallen monarchy to affirm the government's official narrative of prerevolutionary violence, revolutionary struggle and martyrdom (particularly among revolutionary clerics), and postrevolutionary freedom.

Despite the present-day struggle over Iran's carceral record and the importance of the 1979 revolution and its aftermath to the story of incarceration in Iran, the country's modern prison system has its origins in the first decades of the twentieth century. And despite the urgent global resonance of today's political debates on the treatment of Iranian prisoners, political movements challenging Iranian prison violence and torture also originate in this earlier era. It is this making and establishing of the modern carceral state in Iran as well as concomitant transformations in Iranian social worlds and political vocabularies with which this book is centrally concerned. After establishing Pahlavi rule in 1925, long before these contemporary contestations over Iran's prisons, the Pahlavi government established Iran's modern prison system as part of its massive state-building and legal centralization efforts.[12] Just as the Pahlavi government centralized Iran's legal edifice in the late 1920s and early 1930s, codifying an unprecedented and expansive secular penal and criminal legal code, the early Pahlavi state planned for tens of new prisons. The nascent Pahlavi elite saw these new prisons as a solution rather than a problem and a necessary step in the project of transforming Iran into a civilized modern nation-state capable of taking its rightful and sovereign place on the global stage. Those affiliated with the Pahlavi state were proud of their prisons, which they claimed would help end an era of arbitrary despotism and colonial encroachment and usher in a new era of humane and modern punishments. They boasted that these new prisons would end the violence and torture they believed endemic to a "lawless" pre-Pahlavi era and would be capable of finally treating all prisoners equally regardless of their background. Later, Pahlavi statesman Ahmad Hooman, who over his career held numerous posts including deputy prime minister, acting minister of court, and president of the Iranian Bar Association, declared that under Reza Shah—the founder of the Pahlavi dynasty—Iran had finally built modern prisons that would hold prisoners "without any sort of class distinctions."[13] Members of the Pahlavi elite claimed that this "progressive" and "modern" institution—designed and built with input from criminologists and law enforcement specialists from Europe and the United States—could reform criminals into productive citizens and might even end crime altogether.

The foremost of these new modern prisons was central Tehran's Qasr Prison. Qasr's history is emblematic of the changes wrought by the legal and carceral transformations of the last century in Iran. Qasr Prison first opened in 1929 on the grounds of a former Qajar castle and royal gardens and closed its doors to prisoners in 2005 before reopening as a museum and public park in 2008, after over a quarter century of use under the Islamic Republic (figs. 1 and 2).[14] An institution to which this book will return several times, Qasr is a foundational if understudied site of Iranian political modernity. Even before the opening of the prison, when the lands were still largely in their former state as Qajar royal gardens, the grounds around Qasr were consecrated in the project of Pahlavi state nationalism. In 1928, when Iran's first radio masts and towers were built on Qasr's grounds just three years after the Pahlavi monarchy was declared, Reza Shah wrote his hopes for the rest of his reign and for Iran on a piece of paper and buried it in a tin container onsite.[15] A few months later, that site of nationalized hope and kingly aspiration would open its doors to prisoners as twentieth-century Iran's most expansive carceral space. The Pahlavi era would crash to an end just a few decades later with the 1979 revolutionary movement that eventually brought the Islamic Republic to power. During those electric months, revolutionaries and protesters targeted the shah's prisons, Qasr included, as a major recipient of their fury, forcing the release of political prisoners in an effort to materialize their demands for a radically different world.¹⁶ Today, Qasr has again been recast as a museum, and while its walls continue to bear the scars of nearly a century of incarcerated Iranians of all kinds, including those imprisoned by the Islamic Republic, the official story told on its curated placards and signs tells only a partial tale. This book aims to tell a different story.

FIGURE 1. Qasr Prison Museum. Source: Photograph by Golnar Nikpour, 2014

FIGURE 2. Qasr Prison Museum. Source: Photograph by Golnar Nikpour, 2014

PRISONS AND PUBLIC LIFE

This book examines key moments in the establishment of the modern prison system in Iran in the twentieth century, the resulting incarceration of millions of Iranians, and some of the responses among both Iranians and non-Iranians to those prisons. I argue that the making of the modern prison system has led to an elemental and enduring transformation in Iranian life. I further argue that this transformation did not happen in isolation but rather was part of a worldwide trend promoting and entrenching carceral solutions—surveillance, policing, and mass punishment and imprisonment—to a wide host of social issues. It is difficult to overstate the wholesale changes that the modern carceral system has brought to Iran.[17] For most of Iran's long pre-twentieth-century history, forced confinement was a relative rarity, and long periods of incarceration were practically unheard of. When someone did find themselves forced into confinement, it was typically for short periods while awaiting punishment. To put it simply, the types and lengths of punishments handed out in modern and contemporary Iran would have been largely unthinkable in the region in earlier eras. Even in the first years of Reza Shah Pahlavi's rule in the 1920s, after some piecemeal legal and carceral reforms had already taken place, prisoners in the capital city of Tehran numbered only a few hundred.[18]

The number of prisoners across Iran has increased steadily in the past century, including another vast leap after the revolution, culminating in this current era of mass criminalization and incarceration. According to Asghar Jahangir, the former head of the Islamic Republic's Organization of Prisons and National Security Measures (Sazman-e zendanha va eghdamat-e ta'mini va tarbiyati-e keshvar; hereafter the Prisons Organization), there are now at least a quarter of a million prisoners in 268 official prisons.[19] (This number, as high as it is, doesn't account for protesters jailed during the current anti-government uprising, nor does it perfectly account for everyone imprisoned before the uprising, as I will explain in later chapters.) This book traces this extraordinary transformation and expansion. Yet the story I tell here is not simply one of Iranian institution- or nation-building, despite the umbilical relationship between Iran's modern prisons and the history of Iran as a modern nation-state. Rather, I focus on what I call the "public life" of the modern prison. I chart the history of modern surveillance, punishment, and incarceration—that constellation of techniques and institutions of modern power foundational to the carceral state[20]—and argue that far from simply being a site of private suffering, the modern Iranian carceral system emerged as and remains a generative public locus for questions of citizenship, rights, and political belonging and unbelonging.

Some further explanation on what I mean by the public life of the prison is in order. I use this phrase in two linked senses, the first of which refers to the new public conversations that questions of law, punishment, justice, and incarceration elicited in Iran. The central topics of this book—prisons and punishment in Iran—have been of great significance to Iranians themselves. Seemingly as soon as plans for new modern prisons in Iran were formulated in the early twentieth century, Iranians were talking about these prisons, as well as the new forms of mass surveillance and policing that came along with them. After legal and carceral centralization, Iranians had to learn en masse how *not* to get arrested and incarcerated and what to do if they were. Like people all over the world, many Iranians did this through new popular genres such as prison memoirs, academic criminology and penology, newspaper accounts of crime and punishment, and, of course, through face-to-face interactions with Iranian institutions of policing, surveillance, and incarceration.

The modern prison system has also proven foundational for Iranian political and intellectual movements. Throughout the twentieth and twenty-first centuries, Iranians have written on, organized their political activism around, and produced copious art and literature contemplating the relationship between power, citizenship, modernity, and incarceration. From the earliest years of carceral centralization, dissident political parties were formed in Iranian prisons, and jail overcrowding—and the apparent explosion in criminality this overcrowding seemed to indicate—would become a matter of widespread public concern. It was in the aforementioned Qasr Prison that a small group of intellectuals lay the groundwork for the only mass-based party in the history of modern Iran, the communist Tudeh (Masses) Party. One of the party's founding members, novelist Bozorg Alavi, later claimed, "Prison, for us, was truly a school. We learned many things there. Not only about social and political matters, but also ... well, what didn't we learn? For example, I learned Russian in prison. I learned English in prison. In prison ... one read in earnest."[21] In other words, prison was the space in which Alavi and his comrades fully committed to their political lives. This experience is not limited to the Tudeh Party. From the prison communiqués of the Islamist Fadaian-e Islam party in the 1950s written on behalf of its imprisoned leader, Navab Safabi,[22] to the prison writings and paintings of leftist guerrillas like Bizhan Jazani in the 1970s[23] to digital prison mapping projects organized by formerly incarcerated dissidents in the contemporary Islamic Republic,[24] virtually every important modern Iranian political movement has produced work from and about prison. That these movements have theorized liberation from the context of modern confinement is, I argue, reflective of the modern prison's public life.

Yet the public life of the prison does not encompass simply that which dissident Iranians have said or thought in response to modern incarceration. Carceral practices (that is, linked systems of surveillance, policing, punishment, and incarceration) have transformed *all* Iranian social worlds and public life, not just those of the most politically engaged. My argument is not merely that modern carcerality produced new public cultures in Iran—

though of course it did—but rather that modern forms of incarceration have shaped the very notion of the public and of membership in that public. This is the second sense in which I theorize the public life of the prison. Throughout this book I argue that in drawing, redrawing, and policing the line between the "bad criminal" and the "good citizen," carceral techniques of the modern state have broadly shaped Iranian notions of citizenship, freedom, and nationalized inclusion (and exclusion). Labeling its expansion of prisons and prison factories "social work," for instance, the mid-twentieth-century Pahlavi state argued that expanded prisons were necessary to "train and educate" deviant Iranians so that they could "live nobly" as productive citizens in a progressive modern society; their ability to function as citizens was predicated on the expansion of the carceral state.[25] Pahlavi officials also touted the rehabilitative capacity of their new prisons, claiming that these prisons would help transform social deviance into social productivity. The names of Iran's carceral sites were changed in the 1960s to reflect this rehabilitative impulse; the Central Prison for Men and Women (Zendan-e markazi-ye mardan va zanan) was changed to Penitentiary (or place of repentance) for Men and Women (Nedamatgah-e mardan va zanan), while some prisons stopped using the word *prison* (*zendan*) altogether and instead called themselves Place of Counsel (Andarzgah).[26] This euphemistic sleight of hand mirrored the widespread adoption across the global south of the "penitentiary" model of mass imprisonment, in which "penitent" prisoners would learn the error of their ways, along the lines first imagined by Euro/American penal reform movements.[27] This pedagogical project has continued, albeit in different ideological dressing, in today's Islamic Republic. Referring to prisons as "virtue training schools" (*amuzeshgah-e nikiha*), the Islamic Republic has promoted its prisons as necessary spaces in the transformation of antisocial elements into ethical modern Islamic citizens.[28] In other words, the public life of the prison also refers to the way that carceral practices and institutions have worked to shape modern Iranian ideas and norms of national belonging, social deviance, healthy citizenship, and even Islamic ethics.

The Incarcerated Modern charts Iran's transformation from a decentralized empire with few incarcerated persons in the early twentieth century into a modern nation-state with a vast prison network today. How and why did this transformation happen? How did Iranians come to understand their increasingly surveilled and punished social worlds, and how have subsequent Iranian governments touted the benefits of their prisons? What political movements have emerged in the context of prisons or were organized against carceral policies? What sorts of solidarities have these movements demanded? Finally, what does Iran's penal history tell us about the expansion of prisons across the globe? Throughout the twentieth and twenty-first centuries, as the number of detainees in Iran's prisons, jails, and detention centers has exponentially increased, members of both the Pahlavi and Islamic Republic governments have, despite their political differences and against mounting evidence to the contrary, routinely promised that carceral methods would render Iranian citizens safer by simultaneously sequestering and "reforming" criminals into productive and moral citizens.

The wholesale shifts I outline above have been marked by a turn toward what I—borrowing from the recent tradition of critical prison studies—call the "carceral imagination," or a way of seeing the world in which the monitoring, policing, and incarceration of large numbers of people is normalized and viewed as inherent to the project of modernity. *The Incarcerated Modern* analyzes the methods by which mass criminalization and mass carceralization came to be seen in Iran as obvious and necessary responses to a wide host of social issues and a needed step toward placing Iran among the "progressive" and "civilized" nations of the world. I argue that Iran's new modern prisons, meant to showcase Iran's arrival on the global stage during the early Pahlavi era, were integral to this project of state nationalism and centralizing sovereignty. Throughout the book, I outline the processes through which the modern Iranian carceral system took root, showing that even as Iran has undergone profound political upheavals at the highest levels—the 1921 coup that brought Reza Khan to power (he would be crowned Reza Shah in 1925), the 1941 Allied invasion that brought his son Mohammad Reza Shah to power, the 1953 coup that kept the latter on the throne, and the 1979 revolution that toppled his rule in favor of an Islamic Republic—the carceral institutions, imaginaries, and publics inaugurated at the turn of the century have not only remained in place but also expanded in size and scope.

GLOBAL INSTITUTIONS, TRANSNATIONAL METHODS

Although in the main *The Incarcerated Modern* is a history of carcerality in Iran, it also argues that the history of modern prisons is foundationally *global*. Throughout the book, I show that modern carcerality is today a truly world-spanning phenomenon. This means that the history of the prison cannot simply be studied from Euro/American imperial centers, nor can modern prisons such as those found in Iran be treated as peripheral or exceptional to the story. The architectures, economies, and techniques of modern punishment—as well as peoples' responses to modern punishment—are transnational and linked. As I will show, even places imagined to be politically opposed, such as the contemporary Islamic Republic of Iran and the United States, are in fact in many cases today operating from the same carceral blueprints. Throughout the book, I dwell in the previously undiscovered connections between places not typically thought of together—for example, Mashhad, Iran, and Marion, Illinois. Several prisons in the contemporary Islamic Republic, including two maximum-security prisons in Shiraz and Mashhad, were built in the 1960s from blueprints of USP Marion in Illinois, now a part of the US federal supermax system. USP Marion, with its novel experiments in solitary confinement as well as "group therapy" sessions, was built virtually at the same time as its Iranian counterparts as both penal systems experimented with confining and controlling "trouble" populations. These same blueprints were also used for prisons from Israel to New Zealand, revealing the global scope of these carceral logics and architectures and undercutting exceptionalist and Orientalist arguments that would claim that the Islamic Republic's legal and juridical system has a singularly sharia-based pedigree unlike that found anywhere else in the modern world. Without a transnational approach in addressing the question at hand—that is, how and why did the modern prison take root in Iran?—links like this disappear into the historical ether.

To situate Iran's prison history in a broader global framework does not mean to erase its historical specificity but rather to better locate and understand that specificity. A brief example might help better situate this dialectic between the local and the global in Iran's prisons. In the contemporary Islamic Republic, the government has increasingly used new and globally popular technologies such as ankle monitors and biometric surveillance—a fact that links surveillance in today's Iran to cutting-edge surveillance and punishment technologies the world over. Yet in Iran this new tech is often used in novel ways particular to the needs of a modern authoritarian Islamic government. In early 2020, the Tehran Morality Police—the same police force responsible for the arrest and eventual death of Jina Mahsa Amini, the young Kurdish Iranian woman whose death launched an uprising in 2022—began using traffic cameras to not only issue tickets for traffic violations but to also send text message summonses to women for alleged hijab violations. Those who didn't respond to the texts and those who were issued repeat summonses were told that they were in danger of having their cars impounded.[29] This new policy portended the further expansion of similar surveillance tech into the world of "morality" policing. Amid the current uprising, in which the country's hijab laws have been a central recipient of protester fury, law enforcement and judicial officials have ominously promised an escalation in the use of these new technologies in policing issues they see as critical for proper Islamic morality, particularly hijab. The government's specific investment in molding what it views as proper Islamic citizens, then, is reliant on new carceral technologies that are used to surveil, police, and punish behavior all over the world.[30]

It is not only carceral technologies and geographies that are global. Throughout this book, I also examine the transnational solidarities forged by political movements of varying stripes—leftist, Islamist, liberal, nationalist, human rights–seeking, and more—in the face of increased political surveillance, incarceration, and torture throughout the twentieth and now into the twenty-first century in Iran. As early as the 1910s and 1920s, leftist prisoners were linking their struggles to those of imprisoned comrades around the world. For instance, Armenian-Iranian Communist Party member Ardeshir Avanessian was heartened to find "freedom for comrade Béla Kun" scrawled on the walls of his 1920s prison cell, a gesture of solidarity with the imprisoned Hungarian communist leader.[31] In the 1960s, European intellectual luminaries including Bertrand Russell and Jean-Paul Sartre advocated on behalf of Iranian political prisoners using the then-nascent language of human rights, and revolutionary Iranian prisoners, Islamist and Marxist-Leninist alike, linked their own struggles to political movements from Algeria to Vietnam to Palestine. Today, transnational prisoner solidarities remain a critical component in the politics of incarceration in Iran. Angela Davis, one of the founding theorists of the global movement to abolish prisons and among the most well-known revolutionary political prisoners of the twentieth century, wrote in 2020:

As a longtime political activist in the US, my own trajectory has been deeply influenced by progressive and radical resistance in Iran.... As a scholar whose research interests revolve around the emergence and evolution of the prison industrial complex and the central role of structural racism, and as an activist who has helped to organize numerous actions and campaigns over the years asserting the human rights of prisoners, I count myself among those who are especially concerned about the politics of the proliferation of prisons under the Islamic Republic of Iran.[32]

Davis's solidarity is a moving example of the long-standing links global prison activists have made with Iranian dissident movements. The famed Black revolutionary and intellectual also advocated on behalf of incarcerated Iranian dissidents before the 1979 revolution, writing a public letter on the topic of torture and political incarceration in Pahlavi prisons to Prime Minister Amir Abbas Hoveyda in 1972.[33]

Carceral politics do not always produce emancipatory solidarities, of course. Neoconservative political figures have also paid lip service to prisoner abuse in the Islamic Republic in order to further their own favored projects: crippling sanctions, military intervention, and US-government-led regime change (as opposed to Iranian people-led revolution). One emblematic instance came when former US secretary of state Mike Pompeo announced further sanctions on Iranians in 2020 with reference to "torture and other cruel, inhuman, or degrading treatment or punishment" meted out in Tehran's notorious Evin Prison.[34] These new sanctions came two years after sanctions levied by the US Treasury Department against Evin as an entity.[35] There is a distinction, however, between the solidarity of grassroots prison activists like Angela Davis and the worldview of US officials like Mike Pompeo, despite nominally sharing support for Iranian prisoners. That difference lies in the material gaps between horizontal solidarities and the vertical might of US imperial power. To situate the history of Iran's prisons in a global framework, then, is to analyze this history with a clear-eyed understanding of the global hierarchies of political and economic power implied by these differences while leaving open the possibility of the solidarities implied by Davis's half-century-long support for Iranian prisoner movements. Such understudied connections to global architectures, economies, discourses, and political movements belie an understanding of contemporary mass incarceration and carceral modernity that would divide global regimes of punishment along political fault lines despite shared institutional, political, and conceptual histories.

I further argue throughout this book that both techniques of surveillance and punishment and responses to those techniques are not only global but also *historical*; that is, they have developed and varied over time. Modern punishment techniques are not natural, stable outgrowths of forms of governance or static essential cultures or religions—that is to say, we cannot speak coherently of essential forms of "fascist punishment," "liberal punishment," "Islamic punishment," and so on—but are historically contingent (and constitutively transnational) practices that fluctuate and evolve in the shifting arsenal of modern power.[36] Carceral states, along with the prisoners whom they detain, are adaptive and fluid, and their responses to each other have changed over time or in response to external pressures. We can find an illustrative example of this phenomenon in the prison writing of leftist novelist Bozorg Alavi, whose epochal 1940s prison memoirs reveal the degree to which the techniques and practices of both prison-keepers and prisoners in Iran were learned through trial, experimentation, education, and experience. Alavi explains that, in his time in Qasr, the lives of the incarcerated were increasingly regulated and limited by prison officials learning how to detain and discipline their wards more effectively. Just as importantly, he notes, it was within prison that otherwise ordinary people could learn to endure any difficulty:

> The most difficult passions can be endured. A human being can get used to anything. Hunger, cold, all manner of bothers, and even torture—as long as they are repeated—can eventually be tolerated.... I saw prisoners at Qasr shiver through the freezing cold nights with barely a blanket and nonetheless wake up the next morning in good spirits.[37]

In response to this learned endurance, Alavi explains, prison leadership worked to make life progressively more uncomfortable for the incarcerated; if blankets were needed to stay comfortable, blankets would be taken away. If books provided comfort or helped pass the time, these too would be limited. I argue throughout this book that the archive of Iranian prisons across generations reveals both the continuities and learned transformations of the modern prison system in Iran.

Among the most important such learning experiences for the Pahlavi monarchy came in 1951–53, with the rise and CIA- and MI6-orchestrated downfall of popular anticolonial nationalist Mohammad Mossadeq as the country's prime minister.[38] It is now well established that in the aftermath of the US-led 1953 coup that deposed Mossadeq, the CIA and Israeli Mossad helped train the notorious new Iranian intelligence force, SAVAK (Sazman-e ettela'at va amniyat-e keshvar, or National Intelligence and Security Organization), further incorporating transnational policing, interrogation, and security methods into the arsenal of the Iranian state. As I show in later chapters of this book, the United States not only helped train SAVAK in this era but also sent military and police leaders—as well as considerable funding—to their Iranian counterparts in the service of "riot control" and an escalating "war on narcotics." It is no accident that the grisly interrogation tactics and forced recantations now most associated with the postrevolutionary era were first inaugurated in this post-coup escalation of tactics against the shah's political adversaries. Nor is it an accident that post-1979 methods of crowd control and drug-trade control would also be prefigured in this earlier moment.

The 1979 revolution would also serve as an inflection point in the history of Iran's prisons, after which the country's carceral system again underwent significant expansion. This era witnessed a vast increase in the total number of incarcerated Iranians, political dissidents and (mostly) otherwise, such that Iran is now among the most heavily carceral states in the world. The post-1979 state has also expanded the use of mass arrests during protests, forced confessions among political prisoners, and the death penalty for a variety of detainees. Although these methods predate the establishment of the Islamic Republic in Iran, they have come to be virtually synonymous with the violence of the post-1979 state due in part to the dizzying and seemingly ceaseless expansion in their use. Despite this, Iran's Islamic revolutionaries, like their hated monarchic predecessors, have also rhetorically promised a utopian carceral horizon. Just as members of the Pahlavi elite argued that a modernized prison system could end crime and violence altogether, the Islamic revolutionaries have promised that mass arrests of "counterrevolutionaries," from dissidents to drug users, will similarly transform Iranian society, either in teaching antisocial elements to integrate into a utopian Islamic society or in eliminating those elements altogether.

I argue throughout the book that Iran's carceral history is one of continued *escalation* and *adaptation* rather than one of meaningful alteration, let alone eradication, even after a successful revolutionary movement. I also flatly reject the view that would lay the blame for carceral violence in contemporary Iran—promoted by some rights advocates who call the Islamic Republic's prisons "medieval"—at the feet of an apparently retrograde Iranian or Islamic culture or religion, sealed off from modern global trends or internal political vicissitudes.[39] Such arguments are not only politically dangerous but also crumble under serious historical scrutiny. The long history of Iran's carceral institutions teaches us to see the disturbing expansion of the post-1979 carceral state not in isolation but as part of a decades-long story of expanding carceralization with links to carceral practices around the world. Exceptionalizing the prisons of the Islamic Republic—that is, seeing those prisons as uniquely and singularly violent or repressive in comparison with prisons around the world—misunderstands the roots of carceral violence in Iran and only works to foreclose possibilities for more just futures. Iran has already experienced one revolution in which prisons were targeted as unjust only to later be expanded; any new effort at social or political transformation would need to dig out the roots of carcerality in order to effect true change.

WHICH PRISONERS?

Throughout the book, I interrogate received wisdom on different forms of incarceration and different populations of prisoners. Despite the significance of political prisoners to Iranian carceral modernity, *The Incarcerated Modern* does not limit its analysis to prisoners of conscience (to use the language founded by Amnesty International) or prisoners of politics detained by subsequent Iranian governments.[40] Instead, in distinction to most of the extant scholarship on Iranian prisons—which has largely taken political incarceration and torture as its major focus—I look at Iran's prisons more broadly and also include a closer look at those who in Persian are typically referred to as Iran's "ordinary," or common-law, prisoners.[41] This long-standing historiographical focus on incarcerated political dissidents in Iran has arisen in part from the herculean efforts undertaken by these same prisoners—often under profound physical and psychological duress—to have their stories heard. In some cases, former imprisoned dissidents have become scholars and have written moving and insightful accounts of their experiences of incarceration.[42] In other cases, important scholarly and philosophical work about torture in Iran has been produced by former prisoners.[43] Still other works, particularly on the brutal prison massacre of 1988, represent the joint efforts of activist-scholars and former prisoners to shed light on events that the Islamic Republic has tried to suppress.[44] The most detailed historiographical excavation on prisons in Iran to date—a pathbreaking monograph by historian Ervand Abrahamian—focuses on the history of torture, forced confessions, and public recantations of incarcerated political dissidents in both pre- and postrevolutionary Iran.[45] In the past several years, there have also been several important new works by Iran-based scholars written in Persian, many of which analyze histories of both political and common-law incarceration in Iran.[46] These texts invariably end the story at the 1979 revolution, however, presumably a direct result of the censorious political climate in the Islamic Republic.

Despite the public focus on political prisoners, it is common-law prisoners who have always represented and continue to represent the vast majority of Iran's incarcerated population, both in the Pahlavi and now in the Islamic Republic periods. It is not simply because large numbers of prisoners have been held on ostensibly "nonpolitical" charges—drug offenses (which both before and after the revolution represent the overwhelming majority of Iran's detainees), sex work and sexual deviance, vagrancy, theft, brigandage, border crossing, corruption, murder, etc.[47]—that I turn part of my attention to those detainees or what has been said about or done with them. Beyond the practical fact of their large numbers, I argue that we must work to denaturalize the entrenched logic through which we conceptually (and thus politically) separate these two populations of prisoners.

The taxonomic divide between "political" and "nonpolitical" prisoners in Iran has historical roots in the different way these detainees have often been treated by subsequent Iranian governments, as well as in the way political movements have advocated on behalf of certain detained populations. The divide has its roots partly in the institutionalizing efforts of the early Pahlavi state, which typically grouped and housed Iranian prisoners into two distinct if uneven categories: "ordinary" prisoners (*zendani-ye 'adi*), who comprised the vast majority of Iran's incarcerated population, and "security" prisoners (*zendani-ye amniyati*), the smaller but significant population typically understood by dissidents and human rights organizations alike to be Iran's political prisoners. So important is this division that political prisoners, who are typically (though not always) housed separately, have been sent to general holding or to small provincial prisons with no other "politicals" as a form of punishment since at least the Qajar era.[48] The "divide-and-conquer" strategy of sending lone dissidents to less central or provincial prisons housing common-law prisoner populations, typically despite the protests of the detainees, remains in use as punishment today.[49] Resultantly, this division perseveres not only in the carceral institutions of the Islamic Republic—which polices the boundary between detained populations while nonetheless continuing to avow, as former chief justice Ayatollah Amoli Larijani did in 2019, that there are no "political prisoners" in Iran[50]—but also in the political work and imaginations of those global human rights advocates and organizations who campaign principally on behalf of Iran's incarcerated dissidents.

Human rights organizations like Amnesty International (AI) have a long-standing record of advocating mostly on behalf of their preferred category of nonviolent "prisoners of conscience," largely bypassing the hundreds of thousands of incarcerated Iranians—not to mention millions of global detainees—who do not fit this narrow classification. (Even Nelson Mandela famously and controversially did not fit AI's definition of the category.)[51] The widespread public focus on Iran's political detainees comes despite the fact that "political prisoners and prisoners of conscience constitute a tiny fraction of prisoners in Iran," a fact noted by the widely cited (and State Department–funded) Iran Human Rights Documentation Center in its 2015 report on Iranian prisons.[52] Yet despite the enduring view that would divide prisoners into hermetically sealed categories of "political" and "nonpolitical"—a logic that tacitly (if not explicitly) imagines common-law prisoners as the "real" criminals, just as it imagines that political imprisonment is only a problem "over there" in illiberal places like Iran[53]—many of the ostensibly nonpolitical charges for which people are detained in Iran, as elsewhere in the world, stem from self-evidently political issues. In other words, the historical processes through which *all* modern states, including Iran, have naturalized the notion that social issues from drug use to sex work to refugee border crossings to certain (but not all) forms of violence demand carceral intervention—as opposed to investment in mental and public health, education, community-building, a stronger social safety net, or various forms of accountability or reparative justice—have themselves been a product of profoundly *political* processes, and relatively recent ones at that. In the words of France's Groupe d'information sur les prisons (GIP), a prison activist group cofounded in the 1970s by French philosopher Michel Foucault, prison is by definition "a political experience, a hostage experience, a concentration camp experience, a class warfare experience, a colonized experience."[54] Thus, while this book centers the particularities of this story in Iranian history, it also endeavors to push our thinking about prisons and prisoners—and what political horizons we struggle toward with and on behalf of prisoners—all over the world.

A brief historical example might illustrate both the historical and moral stakes of my argument. In the 1980s, the nascent Islamic Republic of Iran and Ronald Reagan's United States both inaugurated policies that drove exponential increases in their respective rates of incarceration. In both countries, these new detainees were largely arrested on drug charges of various levels of seriousness. As each country undertook its own war on drugs under radically different political circumstances—the US as part of racist "tough on crime" policies[55] and the Islamic Republic as part of Khomeini's promise to purify Iran of Western influence and "counter-revolutionary" decadence[56]—increasing numbers of socially vulnerable people were ensnared in each state's dragnet. Yet despite the self-evidently *political* nature of policy decisions like these, we do not conventionally think of these drug-related detainees as "political prisoners" in either the Islamic Republic of Iran or in the United States nor do we typically ask why similar expansions of the carceral state targeting drug users were enacted in several places simultaneously. To the contrary, our conventional carceral categories push us to see incarceration in places like Iran and in the United States as fundamentally unlinked and different, with only places like Iran marked by the scourge of torture and political imprisonment, despite overwhelming evidence otherwise.[57] In demanding that we think about these populations of detainees together in Iran, and in analyzing both the victories and limits of discourses and movements for human rights on behalf of Iranian dissident prisoners, this book seeks not only to connect disconnected prisoner histories but also to expand the types of political conversations (and political movements) we are able to have about prisons and prisoners around the world. The stakes of this argument are rendered all the clearer when considering that today's Islamic Republic—not to mention countless other carceral states around the world—has justified its actions against not only "ordinary" criminals but also political dissidents by routinely referring to both as either "mere" criminals or terrorists and thus worthy of often-violent punishment.

WRITING PRISON HISTORIES

Although based on nearly a decade of public and private archival research in several countries across three continents, the writing of this book has never solely been an intellectual exercise. While my work has been inspired by innumerable scholars and writers who work on the history of prisons, policing, and punishment around the world, it has also been deeply shaped by far more intimate matters. I first came to be aware of the history of incarceration in Iran from my extended family, particularly my father and some of his closest friends, who have been surveilled, incarcerated, and even tortured for their political activities in both pre- and postrevolutionary Iran. Whether visible or invisible, all of them have borne the scars of their experiences on their bodies and psyches and live with traumas both shared and private every day. My own life has been shaped by years of hearing their stories—both the bright hope of their days of struggle and the dark despair of their days of forced confessions, broken movements, lost comrades, and dispersed dreams—and of absorbing their insights about life in a modern surveillance state. Incredibly, the setting for both the most dazzling of their aspirations and the most acute of their anguish was often the same place: the prison cell.

My family and I left Iran in the mideighties amid the devastating Iran-Iraq war, eventually settling into diasporic life in New York. As I grew older and found my own political footing, the first protest I attended on my own was a rally in 1999 to free former Black Panther Mumia Abu-Jamal from his then seventeen-year-long incarceration on death row.[58] I was seventeen years old at the time and barely knowledgeable about Mumia's case or the broader politics of racist incarceration and policing in the United States. Still, I skipped a day of college classes on a rainy weekday and joined a small group of wide-eyed young people on a bus from my then home in Manhattan to Philadelphia, which happens to be the city where I now live. Our group met up with a larger assortment of Philly-based organizers and activists and stood outside the city offices for several damp hours, holding signs with two simple demands: "FREE MUMIA!" and "FREE ALL POLITICAL PRISONERS!" Supportive passersby honked their horns and raised their fists with us in solidarity; others, less supportive, shouted racist epithets and obscenities. I was just beginning to learn about Mumia and the movements to which he was linked, but that day left me with a new and indelible certainty that political prisoners exist everywhere, from the city where I was born (Tehran) to the city that I today call my home (Philadelphia).[59] My work, and its myriad intellectual, political, and historiographical engagements, is born of a lifetime of trying to make sense of the seemingly linked but somehow-unseen connections between the stories I heard at home and the struggles and movements I encountered in the broader world. This book, then, in the spirit of Stuart Hall, must be understood as a diasporic endeavor, researched across continents and countries and languages by someone whose personal history has spanned those same continents and countries and languages, in circumstances not of my own making but nonetheless shaped by my ethical, political, and personal engagements.[60]

The political ethos of this book has also been deeply shaped by the rich tradition of scholarship and organizing emerging in the US context challenging contemporary systems of prisons, policing, and punishment to their core. Spearheaded by the work of Black feminist intellectuals and activists such as Angela Davis,[61] Ruth Wilson Gilmore,[62] and Mariame Kaba,[63] among many others, this scholarship, often termed critical prison studies, has been invaluable in analyzing modern and contemporary transformations in the US carceral system and in uncovering the ways that policing and punishment has placed grossly disproportionate pressure on the most vulnerable members of society, reproducing and exacerbating vicious social hierarchies.[64] For her part, Davis in particular has also sought to make connections between racist policing and prisons in the US and similar institutions around the world, including in Iran. She has also written movingly on the possibility of transnational solidarity in the face of these global forms of repression.[65] The work of these scholars and activists represents some of the foundational work critiquing prisons and policing around the world.[66]

Emerging out of Black liberation movements in the US, the abovementioned scholars and writers are linked to the broader movement to abolish prisons, which has recovered the language and legacy of abolitionism from the earlier movement to abolish the institution of chattel slavery across the Atlantic world. The contemporary abolitionist movement draws not only its language but also its moral and political force from its conceptual and material links to these earlier liberation struggles. It is this transatlantic historical context—marked as it is by histories of slavery, colonialism, and anti-Black racism—that gives contemporary abolitionism its profound urgency. Yet this great strength also reveals something of a conceptual conundrum and even limitation for those scholars and activists working outside of Anglophone or Atlantic world contexts: the language of abolition as such simply doesn't have the same historical weight in all global carceral contexts, including (crucially for this book) that of Iran. There is no one word in Persian that holds the same meaning that "abolition" does in the Anglophone context; yet the *idea* of abolishing prisons clearly resonates with certain critiques of prisons, policing, and the carceral state emerging from other contexts, Iran included. Material political links between prison abolitionism and the movement on behalf of Iranian prisoners have already been forged, most recently seen in Davis writing an introduction for Nasser Mohajer's extraordinary volume on the 1988 massacre of incarcerated dissidents in the Islamic Republic. Mohajer and his coeditors translated and collected the writing of numerous Iranians who lived the devastating 1988 prison massacre, in which the Islamic Republic surreptitiously executed several thousand incarcerated dissidents.[67] Some Iranian prisoners have themselves imagined a political horizon beyond the prison. One such dissident wrote of her incarceration in the late 1980s, "During this period, I was deeply involved in serious studies with my circle of friends, who were more or less of the same ideological persuasion. . . . We were concerned with how we were going to deal with political dissidents and our political enemies in the future society. We should not let any of our enemies be arrested. We wanted to destroy the prisons altogether."[68]

The Incarcerated Modern attempts to grapple with the questions of translation and political legibility raised above. Can critiques centering one historical context inform the writing of critical prison histories everywhere? Can (and should) prison abolition be a global project? For those of us dreaming of a world beyond the prison, should we all be dreaming in the same language? For those of us who write critical prison histories, the problem of translation and the question of legibility is more than linguistic minutiae. Historians dwell in what is particular and irreducible; the histories of carceral institutions in North America, the history of race in the US, and the languages coming from movements for freedom in these contexts can't be mapped onto carceral histories the world over. Varying forms of modern incarceration and confinement have distinct histories born of specific material, economic, and political conditions. There are discrete stories to be told about how the modern carceral system was introduced and adopted in different locales and how and whom these institutions have been used to control, confine, discipline, and exploit. There are also stories to be told about how particular detained persons have made lives and politics in the context of forced confinement. As such, this book tells a transnational story of a globalized institution—forged in the global crucible of colonial modernity, capitalism, and competing authoritarianisms—yet dwells in the specific details and archives of carceral institutions of modern Iran. Still, my project is ultimately a critical one, insofar as one of its undergirding proposals is that there is simply no reform that can salvage the modern prison from its foundational modern role as a space of extraordinary violence, discipline, and repression.

Of course, critiques of the modern prison are hardly limited to the North American context. Scholars of modern incarceration around the world have long noted the astounding failures of the modern prison at both the practical and moral level, juxtaposing these patent shortcomings with the institution's equally remarkable historical *success* in spreading globally in a very short period of time. In his pathbreaking book on the history of prisons in China, for instance, historian Frank Dikötter states in no uncertain terms, "The prison is a failed invention of modernity."[69] As Dikötter notes, the modern prison—an institution that he aptly calls a "cathedral of modernity"—emerged promising reform, rehabilitation, and the reduction of crime, distinguishing it from limited earlier forms of confinement, which had no such reformist pretenses. Yet, Dikötter continues, the unfolding of the twentieth and twenty-first centuries have shown the modern prison to be an "incontrovertible failure, in theory and in practice."[70] Dikötter's provocative insight proves no less true in the Iranian case, in which the early nationalist-reformist promise of the modern prison as a "progressive" solution to myriad social ills has given way to a widespread understanding of the prison as a site of habitual violence and social degradation, so much so that the officials in charge of today's judicial system in the Islamic Republic have at least nominally made reducing the prison population a top policy priority. The rise of modern prisons in Iran bears many points of similarity to the trajectory of other self-consciously modernizing countries that adopted the penitentiary model of punishment across the global south, whether colonial, semicolonial (as in China and Iran), or otherwise. As such, this book reveals the extent to which modern prisons were initially built in Iran by nationalist elites who were self-consciously adopting what they viewed as superior Euro/American models in order to transform Iran along "civilized" and "scientific" lines, such that dangerous criminals could be reformed into productive citizens. Now, in the Islamic Republic, the prison's constitutive reformist impulse has been reconstructed with the postrevolutionary state's notion of modern Islamic citizenship in mind. Yet both before and after the 1979 revolution, as in Dikötter's China, the carceral project has been a marked failure in Iran. This book argues that this failure is a defining feature of modern carcerality *as such* rather than a bug limited to Iranian prisons resulting from some particular cultural pathology.

The prison models championed by Iranian nationalists initially used the language and logic promoted by modern European penal reformers, who were themselves in turn enmeshed in the budding fields of positivist criminology and sociology. As historian Clive Emsley notes, English prison reformists of the eighteenth and nineteenth centuries considered themselves to be "progressive and humanitarian" and wrote about their efforts to "humanize" the prison in just those terms.[71] Their reformist language was echoed by later historians, criminologists, and scholars, who typically took reformists and philosophers such as Jeremy Bentham, Gabriel Tarde, and Cesare Beccaria at their word. As this book shows, these classic European criminologists dramatically influenced Iranian criminology and legal theory, as academic criminologists worked closely with the Pahlavi government to enact "humane" and progressive prison policies. Even in today's Islamic Republic of Iran, the academic discipline of criminology remains embedded in the government's approach to law enforcement and punishment at the highest levels. For instance, in June 2020, Mohammad Mehdi Haj

Mohammadi succeeded the longtime head of the Islamic Republic's Prisons Organization, Asghar Jahangir. Haj Mohammadi's qualifications included a master's degree earned in 2005 from the University of Judicial Sciences and Administrative Services (Daneshgah-e ulum-e ghazai va khadmat-e edari) with degrees in criminal law and criminology. The contemporary Prisons Organization has also routinely partnered with academic scholars in Iran and globally to produce research on its various public health programs, revealing the continued imbrication in Iran of academic research, state knowledge production, and the broader promise of carceral reform.

Reformist narratives remain entrenched in modern and contemporary understandings of the prison, in Iran as elsewhere. As Emsley notes, the rosy promises of prisons and prison reform today remain "embedded in many of the popular histories of crime and the institutional histories of police and penal policy. . . . They commonly presuppose a social order based on consensus in which the criminal is an identifiable, alien 'other' that preys upon ordinary, law-abiding citizens."[72] For their part, Iranian prison reformers of the Pahlavi era similarly used the language of progress to promote their own efforts, which were intimately linked to the larger project of Pahlavi modernization and state nationalism. Yet unlike the European reformers from whom they drew intellectually, Iranian nationalists promoted their reformist fixes as *civilizational salves* in a radically unequal world shaped by colonialism. Not only did Pahlavi nationalists and statesmen argue that the modern prison was more humane than what came before in Iranian history; they also argued—precisely after a century of colonial military and economic losses—that as an institution it would help restore Iran to equal footing with the "civilized" European powers, where it belonged. This belief in the civilizational capacity of prisons has also been a global one, promoted by nationalizing governments, prison reformers, and anxious modernizers across the global south.[73] Of similar prison reforms from Japan to Russia to Brazil to France to China, Dikötter writes, "These global developments were dynamically interrelated: portraying their mission as a fight against barbarism and inhumanity, prison reformers around the world operated within a comparative framework in which prison reform was seen as an indicator of a country's progress."[74] We could very easily add modern Iran to that list.

Of course, intellectual and political challenges to this reformist pretense of modern prisons are not new. Although Marx himself never wrote on the topic of prisons or prisoners as such, Marxist writing on the modern prison has perhaps the lengthiest career in challenging the humanist pretentions of the institution, making the case in numerous contexts that ruling-class needs and labor exploitation—and not humanitarianism or reform—drove the modern carceral project.[75] Yet the name perhaps most associated with critiques of liberal prison reformism is that of French philosopher Michel Foucault. Since the 1970s, the study of prisons, earlier dominated by positivist social scientific methods, has been shaped by Foucault's pivotal *Discipline and Punish*. Virtually no scholar of prisons since the publication of that influential work has escaped Foucault's lengthy shadow. Foucault periodizes the history of punishment in France, arguing that earlier, spectacular forms of public punishment—that is, public torture and execution—gave way in the modern era to a dispersed and self-regulating scheme that he terms the "carceral system." In arguing for a diffuse and decentralized understanding of power, he departs from those Marxist theorists who give the state pride of place in their analysis of power. For Foucault, the emergence of the carceral system, which not only includes the prison and its architecture but also penetrates society through surveillance, policing, schools, the military, etc., is intimately linked to the shift from earlier forms of sovereignty to modern forms of disciplinary power through which the modern subject is produced, individuated, and classified. For Foucault, then, power has a creative capacity, making even institutions like the prison not simply repressive but also productive spaces in which new subjectivities are formed. At the same time that the modern subject of discipline is produced in Foucault's prisons, hospitals, schools, and asylums, a typology of criminality also emerges, alongside a typified series of "correctional" behaviors for these newly classified criminals.

My work, like so many studies of prisons after Foucault, has been deeply influenced by the French philosopher and yet departs from several of his key suppositions. Although I take seriously Foucault's lessons on the expansive nature of the carceral and the productive capacity of power as well as his work to destabilize and denaturalize the category of the criminal, my work challenges his model in several ways. First and perhaps most obviously, I join a substantial pool of scholars and writers who have challenged the fundamental Eurocentricity of Foucault's writing, which simply elides the global histories of colonialism, capitalism, and the vast world beyond France in the making of the modern world. Despite significant analytical and theoretical differences, much of the earlier scholarly debate between Marxists, liberals, and postmodernists on the question of prisons, punishment, and criminology largely took Europe as its primary site of inquiry. As a result, scholarship on prisons, policing, and torture was long dominated by studies of Europe and the United States, while in the popular imagination, prisons and punishments across Asia, Africa, Latin America, and even Eastern Europe have often been discussed through an Orientalist lens promoting a culturalist view of violence.[76] Mary Gibson notes, however, that prison studies have more recently been shaped by a new generation of scholars who have taken up the question of carceral modernity as a constitutively global problematic, inexorably linked to but not reducible to colonial networks and hierarchies of power.[77] This investment in the global is not simply a matter of adding local case studies to an otherwise correct Foucauldian (or Marxist or liberal) structure. Studying the histories of modern punishment in global south contexts challenges Eurocentric historiography and theory more fundamentally, shifting not only how we think about the making of the modern world but also how we understand those seemingly set Euro/American histories in the first place.[78] History doesn't simply flow from West to rest; modernity has been built by imbricated global networks structured by capitalist and colonial hierarchies of power but shaped by people all over the world. As such, I argue that understanding prisons in Iran (or, say, Peru, or China, or Egypt) is fundamentally important not just for those local histories but also for the study and understanding of modern carcerality and modern societies, full stop.

The history of the Iranian prison reveals the practical limits of Foucault's model of a self-regulating disciplinary system in which power is always slippery and diffuse. Borrowing from what A. Naomi Paik has astutely argued in a different carceral context, I instead argue that the prison is a "dense node of state power" in which governments can remake or contravene "the rules that define and enable [their] authority."[79] An example might help better illustrate this point of critique. In *Discipline and Punish*, Foucault famously argues that modern forms of governmentality are by definition marked by the disappearance of public punishments and physical forms of torture. Modern power for Foucault is, after all, productive of disciplined subjects rather than centralized and baldly repressive. Yet anyone paying even cursory attention to our contemporary world knows that painful punishments, often termed "torture," are by no means a thing of the past in either illiberal or liberal states. To argue that torture is a vestigial remnant of earlier modes of sovereignty or regimes of power, as Foucault's schema could have us do, is not historically viable. In Iran, under first Pahlavi and now Islamic Republic rule, not only has torture persevered—despite being formally against the law both before and after the revolution—but, as historian Ervand Abrahamian has definitively shown, so have public trials and forced confessions.[80] Similarly, psychological torture including solitary confinement and other forms of destabilizing sensory deprivation—recently termed "white torture" by Iranian prisoners—has become disturbingly commonplace in recent years.[81] Although it is not a "spectacular" (that is, physical and visible) form of torture, white torture—which focuses on destabilizing the mind and psyche of the prisoner—is perhaps even more effective at breaking down detainees than is physical violence alone. The use of torture (conventional and "white" torture alike), forced confessions, and publicized recantations of political detainees in Iran all represent decidedly modern forms of punishment in which physical punishment is not itself applied publicly but nonetheless remains firmly part of public life. In this, my work also draws from that of Darius Rejali, who in his monumental study of the history of torture around the world notes, "Iranians relate to torture as a familiar event of modern life. They know it exists, and they never imagine that it is logically incompatible with telephones, central heating, weddings, elections, and other occasions of modern life."[82]

Moreover, unlike Foucault, who in his well-known philosophical writing is not interested in what prisoners *do together* while in prison, I look at the social worlds and political vocabularies built in carceral contexts.[83] In *Discipline and Punish*, the prisoner is a fundamentally atomized subject of power and yet also part of an undifferentiated mass population disciplined and produced as such by biopower; social worlds beyond those forms in this framework are at best irrelevant and at worst obfuscating. My work, however, is invested precisely in the question of how people live in carceral contexts and in the social worlds and languages they build together. This investment comes from an attention to the particulars of the Iranian archive, which contain plentiful examples of the importance of these carceral social worlds. In August 1979, for instance, Iran's foremost modernist poet Ahmad Shamlu published a one-of-a-kind dictionary of prison slang as part of his famous encyclopedia and lexicography of vernacular language, *Book of the Street* (*Ketab-e kucheh*).[84] Shamlu's *Book of the Street* is an extraordinary attempt at cataloging the poetics of everyday life in modern Iran and is arguably the most thorough written record of modern Iranian vernacular language. Shamlu explains in the introduction to the prison slang dictionary that the words collected therein were culled from the everyday language of "ordinary criminal prisoners," who put a premium on meanings and forms of communication that could elude the omnipresent prison authorities.[85] A sample of the terms includes the following:

> *bala* (literally, "up" or "above," or if in a building, "upstairs"): Military courts.
>
> *sandevich-e pedar* (literally, "father's sandwich"): The unique bread found in prison.
>
> *do va seh* (literally, "two and three"): The situation is bleak. (Used in conversation or in giving information.) For instance, in order to communicate to each other that things are bleak, they say "it is *du va seh*."
>
> *mullah* (literally, "a Shi'ite clergyman"): A long nail used to break a lock.
>
> *sukhteh jushani* (literally, "something that is burned and boiled"): Same-sex sexual activity.
>
> *'ame* (literally, "paternal aunt"): A spy.
>
> *khan dayi* (literally, "uncle Khan"): A senior prison official.
>
> *shazdeh* (literally, "prince"): A prison warden.

This compendium of prison slang—full of ironic meanings, double entendre, nods to prison hierarchies, and references to drugs, sex, friendship, religion, love, and violence—reveals something of the lived experience of prison life in the era of the 1979 revolution. And, although Shamlu's lexicography focuses on Iran's so-called ordinary prisoners, it nonetheless insists that everyday life in the prison is inherently political for *all* prisoners, gesturing to the political dimensions of making new social connections and languages in the context of modern state repression. In this sense, Shamlu's text resonates with the work of Italian Marxist Antonio Gramsci, who understood that the work of state power is always incomplete and that political subjectivities and languages can be formed through resistance to stultifying forms of state power such as the prison.[86]

HISTORICAL AND CHAPTER OUTLINE

The Incarcerated Modern covers three distinct historical eras in Iran—the late Qajar, the Pahlavi, and the Islamic Republic periods—moving from the late nineteenth century to the contemporary era. This historical chronology, during which Iran's carceral state was founded and continuously expanded, covers two monumental revolutionary movements—the Constitutional Revolution of 1905–11 and the Islamic Revolution of 1979—as well as two coups d'état, in 1921 and 1953. This chronology reveals the extent to which the infrastructure of the modern carceral state has undergirded seemingly ideologically opposed governments and disparate leaders, despite instances of transformative political change. The first chapter begins in the Qajar period (1789–1925) under the reign of Nasser al-Din Shah, who ruled from 1848 to 1896 and oversaw partial early efforts to reform systems of law, policing, and punishment. Though the country was never formally colonized by either of its main imperial adversaries (England and Tsarist Russia), both of whom instead took Iranian land in warfare and otherwise used economic means to encroach on Iran's sovereignty, colonialism is nonetheless a key part of Iran's early carceral story. In the late Qajar era, European colonial officers and company men were an increasing presence across Persia—both to protect colonial business interests and to control access to India, the crown jewel of the British Empire. One result of this presence was a steady stream of incidents in which Europeans were targeted for violence or theft by Iranians, leading to increasing anxiety about apparent Qajar "lawlessness." Colonial officers and Iranian reformists alike came to view the Qajars as incapable of dealing with the perceived explosion of criminality across the country and thus unfit to rule. These growing concerns, as well as reformist calls for the rule of law, led to calls for increased policing and punishment, setting the stage for Iran's first small prison network to be built in Tehran in the 1910s.

In chapter 2, I show that the Pahlavi monarchy (1925–79), which came to power in a British-aided military coup d'état in 1921 and formally took the throne in 1925, played a decisive role in establishing the modern carceral system with which Iranians have lived to this day. It was under the first Pahlavi monarch, Reza Shah, that Iran undertook the restructuring and centralization of its legal system in the late 1920s and 1930s. Alongside this process of legal centralization, Pahlavi officials began participating in European prison and policing conferences, eventually planning and building several modern prisons with insights gathered at these conventions. In this era, Pahlavi statesmen began to promote these new prisons as necessary and progressive modern solutions to myriad social and political crises, from lawlessness to colonial encroachment to social deviance. By vastly expanding Iran's prison system and extolling the social virtues of its penal factories and classes, the Pahlavi government championed its prisons as spaces of rehabilitation in which aberrant criminals could be transformed into productive citizens. From its inception, this state-led project was linked to the new academic discipline of criminology, which emerged in Iran on the heels of legal and penal centralization. In this chapter, I further chart the rise of social scientific and technocratic debates on prisons and punishment in midcentury Iran and argue that the findings of this new discipline often mirrored the government's rhetoric, if not their actions, regarding productivity, rehabilitation, gendered citizenship, and progress.

Chapter 3 is the first in the book to analyze prison writing and activism by incarcerated Iranian dissidents, moving to the heightened security environment that emerged after the US-led 1953 coup that reestablished the rule of Mohammad Reza Shah, the second and final Pahlavi monarch. This chapter focuses specifically on Iran's guerrilla movement, which spectacularly emerged on the public stage in 1971 and which shaped the landscape of Iranian political culture in the years leading up to the 1979 revolution. I argue that the guerrilla movement played a decisive role in the public life of the Iranian prison by widely publicizing the image of the shah as torturer among Iranians and non-Iranians alike. If the early Pahlavi state inaugurated the flowering of a modern carceral imaginary in which an expanded penal system was promoted as a progressive solution to modern social crises in Iran, guerrilla discourses turned the imaginary on its head, contending instead that it was precisely the Pahlavi state's carceral record that necessitated the shah's ouster.

In chapter 4, I examine the moment when the public life of the Iranian prison went global as a site of critique for the embryonic international human rights movement. In the 1960s and 1970s, concern with Pahlavi political prisons and torture came to animate global political activists, including intellectuals like Bertrand Russell and Jean-Paul Sartre as well as British parliamentarians and US congressmen. I argue that the growing international prominence of torture and political imprisonment in Pahlavi Iran provided both a rallying cry for a range of Iranian dissidents and a testing ground for the emergent global human rights movement at a time when this movement had not yet cohered into the industry it is today. As such, this chapter seeks to expand the historiography of two prominent and much-debated 1970s revolutions: Iran's 1979 Islamic Revolution, and the so-called international human rights revolution, in which human rights became the dominant global political language through which to challenge state-sanctioned political violence and abuse.

Chapter 5 begins in the midst of the final collapse of the Pahlavi monarchy in early 1979 and the establishment of the Islamic Republic of Iran, led by Ayatollah Ruhollah Khomeini. Although Khomeini once claimed that in a system of true Islamic justice no one would need to be imprisoned "for a single day," the decade between the shah's fall and Khomeini's 1989 death marked the deadliest period of carceral violence in Iran's modern history. This chapter begins by revealing an uncanny moment in the linked histories of Iran's prisons and revolution, during which exultant revolutionaries attempting to free prisoners from Evin Prison accidentally locked themselves into the notorious prison. This moment of chaos grimly foreshadowed what would come next: the immediate use of the most hated of the shah's prisons by the new government to hold significantly more prisoners than ever before, including many of those revolutionaries who had mobilized against the shah.

Chapter 6 begins in the period after the end of the Iran-Iraq war and the 1989 death of Khomeini and brings the story of the carceral state in Iran into the contemporary period. I show that during the 1990s, the technocratic and criminological logics of the late Pahlavi period returned amid Islamic Republic efforts to address several new carceral crises, including overcrowded and overwhelmed prisons and the crisis of prison-based HIV/AIDS outbreaks. I then move forward to the first two decades of the twenty-first century, arguing that in the aftermath of a mass protest movement in 2009, the Iranian government's carceral approach has moved forward on two seemingly incompatible yet connected tracks. First, the government has intensified its use of its carceral tactics, including surveillance, mass arrests, police and prison violence, and forced confessions in its continued effort to suppress public dissent. Second, high-ranking members of the judiciary have publicly avowed that a central goal is significantly *reducing* the number of people in Iran's prisons. I argue in this chapter that despite the seeming contradictions of these approaches, these strategies are in fact linked by the logic of carceral expansion, insofar as both the hyper-policing of the public sphere and efforts to hold fewer people in traditional prisons are increasingly tied together through the Islamic Republic's use of new surveillance and monitoring technologies.

The sheer number of people who have been swept up into jails, interrogation centers, police station holding cells, and prisons in Iran in the past century plus renders the project of writing a single history detailing every aspect of the modern Iranian prison essentially impossible. What this book endeavors to offer is a new method—one that is at once transnational, historical, and diasporic—to the study of modern prisons and the modern carceral state in Iran. In doing so, I argue that the making of the carceral state in Iran, with the modern prison at the institutional center of a vast network of surveillance, policing, and punishment, has indelibly changed the way in which Iranians live, how they relate to each other, and how they relate to their government. The project of carceralization in Iran is now over a century old, but it continues disturbingly unabated today, growing into new directions and using new technologies year after year. Yet despite this bleak fact, this book emanates from a foundational belief that to understand the historical origins of a seemingly entrenched site of social struggle such as the modern prison is to be able to imagine a world beyond those prisons as well. When a story has a beginning, it may very well also have an emancipatory horizon. This project has grown out of a dedication to that liberated future.

One

LAWLESSNESS AND ORDER
The Qajar Roots of Modern Prisons in Iran

IN THE SUMMER OF 1895, JUST A YEAR BEFORE THE ASSASSINATION OF Nasser al-Din Shah, the king of Qajar Persia,[1] an Iranian man identified only as Saduk attacked and attempted to murder his British employer, a Mr. Tanfield, in his bed with a sword.[2] According to Tanfield's account, the enmity between Saduk and his employer began when Tanfield fired Saduk for allegedly stealing a watch, money, and liquor. Tanfield worked for a private British firm called Lynch and Company, which had been granted a concession by the shah in 1888 to run a line of steamers along the Karun River, including to the southern city of Ahvaz.[3] This concession was one among several unpopular and lopsided business deals that Qajar monarchs, under financial duress, granted to British businessmen. The most famous of these economic concessions included the 1872 Reuter and 1890 Tobacco concessions—both also granted during Nasser al-Din Shah's forty-eight-year-long reign—as well as the 1901 D'Arcy oil concession, which would soon change the face of global and Iranian economies and politics.

The lopsided terms of these colonial deals and the corrupt homegrown monarchy they helped prop up famously elicited mass mobilizations by broad cross sections of Iranians at the cusp of the twentieth century. These responses—first the tobacco revolt of 1890 and later the Constitutional Revolution of 1905–11—have rightly been understood as the first mass protest movements in Iranian history.[4] However, the exploitative presence of British concessionaires and colonial officers elicited intimate and quotidian violence as well. Tanfield awoke to find the sword-wielding Saduk perched on top of him, and despite his drowsiness, he managed to fend off a would-be deathblow to his head with his left hand; he escaped with his life, though he lost his hand in the ordeal. When Tanfield was carried to the river to be taken away for safety and for medical care, crowds of locals cheered and celebrated the company man's numerous injuries and possible death.

In a subsequent report to his superiors in England about the Tanfield incident, J. F. Whyte, assistant political agent for Her Britannic Majesty's Consul in Iran, was apoplectic. Decrying what he perceived as the general lawlessness of Qajar Persia, Whyte exasperatedly claimed that the Qajar government seemed not to grasp that its inaction regarding known criminals and violent perpetrators was a problem. Because of "the inactivity of the local authorities," Whyte proclaimed,

> There has been another attack upon an Englishman, Mr. Tanfield, of Lynch and Co., who has been dreadfully wounded and disfigured. . . . I have tried in vain to get the would-be murderer punished . . . nothing whatever has been done in Shuster, where the mob hooted and stoned Mr. Tanfield as he was carried down wounded to the river . . . the local authorities have taken no notice of this brutal demonstration.[5]

Although the colonial archive doesn't capture the actual voices or stated opinions of the Iranian townspeople who were Tanfield's neighbors, their sentiments toward the British colonial presence are apparent in their recorded actions. They didn't view the Tanfield incident as representative of wanton lawlessness or unchecked criminality as did the British but rather experienced it as anticolonial catharsis—a reason to get together and cheer in the face of unwanted intrusion. As Tanfield himself reported:

> While I was being carried from the house to the riverbank at Shuster a large crowd of people followed us rejoicing that I had been killed, stone throwing also began, and a stone passed close to the bed on which I was

being carried. When I was put on the raft they lined the Shuster bank of the river and continued shouting abuse and throwing stones. Four ferrashes [servants] were sent by the Nizam to carry me to the river, but their presence did not appear to have any effect on the crowd.[6]

The colonial archive in late Qajar Persia is replete with incidents like Tanfield's, with innumerable accounts of Persian violence, thieving, and brigandage alongside just-as-common reports of locals' cheering on violence against Europeans. As one emblematic early modern German traveler wrote, "The ruler provides no protection against murder and theft. It is lawless here. An offended party may, if he can, seek satisfaction. Is it possible that so close to the Russian Empire such unrestrained conditions exist?"[7] Not only was there no codified law in Persia, this traveler bemoaned, but there was nothing that in his view even approximated *natural* law: "One would . . . think that a general natural law must be observed, but this is not so. Right now in Persia national laws do not exist, nor do natural laws. The cruel [shahs] have made sure that through their unnatural activities they have justified the injustice of their successors when dealing with present and future subjects."[8]

A seeming paradox thus emerges in the colonial archive of Qajar Persia. European accounts painted Qajar kings as despotic and absolutist in dealing with apparently aberrant or criminal behavior yet somehow viewed Qajar Persia as simultaneously anarchic. European demands were typically for *more* rather than less punishment, at least when the aggrieved parties were European nationals or capital. In their reports back to London and in communication with Qajar leadership, English colonial officers routinely called for a redoubled presence of armed law enforcement, lest English reinforcements be brought in to do the job. Colonial officers stationed in the city of Yazd at the turn of the century, for instance, referenced repeated attacks on Englishmen and complained that the "Persian Government either cannot or will not deal with such situations, which frequently arise." "I think," the same report states plainly, "that time has come when we should [have] Consular guards all through Persia."[9] If the Qajars wouldn't or couldn't police their own country, the logic went, the Crown would have to do it for them.

These European demands for more policing and punishment in Persia led to the implementation of increasingly carceral solutions. Just as crucially, it was also in this era that modernist Iranian reformers and intellectuals became invested in questions of law and legality as well as in techniques of policing and punishment in their reform efforts. As historian Firoozeh Kashani-Sabet aptly notes, these reformist intellectuals were eager to re-establish territorial and economic sovereignty for Persia against encroaching colonial powers, emphasizing legal reform as a "palliative" to their perceived decline vis-à-vis the European powers.[10] This investment in the rule of law, or what scholar Hadi Enayat (echoing Karl Marx) has called the "legal fetishism" of Qajar-era intellectuals,[11] would have increasingly carceral manifestations as Qajar and later Iranian reformists came to see modern prisons—counterposed against despotic Qajar dungeons—as part and parcel of their reformist project and a necessary component of Iran's civilizational leap forward into proper modern nationhood.

This chapter examines these interlinked histories and the forces undergirding them. How and when did modern ideas about imprisonment begin to circulate in Iran? Why were prisons taken up by reformers and intellectuals as potential solutions to various social problems? In this chapter, I show that several dynamics informed the gradual turn to prisons as a preferred mode of punishment in Iran in the late nineteenth and early twentieth centuries. I begin the chapter by analyzing late Qajar systems of law and order, in flux in this period, and show how law and order emerged as a driving concern of Iranian reformists in this moment of political upheaval, colonial exploitation, and Qajar corruption. For late Qajar-era reformers, systems of modern legality and carcerality were seen as integral not only for the political health of Persia in its perpetual fight against the twin ills of internal despotism and external imperialism but also for its global *civilizational* standing. At the same time, Qajar "lawlessness" became a concern of European colonial officers and companies, who made efforts toward creating their own structures of law and order in Persia. For the British, this was a practical matter—they felt compelled to protect their investments—that was undergirded by a civilizational logic in which Persia and Persians were painted as somehow simultaneously absolutist *and* anarchic. Amid these pressures, Iranian modernists and nationalists came to view modern forms of law and incarceration as potential salves to the political and civilizational ills they diagnosed all around the country. What had been a motley assortment of types of legal processes and punishments became slowly but increasingly centralized into carceral solutions—that is, jails and prisons. As I outline below, the late Qajar and Constitutional Revolution (1905–11) periods saw the reimagining of the practice of jailing, the figure of the prisoner, and the space of the prison from piecemeal elements of a hybrid system of law and punishment into essential parts of maintaining order as a properly modern nation. Although full legal and carceral centralization wouldn't happen until the early Pahlavi era of the 1920s and 1930s, the late Qajar period nonetheless set the stage for that more total transformation to come.

LAW AND PUNISHMENT IN THE LATE QAJAR ERA

During the reign of Nasser al-Din Shah in late nineteenth-century Qajar Persia, systems of law, policing, and punishment were in a state of flux. In this period the Qajar monarchy was, despite its reputation as absolutist, in fact quite weak; it lacked centralized state institutions, and its power didn't extend far beyond the capital city of Tehran. This is not to say that the Qajar monarchs were democratically inclined—far from it—but rather that the government simply lacked the capacity or manpower to function as an absolutist state. The Qajars' nonexistent standing military and minimal bureaucratic capacity meant that they couldn't reach the tentacles of the government into most facets of their subjects' daily lives. Unlike the Tanzimat reforms in the neighboring Ottoman Empire, which expanded and further centralized Ottoman military, education, and bureaucratic systems, late Qajar efforts at modernizing reform were fitful at best.[12] As historian Ervand Abrahamian notes, "Even after a half-century of half-hearted attempts to build state institutions, Nasser al-Din Shah ended his long reign in 1896 leaving behind merely the skeleton of a central government."[13] Significant state centralization and expansion would wait until the Reza Shah period.

Qajar rule relied on what Enayat calls a "parcellized" system of local leaders with independent sources of power of varying scope.[14] This included large landlords, tribal leaders, local notables, merchants, clerics, and *kadkhodas* (village heads in peasant regions, with peasants composing the majority of people in Iran in the era). There was no one single system of law or punishment across Qajar Persia; rather, local leaders made localized decisions based on political vicissitudes, community needs, power dynamics, the facts of the dispute, and the local customs of the region in question. The Qajars' widespread reputation as "lawless" and "arbitrary" was in part born of this dispersed and unsystematized network of legal arbitration. As some Qajar-era notables claimed through rose-colored glasses, "Society itself managed to take care of legal matters without interference from the central government."[15] In practice, this unregulated system of legal arbitration emerged as a major source of frustration among ordinary Iranians and the modernist intelligentsia alike.

Yet despite this lack of a centralized and codified legal regime, accounts of "lawlessness" in Qajar Persia tell at best an incomplete tale.[16] Before full-scale legal centralization in the twentieth century, legal arbitration was largely carried out in local contexts. Across Qajar Persia, both *'orf* (customary/civil law) and sharia (Islamic law) courts, as well as tribal councils, were available to adjudicate matters between parties or between the state and individuals. Although there was no formal check on the shah's power, "the *shari'a* and the Iranian-Islamic theory of the 'circle of justice' acted as a kind of informal constitution," with the Shi'a ulama, or legal scholars, delineating the boundaries and content of Islamic law.[17] Schematically speaking, punishments drawn from Islamic law fell into four major categories. *Hudud*—a term literally meaning "limits"—were fixed punishments as specified in sharia for certain actions such as theft, alcohol consumption, adultery, etc. Retaliatory punishments, or *qisas*, were granted to victims or the family members of victims (for instance, in cases of murder) to be meted out to the perpetrator in equivalent fashion. *Diyat* (monetary compensation) and *ta'azirat* (punishments at the discretion of the judge) rounded out this list.[18] As Abrahamian notes, although in theory *'orf* and sharia courts presided over distinct legal spheres, with *'orf* courts overseen by the shah and his governors and attending to matters of the state and sharia courts presided over by clerical *qazis*, this schematic division did not rigidly hold in practice. Complainants would sometimes be referred between the two types of courts, shahs appointed the *qazis* who presided over sharia courts, and *'orf* courts at least nominally purported to follow sharia.[19]

This hybrid legal form, in which the state and its constituents had to negotiate the unruly needs of competing and overlapping legal orders, was common in early modern Islamicate empires beyond Qajar Persia. Historian Fariba Zarinebaf notes a similar division in her study of crime and punishment in early modern Ottoman Istanbul, in which the divide between customary and Islamic legal structures was also messy in practice.[20] Despite these cross-regional similarities, however, the Shi'a ulama of nineteenth-century Qajar Persia enjoyed significantly more independence than did their Sunni counterparts in the Ottoman Empire. First, there was a latent bias against ʿorf judgments among the Shiʿa ulama—what Enayat calls an "ideological predilection" against customary law in Shiʿism.[21] Further, as Islamic law scholar Wael Hallaq notes, "By the time of European encroachment, the [Persian] legal establishment and its personnel ... stood in a more powerful position *vis-à-vis* the political establishment than ... their Ottoman counterparts (whose power was manifestly dependent on the political sovereign)."[22] This relative power of the Shiʿa legal scholars was itself a function of the weakness of the Qajar state and the development of a relatively independent hierarchy of Shiʿa ulama. Of course, beginning in the early nineteenth century, neither customary nor sharia courts had any jurisdiction in matters involving European nationals. After the humiliating 1828 Treaty of Turkmenchay and the 1836 Persian-British treaty—the results of disastrous wars with Iran's chief colonial rivals—foreign subjects and their property were taken out of the legal prerogative of Persian courts altogether, a sore spot for generations of Iranian nationalists to come.[23]

In customary courts, the hierarchy of decision-making was at least nominally standardized, even though law itself was not codified, with the shah's decree at the top of the juridical chain. Below the shah were his regional deputies (*navaban*), regional governors (*valian*), and village leaders (*kadkhodas*). Village *kadkhodas* were authorized to arbitrate in minor cases, while for more serious disputes, whether in terms of money, state matters, or degree of the action, the accused party would typically be referred to ruling state magistrates or higher-ranking representatives of the crown.[24] In tribal contexts, self-contained decisions regarding punishment were similarly made by councils of tribal leaders. Legal rulings were usually made by provincial officials as a sort of mediation between aggrieved parties, with arguments and witnesses heard and input taken. As one European missionary described in the late 1890s, "The city government ... the beglar-begi or mayor, and the kand-khudas [*sic*] or alderman ... hold court in their own houses, have their own prisons, decide cases, and punish with fines, the bastinado or imprisonment in chains."[25]

Although this system of legal arbitration was derided by both Europeans and Iranian reformists as arbitrary, there is evidence of some degree of public accountability in cases decided by local leaders and judges, at least insofar as these leaders did not want to arouse public ire by handing down obviously unfair judgments. One observer described the typical process of adjudication in the 1880s, with its eventual form of justice, thus:

> Plaintiff and defendant state their cases, either themselves, by a friend, or infrequently by a vakeel or substitute, often a professional lawyer. Documents and opinions are examined, witnesses heard and at times on oath; a whispered conference takes place between the governor, the vizier, and the chiefs of the law and religion.... [The governor] now delivers judgement on the merits of the case, generally a fair one.... He dare not give a manifestly unjust decision, for public opinion would be too strong for him, and an appeal to the King might cause him to be heavily fined.... Thus by a torturous path substantial justice is after a time obtained, but, as we stated at first, law is usually avoided by a recourse to friendly arbitration.[26]

Some commentators noted the relative quickness of this legal and punishment process. If the arbiter required it, punishment would be meted out swiftly, and the matter was then considered over. As one observer noted, justice in Qajar Persia was typically "administered by the provincial governors upon common-sense principles.... 'Strip him and let him go' is the rule in criminal justice in Persia, and most crimes are merely punished by an imprisonment of a few days or weeks, and a more or less severe beating. Justice is rough but rapid, and the worst punishments still in force are not looked upon by the Persians themselves as cruel or vindictive."[27]

In cases of murder, sharia courts would routinely turn over the accused to the family of the murdered to mete out justice. The details of a given case—that is, the identities of the accused and the complainant, the relative wealth of the accused, the situation in which the infraction occurred—were more important than the abstract type of transgression. There is considerable evidence that different punishments were meted out to the accused if the aggrieved party was a powerful person, even in similar cases.[28] A number of the above points are illustrated—if embellished in somewhat contradictory fashion—in the account of a German traveler in the late eighteenth century:

> Whoever is found guilty of murder, theft, or other important felonies, his life and goods are the mercy of the subject's Khan. The relatives of a murdered man often get permission from the governor to take revenge

on the murderer by killing him in any way they like, which often happens. Frequently, the Khan dictates the punishment and the usual ones are the bow string or the axe. More often things are more lenient. The accused who is able to give good presents can get away with the whip on the feet.[29]

Bribing local authorities for more lenient outcomes was typical. As one European missionary noted, with rather more self-awareness about the similarities between "East" and "West" than was typical for others of his ilk, "Wine-sellers, thieves, and lewd men and women are levied upon for hush-money, *à la* Tammany [Hall, in New York]."[30]

Given the diffuse nature of the juridical order, it should come as no surprise that punishments for various infractions were heterogeneous in both nature and intensity. Yet despite the legal patchwork, there were several common practices and techniques of punishment throughout the period. By far the most widespread of these was the *falak*, or bastinado—the whipping of the soles of prisoners' feet, sometimes followed by forcing them to walk on these bloodied and swollen appendages. In certain prominent cases, this punishment was meted out in public squares (fig. 3). European and American travelers were often horrified by the practice, as was an American missionary and reverend by the name of Justin Perkins, who lived in Qajar Persia for eight years. An unsettled Perkins wrote in 1837 of his experience seeing a man receive the bastinado, "As soon as I had sufficiently recovered from my shock of horror at the scene, to speak composedly, I inquired the crime, and was told that the prisoner had been fighting. He doubtless deserved punishment, but this frightful method of administering it often makes me sigh for the *land of my kindred*, a *land of wholesome* laws, and of efficient yet *humane* administration" (emphasis in original).[31] This would not be the last time the idea of humane punishments would appear in the Iranian context.

The bastinado has been a remarkably durable form of punishment across centuries and forms of governance in Iran—it was popular before Qajar rule and has remained disturbingly widespread in both the Pahlavi and Islamic Republic periods. As Assyrian-Iranian Joseph Knanishu noted blithely in 1899, "This [the bastinado] is the most common form of punishment in Persia and one that almost every one is liable to receive at some time or other." Not every use of the bastinado was the same in terms of style or severity, though there were some common traits of the practice and the method by which it was carried out, as Knanishu explains:

> There are different kinds and sizes of bastinadoes in different places but the most common and simplest one consists of a beam like piece of timber which is raised about two feet above the ground. When the magistrate has given orders to have this punishment inflicted upon some offender ... the magistrate's servants take the offender and laying him down take off his shoes and stockings and bind his feet to the piece of timber. Then one servant standing on the right side and another on the left, each with a flexible stick in his hand, begin striking the soles of the offender's bare feet by turns. Whether this punishment is mild or severe depends entirely upon those who execute it.[32]

Other sources attest to versions of the bastinado wherein the whipping was done by bunches of sticks rather than one larger rod. A Detroit-based Iranian student named Melik Vartan describes the practice for a feature on Qajar Persia in a 1902 edition of the *Detroit Free Press*:

> Around [the offender] gather some half dozen prison attendants, hard featured men, under the command of the sheriff. Each carries a bundle of stout sticks with which he strikes with all his might upon the bare feet of the unfortunate wretch whose cries of agony and appeals for mercy are taken up in chorus by other prisoners awaiting their turn for punishment.... The amount of punishment given is regulated in a curious way. A judge in pronouncing sentence upon a criminal awards him not so many blows, but so many "sticks." A stick is used until it is broken, and is then cast aside. Accordingly a man who has received a sentence of a hundred sticks will be beaten until each of the hundred sticks are broken.[33]

The archive is replete with references to this practice. One seventeenth-century traveler to the Safavid court noted, "On the 14th, the King caused Two hundred Bastinado's [sic] to be given ... to the Captain of the Gate of the *Harem*," with whom he was displeased.[34] Another traveler noted the practice in the early Qajar era: "When [Fath 'Ali Khan] demands money and the subject does not pay it on time, heavy corporal punishment is certain. When a short while ago the chief Armenian priest sold some flour to a few of the

FIGURE 3. Public bastinado of an unidentified man in Zanjan. Source: Photo archive no. 0-3304-0-1ع. The Institute for the Study of Contemporary Iranian History Archives, Tehran.

followers of Aghasi Khan ... Fath 'Ali Khan had him publicly beaten on the feet."[35] Some accounts claimed that a prisoner could be whipped on the feet so brutally that death would result from the punishment.[36] By the Nasseri period (1848–96), however, bastinado to the point of death was seemingly rare. As one traveler explained, "The bastinado is administered upon the bare soles of the feet. Save by the King's express order, it is never nowadays carried to a fatal issue; in twenty years I never heard of a fatal beating. The ordinary application of the bastinado means what we should term a 'good hiding'—nothing more.... The bastinado is usually administered to all small delinquents who are not fined. It is the punishment of peccadilloes."[37]

The Qajar archive also notes numerous other eyebrow-raising corporal punishments, although many of these were undertaken relatively infrequently with some perhaps no more than rumors or one-off affairs. In his six-volume social history of the history of Tehran, Ja'far Shahri provides an extensive list of such Qajar-era punishments, executed by the state's *mir ghazab* (masters of wrath) and their *farash* (lackeys) on the orders of the shah or a local leader or dignitary. Shahri's sometimes salacious inventory of painful punishment techniques includes branding, flogging, beating, bone breaking, sleep deprivation, starvation, dehydration, burning, aural torture, rape, and execution. It also includes more imaginative punishments, such as hanging the prisoner upside down and hitting him with a stick, putting the prisoner into ice water, forcing the prisoner to drink "an entire pail of water," sitting the prisoner on hot bricks until they are thoroughly "kabobed," tying a rope around the prisoner's neck with the other end tied to a horse and making the prisoner run after the horse or have their neck snapped, force-feeding the prisoner feces, plugging the prisoner's urethra to make urination impossible, gluing the prisoner's anus shut, making the prisoner walk on broken glass or nails, removing the prisoner's eyes, burning the breasts of female prisoners, pouring pepper into the eyes of prisoners, sticking sharp objects underneath the fingernails of the prisoner, firing the prisoner out of a cannon, cutting off the prisoner's ears, and other such gruesome techniques.[38]

On the infamous *mir ghazab*, Abrahamian writes, "Wearing black hats and bright red coats, the Masters of Wrath led royal processions and displayed to the public the brute power of their sovereign. In appointing provincial governors, the shah bestowed on them both a Mir Ghazab and a jeweled dagger to symbolize his royal prerogatives over life and death."[39] Commentators of the era also routinely referenced the trademark red coats of the *mir ghazab*, which elicited fear and loathing in the populace. As the Assyrian Knanishu noted in 1899, "These executioners are easily recognized because they have to wear red clothes. The people look upon them with a great deal of horror, and they are indeed hard men."[40] In his 1886 travelogue, Englishman C. J. Wills, who lived in Persia for a decade and a half, noted the capacity of the *mir ghazab* and their assistants to both entertain and terrify onlookers, "The King never stirs without several gentlemen in red coats (executioners) and an ominous band of burly ruffians termed farashes ... each carrying a good switchy stick four to six feet long. These, to keep their hands on, they invariably ply upon the backs and legs of a good-humoured and grinning crowd; but when used in earnest it is another matter, and the shrieks of the victim soon attest the reality of the punishment."[41]

Sources of the era note that in "exceptional" cases, punishments such as "blowing from guns or mortars, crucifixion, walling up or burying alive, burning alive" were administered, and "in the few capital punishments of women," the offending party was "usually strangled, or wrapped up in a carpet and jumped upon, flung from a precipice or down a well."[42] Despite these spectacular accounts of grotesque or bizarre forms of punishment, capital punishment for male wrongdoers was typically done via hanging or throat slitting. Although common early in the Nasseri period, spectacular forms of public punishment and executions gradually reduced over the course of Nasser al-Din Shah's reign, in keeping with global norms. Some claimed that Nasser al-Din Shah did not enjoy watching capital punishments at all; as one source noted, the shah "is very averse to the shedding of blood, and has abolished the old custom of the monarch's presiding at capital punishments."[43]

The relatively few women who were put to death were typically poisoned or strangled.[44] As one female traveler of the era noted, "No women are ever imprisoned, although if mixed up in a crime they will probably be poisoned, but . . . such cases are of the rarest."[45] By far the most prominent woman to be executed in nineteenth-century Persia was the revolutionary women's activist, poet, and Babi firebrand Fatemeh Zarrin-Taj Baraghani, also known as Tahereh Qurrat al-'Ayn, who was punished for her transgressive political, social, and theological views by being strangled to death and thrown into a well in 1852. Qurrat al-'Ayn was executed as part of a brutal assault against disciples of the egalitarian and heterodox Babi movement in what was nineteenth-century Iran's most severe and sustained campaign of political violence.[46]

JAILING PRACTICES IN THE LATE QAJAR ERA AND INKLINGS OF MODERNIZING REFORM

Although Iran's first modern prisons would not be built until after the Constitutional Revolution of 1905–11, there were facilities used for detention dotted across the towns and cities of Qajar Persia. These sites were not typically built with incarceration in mind, as modern prisons later were; many were built as munitions forts or citadels.[47] These were colloquially known as *zanjirkhaneh* (house of chains) and often located in city squares, acting as holding cells for male offenders including drunks, thieves, and others accused of various public nuisances. (Some sources also attest to the use of the word *dustaqkhaneh* for these dungeons, a word of Azeri Turkish origin.) These were quite unlike the imposing modern prisons that were to be built in just a few decades' time. These facilities held relatively few persons for what were usually short lengths of time, until a detainee was either granted his outright release or given his actual punishment. In these facilities, prisoners typically had to pay for their own comforts and necessities. As Wills noted of these structures in 1886:

> The Zanjir-khana ... is an apparently insecure structure having a mud wall about ten feet high. Half-a-dozen soldiers occupy the gateway; their unloaded muskets are piled in a corner. Three of the men are asleep under rugs. The other three, the guard on duty, are warming their hands over a small earthen pot full of charcoal. Each man is provided with what is termed a shisht-per, a heavy bludgeon surmounted by an iron head having six projections: a simple weapon, but one with which you might stun an ox. The sentry salutes on seeing a European, and immediately seizes one of the rusty muskets. He calls to the gaoler, who is a hungry-looking man in a dirty cloth coat. We have come to see the gaol; and this man the governor of the prison, has no objection; for he knows he will get a fee.... Fees from the prisoners, fees from the friends of the prisoners, fees perhaps from their enemies.[48]

Further, some local *kadkhodas* or other regional notables had simple jailing facilities—sometimes just small rooms—in their homes. A Belgian-born woman by the name of Carla Serena noted in her 1883 travel writing that small jailing facilities were also scattered in the private homes of some wealthy individuals, evidently used to confine wayward servants of the master of the house.[49]

Europeans routinely decried what they saw as unjust Persian punishment practices, championing the "civilizing" effects of European legal influence on the Qajar state. For instance, George Curzon—the famed British colonial officer who would go on to be viceroy of India—described the "barbarity" of the "merciless and Oriental" approach to punishment in Persia and celebrated what he saw as the "increasing influence of civilized opinion" in the country.[50] Yet some Iranians expressed similar judgment of *European* punishment norms, including long-term prison sentences and heavy prison labor. In an 1885 article in the London-based newspaper *The Globe*, Sultan Morad Mirza Qajar Hessam ol-Saltaneh, the shah's late uncle, was quoted as defending his country's punishment practices by comparing them favorably to European prisons. "I punish in such a way," the Qajar noble once stated, "that his punishment will not be forgotten and his fate will be a terror to evildoers. Unlike you Europeans, I don't shut the man up for years."[51] Nor was it only the Qajar elite who expressed such a view. Another such encounter was noted by the Englishman Wills, who visited a small Qajar jailing fort that held a few dozen men. Wills described the conditions of the building unsparingly: "The khelwut was a low dank apartment, filthy in the extreme, the air almost poisonous with its ten inhabitants. . . . The three condemned men, ironed as were those outside, were sitting with both feet securely fixed in the kang, or beam. . . . The place was pestilential, and alive with vermin."[52] Yet the Englishman admitted that the officials he encountered were keen to remind him of what they viewed as the brutality of European systems of justice. Wills remarked, "As we left the prison the gaoler said with a smile, 'Ah, sahib!' We are more humane than you are; there are no vindictive punishments here, no long sentences, no lifelong imprisonments; and you see our prisoners do no work—absolutely none."[53] Other European writers also compared punishment norms in terms surprisingly similar to this sarcastic jailer. Englishman S. G. W. Benjamin mused in 1887, for instance, "Is there not many a criminal with us who would gladly pay a given sum rather than linger in prison? On the other hand, are there not some people who would prefer losing a finger—nay, a hand—rather than endure a ten thousand dollars fine or five years imprisonment? All these questions are comparative."[54]

General amnesties of prisoners were relatively commonplace and often granted yearly on Nowruz (Persian New Year) on the first day of spring or upon the appointment of a new provincial governor, although some violence would occasionally accompany these amnesties. As Wills noted, "These occasions are much dreaded; for if the new governor wishes to make an example, then six, a dozen, or a score of prisoners may be executed at once."[55] Curzon noted this practice in more anodyne terms, writing, "There is no such thing as penal servitude for life, or even for a term of years; hard labour is unknown as a sentence; and confinement for a lengthy period is rare. There is usually a gaol-delivery at the beginning of the new year; and when a fresh governor is appointed, he not uncommonly empties the prison that may have been filled by his predecessor."[56] Other sources attest to practices that essentially amounted to decentralized grassroots amnesties—that is, people going to local jailing facilities and demanding the release of certain prisoners held therein, often on Nowruz or important religious holidays. Another European traveler noted this practice with great disdain:

> During the last few days of Moharram it is also common for the rabble to go to the prisons and insist on the release of criminals whom they demand by name. In order to prevent the storming of the prison and save his own life the jailer is forced to yield. In 1884 sixty-five men were thus set at liberty. So much is this an annual custom that the authorities dare not as yet interfere to prevent it, although the progressive spirit dominant during the present reign will undoubtedly check it before many years. Fortunately for the credit of the government and the well-being of society, means are taken to track and recapture these men immediately after the excitement has subsided.[57]

Government-granted general amnesties would continue throughout the twentieth and into the twenty-first century. In his celebrated prison writings of the Reza Shah period, for instance, novelist and leftist political prisoner Bozorg Alavi describes the anxious mood among prisoners awaiting the possibility of such amnesties.[58] In today's Islamic Republic this tradition has been codified in the constitution in Article 110 as a function of authority vested in the office of the leader (or leadership council). The relevant clause of that article grants the leader power in "pardoning or reducing the sentences of convicts, within the framework of Islamic criteria, on a recommendation from the head of the judicial power."[59]

The most well-known jailing facility of the Nasseri period was Tehran's royal dungeon Anbar-e Shahi, "The Shah's Cellar," located in the southeastern corner of Citadel Square (Maydan-e arg) in Tehran. Over its existence, Anbar-e Shahi housed all manner of prisoners, though it was most famous for housing those accused of crimes against the person of the shah or the Qajar government. The dungeon's structure was modest: a covered walkway about four meters wide and fifty steps long gave way to a small door. Once through the door, prisoners would see the prison yard, approximately five meters wide and fifty meters long. To the south of the yard stood archways, behind which was an interior space about eight meters wide and the same length as the yard. This latter space is where prisoners were housed, although they would also be taken outside to the yard, albeit in heavy chains.[60] This facility was colloquially known as the *falakeh* in part because *falak* (bastinado) was carried out there; new jailing facilities built in later decades on the same site would be burdened with the same grim nickname.[61] Anbar-e Shahi, which was used throughout the Constitutional period, would become particularly notorious among constitutionalist opponents of the Qajar monarchy and would remain synonymous with Qajar despotism for decades to come.

Before the twentieth century, even a year would in most cases have been considered a long time to spend in forced detention in Iran, though there were noteworthy cases in which detainees spent longer periods jailed. The political turmoil of the 1890s tobacco revolt and rising anti-Qajar and anticolonial sentiment in the last years of the nineteenth century led to some political cases featuring longer prison stays. One such case was that of Mirza Mohammad-'Ali Mahallati, also known as Hajj Sayyah, or "The Traveler," who was arrested and spent twenty months incarcerated in Tehran. Hajj Sayyah, who earned his sobriquet by traveling the world for eighteen years, was a ferocious critic of Qajar autocracy, a friend of famed anticolonial Muslim firebrand Jamal al-Din al-Afghani, and a probable freemason. Hajj Sayyah was also the first-ever Iranian American: he lived for ten years in San Francisco, reportedly met several times with US president Ulysses S. Grant, and was naturalized as a US citizen in May 1875. Upon returning to Iran after his travels, including stops in Japan, China, Burma, India, Mecca, and elsewhere, Hajj Sayyah returned to Persia in 1877 and began political activities that would eventually lead first to his exile to Mashhad—probably on the direct order of the shah—and then to his 1891 arrest.[62]

Hajj Sayyah would eventually write a long account of his remarkable life, politics, and travels, including a chapter on his lengthy stay in a late Qajar prison—the first prison writing of its kind in modern Iranian history.[63] The circumstances of his arrest reveal the explosive social and political climate of the day and shed light on punishment practices during the last years of the nineteenth century in cases involving political prisoners. Hajj Sayyah was arrested because Mirza Reza Kermani—the future assassin of Nasser al-Din Shah and acolyte of al-Afghani—was arrested and tortured into implicating The Traveler in the circulation of reformist agit-prop around the country. Upon Hajj Sayyah's arrest, officials also arrested two unrelated Babis, simply to confuse the situation and cast doubt about those who were detained.

Hajj Sayyah's experience is both illustrative of late nineteenth-century punishment practices and a striking portent of methods of political incarceration to come. When officials first entered Hajj Sayyah's home, they searched his belongings and papers looking for incriminating materials, trying to read scattered papers that he had burned the night before. Hajj Sayyah's arrest and interrogation began with threats and continued with Qajar officials questioning him about political pamphlets containing a key demand: for the shah to govern by the rule of law. Hajj Sayyah describes his imprisonment in harsh terms, as filthy, stinking, and fundamentally unjust. He is made to pay for his own food when hungry. There were other distinctly Qajar elements to his incarceration, namely his experience being held in *kundeh* and chains.[64] The device known as the *kundeh*, or stocks, became a particularly vivid symbol of Qajar brutality in the budding nationalist imaginary. Most extant images of Qajar prisoners into the era of the Constitutional Revolution show them bound together in the *kundeh*, which held prisoners together in rows of a handful to dozens of persons (fig. 4). Photographic evidence from the late nineteenth century also reveals that other variations of this practice existed wherein prisoners were bound together using large rocks around their ankles rather than classic wooden stocks (fig. 5). A punishment practice derided by Iranian constitutionalists and Europeans alike, the practice of binding prisoners together in the *kundeh* or with chains around the neck would be banned in Iran in the early twentieth century by Swedish officers brought in by reformists in the government to transform the Iranian police force along European lines.

The Constitutional Revolution of 1905–11, the first of two monumental revolutions in Iran in the twentieth century, marks a shift in the legal mores of the country. Mobilized by calls for justice (*'adalat*), a diverse cross section of Iranians fought for and won a constitution and a parliament, only to have those gains partly rolled back by Qajar and clerical reactionaries in

FIGURE 4. Late Qajar prisoners with ankle binding (*kundeh*) and chains around their necks. Source: Postcard from the personal collection of Golnar Nikpour.

alliance with Russia and Britain, who carved the country into spheres of influence in 1907. For budding Iranian nationalists of the late Qajar era—most of whom were sympathetic to the twin projects of state modernization and constitutionalism—the movement was an effort to eradicate the twin evils of internal Qajar despotism and external colonialism. Earlier legal reform efforts under the Qajars had been piecemeal and abandoned by fickle kings; the Constitutional movement was, in part, a response to these earlier failures, as well as a continuation of earlier efforts at mass mobilization, such as the tobacco revolt. For many nationalist intellectuals, the common punishment practices of the last Qajar century were clear proof of Qajar capriciousness and tyranny; in their championing of the rule of law, they often deployed disturbing accounts of Qajar punishment practices to mobilize support for the nationalist cause.

FIGURE 5. Late Qajar prisoners with rocks binding ankles and chains binding necks. Source: Photo archive no. 0-61650-0-235ف. The Institute for the Study of Contemporary Iranian History Archives, Tehran.

In his epochal account of the Constitutional Revolution, iconoclastic intellectual Ahmad Kasravi paints the archetypal nationalist picture of the aforementioned Anbar-e Shahi, the prison most associated with torture and political incarceration in the era leading up to the Constitutional Revolution. Kasravi laments the degrading treatment of prisoners jailed in the dungeon, explaining that in this space, prisoners were chained to each other at the neck and around the ankles and forced to urinate while in these group chains.[65] Meanwhile, in his own influential early twentieth-century work of nationalist historiography, *The History of the Awakening of the Iranians*, Nazem al-Islam Kermani writes of late Qajar-era jailing facilities: "Prison is a term that refers to a dark, humid, and filthy room with nothing to be found all day and all night but a *kundeh* [stocks] for one's feet and chains around one's neck."[66] This influential intellectual tradition portrayed the Qajar era as an arbitrary age of oppression, in which unpredictable rulers meted out punishments across Iran by their most vicious whims. Unsurprisingly, many of the extant images and artworks depicting brutal and spectacular punishments during the Nasser al-Din Shah period were produced during the Constitutional period and not during the era that they were said to depict.[67] This image of Qajar-era punishment would influence Iranian intellectuals into the late Pahlavi era. Even as dissidents lambasted Pahlavi prisons as sites of torture and oppression, some scholars and statesmen continued to reference Kasravi's influential account as proof of the good the Pahlavi government had done in humanizing and civilizing Iranian punishment practices.

CARCERALIZING REFORMS, CARCERALIZING SPACE

As evidenced by Hajj Sayyah's memoir, disgust with Qajar repression was building to a fever pitch among modernist intellectuals at the dawn of the twentieth century. These demands for reform came on the heels of earlier scattershot efforts at legal reform during the Nasseri period. Famously, Nasser al-Din Shah's first chief minister, Amir Kabir, attempted a slew of modernizing reforms—including an effort to curtail the influence of the ulama and banning torture—before being summarily executed by the young shah in 1852. (Torture would go on to be repeatedly banned under Qajar, Pahlavi, and now Islamic Republic rule, though its use has not yet been ended.) Budding modernist sentiment and continued colonial encroachment pushed Nasser al-Din Shah toward making some limited European-style reforms of law enforcement in Tehran. In 1878, after his second voyage to Europe, the shah decided to create the nation's first European-style police force, hiring the Italian-born Austrian Conte di Monteforte as an advisor. With di Monteforte's arrival, policing in Tehran was partially reorganized, and a modern-style police force, at that point called the *nazmiyeh*, was officially formed. As with many other legal and carceral reforms, even into the contemporary period, efforts were limited to Tehran, and the situation in the provinces remained quite different than in the capital city.

The *nazmiyeh* remained relatively small in strength and number, ranging from 250 to 400 members over the next two decades. Still, di Monteforte, who was eventually made Tehran's chief of police, took steps toward reorganizing policing in the capital city along European lines, writing the *nazmiyeh*'s first formal police codes and standardizing police uniforms to look like those found in Vienna.⁶⁸ Di Monteforte's efforts also included a suggested penal code with set sentences including lengthy prison sentences, some upward of ten years, or the death penalty in the case of serious infractions.⁶⁹ Foreshadowing efforts that would be undertaken in earnest during the Pahlavi era, di Monteforte also suggested institutionalizing a system of prison labor—including activities like shoe making, sewing, and carpentry—in Tehran's royal dungeon. In di Monteforte's view, this could have the effect of disciplining and reforming those who had been detained, with the hope that they would not return to their criminal ways after their release.⁷⁰ Although this code didn't gain much practical traction during di Monteforte's tenure, it was an early sign of the reformist ethos undergirding the institutionalization of modern forms of incarceration in the country. The nascent police force was said to be disliked by many Tehran residents during di Monteforte's day. According to one commentator:

> [di Monteforte] has organized a force whose external appearance is neat enough. Riding through the streets of Teheran, the traveler occasionally passes a house in the verandah of which swords are hung and muskets piled, and two or three men in a neat dark-coloured uniform draw up and salute the passing Farangi [European foreigner]. This is a police-station. The police do not seem popular among the inhabitants of Teheran. Their officers are mere lads, very handsome and spruce in their grey uniforms, and fond of riding about with sabres clanking by their sides, but scarcely the sort of people to command the confidence of the public.⁷¹

Still, di Monteforte's accomplishments were such that a street in Tehran was named after him and remained so named throughout the Pahlavi period. Later Pahlavi-era statesmen and legal scholar Ahmad Hooman, who in 1960 would write the first published monograph in Iran on the topic of prisons and prisoners, referred to di Monteforte in positive terms as "orderly and reform-minded" (*monazam va eslah talab*), although he also lamented the limited reach of di Monteforte's reforms, which he attributed to the influence of powerful individuals who endeavored to undermine di Monteforte's efforts.⁷²

Europeans routinely decried the legal and policing reforms enacted by the Nasser al-Din Shah government as inadequate, although their reasons for doing so were different from that of most Iranian nationalists. The British expressed particular frustration at highway banditry, which ate into their profits and placed company men and travelers alike into seemingly routine danger. As one Englishman exclaimed in the 1870s, "Brigandage is flourishing in Persia. Caravans and travelers are plundered at the very gates of Tehran. Want and oppression have turned the most peaceful of the population into highwaymen."[73] There is evidence that the Qajar government took brigandage against Europeans seriously enough to punish perpetrators in cases where brigands were caught.[74] From the point of view of the British, however, the law enforcement personnel charged with establishing order on Persia's highways were as bad as the brigands themselves. In 1907, amid the Constitutional Revolution, English traveler E. C. Williams recounted mistaking some "license carrying" highway patrolmen carrying rifles for a "ruffianly" looking "band of robbers"—the kind that "one hears so much" about.[75] Williams took little relief at finding that these men were patrolmen, avowing, "Our friend the Persian policeman will guard you excellently when it is in his interest to do so; he will steal from you when he thinks it is profitable; and, if possible, he will do both at once, and thus obtain a twofold reward for his services."[76]

These episodes plagued relations between the Persian government and the British well into the twentieth century. The situation only further degraded in the Constitutional period, as Russian military occupation and a devastating civil war hamstrung the central government's ability to control Persia beyond Tehran. An incident stemming from a British public health initiative in the southern province of Sistan—an important region for the British due to its proximity to India—is illustrative both of these tensions and of the new carceral geographies and logics creeping into the country at the turn of the century. In attempting to fight the spread of the plague in 1906, the British were met with resistance from local residents. A telegram from the British consulate at Sistan reported, "A mob of Persians, incited by a fanatical native doctor, attacked the British Consulate at Seistan, and assaulted the Consul and a British doctor with sticks."[77] The incident soon became a full-blown disturbance. A few days later, officials at the consulate sent word that a crowd "wrecked [the] dispensary and clods struck Consul and Consulate doctor. Immediate cause was [the] attempt of Customs official to remove plague patient to hospital by force."[78]

The English feared a night attack on their delegation, so they requested fortification by local police or gendarmerie troops, as well as arms with which to protect themselves. Before either arrived, however, they contented themselves by reinforcing their position with "all available Afghans."[79] Eventually, some arms and Persian troops were dispatched on the order of the Mushir od-Dowleh Mirza Nasrollah Khan, Constitutional Iran's first prime minister, who also requested that the British pass along the names of the accused rioters to his office. The English response to this request was prickly: they felt that it was the responsibility of the government to investigate and punish those behind the unrest. Still, they agreed that they would "instruct His Majesty's Consul to give names [of the accused parties] if he is able to do so."[80] Two months after the initial disturbances, the situation had not yet calmed down. When the consulate was finally attacked at night, the consuls groused about what they viewed as "the impotence of the Persian Government to afford protection" as well as "the refusal to allow the importation of a small number of rifles."[81]

Eventually, the demand for armed reinforcement of the consulate was taken to a new spatial—and ultimately carceral—level. In 1908, the English drew up blueprints for a fortified consulate. These blueprints suggested transforming the consulate from a modest building with little adornment into a quintessential space of carceral modernity, resembling both army barracks and a modern prison. The proposed plans included iron bars on windows, iron sheeting of the main gates, strengthened outer walls, a standing number of armed guards, barbed wire fences, and a reinforced perimeter.[82] Fortification of the consulate was never formally undertaken. Yet this spatial reordering is nonetheless illustrative of a modern carceral strategy: delimiting space to produce a social division between the "inside" and the "outside" of both the space *and* the law. Inverting the logic of the modern prison, the fortified consulate would have created a new spatial ordering in which normative legality could only exist within the institution instead of outside of it, with criminality left to remain in the "lawless" space beyond the building walls.

Continued turbulence of this sort pushed reformists in the Qajar government—then nominally ruled by twelve-year-old Ahmad Shah—to invite Swedish advisors into the country in 1910 to help establish and train a national highway gendarmerie. As historian Stephanie Cronin notes, this move was born in part of British demands that the Persian government work toward the "establishment of some sort of force which could guarantee security for trade, particularly in the south of the country."[83] The Constitutional government, worried about its territorial sovereignty in the aftermath of the 1907 Anglo-Russian agreement, which split the countries into spheres of influence between the two European powers, was also keen to expand its military and law enforcement capacity. From its inception, this new national gendarmerie was thus stamped "indelibly with a pro-Democrat, nationalist and anti-Russian character."[84] By the beginning of the Pahlavi period, the situation in Iran's regional highways was, according to some European company men, much improved. In 1926, an M. Svend Langmack, representative of a trading company in London, claimed, "Though we send both goods and money far into the interior of Persia by strangers whom we do not know and never see, we never lose anything." Langmack credited this safety not to any particular law enforcement force or the gendarmerie, however, but rather to that old custom the bastinado.[85]

In 1912, the reformists in the government would also invite Swedish officers under the direction of reserve lieutenant Gunnar Westdahl into the country to restructure Tehran's police force. Among the personnel Westdahl brought with him to Persia was an expert prison warden. In their decade in Tehran, Westdahl's Swedish officers expanded Tehran's police force and introduced some of the basics of then-current European evidentiary norms, including fingerprinting and interrogation tactics. Under Swedish tutelage, the Tehran police also collected data, including photographs, on vagrants, the homeless, and those suspected of belonging to the criminal underworld.[86] As Elahe Helbig has argued, prisoner photographs had already become a key "technology of institutional violence" against prisoners in the late Qajar era, even before the coming of the Swedish to Tehran. Yet it was under Swedish tutelage that prisoner photographs were increasingly used as a systematized method of surveillance for the expanded police force. By 1925, a League of Nations report revealed that the reorganized Tehran *nazmiyeh* had grown to approximately one thousand members in size.[87]

During their time in Iran, the Swedish officers under Westdahl also oversaw the building of a small modern prison network in Tehran's Tupkhaneh Square (Maydan-e tupkhaneh; literally "Cannon Square"). Tupkhaneh Square had until recently been used for public whippings and executions.

The Qajars first built the square in the 1860s and had public punishments moved there near the turn of the twentieth century. For their part, the Constitutional government did not shy away from public executions in this arena, particularly against those who conspired against it, though these executions were increasingly met with global opprobrium. After one such public execution, a 1910 report in *The Times* stated:

> No one questions the right of the Persian Government to inflict the punishment of death upon those condemned, as in this case, in the ordinary course of justice, but it is not too much to expect that the Constitutional Government, which professes to be actuated by principles of humanity and which invites the sympathy of Europe in its laudable task of regenerating the country, shall take every step to prevent the recurrence of such a brutalizing spectacle, which can only be described as public torture.[88]

The routine of public executions in Tupkhaneh Square would end not long after this execution, as public executions were nominally banned in Iran until the Islamic Revolution of 1979. There is evidence, however, that traditions of localized community justice including public executions continued into the Pahlavi era.[89]

The Tupkhaneh Square prison network eventually included a small interrogation center, the Central Police Prison, and the first dedicated women's jailing facility in Iran. This women's facility would remain Iran's main women's prison well into the Pahlavi period, although women would begin to be jailed in police jails in other big cities such as Isfahan during this period as well.[90] By 1925, there were three medical officers who attended to those in the prison infirmary in these facilities—a chief medical officer and two medical assistants. One medical assistant was tasked with visiting the prison infirmary daily, the other with keeping records and inspecting police posts throughout the day. This early prison infirmary consisted of seven beds— five for men and two for women—small rooms for dressing wounds, and a dispensary.[91] Along with inaugurating these new carceral sites, the Swedish officer era also ushered in new formalized prison regulations, which haltingly but enduringly changed the culture of Iran's carceral system.[92] These regulations ended the practice of putting chains around the necks and blocks (*kundeh*) around the legs of prisoners, who were now granted mandated hour-long outdoor breaks and visitor periods. The Westdahl-initiated regulations attempted to routinize prison life in the capital city for the first time. The regulations included standardized eating and sleeping hours, and prisoners were also newly made to wear standard-issue uniforms modeled on those found in European penal institutions. Standard-issue uniforms would remain in use into the Pahlavi period (fig. 6). The reforms also significantly expanded the amount and kind of information collected on each prisoner upon their arrest and jailing. For the first time, case files (*parvandeh*) were collected on individual detainees, with information regarding the individual's background, physical characteristics, and legal history. Yet these changes, while foundational in beginning to shift norms of law enforcement and penal life in the capital city, were limited to Tehran and only hinted at the wholesale changes still on the horizon in the Pahlavi era. It is to those changes, and the establishment and entrenchment of the modern carceral system in Iran, that I turn my attention in the next chapter.

FIGURE 6. Prisoners from the early Reza Shah era wearing standardized uniforms. Source: Photo archive no. 1-30-0-118ص. The Institute for the Study of Contemporary Iranian History Archives, Tehran.

Two

THE CRIMINAL IS THE PATIENT, THE PRISON WILL BE THE CURE
Building the Carceral Imagination in Pahlavi Iran

BY THE DAWN OF THE REZA SHAH PAHLAVI ERA IN 1925, LEGAL REFORM had long been established as a major concern of Iranian intellectuals trying to combat European colonial encroachment and Qajar malfeasance. At the end of the nineteenth century, reformists influenced by European ideas of statecraft as well as by events in the Ottoman and Russian Empires were arguing that *qanun*—law—was the only way to progress as a nation and stave off further territorial or economic loss to the European powers.[1] During the Constitutional period of 1905–11, legal reform remained a concern of constitutionalists, reformists, and revolutionaries, although differing notions of law and order, drawing alternately on European models and on various interpretations of sharia, were advanced by the diverse groups and classes who supported the abstract call for justice.[2] Social and moral norms were also changing, as nationalists increasingly looked to diagnose and address what they saw as the social ills of the country, including opium use and prostitution, through legal means. As Maziyar Ghiabi notes, "Constitutionalists referred to opium addiction as one of the most serious social, political ills afflicting the country. They were actively advocating for a drastic cure of this pathology, which metaphorically embodied the sickness of late Qajar Iran."[3] Despite revolutionary efforts, however, the Constitutional experiment halted neither European intrusions nor Qajar corruption, nor did it succeed in establishing the stable Constitutional government for which the movement fought. Yet despite the enduring sentiment that the post–Constitutional Revolution era and the last years of Qajar rule were marked by legal and political chaos, significant albeit piecemeal legal reforms along European lines were undertaken in that time—most notably, the 1912 Law of the Principles of Criminal Trials and the temporary Penal Code of 1917, which (again) formally prohibited physical torture and the shackling of prisoners.[4]

By the time Reza Khan appeared on the national stage in 1921, Iranian reformers were anxious to unify Iran's disparate social and political forces.[5] For many nationalist intellectuals, the soon-to-be first Pahlavi monarch seemed to be just the sort of strong figure capable of restoring Iranian sovereignty against the threat of continued European encroachment. Where once the overriding call among Iranian nationalists was for justice (*'adalat*), the early 1920s saw an amplified demand for a powerful, centralizing figure, a "Mussolini who [could] break the influence of the traditional authorities, and thus create a modern outlook, a modern people, and a modern nation."[6] Reza Shah understood the value of at least appearing to govern by the rule of law for both the emerging modern middle class in Iran and the international community of states. For most Iranian nationalists of the era, coming off the disappointments of the Constitutional period, Reza Shah represented Iran's last best hope for finally ushering the country into the type of modern system of law and order that had long been the desire of reformist political projects. For the shah, international appearances were especially important in the wake of Iran's abrogation of capitulations in 1928—particularly the law that had protected foreign nationals accused of wrongdoing from the Iranian justice system. As historian Hadi Enayat notes, in the wake of the abrogation, "the shah felt it necessary to show the international community that his government was based on sound and predictable legality."[7] New legal codes and expansive modern prisons were the centerpieces of that outward-looking project.

This chapter addresses several of the important carceral transformations of the Pahlavi era (1925–79), analyzing the close relationship between the civilizational anxieties of early Pahlavi reformers and the establishment of modern forms of policing and incarceration in the country. As I show, during Reza Shah Pahlavi's reign (1925–41), the government undertook the dramatic centralization of the state's legal and judicial systems as well as a vast expansion of Iran's then-fledgling prison network. Later, under Reza Shah's son Mohammad Reza Pahlavi (1941–79), Iran's carceral system would further expand as US military advisors were brought into the country to shape carceral and policing institutions. It was also during the Pahlavi era that the issue of political incarceration and torture would emerge as central motifs of Iranian opposition movements across the political spectrum, eventually contributing to the 1979 revolution that ended Pahlavi rule. Yet despite the notoriety Pahlavi prisons would achieve in their own day, Pahlavi statesmen, law enforcement officials, and some intellectuals applauded Pahlavi legal and penal reform, arguing that the Pahlavi government had made punishment rational, civilized, humane, and modern.

LEGAL CENTRALIZATION AND PRISON EXPANSION UNDER REZA SHAH PAHLAVI

The centralization of modern Iran's legal system was undertaken swiftly by the newly crowned king, who in 1927 appointed Minister of Justice Ali Akbar Davar to lead and reform the judiciary, which had first been established during the Constitutional era. Davar, the son of a Qajar statesman who received his law degree from the University of Geneva in 1920, transformed Iran's legal and judicial structure root and branch.[8] Two days after his appointment, Davar dissolved the existing judiciary and undertook a complete overhaul of the 1911–12 organic, civil, commercial, and criminal codes, which had themselves been partial efforts to standardize Qajar Persia's decentralized systems of legality.[9] The wholesale changes in the legal codes of the Davar period, largely undertaken between his appointment and 1931, irrevocably transformed the Iranian political and legal landscape by centralizing law, reducing the power of the sharia courts, and establishing an overhauled judiciary with new personnel and new codes of conduct. This new secularized judiciary would remain in place until the 1979 Islamic Revolution, after which Shi'a jurists systematically replaced the secular legal elites elevated to positions of power during the Pahlavi period.

Legal centralization happened in the same era as the expansion of the modern prison system in Iran. In the early 1920s, most prisoners in Tehran were held in the small prison network first established under the aegis of the Swedish officers. By the late 1920s, the nominally "temporary" Central Police Jail, in which police often interrogated suspects, housed twice as many prisoners as was originally intended (fig. 7). This small jailing network included the notorious if generically named Prison Number One and Prison Number Two. Noteworthy political detainees such as Ardeshir Avanessian of the Iranian Communist Party would be held in these numbered facilities in the 1920s. Avanessian described these spaces in stark terms: "The walls were thick, the rooms were small and dark, full of lice and cockroaches ... blood and a thousand other forms of filth were stamped on the walls."[10] Prison Number One was particularly notorious among those who were held there for its "dark imprisonment," which Avanessian likened to being buried alive.[11] Political prisoner Ali Dashti unfavorably compared the prison's cells to coffins.[12] His grim experience in prison so rattled Dashti—an eclectic champion of Reza Shah who was later imprisoned by him on multiple occasions and who spent one early prison stay translating Gustave Le Bon—that he cursed the very person who invented prisons in the first place. "How cruel and oppressive," he wrote despairingly, "was the person who invented the prison in this world!"[13] Despite his antipathy to the institution of the prison, Dashti would become quite familiar with them by the end of his life, serving sentences under both Pahlavi shahs and in the Islamic Republic. Dashti, who also served in Mohammad Reza Shah's government, was imprisoned for a final time in 1980 in Evin Prison two years before his death.[14]

Existing facilities were simply not enough to meet the mushrooming demand for carceral space brought about by a changing legal order. Ali Dashti described penal overcrowding thus: "There are four bloody walls into which hundreds of human beings have been poured like animals."[15] Just before the Davar-led restructuring of the judiciary, old Qajar buildings and ruins were bequeathed to the *nazmiyeh* by the central government to turn into jailing facilities.[16] The Pahlavi government also planned to build tens of new prisons to address the need for more space: five large prisons of 2,700 square meters for one hundred prisoners; fifty medium-sized prisons of 1,400 square meters for fifty prisoners; thirty small institutions of 1,000 square meters for thirty prisoners; and several very small prisons of 200 square meters.[17] As scholar Maryam Alsadat Hosseini notes, this era is of particular importance in the history of Iran's modern prison system precisely because of this foundational effort.[18] Some of these planned prisons were never built, while others were built only in subsequent years. Large cities, especially Tehran, received the lion's share of these modern prison spaces. Smaller village and provincial prisons remained several paces behind those in the capital city, and in some cases lacked the most basic amenities like water and electricity well into later decades. On the whole, the Reza Shah era oversaw the first dramatic expansion of prison space in modern Iran, establishing the carceral system with which Iranians have lived until today.

The Reza Shah era not only built the new prisons with which Iranians

FIGURE 7. Tehran police interrogating detainees in the Central Tehran Jail, Reza Shah era. Source: Photo archive no. 1-87-0-124ب. The Institute for the Study of Contemporary Iranian History Archives, Tehran.

would soon learn to live but also changed the very language with which Iranians would speak about incarceration. Before this period, the most common word used for jails of any kind among Persian-language speakers was the word *mahbas*, a word of Arabic origin taken from the Arabic root *h-b-s*, which carries the meaning "related to imprisonment." The premodern literary genre of prison poetry was known as *habsiyeh* (from the same root); Nima Yushij, the towering founding figure of modernist poetry in Iran, published his poem "Mahbas" (Prison) as late as 1924. Yet not long after this point, the word *zendan* became the most common word by which Iranians referred to prisons and jailing facilities; it remains the most common word for prison used by Persian speakers in Iran today. The word *zendan* probably has its roots in the Avestan language, with component parts meaning weapon (*zan*) and denoting a space or place (*-dan*). Variations of the compound word *zendan* can be found in other early Persian languages, inscriptions, and texts, including Manichaean Parthian and Middle Persian. There are also interpretations of the root of the word *zendan* that link it to the Arabic word *zandiq*, which is itself a loanword from Middle Persian and was used in the early centuries of Islam to denote a heretic. By the eighth century in the Abbasid Empire, a *zandiq* could be a heretic of any sort, but in earlier centuries it was specifically used to denote the Manichaeans of the Sasanian Empire; there is an outside possibility that the word *zendan* is derived from this usage.[19]

In the modern era, *zendan* is one word among thousands that was promoted and popularized during Reza Shah's reign through the work of the Farhangestan-e Zaban-e Iran (the Persian Language Academy), a state institution first set up in 1935 to "purify" Persian by eradicating foreign (and especially Arabic) loanwords from the Persian language.[20] For Reza Shah, like the Iranian nationalists who first popularized this idea before his reign, the so-called purification of the Persian language was explicitly part of an ethnonationalist imaginary, in which the forced Persianization of non-Persian ethnic minorities across Iran went hand in hand with stripping Persian of hundreds of Arabic loanwords that had circulated as part of the living language for centuries. This shifting terrain of carceral language and the broader project of language "purification" further reveals the civilizational logics in Reza Shah's project of statist nationalism. It wouldn't be the only time the Pahlavi government would change the manner in which it referred to carceral sites in its efforts to promote the legitimacy of its penal reforms.

GLOBAL NETWORKS, IRANIAN PRISONS

In 1925, members of the Iranian police force including Mirza Abdollah Bahrami and Lieutenant Colonel Abdollah Khan Saif, then Qazvin chief of police, traveled to the International Penal and Penitentiary Conference in London.[21] The 1925 event was the ninth such conference held by the International Prison Commission (IPC), an organization that had first convened in London in 1872. The commission was formed with the mandate to collect international prison statistics and to recommend reforms on prison management and prisoner rehabilitation. 1925 was the first time an Iranian delegation participated in an IPC conference but not the first time an Iranian government had interacted with the organization. In 1876, following a conference in Stockholm, the IPC sent questionnaires on what they called the "penitentiary question" to governments around the world and received a response from the Qajar government, although evidently nothing meaningful came of this early exchange.[22]

For Sir Evelyn Ruggles-Brise, British prison administrator and president of the IPC, the work of the commission was no less than an undertaking in the service of civilization and humanity. On the eve of the 1925 conference, Ruggles-Brise boasted that the ICP was a "confederation of most of the civilized States of the world" [23] working "quietly and unostentatiously, to introduce a greater humanity" to punishment systems around the world.[24] Ruggles-Brise claimed the commission was the torchbearer of "a world-desire for a rational and equitable 'system of punishment.'" For Ruggles-Brise, this "world-desire" was itself "due to the progressive widening of the circle of humanity" in recent years.[25] Ruggles-Brise and the commission routinely referenced the work of French sociologist Gabriel Tarde, whose work had grown influential in criminological discourses of the era. Tardian criminology argued that social factors—rather than biological or essential attributes, as in Lombroso's criminological theories—were the foundation for understanding and curtailing criminal behavior. Moreover, arguing against the Durkheimian structuralist functionalism popular in European sociology of the day, Tardian criminologists emphasized the need to understand not only social structures but also the individual personality and psyche of each detainee, opening the door for the rising influence of criminal psychology.[26] For Ruggles-Brise and the IPC, these insights highlighted the interconnected social stakes of their work. Noting recent successes in prison reform in Siam and Japan, Ruggles-Brise credited the commission for bringing together statesmen and reformists from around the world to promote "the continental system" of prison administration. "Members of different nations breathing in the same civilizing atmosphere come to regard each other as *compatriotes sociaux* in the work of humanity," Ruggles-Brise declared.[27] For the IPC, the London conference would be an important step toward bringing new participants, Pahlavi Iran included, into that civilizing atmosphere. The insights gleaned from the conference and from European criminological trends—as well as the civilizational logics buttressing those insights—would influence Iranian carceral trends for decades to come.

The immediate effect of the London conference was to convince the Iranian delegation of the importance of building state-of-the-art modern prisons in Iran. Following Iranian participation in the conference, Reza Shah chose Tbilisi-born architect Nikolai Markov to design a new prison on the grounds of the former Qajar palace at Qasr in Tehran. Before becoming an architect, Markov started his professional career as a military man. He served as an officer in the Imperial Russian Army tasked with fighting Bolshevism and was later captain in the Iranian Cossack Brigade, the branch of the Qajar military in which Reza Shah also served.[28] Other individuals eventually linked to the new Pahlavi law enforcement apparatus also spent time with Reza Shah in the Cossack Brigade, such Mohammad Hossein Ayrom, who was made chief of police in 1931. Before his time in the military, Markov studied architecture and Persian literature at the University of St. Petersburg, showing interest in and aptitude for both classical Islamic architecture and modern design. In part through ties forged with Reza Shah in their Cossack Brigade years, Markov was granted the task of designing Iran's Ministries of Finance, Defense, and Justice, the post office, and several schools, factories, embassies, churches, and mosques across the capital. Markov, whose mandate was to design Qasr such that it would be suitable for Iran's climate and culture, brought a mix of Iranian design elements and European and American architectural frameworks into his design of the prison.[29] His influence was such that prisoners and statesmen alike would refer to Qasr as "Markov's prison" for years to come.[30]

Qasr Prison in Tehran was by far the most famous prison built during Reza Shah's reign (fig. 8).[31] Launched under the direction of Tehran chief of police brigadier-general Mohammad Dargahi and built on the grounds of a former Qajar castle, Qasr opened its doors on December 2, 1929, with seven cellblocks, 192 rooms, and the initial capacity to hold an estimated eight hundred to one thousand prisoners.[32] Upon opening, Qasr also included fourteen yards, used ostensibly to categorize prisoners by age and type of crime and meant to safeguard against the "corruption of morals," although this separation was not always strictly enforced.[33] Qasr alone represented a significant expansion of Tehran's carceral capacity. Just before the Davar-led legal and judicial overhaul, there had been only about four hundred total prisoners held in Tehran, but within a few years the need for carceral space had already doubled.[34] The prison would expand further several times over the next decades, though it would remain plagued by overcrowding from its first months until its closing in the mid-2000s. Incredibly, just two days after Qasr

FIGURE 8. Qasr Prison, 1930s. Source: Photo archive no. ع1-0-4779-0. The Institute for the Study of Contemporary Iranian History Archives, Tehran.

held its opening ceremony and for reasons that remain contested, Dargahi was dismissed from his post and became the first person to be imprisoned in Qasr. He would be released several months later and, briefly back in the good graces of Reza Shah, given a ranking military post until he again fell afoul of the monarch and was dismissed in 1937.

Fazlollah Bahrami, then head of the Department of Prisons, claimed that the London conference had convinced the Pahlavi elite that new modern prisons were necessary not just for the good of Iran but for the good of the prisoners themselves.[35] In an essay in the Tehran police journal, Bahrami explained that with the new prisons, Iran's penal system had been "reformed and corrected . . . fundamental steps [had] been taken to improve the situation for prisoners."[36] Yet Qasr was not built solely or even chiefly with Iranian prisoners in mind. Reza Shah intended Qasr to be proof to the entire world that Pahlavi Iran was a civilized modern state. In the late 1920s, Iran's legal system was under international scrutiny due to the shah's abrogation of capitulations to foreign powers in 1928. According to a 1935 message from US diplomat J. Rives Childs to the US secretary of state, Qasr was meant to "provide suitable accommodations for [foreign] prisoners consequent upon the abandonment by the Powers of their capitulary rights."[37] One US citizen eventually held at Qasr, traveler Richard Halliburton, did indeed find the prison suitable. Halliburton described Qasr as having "well-lighted, scrupulously clean corridors of steel and concrete, lined with large sunny compartments" with cells that were "well heated and furnished with a cot, a table and chair, all new and all well made."[38] Other characters of global renown, including T. E. Lawrence (more famously known as Lawrence of Arabia), also found their way to Qasr in these early years; a room in today's Qasr Museum remains dedicated to the famed Brit.[39]

THE PRISON AS PROBLEM

Despite the early hopes of reformist statesmen, Qasr quickly became an object of public criticism, as the prison seemed almost immediately to reveal the limits of Pahlavi carceral modernization rather than its successes. In the aftermath of legal centralization, updates appearing in Iranian newspapers more frequently informed readers of happenings in criminal court, particularly in the event of salacious cases.[40] Critiques of Iran's police and prisons also began to emerge. While political communiqués[41] and prison memoirs[42] by political prisoners have gained the most subsequent attention, not all critiques of modern policing or punishment were written by members of opposition parties. In fact, for some modernists, it was not the government or its institutions that deserved critique but rather its misbehaving *citizens*. As one writer of the era complained, "In our nation there are still people who don't pay enough heed to the importance of the police officer, who is the representative and executor of the law [*qanun*] in the country. Perhaps there are even police officers who do not realize their own worth."[43] For this writer, the modern rule of *qanun* had not yet been achieved in the country because of Iran's intransigent and not-yet-properly-modern citizenry, not because of the failings of Iranian law enforcement officers themselves.

Others critiqued Iran's expanding carceral network directly. In 1946, a Tehran-based publisher released *Come with Me to Prison* by Hedayatollah Hakim-Elahi, an Oxford-educated journalist, Islamic humanist, and critic of the Pahlavi government.[44] Dedicated to the prisoners of Iran "whose only crime has been poverty and the lack of power," *Come with Me to Prison* is an occasionally salacious work of reformist agit-prop written after repeated visits by Hakim-Elahi to Qasr and Tehran's Central Police Prison. The book compiled Hakim-Elahi's serialized newspaper writing and was one of several similar titles—*Come with Me to the Red Light District*, *Come with Me to the Asylum*, and *Come with Me to School*—written by the author in this era. *Come with Me to Prison* went through three printings, and the publisher boasted that it couldn't keep up with reader demand.[45] As Jairan Gahan notes in her work on Hakim-Elahi's writing on Tehran's red-light district, Hakim-Elahi had ties to Muhammad Baqir Hijazi, who was then editor at the newspaper *Vazifeh*. This newspaper, for which Hakim-Elahi also wrote, was "an Islamic opposition publication that advanced a humanitarian idea of Islam" and that "regularly printed articles about the role of compassion in Islam."[46] *Come with Me to Prison* gestures to the budding sentiment that Tehran, lined with prisons, mental institutions, and brothels, was not only the capital of modern Iran but also the nation's capital of sin. To live in modernizing Pahlavi Iran, Hakim-Elahi seems to imply, was to live among criminality and vice. And yet Hakim-Elahi's work is reformist, not antimodernist; his prescription for the ills that had befallen innocent Iranians in the capital city falls along the legalist lines promoted by Iranian reformers for decades, albeit with a moralist bent.

Come with Me to Prison follows the experience of what the author calls a "typical" Iranian prisoner. Upon capture, Hakim-Elahi explains, the prisoner was first taken to Tehran's Central Police Prison, a facility at that point meant to be a temporary stop for unsentenced arrestees. This is where the accused was meant to remain until sentencing, after which he would be transferred to Qasr. According to Hakim-Elahi, however, this was not the case in practice. Some prisoners were granted their outright release without arraignment because they understood the state's meaning of "freedom": freedom to pay the bribe.[47] This is not the rule of law, Hakim-Elahi protests, but the "rule of money" (*hokumat-e pul*).[48] Hakim-Elahi claims that corruption was even more rampant at Qasr. Upon arrival, detainees were given one pair of pants and a striped shirt and taken to the "grimiest" section of the prison, cellblock 2. The cellblock in which the detainee was eventually housed, Hakim-Elahi explains, was decided either through bribes or social status. Hakim-Elahi was not the only writer to mention differentiated treatment between prisoners; such discrepancies were noted by the era's political prisoners, who were often given preferential treatment due to their class positions and educations. Members of the Iranian elite who fell out of favor and were thrown into Qasr also recounted receiving favored treatment. Firuz Nosrat al-Dowleh, who had a hand in the prison's establishment but like Brigadier-General Dargahi was himself imprisoned there not long after, marveled at the polite behavior of the guards and the peaceful gardens on Qasr's grounds.[49]

Hakim-Elahi describes the prison quite differently. Detainees, both male and female, were routinely whipped or punched.[50] Illicit drugs were a major problem. Crime bosses were allowed to move around the facility freely. Another Qasr prisoner from the 1930s confirmed Hakim-Elahi's account, writing, "There were no locks whatsoever on our doors, and we soon found that the guards took no notice of prisoners wandering in and out of their cells, making social calls upon their neighbors at any hour."[51] (Ahmad Hooman, a Pahlavi-era legal scholar and onetime head of the Iranian Bar Association, disputes this claim, writing that every cell in Qasr had a heavy-duty lock on its doors.)[52] Hakim-Elahi describes the culture of Qasr sardonically, writing,

"The angel of freedom [*fereshteh-ye azadi*] is in flight at Qasr. Long live this democratic government [*zendeh bad hokumat-e demokrasi*]".[53] For Hakim-Elahi, the failure to maintain the rule of law in prisons is tantamount to a larger failure to bring about those political demands—freedom, justice, legality, etc.—that had for so long animated Iranian reformers.

At the time of *Come with Me to Prison*'s writing, there were nine cellblocks at Qasr.[54] Cellblock 3 housed the infirmary, and a small prison factory was housed in cellblock 7. Each cellblock had a café and grocery staffed by prisoners. Years prior, Brigadier-General Dargahi had pushed for a modernized infirmary for Tehran's carceral network.[55] Better health services had been part of the modernist promise of Qasr, but Hakim-Elahi's description of the Qasr infirmary indicates failure in this regard. Meanwhile, he notes, the wages paid to prisoners who worked in the small prison factory were often coerced out of the workers' hands by guards and prisoners with links to organized crime.[56] Prisoners of all stripes routinely complained of being held without sentencing, or in some cases even after their sentences had expired.[57] During Hakim-Elahi's visit to the women's prison, he found that only five of the fifty-seven women detained there had been sentenced.[58] Overcrowding stemmed in part from the sheer number of new criminal cases in the aftermath of legal centralization, which far exceeded the Iranian judiciary's ability to attend to them in a timely fashion. This backlog was such an issue that concerned citizens anxiously wrote to Iranian newspapers with ideas for relieving the judicial logjam for Iran's "heroic" but overburdened judges.[59] Remarkably, in the years after a government-initiated prison reform program in the 1950s, state literature would admit that many of these issues—drug use, organized crime, overcrowding—had all been major problems in Pahlavi prisons in years prior.[60]

Female and juvenile incarceration also emerged in this era as a site of reformist anxiety. Hakim-Elahi explains that many of the women held at the women's prison were there with their children in tow, and other women spent their days worried about youngsters at home. The conditions at the juvenile prison were equally grim.[61] This situation, Hakim-Elahi indicated, had deleterious effects on Iranian family life. Documentarian Kamran Shirdel, a 1960s critic of Pahlavi state modernism, paints a comparable picture of Tehran's women's prison in his 1965 film *Women's Penitentiary*.[62] *Women's Peni-*

tentiary includes footage of imprisoned women raising their young children behind bars or worrying about their families beyond prison walls. A social worker interviewed in the film admits that having mothers in prison leads to "psychological and emotional problems" for their children. In their emphasis on broken families and damaged children, critiques such as Hakim-Elahi's and Shirdel's offered damning appraisals of the Pahlavi government, in part because they challenged the state using a long-standing discourse of Iranian nationalism: patriotic motherhood.[63] Instead of raising the next generation of healthy patriots and citizens, these critiques indicate, Iranian women were raising the next generation of criminals and recidivists. Years later, the Islamic Republic would similarly elicit protests regarding young children forcibly incarcerated with their mothers. "With such rancour and violence," one such critic wrote of a child growing up in Islamic Republic prisons, "what type of future await[ed] him?"[64]

Hakim-Elahi was skeptical of official efforts to improve the women's prison, including those made by the shah's twin sister Princess Ashraf Pahlavi, then perhaps the most powerful woman in Iran. In September 1946 Princess Ashraf visited the women's prison and met with both officials and detainees (fig. 9). Hakim-Elahi claims that prison officials simply gave the filthy women new *chadors* (veils), and that Ashraf was satisfied by these surface efforts. More sympathetic press of the day took a different view on the princess's visit. One such article was published in the popular newsmagazine *Khandaniha* (Readables), a long-running *Reader's Digest*–style journal that reprinted news from other sources alongside its own reports.[65] The *Khandaniha* report puts the official number of detainees in the women's prison at the time of Ashraf's visit at sixty, close to Hakim-Elahi's claimed total of fifty-seven, and provides a benevolent and uncritical account of the princess providing comfort and compassion to suffering female detainees and their children. The report claims that of the women being held, eleven were incarcerated on the charge of murder, ten were incarcerated on the charge of "actions inconsistent with chastity," twenty-four on charges related to theft, and the final fifteen on fraud. Yet even this sympathetic account admits that among the detained women, at least fifty were still unsentenced and uncertain of their status. Upon leaving the prison, Ashraf is reported to have taken the names of all the children, in whom she took charitable interest, to osten-

FIGURE 9. Princess Ashraf Pahlavi visiting female prisoners in September 1946. Source: Hedayatollah Hakim-Elahi, *Ba man beh zendan biyaid* [Come with me to prison]. Tehran: Sherkat-e Sehami, 1325/1946.

sibly introduce them to relevant educational institutions.[66] In Hakim-Elahi's view, little meaningful change would come of such halfhearted efforts.[67]

The concept of female and child criminality—particularly the idea that children were learning to engage in lives of crime rather than going to school—challenged the modernizing state to its core. For their part, Pahlavi state institutions publicized child criminality as a dangerous failing of absentee *parents*, who through negligence let their children fall under the control of corrupting forces. A 1960s radio program broadcast by the National Police

Force, for instance, interviewed a twelve-year-old pickpocket who explained that he had been abandoned by his father and left unattended by his mother, leaving him to learn the art of delinquency from street thieves.[68] *Come with Me to Prison* ironically notes that Qasr is a "giant school of ethics" in which one must learn a "strange science": the science of criminal behavior.[69] This claim echoes a common refrain by political prisoners who asserted that they received their own educations at Qasr, albeit to different ends. In the prison, Hakim-Elahi's prisoners cement their status as recidivists: a master lock breaker teaches prisoners how to break locks with silk, and a murderer teaches them how to slit throats without making a sound.[70] Yet for all these critiques, Hakim-Elahi believed in the promise of the modern prison. In particular, Hakim-Elahi argued for the development of Iran's prison factories—echoing Iran's prison reformers since the age of the Conte di Monteforte. Instead of a "factory for pickpockets" and a "university for thieves," Hakim-Elahi insisted, the prison should reform incarcerated persons into useful citizens by making "honest" labor available to them.[71] It is precisely this expanded carceral project, wherein prisons were promoted as a reformist salve for social ills, that the Pahlavi state would take up in subsequent years.

IRANIAN CRIMINOLOGY AND THE SCIENCE OF PRISONS

In 1931, the same year that the government passed a law banning any political organizing with a "communitarian" (i.e., communist) outlook, the University of Tehran first opened its doors. In 1946, the first sociology course was offered at the university, and in 1958, the Institute for Social Science and Research (ISSR) was established there.[72] The initial plans for the ISSR were drawn up by the Geneva- and Paris-educated intellectual Ehsan Naraqi, whose connections to the European academy as well as international institutions like the United Nations and UNESCO helped the institute secure international funding and draw visiting international scholars.[73] (Naraqi would go on to be imprisoned in the Islamic Republic after the 1979 revolution.)[74] After the institute's founding, other universities, including Pahlavi University in Shiraz, Mashhad University, Tabriz University, Isfahan University, and the National University of Iran, also began to offer courses in the social sciences.[75]

From its inception, the Iranian academy was linked in complex ways to the project of Pahlavi state modernization. As historian Cyrus Schayegh has astutely noted, the language of the modern sciences—and the positivist logic of this discourse—was first adopted by members of the Pahlavi elite and the new Iranian middle class as part of the Pahlavi government's "modernist urge to hasten Iran's modernization and improve its administration."[76] In the postwar era, the language and logic of the social sciences would also be adopted by members of the Pahlavi elite. Criminology, as well as its offshoots criminal psychology and penology, emerged in the middle of the twentieth century as a distinct field in this broader academic and social context. From its inception, Iranian criminology had a global horizon. In 1950 Iran sent its first representative to the second International Congress of Criminology, convened by the International Society of Criminology in Paris and host to 760 participants from sixty nations.[77] This intellectual investment in academic criminology and "scientific" approaches to crime would become crucial to Pahlavi prison reform efforts, which mobilized technocratic logics from the medical and social sciences to legitimize state practices.

Academic writing on prisons in Iran was initially limited. An index of books published in Iran up to 1958 reveals several academic and popular texts on the topic of modern law and legal reform, many published through the University of Tehran law school, but none appear to be focused solely on prisons and few on crime or criminality as such.[78] There was, however, budding interest in *elm-e zendan*, or "prison sciences," in Iran's universities. In 1957, a student at the University of Tehran college of law named Abolhasan Behpur completed a doctoral dissertation entitled "Prisons and Prisoners."[79] This text appears to be the first monograph-length treatise on prisons by an Iranian scholar, and as such, it is worth analyzing at length. Behpur, whose thesis borrows liberally from but never cites classic European criminology, introduces his research on criminal law and prisons in Iran with a general social theory of law. For Behpur, every individual was a cog in a society. In order to maintain the health of society, each individual had to fulfill certain duties. Yet despite this basic principle, there would always be individuals who, due to a lack of moral character and limited "love for humanity" (*bashar dusti*), transgressed social norms.[80] "Just as an individual needs air to breathe in order to live," Behpur argues, "so does a society need laws."[81]

Behpur argues that the purpose for punishment is twofold: meting out justice and safeguarding society. Paraphrasing Italian criminologist Cesare

Beccaria's argument, the author insists that a just punishment must be proportionate. That is, the severity of the punishment must match that of the crime. Further, Behpur argues, an effective punishment must be rational, successfully dissuading others from undertaking similar activities.[82] But what should society's response be "when faced with a thief, a traitor, a swindler ... or those who have committed manslaughter or tens of other crimes of this sort?"[83] For the author, the answer is simple: prison. For Behpur, the history of punishment was a progressive march from the inefficient and inhumane toward the socially useful, civilized, and just; none of Shirdel's noir critiques of the dark underbelly of modernization are apparent in his analysis.

Behpur argues that punishments, in Iran as elsewhere, were once meted out according to the whims of tyrannical rulers rather than by law. In this primordial, prelegal era, "no one paid attention to 'criminal law' or 'the reform of the criminal,' issues which are of paramount importance in the laws of progressive [*motaraqi*] nations today."[84] Earlier prisoners were thrown into "terrifying, dank, underground dungeons," spaces in which the life of the prisoner was rendered "worthless" and concepts like "law" and "rights" had no meaning. Behpur argues that Iran was mired in just such a prelegal dark age before Reza Shah. Neither Islamic law nor Persianate notions of the circle of justice appear in Behpur's schema, even in passing or by way of critique—simply a before and after Reza Shah's program of legal modernization. He continues, "In prisons of old so much did they torture . . . that [prisoners] would be forced to confess whether or not the individual had committed a crime." According to Behpur, this was no longer the case, as torture in Iran had been put to an end.[85] To prove this, Behpur quotes Article 131 of the Pahlavi penal code—the anti-torture article—at length. "Human societies gradually moved towards progress and civilization," Behpur proudly argues, such that "today, punishments must be applied with regard to the law."[86]

Despite Behpur's triumphalist tone, Pahlavi prisons emerge in his work as sites of anxiety at the same time as they were lauded as markers of civilizational progress. He notes, for instance, that Pahlavi prisons lagged behind those in other "progressive nations" in securing both the physical and psychological health of prisoners.[87] Prisoner health and the effects of that health on Iranian society more broadly are essential concerns in this era's criminological texts, many of which share Behpur's concern that Iran was lagging in this regard. An unpublished 1959 dissertation by a scholar named Mahmud Qahremani, for instance, argues that prisoner psychology was not merely a health issue but more critically a broader issue of that ever-elusive reformist desire: justice. Unfortunately, according to Qahremani, the Iranian criminal system of the 1950s rarely took stock of the accused individual's mental health and capacity for healthy reasoning during sentencing. This evident legal lacuna was, for Qahremani, also a *moral* lacuna, insofar as the state had both ethical and legal responsibility for the care of its citizens.[88] Nowhere was this more evident than in the carceral system, Qahremani reminds readers, insofar as it supervised both *mentally* ill and *socially* ill persons.

Referring to the writing of French sociologist Gabriel Tarde, whose work had been championed by the International Prison Commission in the 1920s, Qahremani insists that the Iranian judicial and penal systems needed to better incorporate lessons from both the fields of sociology and psychology if they were to function justly and optimally. Qahremani's emphasis on individual detainees' mental health is drawn in part from Tarde's insight that criminal justice systems must take both social and individual contexts into account as well as his emphasis on a sociology that would incorporate the psychological sciences. According to Qahremani, the Iranian criminal justice system still too often looked only at the accused's list of offenses rather than taking stock of their mental health and asking whether they could be held criminally responsible for their actions. Those with mental disorders, the young scholar notes, should not be held responsible for their crimes because they did not have a "unity of personality" (*vahdat-e shakhsiyat*). Criminal justice in Iran needed to incorporate lessons from the modern psychological sciences and sociology, Qahremani argues, because these revealed that mentally ill persons must be cared for differently than healthy persons who know right from wrong.[89] For Qahremani, prison is an ideal site of care and of rehabilitation—an answer to the question of how to treat and even cure harmful social pathologies.

Among the most influential legal scholars in Iran in this period was the aforementioned statesman and onetime president of the Iranian Bar Association, Ahmad Hooman. As a professor at the University of Tehran, Hooman wrote extensively on law, crime, punishment, and criminal psychology, taking up some of the issues referenced in Qahremani's thesis. In an essay called "Psychological Disorders in Iran's Criminal Courts," for instance, Hooman addresses a wide array of diagnoses, including schizophrenia, "reactive disorders," and "functional psychoses," as well as their importance in matters of criminal liability. He examines approaches to mental health issues and criminal justice with reference to European and US norms such as the so-called McNaughton rule, the legal standard established in the United Kingdom in the 1840s exempting the "insane" from the same standards of criminal liability, and the Durham rule, which similarly exempted those with mental illness from criminal liability in the US.[90]

In 1960, Hooman wrote a monograph called *Prison and Prisoners*—the first published monograph by an Iranian scholar to take up the sole topic of prisons. Like most other criminological texts published in Pahlavi Iran, the text focuses more on general trends in the "science of prisons" than on Iran's legal or penal system specifically. Hooman was very much among the modernist legal thinkers empowered by the Davar-era changes to the judiciary, and as such he dedicated the book to Davar—the person whom he claimed was the first in Iran's history to "[pay] attention to the state of prisons and prisoners."[91] Hooman is clear-eyed in his appraisal of the current state of Iranian prisons. "There is no doubt," Hooman admits, that when it came to prisons, things "are not in a good state in our country and the means to discipline and reform prisoners . . . don't exist." His book is an effort, he explains, to help students gain facility with the criminological theories necessary to improve this state of affairs.[92] "If this book directs the attention of our dear students to matters of discipline and the reform of prisoners and prisons and prepares them for this social service [*khedmat-e ejtema'i*], that will be reward enough for my labor," Hooman avers.[93]

As criminology further established itself as a regular academic pursuit in Iran, the psychomedical logics hinted at by these earlier texts became all the more commonplace. A 1973 monograph written by Taj Zaman Danesh, one of Iran's foremost criminologists both before and after the revolution, represents the culmination of two decades of criminological thinking in the country. In Danesh's work, acts deemed criminal are described in pathologized terms: "The criminal is like a patient [*bimar*], and just as a doctor orders various tests on the patient in order to diagnose their disease, the judge must collect information for a file on the individual personality of each offender, in order to discover the reasons and motivations for the crime."[94] The Swiss- and French-educated Danesh, who was a prison reform advocate as well as a University of Tehran professor, worked directly with Pahlavi law enforcement institutions to advance reformist aims. The link between the government and academia is made clear by Danesh's relationship with the Tehran Police Academy, where she taught, and which republished some of her writing expressly for use by its cadets.[95]

This wasn't the only link between police training in this era and the field of criminology, as the national police department also built a small museum of criminology, where police academy cadets were taken to learn about fingerprinting techniques and "scientific" police methods and see "paraphernalia used in committing various crimes."[96] These modern policing methods, of course, amounted to a significantly more intensive surveillance state for *all* Iranians, affording a remarkable new ability to collect and use data from millions of Iranian citizens—a project hinted at in the prisoner dossiers of the Swedish officers and expanded in subsequent decades. By the mid-1960s, for instance, Iran's National Police Bureau of Identification held a repository "with over 5,000,000 photographs and fingerprints classified according to the Henry system on file.... Given the proper classification, any card [could] be produced in fifteen seconds."[97] Yet in Danesh's scholarship, the modern surveillance state is cast as a healer-reformer of individual prisoner pathologies rather than as the authority who simply punishes without regard for prisoners' health. This preoccupation with prisoners' bodies and psyches represented a new strategy of power that was at once invested in technologies of the body and in the management of populations.[98] For criminologists (and the government that employed them), the expanding prison populace represented both a source of latent danger and a site of experimentation with methods of discipline and reform. And for both academic criminologists and the Pahlavi government, social ills from drug use to vagrancy were increasingly subjected to heavy surveillance and carceral thinking. In other words, modern prisons were recast as therapeutic institutions that could heal or even cure and thus eradicate these social ailments.

PRISON REFORM UNDER MOHAMMAD REZA SHAH

On October 9, 1954, just a little over a year after the CIA-led 1953 coup that deposed the popular prime minister Mohammad Mossadeq and placed Mohammad Reza Pahlavi back on the Peacock Throne, the Iranian cabinet approved the bylaws for the Institute for the Cooperation and Industry of Prisoners (ICIP; Bongah-e ta'avun va sana'i-e zendanian), a state-run organization mandated with founding prison factories and education facilities and supporting the families of the incarcerated.[99] With financial backing from another state institution, the Organization for the Protection of Prisoners (OPP; Anjoman-e hemayat-e zendanian), the institute initiated a prison labor and education program that the Pahlavi elite advertised as an important modernizing victory. It wasn't until 1959 that the institute secured funding for the machines and tools necessary to begin its work in Iran's prison factories. That year, through the OPP, the Pahlavi government gave machines, tools, and capital in excess of 285,000 rials to the institute to put toward expanding those factories. The institute established new factories in both the men's and women's prisons, with workstations for sewing, metal works, automobile repair, furniture building, shoemaking, purse making, embroidery, basket weaving, belt making, straw mat making, rug making, sock knitting, frame building, hair and makeup, handicrafts, and fine arts.[100] By 1965 there were at least 30 skilled experts or technicians in the Qasr Prison factory who taught skills classes and worked in a management capacity. There were also an estimated 850 male, 95 female, and 45 youth workers in prison work programs throughout Iran.[101]

The institute credited its founding to the progressive nature and reformist zeal of Mohammad Reza Pahlavi, whom they claimed had reformed Iranian prisons along "civilized" and "humane" principles.[102] After 1963, these successes were situated by institute officials in the broader context of the shah's White Revolution reforms, a spate of top-down reforms including infrastructure projects, literacy and health services, and women's enfranchisement undertaken with input from American economic consultants.[103] A 1965 speech given at the eighth general conference for the OPP by the then national chief of police Major General Mohsen Mobasser, whose police force numbered approximately thirty thousand and whose office oversaw the Iranian prison system,[104] revealed the extent to which the language of the social sciences, as well as language popularized by Marxist intellectuals, buttressed the organization's view of Iran's prisons. Highlighting the "humanitarian efforts" (*talashha-ye ensani*) of those working to improve the lives of prisoners in Iran, Mobasser invoked the "language that is common today and is called dialectics" in order to "scientifically explain" the government's prison expansion and reform efforts. "The dialectical method," the chief of police continued, "teaches us that every phenomenon must be studied in a state of flux, transformation, and evolution [*takamol*]."[105] Instead of merely punishing for the sake of punishing, Mobasser stated, civilized and rational modern nations such as Iran under Mohammad Reza Pahlavi meted out punishment scientifically, humanely, and effectively.

That the national chief of police would reference the dialectical method in a speech about law enforcement deserves further comment. Dialectics and the dialectical method, a foundational philosophical language with roots in ancient Greek thought, had by the time of Mobasser's speech long influenced modern intellectual movements owing to its transformative theorization by German philosopher Georg Hegel and especially its perhaps even more influential theorization by Karl Marx. For later Marxists and Marxist-Leninists, "dialectical materialism"—a phrase never actually used by Marx himself but popularized by some of his later acolytes—turned the Hegelian abstraction of idealist dialectics on its head, providing a necessary materialist theory for historical change. It is hard to overstate the Marxist valence of the language of dialectics in this mid-twentieth-century context, Iranian or otherwise. Lenin and Stalin both wrote extensively on dialectics and dialectical materialism, which Soviet theorists popularized as "diamat." By the time of Mobasser's mid-1960s speech, Marxist-Leninist theories of dialectics had dramatically shaped the theoretical scope of several strains of Marxism—from Stalinism to Maoism to Western Marxism and the Frankfurt School and beyond—as well as innumerable leftist political movements across the global south, Iran included.[106]

So just how did an Iranian police chief working for the avowedly anticommunist government of Mohammad Reza Shah come to deploy this seemingly unlikely philosophical language? Some background on Mobasser himself might help solve this apparent riddle. Born in Tabriz in the year of the Bolshevik Revolution, Mobasser came of age in the era in which the newly coronated Reza Shah was using the expanding carceral arm of the state to suppress and dismantle the Communist Party of Iran and other political opposition, imprisoning much of this opposition in Qasr under the aegis of the 1931 law banning any political activity that hinted of communism. As a young man, Mobasser graduated from the Tehran military academy and eventually grew into a key figure in military intelligence and law enforcement during the reign of Mohammad Reza Pahlavi. After a series of key appointments, during which he had direct experiences of the 1953 coup, the era of suppression that followed, and the 1963 Khomeini-led protests of White Revolution reforms, Mobasser was placed in charge of the civilian Tehran police force. Two years later, he was appointed deputy chief of police of the National Police Force (Shahrbani-ye kol-e keshvar), and in 1964 he was made chief of police of that same force, where he would remain until 1970.

Mobasser also worked closely with the International Police Academy and Agency for International Development in the Office of Public Safety of the United States State Department, helping send Iranian cadets to train with that academy and even giving the academy graduation speech in Washington, DC, in 1967. In that speech, Mobasser lauded the academy's work, stating, "As Director of the National Police of Iran, I have observed the results of participation by many of my own officers in this Academy. We are proud of this participation and their contribution to the mutual exchange, the give-and-take of experiences which highlights the Academy's work. This sharing of knowledge is playing an important part in the development and growth of our national police department."[107] Mobasser's career is emblematic of the blurred lines between civilian law enforcement, the military, and intelligence in Pahlavi Iran as well as of the links to policing norms materially supported by the US in this era. It was Mobasser's years serving in military and intelligence posts that gave him his most important firsthand insight into Iranian Marxism specifically and Marxist social theories more broadly.

Mobasser's most significant contribution to midcentury Pahlavi military intelligence is his supporting role in helping suppress and dismantle the military organization of the communist Tudeh Party in his capacity as an intelligence-gathering officer in the Second Bureau (Rokn-e dovvom) of the Iranian army. The Second Bureau, which was modeled on the French Deuxième Bureau and reported directly to the shah, was the military's surveillance and intelligence-gathering force and served as something of an intermediary organization between the era in which the urban National Police Force was tasked with surveillance and the 1956 establishment of a formal intelligence organization in SAVAK.[108] Throughout the late 1940s and 1950s, as Iranian intelligence forces, with an assist from the CIA, dramatically and systematically dismantled the Tudeh Party, arresting, torturing, incarcerating, and even executing party leadership, Mobasser held several high posts in the Second Bureau.

Mobasser knew little about communism or its principles when first assigned to anticommunist army intelligence operations in the late 1940s, later claiming, "Until that point, I must confess that I hadn't paid any attention to what the truth of communism is, or what these people are even talking about. I didn't understand communist ideology."[109] But having been tasked with helping ferret out Marxists in his midst in the officer ranks of the army, where Tudeh sympathizers had made considerable inroads, Mobasser began to research what Iranian Marxists were actually reading and thinking. Feigning sincere interest, he asked a sympathetic army officer to recommend socialist reading material for him. That officer recommended the writing of famed Iranian Marxist Taqi Arani—who was arrested in 1938 and died in prison in 1940—and his foundational journal *Donya* (The world), which was initially going to be called Materialism.[110] Incredibly, before the paranoia that would necessarily overtake the Iranian left in the coming years of suppression, Mobasser procured Arani's writing by simply walking into the Tudeh Party club offices in Tehran and requesting books and journals, including issues of *Donya*. As Mobasser himself later explained, "They prayed to God [*az khoda mikhastan*] for the opportunity to give [military officers] books and have another one join their ranks."[111]

The chief of police was not alone in learning the fundamentals of what were then current Marxist theoretical or organizational trends in Iran from Arani, the famed Iranian Marxist leader of the Group of 53. After Arani's death and Reza Shah's 1941 forced abdication of the throne, it was the formerly incarcerated members of the Group of 53 who would go on to form the nucleus of what became the Tudeh Party. Arani's writing played a foundational theoretical and pedagogical function in midcentury Iranian intellectual trends as well. As Siavash Saffari has noted, Arani "played a key role in introducing Iranians to the theoretical foundations of Marxism and to some of the then ongoing debates in European socialist circles. In particular, [he] used the terminology of dialectical materialism to evoke what European Marxists at the time called *scientific* socialism."[112] Starting well before his arrest and death in prison, Arani's work had been widely read by leftist study groups and student groups in Iran, particularly his essay "The Materialist Concept of History." In the 1930s, before the formation of the Tudeh, study and student groups were formed by the Provisional Central Committee of the Communist Party of Iran. As M. Reza Ghods argues, these student study groups succeeded because "Arani's exceptional humanity and abilities as a teacher attracted many young people to his movement."[113]

Mobasser read Arani's work closely, in time gaining a reputation in the Second Bureau as something of an expert in Iranian communist theory. Yet Mobasser's invocation of dialectics was not simply the whim of one idiosyncratic intelligence officer. As Afshin Matin-Asgari has compellingly argued, during the era of the shah's top-down White Revolution reforms, the Pahlavi elite assimilated and repurposed languages and logics drawn from Marxist theory in general and the Tudeh in particular in a multipronged efforts to defang the influence of the Tudeh in Iranian politics.[114] Not long after Mobasser and his colleagues decimated the Tudeh Party—likely with help from the CIA in decoding the Tudeh's cryptographic code[115]—those same Pahlavi officials were borrowing language born of leftist movements in Iran to promote the intellectual and social scientific bona fides of their policies, including their prison policies.

The policing and carceral reforms that became emblematic of this era, along with the anticommunist law enforcement officers who carried out that work, must further be situated in the context of post-coup efforts by the Pahlavi state to strengthen Iran's institutions of policing, intelligence, surveillance, and incarceration. The founding and training of the notorious Pahlavi intelligence agency SAVAK is the most well-known part of this story. In the immediate aftermath of the 1953 coup, American military officers working for the CIA were sent to Iran to aid General Teymour Bakhtiar, the newly appointed military governor of Tehran, in the building of a bigger and better Iranian intelligence force. The eventual result of this collaboration was SAVAK, which was formally founded in 1956 and would remain an infamous stalwart of Iranian intelligence and law enforcement until the revolution of 1979.[116]

It was not only political dissidents who would experience the impacts of US-trained militarized policing. "Ordinary" detainees who encountered Iranian law enforcement also felt these effects. As Maziyar Ghiabi's work shows, drug users were among those on the front lines of this surveillance. In 1957, just as the CIA was training SAVAK, a United States Federal Bureau of Narcotics supervisor by the name of Garland Williams was setting up a new narcotics squad in Tehran. For Iranian law enforcement agencies and their American backers, "anti-narcotics went hand in hand with the expansion of the intelligence service."[117] The global powers further influenced drug-related policies in Iran, advising and even coercing the Iranian government (among others) to incarcerate drug users, threatening embargos "against those countries which held non-transparent attitudes on illicit drugs."[118] Two decades before the language of the War on Drugs was popularized in the US context, police training literature produced by the US State Department in conjunction with the Iranian National Police Force was already using this language to explain the new surveillance technologies being used in Iran. "New enforcement techniques such as roving flying squads," Mobasser explained in the State Department–published *International Police Academy Review*, "have enjoyed great success [in Iran]. Selection and training of qualified investigators is being increased and the National Police will soon have 25 of these squads to intensify the war on narcotics."[119]

The United States armed forces would further help the Pahlavi government in its efforts to muscle up its systems of policing, punishment, and social control across the country. In 1959, the United States Army sent a military mission led by Colonel Charles Maclean Peake to Iran to oversee reforms to the Imperial Iranian Gendarmerie, although Peake also worked with the Iranian National Police Force and the Iranian Army during his time in Iran.[120] Remarkably, Peake presented his efforts and aims in Iran in the same language that marked the rhetoric of Iranian police and prison personnel in this era, all of whom championed the "humane" nature of Pahlavi carceral reforms. In a memo to his superiors describing his experiences in Iran, Peake claims that the US military mission was deployed to Iran specifically in order to "encourage reform ... and to urge adoption of modern and humane techniques of police and general administration."[121] This would not be the only time US law enforcement agencies applauded Iranian policing and prison reforms. The International Police Academy (IPA), an institution run by the US State Department that helped train Iranian law enforcement, particularly singled out the Iranian Bureau of Prisons as exemplars in its efforts. In a piece penned by Chief of Police Mobasser himself for the IPA's *International Police Academy Review*, the Iranian police chief boasted, "Nowhere is the evidence of progress in professional competence [in Iran's National Police Force] more noticeable than in the National Police Prison system. In the last few years this has been completely reoriented from a punitive to a modern psychologically oriented and humane system."[122]

Yet according to Peake's confidential reports, the US played a role in training the Iranian gendarmerie and army in militarized methods of riot control, particularly after rolling protests broke out in Fars and Khuzestan in response to land reform measures.[123] (Peake blamed the unrest on Minister of Agriculture Hasan Arsanjani, who spearheaded initial land reform efforts in 1962.) According to Peake, US support for Iranian military and law enforcement also took the form of significant financial aid. As Peake notes, "Under a generous and adequate allotment of military assistance which is 3% or less of the total military assistance to Iran to date, the Gendarmerie has been equipped to a standard perhaps slightly beyond the present aggregate skills of the organization. It has first-rate arms, communications equipment, and motor transportation . . . , aircraft, and boats." What failures existed in the program, Peake proclaims, were the result of Iranian cultural defects. The American army colonel ruefully continues, "US schooling has been generous, the effect being less pronounced than one would hope, for there are cultural defects hard to overcome."[124]

How did all of these influences come together in the Pahlavi prison policies of the 1960s? In his aforementioned 1965 speech, Mohsen Mobasser argued that advances in punishment techniques were not simply technical advances for the state but rather leaps forward for the betterment of all people. Echoing the Iranian scholars mentioned above as well as their European criminological influences, the chief of police explained that it was not merely dangerous to punish a detainee disproportionately to their crime, but it would also be dangerous for society if the state were to do so:

> The goal of punishment in earlier society was only retribution [*qisas*] and revenge. . . . As a result, punishments were inhumane [*ghayr-e ensani*], using torturous acts without any results in terms of the reality of crime

[in society]. Not only wasn't any positive result achieved but the vengeful atmosphere also led to the committing of worse and more horrific crimes.... Every day, criminality increased in terms of both quality and quantity.[125]

This economy of criminality became a core ideal of late Pahlavi carceral thinking. Drawing from theories first promoted by European criminologists and prison reformers and later promoted by American sociologists and buoyed by the triumphalist telos of Pahlavi state nationalism, Pahlavi prison discourses promoted the belief that Pahlavi-built prisons would help eradicate—or at least radically reduce—crime in Iran.

After the midcentury founding of the ICIP, members of Iran's government and law enforcement agencies increasingly promoted Iranian prisons as therapeutic and curative rather than punitive in nature. In his 1965 speech, Mobasser outlined the by now familiar metaphor of crime as curable pathology:

> Just as the doctor fights against a dangerous disease by before anything learning about its root causes . . . a criminologist or judge . . . must certainly use this same method in the fight against criminality. Just as a doctor can't operate on a patient suffering from rheumatism by simply amputating their arm, a judge can't simply eliminate or imprison one murderer or thief in the fight against murder and theft in general.[126]

According to a 1967 report in *Kayhan* newspaper, Mobasser spread a similar message to Iran's prison wardens that year. The chief of police told prison officials that Iran's prisoners were simply sick people and were to be treated "humanely" so that they could be cured of their criminal impulses.[127] Mobasser wasn't the only member of the Pahlavi elite to spread this rehabilitative message. No less a personage than Queen Farah remarked in 1968, "Most prisoners are capable of reform and cultivation [*tarbiyat*] and are regretful of their criminal actions."[128] In this telling, Pahlavi prisons were spaces where the incarcerated were sent "*as* punishment, not *for* punishment" (emphasis added). If prisons didn't treat prisoners humanely, then the whole of society would suffer. The empress made this point explicit: "If prisoners see nothing but violence [*khoshunat*] inside of prison, and their families outside are in distress and have no refuge, then those prisoners will become cynical towards society and their antisocial aspects will predominate and they will again turn to crime."[129] Prison bore the responsibility for either the recuperation of the incarcerated or their further descent into social pathology.

The institute routinely touted its work as representing great leaps forward for health both physical and mental, hygiene, and dentistry in Iran's prisons. It further boasted that drug abuse and epidemic diseases among prisoners were both nearly eradicated by Mohammad Reza Shah's efforts. Yet evidence from prisons of this era reveals the significant limits of Pahlavi prison reform efforts. Vakil Abad Prison in Mashhad, today referred to as the Central Mashhad Prison, opened its doors in the late 1960s with a ribbon-cutting ceremony headed by Queen Farah Pahlavi but was within a few years already "dropping to pieces; the electrics, the plumbing, the showers, the toilets, the locks, the heaters, the fly-screens, the whole place was a mess."[130] At the infirmary at Vakil Abad, a large facility whose incarcerated population has from the beginning held disproportionate numbers of Afghans and those held on drug-related charges, "most of the medicines had expired, especially the antibiotics, which were rejects or unsold stock sent back by pharmacies and hospitals all over the country."[131] Drug use, violence between prisoners, organized crime activity, and of course severe overcrowding also remained issues in prisons in Mohammad Reza Shah's era despite formal insistence to the contrary.

Despite these obvious difficulties, Pahlavi law enforcement and prison officials continued to champion the therapeutic and restorative capacity of Pahlavi prisons. In another speech given in 1968, Chief of Police Mobasser again lectured on the necessity of viewing crime as a social disease and boasted that Iranian society had been utterly transformed by Pahlavi efforts:

> There have been remarkable changes in the science of criminology. The prison system has totally been transformed, such that today the prison is no longer a place meant for the negation of freedom. Instead, the prison is a treatment center in which criminals and lawbreakers are taken ... after which the social illness with which they enter is cured.[132]

But by what mechanism did the state claim to guarantee the transformation of the "bad" criminal into the "good" citizen? The answer for the Pahlavi government in this era was labor. Prison labor was promoted as being capable of restoring a prisoner's health, honor, social standing, and moral compass.

Labor, which was imagined in gendered terms with the division of labor for men and women strictly defined, offered a means through which to remake not only the criminal's body and mind but also his or her subjectivity. Male prisoners were put to work in factories or on farms, while women were taught sewing and embroidery (fig. 10). The institute viewed teaching female prisoners sewing, cooking, and home management as integral to its mandate, because women needed to be prepared for future lives as homemakers.[133] The stated goal of Pahlavi prison reformism was the embodied production of healthy, normative, modern citizens. Upon release, the new citizen's body would be healthy, strong, laboring, and gendered. In 1975, the Pahlavi government further turned these reforms into mandated prison policy with a new prison code—the Regulatory Code Governing Prisons and Affiliated Industrial and Agricultural Institutes. As a result of this code, detainees under

FIGURE 10. Workers in the Qasr Prison factory making shoes, mid-1940s. Source: Hedayatollah Hakim-Elahi, *Ba man beh zendan biyaid* [Come with me to prison]. Tehran: Sherkat-e Sehami, 1325/1946.

thirty years of age were required to participate in vocational training as well as physical exercise.[134]

Labeling its expansion of prison labor "social work," ICIP literature asserted that its goal was not profit-making, despite the organization's close accounting of its bottom line.[135] Rather, it positioned itself as the state's means to "train and educate" those Iranians who had fallen on the deviant path so that they could eventually "live nobly."[136] Despite their insistence that they were uninterested in profits, ICIP materials boasted of raising 4,807,594.23 rials in a decade's time. According to the institute, however, prison labor not only benefited government institutions but also aided the prisoners themselves. Institute literature claimed that 25 percent of prisoner wages would be set aside in bank accounts at Iran National Bank, another 40 percent sent to prisoner families, and 10 percent given to prisoners for daily expenses. The Pahlavi government made use of the supply of cheap prison labor, putting the incarcerated to work for the benefit of other state institutions. In 1963, prisoner-workers made new tables, chairs, benches, cabinets, bookshelves, and clothes for police officers all over Iran for "half the cost" of non-prison labor.[137]

The Pahlavi state opened several new prisons in this era, many planned specifically to expand the prison labor program. Qezel Hesar Prison, which was located eleven miles from Tehran in Karaj and opened its doors in 1968, was built with both maximum- and minimum-security wings and outdoor farm facilities for crop management and animal farming.[138] In 1969, the journal of the Tehran police claimed that Qezel Hesar, which it euphemistically referred to as a "work and training center," was one of the "model" prisons of the world due to its capacity to put prisoners to work in the fields of metalworking, carpet weaving, appliance manufacturing, and more.[139] The same article boasted that a conjugal visitation space had also been added to the facility in order for prisoners to meet with their wives so their sexual lives would not be disrupted—a boon for prisoner and wife alike, according to the author. (Qezel Hesar, which was among the sites of the 1988 prison massacre, remains among the biggest prisons in the Islamic Republic.) Other prisons built in this era—specifically, two-thousand-capacity facilities in Mashad and Shiraz—were based on blueprints first used at Marion Penitentiary in Illinois in the United States.[140] The relationship between the Iranian prison facilities and the now infamous Marion Penitentiary is one upon which it is worth dwelling. Though it is now the smallest prison in the US federal prison system, USP Marion has long served as an important if troubling blueprint for carceral sites around the world. Opened in 1963, just a few years before its design was transported to Iran, Marion's blueprint was used almost immediately internationally for prisons in locations including New Zealand, Israel, and the United Kingdom. As Greg Mewbold writes about Paremoremo, the New Zealand prison based on USP Marion, these prisons illustrate "how substantially American social trends have become an international phenomenon and how, more particularly, American modes of criminal justice have been adopted in other parts of the world."[141] The methods of social control used in USP Marion, including novel experiments in solitary confinement and "group therapy" in which prisoners were made to express penitence for their deviant behavior, were also exported and used in a variety of national contexts, Iran included, all looking for new means to control "trouble" populations.

Despite the hopeful rhetoric of the ICIP, which claimed that criminality in Iran would be radically reduced or even eradicated through "progressive" carceral methods, the numbers of incarcerated Iranians steadily increased under Mohammad Reza Pahlavi. Official statistics kept in Iran in this period, for instance, show year-over-year increases in the number of arrests brought by the police, from 59,315 in 1968 to 151,024 in 1973.[142] Rather than being "cured" of the social contagion of crime, as these technocratic state discourses promised, vulnerable members of the Iranian citizenry instead underwent what scholar Lisa Cacho has termed the process of criminalization. In Cacho's theorization, criminalization is not merely the process by which some individuals or communities get marked as potentially criminal but rather the processes by which specific *actions* are newly categorized as "crimes," thus rendering populations who have historically undertaken those actions vulnerable to state intervention and violence.[143] In Pahlavi Iran, drug use, some nonnormative sex acts, border crossing and smuggling, and reading politically radical texts (to give just a few examples) were all criminalized and carceralized over the course of several decades. Later, in the postrevolutionary Islamic Republic era, many of these same acts have remained objects of state intervention, and other acts (certain forms of gendered dress, for instance) have been newly criminalized. In other words, carceral modernity in Iran has not addressed the problem of an essential criminality; it has produced "criminals" in need of carceral intervention and discipline by the state.

In the following two chapters, I turn to dissident movements in the late Pahlavi period and their experiences with torture and extrajudicial violence. Few if any of these tortured dissidents mentioned the ICIP's supposed mandate to treat prisoners "humanely." Yet I argue here that the expansion of torture under the Pahlavis should be viewed neither as a paradox nor as hypocrisy, despite the government's formal outlawing of torture and their rhetorical commitment to "humane" punishment. Nor should it be viewed, as it was by many dissidents of the day, as *only* a political response in the wake of the 1953 coup meant to elicit information on opposition movements—though information was typically its primary immediate aim. Instead, I end this chapter by suggesting that it is no coincidence that the use of torture expanded in Iran precisely in the era in which the body and psyche of the prisoner were taken as pliable objects to be molded and refashioned "scientifically." The discipline and cultivation of the bad prisoner into the good citizen, so important to Pahlavi prison reformism, was pushed to its logical extreme through the more aggressive application of state violence through torture. And, with the establishment in the 1960s to 1970s of forced public recantations, in which "reformed" political prisoners were made to profess allegiance to the state against their former comrades and to disavow their formerly held beliefs, Empress Farah's above comment that "all prisoners are capable of reform and cultivation" takes its most sinister shape.

Three

LIKE A FERTILE STORM
*Prisons and Revolutionary Worldmaking
in the Iranian Guerrilla Era*

THE LATE 1960S USHERED IN A NEW ERA AMONG IRANIAN DISSI-
dents, many of whom were driven by the belief that the old methods and
parties were no longer sufficient in the increasingly stultifying conditions
of Mohammad Reza Pahlavi's Iran. In this era, Iranians, particularly a new
generation of students, leftists, and young Muslims, agitated for a militant
politics of action that they believed would lift the pallor that had fallen over
Iranian opposition movements in the wake of the 1953 coup and the state
repression that conspicuously marked its aftermath. For these young militants, the first step in changing Iran's political culture and state structure
was to puncture what they saw as its oppressive and defeated mood. The
only way to do so, they argued, was to take up arms and fight. "In brief and to
put it simply," Marxist guerrilla leader Hamid Ashraf wrote, the aim of Iran's
new militants "was to break the atmosphere of repression . . . and to show
the people of our country that the only possible way of struggle is armed
struggle."[1] The inaugural salvo of this new militancy took place on February
8, 1971, when a small group of armed Marxist guerrillas stormed a gendarmerie post in the northern Iranian village of Siahkal near the Caspian Sea.

The event that came to be known among sympathizers as the Siahkal resurrection was a political lightning bolt for other fledgling Iranian dissidents and would-be revolutionaries. As one young comrade of Ashraf's put it in 1973, Siahkal was "like a fertile storm that then became a turning point in politics. The old dead ends were destroyed and a new path was opened for the freedom fighters [*mobarezin*] of Iran. Armed struggle ... put an end to conjectural studying and theorizing behind closed doors."[2]

Upon their emergence, the Iranian militants of this new generation were greeted by a colossal show of power by Mohammad Reza Shah's armed forces and particularly SAVAK, resulting in the arrest, torture, incarceration, forced confessions, and death of thousands of politically active Iranians. Practically speaking, the shah's government, which was always fearful of communist efforts in its midst, decimated the guerrilla movement over the course of the decade, putting together a response as ferocious as its treatment of the Tudeh Party mentioned in the previous chapter. Never massive to begin with and centered in just a few cities in Iran, the guerrilla movement found itself at a low point when the revolutionary mass movement the guerrillas had long dreamed of flowered without their leadership in 1978–79.[3] The guerrilla movement didn't bear state violence quietly. Throughout the 1970s, Iranian guerrillas and their sympathizers decried extrajudicial Pahlavi violence and publicized accounts of their torture and ill treatment in the shah's prisons, and through these efforts, their struggle gained attention from a growing body of revolutionary students, militants, fellow travelers, and some dissident clerics. The guerrillas mapped Iranian prisons and interrogation centers onto the same revolutionary cartography as global sites of repression and resistance from Palestine to Vietnam to Cuba. Over the course of the movement's short and tumultuous existence, guerrilla entanglements with the disciplinary and carceral arms of the Pahlavi state came to be central to the guerrillas' emancipatory vision for Iran and to their project of revolutionary worldmaking. The guerrilla movement also flipped the carceral script promoted by the Pahlavi government and its prison technocrats; rather than that which marked the Pahlavi state as progressive and humane, prisons became that which marked the shah as unfit for rule.

This chapter examines the history and scattered archive of the Iranian guerrilla movement through its foundational experiences with Pahlavi policing and incarceration, arguing that the public life of the Iranian prison took new shape in the guerrilla era. The guerrilla movement, while small in numbers, had an outsized role in both publicizing Pahlavi prison conditions and torture and in producing a diffuse and subterranean revolutionary culture and aesthetic that left a lasting mark on Iran's political landscape. While several scholars have noted the practical reality of the widespread torture and imprisonment of Iranian militants and revolutionaries before 1979, and others have studied the development of the guerrilla movement in the context of Iran's revolutionary movement more broadly, there is no study that focuses on the importance of state violence, particularly torture, to guerrilla theory, material cultures, and praxis.[4] Yet it was through these entanglements between the shah's prisons and interrogators and the imprisoned guerrillas that Iran's guerrilla movement most publicly theorized state power and embodied discipline and a revolutionary horizon of possibility.

I further argue that the guerrilla encounter with Iran's carceral system represents a crucial chapter in what I have been calling the public life of the modern Iranian prison, insofar as guerrilla publicity of Pahlavi prisons played an indispensable role in establishing the shah's reputation as repressive autocrat. The enduring image of the shah as torturer, later taken up by international human rights advocates (to whom I will return in the next chapter), comes in no small part from the entanglement of Iran's guerrilla movement with the disciplinary and carceral arms of the Pahlavi state. It was in many instances the guerrillas who most vociferously publicized and literally bore the scars of Pahlavi torture. If, as I've argued in this book, the early Pahlavi state inaugurated a modern carceral imaginary in which an expanded penal system was promoted as a necessary and progressive solution to various social crises in Iran, guerrilla discourses turned that imaginary on its head, contending instead that it was precisely the government's carceral record that necessitated the shah's ouster.

This chapter shines a light on these overlooked carceral archives and histories, arguing that our historical understanding of prerevolutionary Iranian prisons continues to owe a great deal to prerevolutionary guerrilla movements. In addition to its argument regarding the public life of the Iranian prison, this chapter also makes two interventions into the historiography of the guerrilla movement. First, I argue that although guerrilla prison writing has sometimes been read as either simple propaganda or the marginalia of an ultimately failed movement (insofar as the guerrillas didn't seize state power), it constitutes an important if understudied corpus of Iranian revolutionary political history and theory in its own right. This chapter seeks to add to the scholarly conversation on the Iranian guerrillas by further excavating and expanding the archive of the movement, much of which is dotted across private and public archives around the world. Rather than focus on major Marxist guerrilla theorists like Bizhan Jazani and Masoud Ahmadzadeh or Islamist intellectuals who influenced the movement like Ali Shari'ati, who have received the lion's share of the movement's historiographical and theoretical attention to date, this chapter looks much more closely at the "minor" archive of the guerrillas—pamphlets, prison poetry and songs, broadsides, cartoons, and other typically anonymous subcultural ephemera and material culture. I argue that this revolutionary ephemera, a great deal of which is invested in addressing incarceration and political violence, was integral to producing Iran's revolutionary conditions of possibility even as the guerrillas themselves were marginalized by the ulama-led government that took and consolidated power from 1979 to 1982.

My final aim in this chapter, beyond what I have outlined above, is to address and reconsider how scholars of Iran have understood "success" and "failure" in discussing Iran's revolutionary political movements. The historiography of Iran's guerrilla movement, both the Marxist-Leninist left and its closely-related Marxist-Islamist cousin (sometimes known as the "Islamic left"), has often been understood using the rubric of "failure"—failure to avoid Pahlavi repression, failure to seize state power, failure to stop the clerical movement, failure to foresee the violence of the postrevolutionary clerical government, failure to anticipate a need for democratic rights, failure to turn its revolutionary hopes into a lasting program for social justice.[5] These critiques have merit, but they also have some analytic limitations. The rubric of failure and the language of loss—themselves poignant legacies of an English-language scholarly tradition born in part in a condition of postrevolutionary exile—obscure our contemporary analytical need to address and examine these histories beyond what they did not or could not accomplish and to instead retrain our sights on the transformational openings they produced in their own day.[6] Drawing from Manijeh Moradian's "methodology of possibility," which she theorizes in the context of Iranian student revolutionaries living in the United States, this chapter investigates if and how guerrilla efforts changed the terrain and language of the possible in Iranian politics. What were the worldmaking implications of these guerrilla efforts? How did the guerrillas push Iranians to think differently about institutions of the modern state such as the prison? The rubric of failure examines doors closed and paths foreclosed; this chapter looks to dwell in moments of opening and possibility in an era that Behrooz Ghamari-Tabrizi (recalling Foucault) has reminded us was one at the threshold of novelty.[7]

Before continuing, some further notes on both terminology and archive are in order. I draw my use of the term "worldmaking" from political theorist Adom Getachew, who in her work *Worldmaking after Empire* argues that Third Worldism, Pan-Africanism, and Black internationalism should not be remembered solely as nationalist projects committed to postcolonial self-determination but rather as projects invested in fully remaking an unequal world.[8] Getachew reminds readers that European imperialism and capitalism were themselves global in scope and thus worldmaking forces and that revolutionary Third Worldisms similarly sought to remake the world by upending entrenched relations of power. I use her insight here to insist that the Iranian guerrilla political imaginary had worldmaking—and not merely nation-making—implications of its own, although the guerrillas also worked to diagnose the Iranian (and in some cases Shi'a) particularities of their condition in what they considered to be an autocratic semicolonial state. For the guerrillas, this ethos was at once diagnosis and cure: ordinary Iranians were shackled by both a torturing autocrat and by global imperialism, they believed, and the means by which this unequal and unjust world could be remade was through asymmetrical armed struggle.

Yet it is not only in the theoretical texts written by relatively well-known Iranian guerrilla theorists that one encounters this worldmaking impulse; guerrilla responses to Pahlavi prisons and torture were also foundational to the militant movement's ethical and political imagination. Guerrilla pamphlets and broadsides, self-published and circulated under conditions of political repression, self-consciously created alternatives to state-sanctioned narratives of Iranian politics, history, and carcerality in real time. By mapping Iran's prisons, outlining interrogation and torture tactics in detail, and offering alternative readings of Iranian history and politics, the guerrilla movement produced not only a separate archive from that of the state but a subterranean *archive-in-opposition*. Guerrilla discourses provided an oppositional history-of-the-present; guerrilla organizations attempted to explain the contemporary Iranian condition in terms that directly challenged the Pahlavi government's official narrativization of the past, present, and future of the country.

In what follows below, I outline the history of the guerrilla movement and some important public encounters between the guerrilla movement and Pahlavi carceral, legal, and disciplinary institutions. How did the shah's government respond to these young militants? How did the guerrillas respond in turn, and by what means and to what ends did these encounters produce new public cultures of repression, resistance, and political reimagining? From there, I outline the history of Iran's political prisons in this era, examining the social world of the prison as lived by members of the revolutionary movement, Marxists and Islamists alike. These carceral social worlds are a crucial part of the story insofar as they represent the space through which Iranian dissidents most viscerally came in contact with Pahlavi state power. Further, political prisons were also a fundamental arena for political organizing and education in this era. Finally, I examine the archival traces and material afterlives of Iran's guerrilla subcultures. As noted, these materials were typically produced clandestinely in ephemeral formats—flyers, broadsides, pamphlets, copies of copies—and passed through networks of students, revolutionaries, political prisoners, and activists both inside and outside of the country. Given its diffuse and do-it-yourself nature, and the political vicissitudes of postrevolutionary Iran and its diaspora, the archive of the guerrilla movement is both scattered and by definition incomplete. As such, this chapter's aim isn't to achieve an impossible completionism but rather to dwell in the ephemerality of these revolutionary subcultures and consider the types of political openings these materials produced. Although the story I outline below transpires before 1979, the stakes and legacy of this history are not limited to the prerevolutionary era: without closely examining these guerrilla-era prison histories, we can neither understand the political attachments of the prerevolutionary era in Iran nor can we fully grasp the continued importance of Iranian prisons and political prisoners in the contemporary Iranian political imagination.

THE PUBLIC LIFE OF THE GUERRILLAS

The inaugural guerrilla action at Siahkal was undertaken by a fledgling Marxist organization soon known as the Organization of Iranian People's Fadai Guerrillas (Fadaian, or OIPFG)[9], a group composed of small blocs that had its beginnings in reading circles founded in the early 1960s.[10] Despite the pride of place Siahkal would soon enjoy in narratives of resistance to the Pahlavi government, the operation was a practical failure for the young armed Marxists, resulting in the arrest, trial, and eventual execution of all of those who participated. Yet in the aftermath of the arrests of the Siahkal guerrillas, student activists and other budding guerrilla groups—most notably the Marxist-Islamist People's Mojahedin Organization of Iran (PMOI)— were inspired to take concrete action for the first time.[11] For the next several years, Iranian guerrillas attacked other strongholds of Pahlavi power, assassinated members of the state, and performed numerous acts of political violence and sabotage. For the guerrillas, these armed operations had two disparate aims. Any given action had an instrumental goal, such as occupying military posts and seizing weapons or targeting specific individuals for assassination. Beyond these practical concerns, however, was the conviction that armed actions created popular ripples that far exceeded their limited military significance. Following the logic on single sparks and full-blown fires extolled by global guerrilla movements around the world in the decades after the Chinese and Cuban Revolutions, the Fadaian theorist Bizhan Jazani termed these militant actions "armed propaganda." For the early Fadaian, these spectacular acts of political violence would have the effect of bringing the revolutionary cause, as well as the guerrillas' vanguard role therein, to the public eye, igniting a mass movement.[12]

Yet public information on the guerrilla movement spread, perhaps paradoxically, through both guerrilla and Pahlavi state machinations, as both the government and the movement publicized their entanglements to broader audiences. Subverting Foucault's insight that modern punishment is an unseen phenomenon that happens out of the public eye, the shah's government staged military tribunals for arrested guerrillas, in several cases publicly, despite—or perhaps because of—evident signs of torture.[13] From the majority of trials, which were held in secret, official newspapers published a steady stream of forced recantations featuring defendants disavowing their militant parties and beliefs. As Ervand Abrahamian notes in his study of forced recantations in modern Iran, the era of public confessions—officially called "interviews" and publicized widely on radio, television, and newspapers—started in earnest in the aftermath of Siahkal.[14] The Pahlavi government also held some public trials for the benefit of international observers, as internationalist advocacy on behalf of Iranian prisoners increased both among the international left and among global human rights advocates. For the Pahlavi government, these trials and the recantations they elicited were meant to project state power and stability, yet ironically, many young Iranians learned of and came to sympathize with the revolutionary movement through these state-sponsored means. Even the 1971 Siahkal operation, despite its eventual place in opposition lore, gained little public notice at first. It was not until the trial and execution of those who undertook the mission that the operation came to be popularly known, even in dissident circles.[15]

For the guerrilla movement, trials and military tribunals provided opportunities for publicity and propaganda, particularly in instances when defendants refused to confess to any wrongdoing despite obvious signs of physical duress and apparent torture. One particularly important such trial happened not long after Siahkal, when members of the budding Mojahedin-e Khalq Organization—whose worldview in these foundational years promiscuously blended Marxist class analysis with Shi'ite tropes and narratives—planned an even more spectacular act of political violence against the monarchy, conspiring to explode Tehran's main electrical plant and ruin the festivities planned for the shah's 2,500 years of monarchy celebration in August 1971. Before they could carry out their plans, over a hundred members of the group were arrested by SAVAK; their downfall was sealed through an attempt to acquire dynamite from a communist former prison-mate of some in the organization who had turned into a police informant.[16] Charges against the first arrested members of the group, including arms smuggling, plotting to bomb buildings, and conspiring with foreign agents, were published in *Ettela'at* newspaper in February 1972.[17] In 1972, sixty-nine of those arrested, including Naser Sadeq, a member of Mojahedin's Central Committee, were put on trial. Global observers noted evident signs of torture of the accused, as "inquiry about police practices from the outside world" dogged Pahlavi efforts to try the defendants.[18] It was in this heightened climate that several members of the group's Central Committee gave impassioned speeches condemning the Pahlavi government and lauding armed guerrilla action. Sadeq's fiery statement introduced listeners to the name of their organization: the People's Mojahedin Organization of Iran. Transcripts of these statements began circulating among university students and politicized Iranians by word of mouth and via printed pamphlets and broadsides, and the eleven people sentenced to death were made into instant martyrs for the movement.[19] The Mojahed guerrillas presented the shah's prisons and interrogation centers as exemplary of the violence and despotism of the shah's government on the whole; in these courtroom defenses, Iranian prisons (and SAVAK interrogators) were irrevocably linked to a political and moral order increasingly seen by this generation of young militants as unjust.

Although the Fadaian and the Mojahedin received the bulk of the eventual publicity, small militant groups also surreptitiously circulated their comrades' final courtroom statements in the hopes that their words would inspire further revolutionary action. The defiant early 1970–71 courtroom statements of Marxist guerrillas Houshang Taregol of Arman-e Khalq (The People's Ideal) and Shokrollah Paknejad of the short-lived Palestine Group circulated both inside and outside of Iran, thanks in part to other Marxist guerrillas and to a large expatriate Iranian student movement.[20] Although these groups were minuscule even in the context of generally small militant organizations, their tortured or executed members became narratively important to the guerrilla movement. Taregol, who was executed, became a martyr for the cause, as guerrillas linked to the Fadaian publicized not only the Arman-e Khalq leader's courtroom defense but his biography, highlighting small-town roots, working-class links, and militant actions.[21] For his part, Paknejad, who was arrested with seventeen other members of his group in 1970 before Siahkal, was executed in 1982 by Khomeini's government.[22]

These courtroom defenses often shared similar worldviews and structures: an indictment of the shah's despotism and reliance on imperialist powers (particularly the US), the guerrilla's love of the Iranian people, and myriad references to the brutality of Iran's prison and the effect those prisons had on further strengthening the guerrilla's resolve to fight to create a new political order. In Taregol's final defense, which took place after the 1970–71 arrests of members of his group, the young revolutionary inverted the military trial's desired logic of forced confession.[23] "I confess," Taregol defiantly stated, "that during my year of detention the sparks of struggle in my soul turned into burning flames." Later in his defense Taregol linked the seeming pedagogical and disciplinary function of the shah's prisons to his own revolutionary education and training in that institution. Describing brutal prison conditions including the vicious beating to death of an "ordinary" prisoner the young guerrilla witnessed, Taregol continued, "I wrote [about poor prison conditions] in response to you who are so certain that you disciplined [*tarbiyat*] me during my one year in prison. Of course, there is no doubt that I was trained [*tarbiyat*] in prison, as it was in prison that I saw the foul manifestation of our present system."[24] The notion of *tarbiyat*—a word that in Persian can mean discipline, education, training, or some combination thereof—was an important one throughout guerrilla prison texts, connoting both the painful disciplining that guerrillas endured at the hands of their torturers and the revolutionary discipline that they embodied in order to prevail over those same torturers. As noted in the last chapter, it is a key term in Iranian prison discourses more broadly—as when Empress Farah said in 1968, "Most prisoners are capable of reform and cultivation [*tarbiyat*]."[25]

Of Iran's numerous 1970s political trials, it was the televised trial of Khosrow Golsorkhi and Kermat Daneshian in 1973–74 that had the most dramatic public impact. Golsorkhi (a poet and journalist), Daneshian (a filmmaker and journalist), and the so-called Group of Twelve with whom they were arrested, tortured, and tried became symbols of revolutionary heroism and martyrdom in the aftermath of their trials and executions.[26] These twelve men and women, largely artists, writers, and journalists, many of whom had never met before their arrest, were arrested in 1972 for allegedly plotting against members of the royal family. As it did with other such cases, the government published accounts of the trial as well as the forced recantations of members of the Group of Twelve in *Ettela'at* newspaper. The government also decided to theatrically televise the military court proceedings, in evident expectation of recantations from all of the accused. This added to the prevailing sentiment that SAVAK embellished the danger from the Golsorkhi group and saw the public trial as a way to score a clear victory against the rising tide of public militant action in Iran.[27]

Televising the trial backfired spectacularly. Although most of the group confessed to crimes against the state, personally apologized to the shah, and were given reduced sentences, Golsorkhi, Daneshian, and three others refused to do so despite signs of physical abuse and the looming threat of death. Golsorkhi and Daneshian's statements went further than statements from those who only declined to recant their views: the two young writers offered all those listening full-throated and poetic defenses of revolutionary Marxism and armed struggle. As Hamid Dabashi has noted, Golsorkhi's statement not only championed Marxism-Leninism but also drew movingly from Shi'a iconography and tropes, recasting the first imam, Ali, as a proto-revolutionary in his own right and the fight against the Shah as a modern-day Battle of Karbala; in other words, the promiscuous mixing of Marxist and Shi'a tropes was not limited to the Islamic left.[28] The two men were executed soon after, and three others who didn't apologize or recant their views were sentenced to life in prison. After the fall of the shah in 1979, the trials of Golsorkhi and Daneshian were broadcast in full on revolutionary television, this time spliced with footage of interviews with Iranian workers.[29] The post-revolutionary broadcast of the trial had the effect of flipping the intended prerevolutionary royalist logic of the military tribunal: the crime in question was no longer conspiracy against the state, and the trial and sentence were no longer against the Marxist writers. Instead, it was the shah's government that was deemed criminal. Other military tribunal defenses of tortured or executed guerrillas continued to circulate globally both before and just after the revolution, revealing the centrality of Pahlavi carcerality and the guerrillas' role both in publicizing it to the Iranian revolutionary imagination and in the making of the shah's bloody global reputation.[30]

THE INCARCERATED MOVEMENT

The guerrilla era introduced a new generation of Iranian dissidents, the majority of whom were below the age of thirty-five, to Iran's ever-expanding carceral system.[31] The 1960s and 1970s saw growth in Iran's prison system, with several maximum-security prisons and interrogation centers opening their doors across the country in the late 1960s and 1970s. In this era, despite substantial and consistent expansion starting in the 1920s, Iran's prisons continued to suffer from brutal and seemingly intractable overcrowding. According to one prisoner, the general wing in Qasr Prison in Tehran was "crowded, tumultuous, and noisy," while "the temporary wing [for Qasr's political prisoners] was exceptionally crowded" with prisoners "all crammed into tiny rooms together. There was such a shortage of space that some . . . had to sleep in the prison corridors."[32] This overcrowding plagued Qasr in the post-coup era despite the prison adding two new blocks—one for women and one for "politicals."[33] Despite efforts to keep political prisoners in solitary confinement during interrogation, Pahlavi prisons and interrogation centers also experienced perpetual shortages of such cells.[34] Overcrowding was not limited to political prisons or to the prisons of Tehran. For instance, in the Abadan prison, where Group of Twelve member Abbas Samakar was exiled as punishment, and which almost exclusively housed common-law prisoners on ostensibly nonpolitical offenses, detainees were forced to stand shoulder-to-shoulder in one painfully crowded yard area all day.[35] Despite being the only political prisoner in the Abadan prison, Samakar was treated with respect by the other prisoners due specifically to his association with Golsorkhi, revealing the extent to which those political dissidents who withstood Pahlavi torture were held in esteem even by those prisoners not viewed as political prisoners as such. Something else linked Samakar's exile to common-law prisoners in Iran: the practice of exiling Tehran-based prisoners to remote prisons, particularly those in the south, was a long-standing tradition in Iran for political and common-law prisoners alike. Common-law prisoners during the Reza Shah era, for instance, were sent from Qasr to Bandar Abbas throughout the 1920s to 1930s.[36] During the Mohammad Reza Shah period, clerical dissidents such as Sadeq Khalkhali also experienced internal exile, in Khalkhali's case to several different small and far-flung locales.[37] The practice of internal exile predates the Pahlavi period, as those who ran afoul of Qajar shahs and nobles were often given such treatment, and it continues in the Islamic Republic, revealing the extent to which punishment logics born before the entrenchment of the carceral state have been folded into the project of modern carcerality.

The most notorious of the new prisons built in the 1970s was Evin Prison, designed in 1971 by famed Iranian architect Amir Nosrat Monaqah and situated in northern Tehran at the foot of the Alborz Mountains.[38] When Evin first opened its doors in 1971, it had an initial capacity of 320 detainees. Three hundred of these prisoners were to be held in two large communal blocks, with the other 20 to be held in solitary cells. By 1977, however, Evin had expanded many times and held over 1,500 prisoners, with 100 or more prisoners held in solitary confinement.[39] Yet as early as 1972, the just-opened Evin was so overcrowded that, at times, prisoners were made to sleep in makeshift tents outdoors.[40] Evin was not the only new prison or interrogation center to deal with immediate overcrowding. At the newly opened Komiteh-ye Moshtarek-e Zedd-e Kharabkar (Joint Anti-Sabotage Committee) interrogation center in Tehran, the minuscule solitary cells were made to hold up to four or five men each.[41] The Komiteh, which became the primary entry point into the carceral system for political arrestees starting in 1971, was run cooperatively by the police force, the gendarmerie, and SAVAK in an effort to coordinate efforts in an era of interagency rivalry; its gruesome reputation throughout the 1970s rivaled only that of Evin.[42] Before the opening of the Komiteh, newly arrested political detainees would typically first be taken to Qezel Qalʻeh Prison in Tehran, also sometimes known as Qezel-e Sorkh, or the Red Castle, where they were held with covers over their heads in interstitial spaces while awaiting interrogation.[43] Qezel Qalʻeh was first turned into a prison after the 1953 coup by Taymour Bakhtiar, the first head of SAVAK; it was originally a weapons depot. In 1960, Pahlavi statesman and legal scholar Ahmad Hooman explained that the site was opened specifically with the incarceration and interrogation of Tudeh officers in mind and that significant construction was done on the space to make it appropriate for this task.[44] This prison closed its doors in 1971 after nearly twenty years of housing political detainees.

Unsurprisingly, cleanliness, hygiene, and health were constant concerns in the teeming prisons and interrogation centers of the era. A former Muslim student activist describes mid-70s conditions in the Komiteh prison as "damp and poorly lit, to the extent that it was often difficult to see anything at all upon entering the cells. The floors were carpeted with rugs that had two layers—one layer the fabric of the carpet itself, and one layer the filth and blood that had caked onto the rug from the feet and bodies of prisoners."[45] Conditions were often dire for prisoners, both dissidents and common-law prisoners, who needed medical attention. At the infirmary at Vakil Abad Prison in Mashhad, a large facility whose incarcerated population included those held on felony charges, drug users, smugglers, a few political prisoners, and a large number of particularly ill-treated Afghan prisoners, "most of the medicines had expired, especially the antibiotics."[46] Meanwhile, at the Abadan prison, prisoners were made to share one filthy plastic hose as a communal *aftabeh*, much to the consternation of prisoners.[47] "Naturally," one former prisoner writes, "it was impossible to clean oneself and still manage to avoid catching every illness."[48] Throughout the 1970s, late Pahlavi prison conditions were described in much the same way as those that led a commentator from the earliest years of Mohammad Reza Pahlavi's rule to exclaim: "Dying in prison is basically nothing. The infirmary is there to help poor people die."[49]

After Qezel Qal'eh's 1971 closing, political detainees would typically enter Iran's carceral system through the Komiteh interrogation center, Evin Prison, or regional SAVAK-run jails and interrogation centers outside of Tehran. Political prisoners were often housed in solitary confinement in the aftermath of their arrest and were allowed into general holding cells upon the end of their first interrogation period.[50] At different points in the guerrilla era, solitary cells for political prisoners could be found in Tehran at Evin, Qezel Qal'eh, and the Komiteh, as well as in several smaller SAVAK-run sites outside of the capital. Interrogations featured a dizzying array of painful punishment techniques including beating, electric shock, burning, fingernail removal, forced immobilization, sexual assault, and, of course, the enduringly popular bastinado, or whipping on the soles of the feet. After often lengthy and painful interrogations, prisoners would typically be moved to general holding cells to await trial, sentencing, and transfer to the political wing of Qasr, where they would ostensibly serve out their sentences.[51] By 1973, however, this was not usually the process for most political prisoners who had been condemned to death. Such prisoners were typically held in solitary confinement until the moment of their execution, even in cases of rampant overcrowding. According to one former prisoner, this policy changed due to the influence that earlier condemned prisoners, particularly members of the aforementioned Arman-e Khalq group, exhibited on their comrades in general holding.[52] And, as has been the case throughout Iranian carceral modernity, the letter of the law regarding sentencing and quick trial was often disregarded in this era, leaving numerous prisoners unsentenced, untried, untransferred, or simply forgotten while awaiting their fate.

Despite these hardships, and despite increasingly heavy regulations in the aftermath of Siahkal, prison often served as a political training ground for young Iranian militants, with discussion circles held when possible and new party connections forged behind bars. In a practical sense, Pahlavi prisons were important in Iranian political life in the 1960s and 1970s in part because this is where many politically active Iranians—mostly leftists but also both lay and clerical Islamists—spent critical months or years of their lives. To stave off boredom and maintain bodily discipline, militant prisoners tried to exercise in groups, naming certain exercises after fallen comrades.[53] Marxist detainees memorialized their fallen comrades in the Arman-e Khalq group, while others memorialized earlier figures killed by the shah's security forces. For instance, Abbas Samakar, one of the men arrested with Golsorkhi and Daneshian's so-called Group of Twelve, recalls that while in the general wing at Qasr, he and his comrades did group workouts in which one exercise was named the "Vartan move," after Vartan Salakhanian, a rank-and-file member of the Tudeh Party who, along with scores of his comrades, had been arrested, tortured, and executed in 1954 in the era of post-coup repression.[54] These embodied rites had the effect of linking even novice imprisoned militants to earlier dissidents who had been tortured or killed for their cause and further linked the prisoners to a poetics of resistance beyond prison walls. Salakhanian, after all, had also been memorialized by Iranian modernist poet Ahmad Shamlu in his poem "Vartan's Death," which hauntingly depicts the silences around such extrajudicial executions.[55]

As guerrillas frequently noted in their prison writings, targeted physical activities also had important practical outcomes: they expended energy that might otherwise be manipulated by prison guards and interrogators during difficult interrogations. Guerrillas were particularly invested in the maintenance of physical routines, which were thought to help incarcerated militants better control their minds in the face of painful interrogations and anarchic prison life. One anonymous 1971 Mojahedin pamphlet explained to readers—that is, to political sympathizers and potential future prisoners—that guerrillas in solitary confinement should exercise as regularly and rigorously as possible so as to tire themselves out, release anxiety, and even sleep in between torture and interrogation if possible.[56] For their part, especially in the aftermath of Siahkal and as guerrilla activities increased, Pahlavi prison and intelligence officials worked to disrupt any continuity or routine that prisoners made for themselves behind bars.

Muslim political prisoners formed their own social and intellectual circles in prison. Individual and group Qur'an recitation and the singing of religious songs helped pass the time.[57] A text by one Muslim guerrilla recommends Qur'an recitation for prisoners in solitary confinement as a means to remember their connection to a higher power.[58] As leftist prisoners often noted in their writing, practicing Muslim prisoners would help *all* prisoners keep a daily sense of time in dark facilities by awakening for morning prayers.[59] Among Muslim prisoners, prayer groups were common when not banned by the prison authorities, as were discussion circles in which prisoners discussed the work of dissident clerics or theorists such as Ali Shari'ati, the influential and eclectic lay Islamist revolutionary. Shari'ati, the anticolonial thinker often referred to as the ideologue of the revolution, himself endured two prison terms before his 1977 death. His first imprisonment was in 1964, first in Khoi Prison in Azerbaijan and later in Tehran. His second imprisonment was at the Komiteh in Tehran from 1973 to 1975.[60]

By 1972–73, prison officials acted in response to these communal activities, and group prayer was actively suppressed at Qasr when it was apparent that these prayers had distinctly political and organizational ramifications.[61] Young Muslim militants, many of whom were politicized on campuses and in cities in which they intermingled with leftists, found themselves increasingly influenced by politicized members of the ulama whom they met in penal institutions and whose influence eventually pushed them to associate only with other Muslims.[62] Ironically, these prayer and discussion groups often brought together incarcerated militants, clerics, and students who otherwise would not have been able to meet in the heavily surveilled outside world. Revolutionary cleric Ayatollah Hossein-Ali Montazeri describes this atmosphere of education and exchange in prison in his memoir: "During the Shah's period, prison was similar to a classroom. Anyone who wished to become skilled and more mature should go to prison where one has the opportunity to see and converse with many people, an opportunity which for many does not exist outside the prison walls."[63] As historian Sussan Siavoshi notes in her biography of Montazeri, the dissident cleric found his time in the shah's prisons invigorating insofar as it allowed him to share and exchange ideas with likeminded members of the ulama and even with unlike guerrillas, whom he met during his incarceration at Evin.[64] In 1975, the intermingling of religious and Marxist prisoners would end when, under the influence of militant clerical revolutionaries and prisoners, Islamist prisoners began to strictly observe the practice of not eating or sharing space with "unclean" Marxist unbelievers.

As with earlier political prisoners in Iran, incarcerated guerrillas shared books when possible, creating a makeshift library in wings 4 and 5 of Qasr's political prison general holding cells in the early 1970s. All of these books, which included literary, historical, sociological, and economic texts, were held in these wings and then loaned out systematically among prisoners. A schedule was posted to the wall of the wing wherein prisoners could request a book for two hours at a time; when their two hours were up, prisoners returned books so they could be loaned to the next borrower.[65] A number of books, including Nasser Khosrow's travelogue, issues of Iranian intellectual journal *Ketab-e Hafteh*, and a handful of foreign magazines such as *Time* and *Newsweek*, were available in the general holding cells of Evin Prison in 1971–72.[66] One Marxist student and translator who read anything that he could find in his time at the Komiteh prison in 1973 notes that his father, a rank-and-file member of the communist Tudeh Party in the 1950s, had spent *his* time in Qasr Prison reading *Les misérables* aloud to the those incarcerated on petty theft and drug charges with whom he had been temporarily housed as punishment.[67] Another former leftist guerrilla notes that prisoners in Qasr in the early 1970s endeavored to pass around tiny scraps of paper with Lenin's *What Is to Be Done* through a complicated and surreptitious scheme enacted while using the bathroom. As with group prayer, these activities were increasingly suppressed in the context of rising guerrilla actions after Siahkal.[68] The atmosphere in Pahlavi prisons would again change in the late 1970s, when outside pressures led to the relaxation of some of these measures and the shah allowed outside observers, including the Red Cross, to visit some of Iran's most notorious prisons.[69]

MATERIAL CULTURES

In a context in which state institutions had a stranglehold on news media, Iranian dissidents produced a vibrant material subculture aimed at countering official Pahlavi state narratives of civilizational and national progress. These materials, circulated as pamphlets, tapes, records, poetry, and flyers, endeavored to engender revulsion toward the shah's prisons and SAVAK-led torture chambers and concomitantly evoke esteem for Iranians resisting their oppressors and torturers. Some scholars have noted the transformational importance of cassettes recorded by Ayatollah Ruhollah Khomeini in exile and circulated among Iranians in the immediate lead-up to the mass movement and revolution of 1979.[70] Others have noted the importance of posters on the aesthetics of the revolution.[71] Less has been written about the broad circulation of other revolutionary ephemera and media throughout the 1970s, both inside and outside of Iran. This now-scattered material culture included cassettes, records, pamphlets, manifestos, books, posters, and more, none of which were mass produced or freely distributed in Iran but which nonetheless worked to circulate revolutionary ideas and aesthetics over the course of the decade.

Opposition political cartoons, for instance, routinely depicted Mohammad Reza Shah as the embodiment of the false promises of Pahlavi state modernity and nothing less than the king of torture. One such political cartoon depicted the shah in his customary military regalia standing in front of a prison lined with the bodies of dead prisoners and stating, "My nation doesn't like progress!" (fig. 11). Such cartoons not only challenged specific Pahlavi prison practices but also contested the Pahlavi government's boasts of leading Iran's leap forward into a "Great Civilization." Whereas the Shah touted his White Revolution reforms as the pinnacle of modern advancement for the country—while simultaneously disavowing the borrowed leftist provenance of the language of these top-down "revolutionary" reforms—dissidents and guerrillas challenged the real-world effects of Pahlavi state modernity.[72] Such cartoons linked the shah viscerally and bodily to Iranian prisons and the violence therein, as in one example featuring the shah removing a thin mask of humanity to reveal a ghoulish and skeletal prison behind (fig. 12). In the revolutionary imagination, Mohammad Reza Shah came to stand in for Iran's notorious prisons body and soul, with his well-manicured and highly curated modern veneer barely hiding the terrifying reality within.

Dissident ephemera and word-of-mouth prison songs were powerful practical vehicles for communicating revolutionary sentiments. In these materials, the trope of Iran-as-prison circulated widely, with the guerrillas, often likened to the burning flames or the rising sun, ushering in an emancipated future. According to one former leftist prisoner imprisoned from 1973 until 1979, cassette tapes of movement music recorded by those on the out-

FIGURE 11. "My people don't like progress!" From *Taqut nameh*, a revolution-era pamphlet full of similar political cartoons. Source: The International Institute of Social History Archive, Amsterdam, Holland

FIGURE 12. Political cartoon depicting Mohammad Reza Pahlavi as a prison ghoul. From *Taqut*. Source: The International Institute of Social History Archive, Amsterdam, Holland

side were circulated among prisoners in Qasr whenever conditions permitted it.[73] Outside of the prison, poems, pamphlets, and multimedia releases were covertly passed between movement sympathizers, the guerrilla rank and file, and sympathetic students both inside and outside of the country. Whether produced by Muslim or Marxist-Leninist revolutionaries, certain themes and tropes were shared across this carceral archive. Revolutionary discourses often focused on the act of martyrdom, extolling the virtuous sacrificial acts of those who had already given their lives for the movement and for a brighter future. One Islamist prison song from 1970 typifies this type of emancipatory lamentation: "Let us remember our martyrs / Who have gone on the road of love and hope / They are the spellbound stars / That lead us on the way to white morning."[74] These prison poetics created sentimental, moral, and political ties among those inside the shah's prisons and those who came into their political orbit, including a sizable population of students and intellectuals to whom these pamphlets and broadcasts were most regularly circulated. These songs provided interpretations of the past, present, and future: the past as lost opportunity, the present as both repressive prison (and opportunity for struggle and martyrdom), and the future as a revolutionary time transformed by the acts undertaken by heroic guerrillas in the darkness of the present day.

One typical example of this guerrilla prison ephemera is a pamphlet called *Beh aftabkaran: Ghazalsorudeha az band* (To the sunplanters: The songs of the cell), which features songs and poems written in Qasr and the Komiteh interrogation center by incarcerated members of the Marxist Fadaian.[75] The Fadai guerrillas were called *aftabkaran* by sympathizers, a Persian-language portmanteau best translated as "sun planters" (the phrase can be translated literally as sunshine planters). The notion that these revolutionary *aftabkaran* planted the seeds of a dawning emancipatory future directly contradicted the guerrillas' representation in official Pahlavi discourses as *kharabkaran*—troublemakers, saboteurs, and terrorists. The longer version of this Fadai sobriquet was *aftabkaran-e jangal*, or "sunplanters of the forest." Through this simple reference to the *jangal*, or forest, the Fadai guerrillas affectively connected their struggle to both national and global political movements. The Iranian reference point was the 1915–21 Jangal movement, a social democratic struggle for autonomy against colonialism and royalist despotism led from the forests of Gilan against the Qajar monarchy by constitutionalist hero Mirza Kuchek Khan.[76] Of course, as Rasmus Elling has noted, unlike the Jangal movement, "most of the Fada'is' formative experiences with political activism in the 1950s and 1960s took place in urban space ... the Siahkal attack was the exception to a prerevolutionary history of largely urban activity."[77] The second reference point was the rising global tide of Third Worldist revolutionary guerrillas, who often championed the mountains and the forests around the world as their natural homes. Iranian guerrillas saw revolutionary movements from Algeria to Cuba to Brazil as intimately linked to their own.⁷⁸

Guerrilla poetics also articulated and dwelled on the particularity of Iran—and in the case of Islamist dissidents, Shi'ism—linking their struggle to armed national or religious movements of past eras. It is in this context that guerrilla prison poetics routinely likened the appearance of armed struggle in Iran to the arrival of the dawn after a long and arduous night, while often likening that night to a dark prison cell. Throughout these guerrillas' carceral discourses, Iran was often reimagined as an imprisoned nation. As one Fadai prison song declares:

> After that / Heavy month of Mordad / Your anger is asleep / In the ashes of summer / Oh my homeland, oh my Iran / Oh my homeland, oh my prison / The flame of the sun is radiant / Over the red storm of revolution / Like the guerrilla who marches ahead with anger and blood / From heart and iron and smoke and plow and plough / The monarchy shall topple / Shall topple.⁷⁹

For the guerrillas, Iran was a sleeping prison-nation in the aftermath of the 1953 coup, which occurred in the Iranian month of Mordad. As was typical throughout Fadai writing, the sun was a stand-in for the revolutionary movement, heroically breathing fire and life into the slumbering nation and forcing the monarchy to fall. This simple poem reveals something of the guerrillas' teleological historiographical imagination, wherein the politics of the post-coup era are narrativized as a moment of darkness, with the guerrilla movement providing the awakening spark. Notably, the Khomeini-led protests of 1963—which involved significantly higher numbers of dissidents and protesters than the mission at Siahkal—are absent as a moment of narrative relevance.

Revolutionary media wasn't limited to the printed word, nor was it solely circulated clandestinely in Iran. In the 1970s, leftist revolutionaries and fellow travelers outside of Iran released several vinyl records featuring prison imagery and music and decrying Pahlavi torture. Although these records were pressed, released, and largely distributed outside of Iran, copies made their way back to Iran through the same networks of students, activists, and revolutionaries that smuggled other dissident materials across the border. While doing field research in Iran, I found copies of vinyl records produced by the expatriate Iranian student movement in several private archives. The private record vendor based in Tehran who sold me copies of some of these records informed me that these prerevolutionary student-produced records turn up in Iran with surprising frequency. One such vinyl record, released in 1975 by the Europe-based Confederation of Iranian Students, National Union, or CISNU, also featured the common visual trope of the era on its cover: a map of all of Iran behind thick prison bars (fig. 13).⁸⁰ Another record, released and

FIGURE 13. *Solh va danesh* EP. Source: Confederation of Iranian Students (National Union) 1354

distributed in 1973 by CISNU in support of the guerrilla movement, featured a well-known cover image of an Iranian political prisoner on the verge of death. A quote from Shokrollah Paknejad of the Palestine Group's military tribunal defense was translated into several languages and adorned the back cover of the album. In that defense, Paknejad promised, "In the face of the use of bestial oppression, in spite of the cruel actions of SAVAK agents against political prisoners . . . the struggle will be carried on to victory."[81] These revolutionary records also included collaborative works, such as a 1979 album coreleased by Iranian students in Canada in collaboration with several other national liberation groups called *Long Live International Solidarity*, featuring Iranian guerrilla songs side by side with movement songs from Haiti, Palestine, India, Canada, Kampuchea (Cambodia), Zimbabwe, and more.[82]

REVOLUTIONARY EDUCATION

As the militant movement grew, so too did painfully intimate knowledge of the Pahlavi security apparatus—a fact that prompted revolutionaries to prioritize sharing information on Pahlavi arrest practices, interrogation methods, and prison conditions. Guerrilla prison writing produced in the aftermath of Siahkal and the widespread repression of Iranian dissidents largely fit into two categories with, to some extent, distinct functions and audiences. The first was outward-facing writing that was nominally addressed to "ordinary" or unaffiliated readers, meant to expose them to the cruelty of Pahlavi prison conditions and the bravery of the guerrillas. The second was inward-facing and addressed to other guerrillas and revolutionaries who might find themselves in similar situations. The latter texts functioned essentially as revolutionary advice literature or as training manuals—that is, as writing addressed to other militants or would-be militants instructing them on how to avoid arrest or how to behave if arrested. Guerrillas counseled each other to dress neatly and act naturally during missions so as not to arouse police suspicion.[83] Maps of Iran's prisons and interrogation centers, including Evin, Qasr, and the Komiteh, circulated in guerrilla publications, without which little would have been known about these spaces during this era (fig. 14).[84]

Guerrillas intimately understood that arrest and incarceration were unavoidable aspects of revolutionary activism, so they came to argue that the

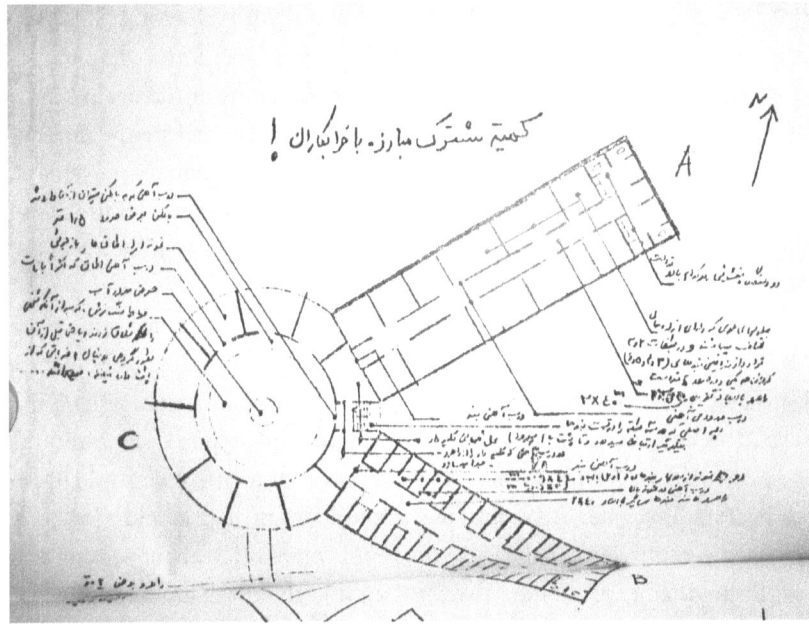

FIGURE 14. "Komiteh-ye moshtarak mobarezeh ba kharabkaran!" Drawing of Komiteh Interrogation Center. Source: ʿAsr-e ʿamal, no. 5, 1973, p. 5

shah's prisons should be conceptualized as a vital front in the struggle. As one anonymous member of the Mojahedin-e Khalq argued in 1972 in the wake of the widespread arrest of much of their leadership, an arrested guerrilla shouldn't assume that their struggle is over simply because they had been detained. On the contrary, the Islamic leftist militant insisted, a new and equally important battle against the enemy was begun upon entering prison.[85] Scholars have noted that the reason detained dissidents endeavored to remain tight-lipped under interrogation was to deny the shah's intelligence apparatus any practicable information that might endanger their comrades.[86] Indeed, information was the central concern for the guerrillas and their interrogators alike. Yet for the guerrillas, tight-lipped resistance under torture was also believed to have broader political ripples. As one guerrilla noted, "If resistance under torture takes the form of a [movement-wide] tradition, the enemy will be disappointed by the process of torture and will eventually find no gain in torturing. Little by little, with resistance, torture will decrease."[87] In this theorization, it was with this certain decrease of torture that mass mobilization would become possible. From this perspective, then, not divulging critical information while under torture not only had concrete implications for the immediate safety of an arrestee's comrades but also had implications for the future of a mass revolutionary movement. In guerrilla carceral discourses, to resist torture was to succeed in ending the vicious cycle of torture altogether and to assure the massification of the movement.

In order to withstand torture, guerrillas and would-be militants were often reminded to study and prepare for SAVAK's psychological tactics. Here, as throughout the guerrilla era and across guerrilla organizations and texts, the concept of discipline was of paramount importance. Militants were urged by their comrades not to believe everything they were told by interrogators. Psychological techniques are used on the battlefield of torture, guerrilla writers claimed, because torture "is more often about scaring and shattering the nerves of the prisoner than it is about the use of bodily violence [*khoshunat-e jesmani*]."[88] But just as torture has the capacity to transform the prisoner into a collaborator, so too does it have the capacity to break the *torturer* if the incarcerated militant is capable of withstanding the punishment long enough to frustrate his or her interrogator:

> The torture-battle is tied to the psychological state of both participants. The interrogator will only continue torturing as long as he believes that the complete surrender of the prisoner is possible. Thus, the prisoner must show precisely enough fortitude throughout the interrogation so as to convince the interrogator that life is not important for him/her, that submission is impossible, and that indeed his/her ultimate goal is to be martyred in their hands. If convinced of this, the state is will be disappointed in its efforts and will invariably shorten the length of time the prisoner is tortured.[89]

In these texts, handed person-to-person among students and militants, the guerrilla body in pain was represented as bearing a crucial responsibility. By not capitulating, the tortured militant could serve not only as political vanguard for a not-yet-born mass movement but also as a surrogate for future prisoners, absorbing pain so that other bodies wouldn't have to. This straightforward calculus is stated no uncertain terms: "Any resistance truly causes the torture of others to be lessened, while any confession will invariably lead to the torture of others."[90] In this embodied economy of pain, the imprisoned guerrilla is performing an essential and transformative world-making labor, upending extant power relations to produce a world in which torture is no longer possible.

Although book-length guerrilla texts were rare in this era in which short pamphlets, broadsides, and subterranean "night letters" could be copied and circulated more easily, the Fadaian published at least two book-length prison memoirs in the 1970s as part of their efforts to educate their rank and file and to spread their revolutionary message. The first, the 1972 *Khaterat-e yek cherik dar zendan* (Memoir of a guerrilla in prison), was written by a young Fadai militant named Yusef Zarkari after his arrest and imprisonment during the wave of resistance and repression that followed Siahkal.[91] The second and much more well-known memoir is the 1974 *Hamaseh-ye moqavemat*, or *Epic of Resistance*, by female guerrilla Ashraf Dehqani, whose memoir was published in the aftermath of her implausible escape from Qasr two years after her 1971 arrest.[92] In part because of the exposure garnered by her spectacular escape, and in part because of Fadaian efforts to publish and publicize her exploits, Dehqani's memoir became (and has remained) one of the guerrilla movement's most widely read texts. It is in large part because of the reputation garnered from this book that Dehqani is described by scholar Peyman Vahabzadeh as a "household name" among politicized Iranians.

Although Zarkari's text doesn't share the renown of Dehqani's, there is some evidence that the Fadai guerrillas would have given Zarkari's text the same expansive treatment they gave Dehqani's had they had the means to do so in 1971–72. Years later, Dehqani herself wrote that "after the publication of *Epic of Resistance*, Comrade Hamid [Ashraf, then leader of the OIPFG] spoke approvingly of the appropriate and attractive print of that book with its red-colored titles and professional lettering, and said yearningly ... 'Would that it had been possible to publish Comrade Yusef Zarkar's book as nicely and with such nice lettering ... unfortunately, at the time such a thing was impossible.' "[93] Although they circulated with different degrees of success, both texts proved important to the guerrilla movement and its understanding of Pahlavi prisons. It is to these two important if understudied texts, and their sometimes-contradictory theories of the guerrilla body in pain, that I now turn.

YUSEF ZARKARI'S MEMOIR OF A GUERRILLA IN PRISON

Yusef Zarkari was born in 1952 on the eve of the US-led coup in Iran and raised in Tehran by an Azeri Turkish-speaking family. Zarkari's father died when he was just nine, causing material hardship for the Zarkari family. In 1971, the nineteen-year-old Zarkari was arrested by SAVAK and interrogated, tortured, and imprisoned after only a short time as a member of the Marxist Fadaian.[94] According to his own recounting of events, Zarkari convinced his SAVAK interrogators of his general ignorance of the armed movement by turning his captor's ethnocentric assumptions about the inferiority of Azeri Turks against them and pretending to be a dim-witted and trusting youngster led astray by manipulative associates. Through these machinations, Zarkari earned his outright release in 1972 after just a brief period of incarceration. This freedom, however, would be short lived; Zarkari immediately rejoined the Fadaian and was killed in a shootout with state forces in Isfahan a year later at the age of twenty-one.

With the guerrilla movement growing in popular exposure and sympathy after Siahkal, other would-be militants and groups sought to join efforts with the larger Fadaian and Mojahedin. It is this inexpert but increasingly militant readership that Zarkari addresses in his prison writing, recounting the details of his arrest and incarceration in order to communicate hard-won lessons at a time of increased police presence across universities, youth clubs, and religious centers. As Zarkari notes of the immediately post-Siahkal guerrilla movement, "The armed movement was an undeveloped organism that was forced to mature under the crushing blows of the antirevolutionaries."[95] Written to address the urgent necessity of educating these inexperienced but headstrong young militants, Zarkari's message largely focuses on practicable advice for the young movement with little attention to the usual excoriation of the Pahlavi government typically found in the era's guerrilla texts.

Zarkari meticulously recounts the circumstances surrounding his arrest, which he believed to have stemmed from a lack of attention to basic detail. Focused attention and discipline, touching on everything from comportment to dress to timeliness, is the obsessive theme of his writing. Zarkari's text lists numerous examples of comrades killed in the shah's prisons or in shootouts with the authorities, warning that their fate awaited those who didn't studiously follow his advice. These fallen comrades were, for Zarkari, revolutionary martyrs to be remembered and lionized. Still, the young comrade understood the *practical* limitations of losing too many guerrillas to early martyrdom and repeatedly emphasizes that avoiding their errors in judgment or preparation was of paramount importance if the revolutionary struggle were ultimately to be won.

Typically, rank-and-file members of Iran's guerrilla organizations had contact with very few other members of their respective groups. When new actions were decided on by organizational leadership, the selected guerrillas would meet at set times and places to get their new assignments or information. Sometimes these meetings would take place with only one other associate. One tactic deployed with success by Pahlavi security forces was to pressure recently arrested militants to share details of their next scheduled meetings. The arrested militant would be taken to their appointment as bait while security officers lurked in the wings. When the unsuspecting guerrilla arrived at the meeting spot, SAVAK officers would come out of the shadows to make the arrest. This process was then repeated with the new detainee. Zarkari described this process in painstaking detail in the hopes that the information would provide other guerrillas with a clear plan to avoid capture.

Zarkari's advice was straightforward: always be on time, never forget or miss a meeting, wait at the precisely agreed-upon spot, and have an intimate sense of the ordinary comings and goings of the meeting spot well in advance.[96] He encouraged guerrillas to stake out locations and learn every possible entrance and exit in the area before meetings. Before undertaking any action, Zarkari explains, a guerrilla must consider scenarios from every angle: "When you are on your way to a meeting, think about what you are doing. . . . Who will I see at this meeting? Is it the first set meeting time or second? Is there anything that implies that the situation is suspicious? Do I know the area of the meeting well? Do I have enough cyanide [to take if I am caught]? Is my weapon completely ready?"[97] Zarkari reminded readers to remain in regimented contact with any member of the group with whom one was planning an action. If a comrade otherwise in routine contact fell even briefly out of touch unexpectedly, it would signal that incriminating evidence should be destroyed. If a comrade missed a set appointment time—typically appointments were set two at a time—the next appointment should be skipped. Zarkari lamented his own inattention to these details at the time of his arrest and warned readers repeatedly to not make the same mistakes.

Upon his arrest, Zarkari was first taken to Evin Prison in Tehran. During his interrogation, Zarkari was repeatedly punched, kicked, slapped, burned, and, of course, whipped on the soles of the feet. In his writing, the young guerrilla outlines every physical abuse and every interrogation question asked both in person and in writing:

> Q: Who do you have meetings planned with, and when and where? A: With a person whose name I don't know.... Q: How will this person arrive at the meeting place? A: It's not clear. He comes a different way each time. Sometimes on foot, sometimes on a motorcycle, sometimes on bicycle.... Q: What color is his motorbike?... Q: If you are not successful in your first meeting, when is the time and place for the second meeting? ... [Written questions:] 1. Your identity is completely known to us. List all of your activities in detail below. 2. Write all of the specifics of your relationship to Person A. 3. Write all of the details regarding Person B, including his address. 4. Write the names of all of the [political] books and pamphlets you have read. 5. You have been accused of membership in a group with communal outlook and procedures. Detail all of your activities with this group.... 7. Detail all information regarding any cellars and secret storage spaces, arms and explosives, photocopiers and typewriters, or pamphlets, books, and publications.[98]

The information Zarkari shared shouldn't be taken for granted as organizational common sense for the guerrilla movement after Siahkal. Rather, it was through these multiplying entanglements with the state security apparatus that a militant common knowledge about Pahlavi policing and its prisons arose. Guerrillas outlined straightforward strategies on how to endure painful punishments in their pamphlets and broadsides; for instance, militants were often warned not to eat or drink if offered food after arrest in order to pass out quickly during torture.[99] These crash courses in guerrilla education were also passed through word of mouth. Among student activists, older and more experienced comrades would pass along strategies in meetings on university campus. For instance, one former University of Tehran student activist with eventual ties to the Fadaian was told to wear as many layers of clothing as possible when attending his first street protests in order to better withstand beatings from police and SAVAK agents.[100]

With the clandestine person-to-person circulation of these texts (or face-to-face transmission of knowledge), even those being arrested for the first time experienced incarceration as an uncanny déjà vu. For instance, in 1973, one anonymous leftist guerrilla described a scene in which, because he had read Zarkari's prison writing, the "atmosphere [upon first entering jail] was extremely familiar. In the face of all of [SAVAK's] actions, I was prepared. I was only surprised when they would leave out a step."[101] Other young dissidents, especially those who sympathized with the armed radicals but who were not members of any revolutionary group themselves, described the mixture of pride and fear that they felt upon being thrown into prisons whose names they'd heard for years. Upon finding herself in the Komiteh and reading "the carved writings of legendary dissidents on the walls of the cell," Shahla Talebi notes having "simultaneously felt proud, burdened by the responsibility of living up to the level of their resistance, and somewhat out of place."[102] Alongside this emergent militant common knowledge came a shared sense of humor. For example, beginning in the late 1960s, young political prisoners, many of them drawn from student activist groups across Tehran, referred to the aforementioned Qezel Qal'eh as "Hotel Saqi" or "Café Saqi" after Saqi, the prison's notorious warden.[103] Another former leftist student recounted taking his jailed comrades' food and other supplies after they had been arrested, and then later having Saqi greet him by name and sardonically welcome him to his friends' party when he was himself arrested some weeks later.[104] This was more than mere gallows humor. Prison had become a social space for young revolutionaries to congregate in a surveillance state.

A driving question for the guerrilla movement was how to minimize, endure, or overcome torture when inevitably faced with it. Unsurprisingly, given the extent of painful physical punishment members of the movement experienced, guerrilla carceral discourses directly and repeatedly addressed the question of the guerrilla body in pain. For Zarkari, to not divulge some sort of information while in extraordinary pain was all but impossible and fundamentally unlinked to a prisoner's dedication to the movement. What, then, could one do in order to prepare for torture? Zarkari recommended that guerrillas invent false stories *before* arrest and to practice "confessing" these so that they would spill out of them as though they were the truth during interrogation. Zarkari's strategy has remarkable implications for a theory of the body in pain. In his schema, one could not simply *be* a committed revolutionary under torture but rather must *practice* for the moment when one is tested through pain. Discipline, a key idea for Zarkari, is an embodied practice in which the militant transforms him- or herself through repetition before interrogation, rather than something he or she simply *has* (or doesn't have) when faced with torture. This theorization of disciplinary practice has resonances to feminist theorist Saba Mahmood's work in a much different context. For Mahmood, ethics should not be viewed as a set of universal values. Instead, ethics is a set of techniques and practices (rather than beliefs) that have transformative capacity. To put it simply, an ethics of practice has the capacity to transform the self.[105]

ASHRAF DEHQANI'S *EPIC OF RESISTANCE*

Zarkari's theory of the body of pain differs considerably from that of fellow Fadai guerrilla, famed female militant Ashraf Dehqani, whose *Epic of Resistance* describes her arrest, imprisonment, and improbable escape from Qasr in 1973. Dehqani is among the most widely known names from Iran's guerrilla decade, and *Epic of Resistance*, which circulated widely among global revolutionary and Third Worldist audiences in several languages, is her most well-known text.[106] Dehqani was lauded as exemplary in guerrilla discourses precisely because her fortitude under torture was so extraordinary and her escape so incredible. For instance, one anonymous Mojahedin author writes, "In trying to torture her, Ashraf's torturers were themselves tortured. All of them exhausted themselves, and still she said nothing."[107] Born in Azerbaijan in 1949, Ashraf Dehqani was politicized in the mid-1960s through the influence of her older brother Behrouz, a friend of the leftist writer Samad Behrangi.[108] Along with her brother, Dehqani joined the guerrilla movement in its infancy. In 1971 she was arrested, interrogated at Evin, and eventually imprisoned in Qasr, from which she managed to escape in 1973.[109] Unsurprisingly, Dehqani's escape from Qasr was the topic of a great deal of guerrilla lore. The Iranian opposition was perpetually caught between wanting to advertise the absolutist brutality of SAVAK torture and the shah's prisons and wanting to show weaknesses in the armor of the state carceral apparatus. Dehqani's story was so popular because it managed to do both.[110]

Despite Dehqani's renown, *Epic of Resistance* has received relatively little scholarly attention.[111] There are, I believe, two major reasons for this. The first is political and related to Dehqani's refusal to abandon the principle of armed struggle long after her comrades had done so in the changed post-1979 context. Some scholars have thus concluded that Dehqani's later theoretical writing is "banal," "naïve," and "unsophisticated," and essentially left it at that.[112] The second and key reason for the scholarly inattention to Dehqani's prison writing—as well as guerrilla prison writing more generally—is in the perceived intellectual insignificance of prison writing to Iranian Marxism specifically and to Iranian political theory in general. Unlike the work of guerrilla theorists such as Masoud Ahmadzadeh or Bizhan Jazani—who himself wrote theoretically sophisticated texts and produced revolutionary paintings in prison—these prison writings do not present themselves as political theory as such. Yet this prison literature circulated widely among militant young Iranians and their international sympathizers in the 1970s. I argue that these prison texts represent a *theoretical* as well as material contribution of the guerrilla movement, insofar as they best reveal the powerful nexus of praxis, ethics, and affect typified by the movement at the height of its popularity. The overlooking of these prison texts has led to a critical oversight of the *popular* effects of the guerrilla movement on the political ethics in this era in which torture became practically synonymous with the shah's rule.

Epic of Resistance is a work of political propaganda, but it is also a meditation on the political effects of the guerrilla body in pain. Upon her arrival at prison, Dehqani was, like all detained militants, primarily concerned with withstanding the pain long enough to give her comrades an opportunity to find new hideouts.[113] Yet it is not simply for this instrumental reason that she claimed to bear the pain of torture. As mentioned above, Zarkari acknowledged that torture is impossible for even committed militants to endure. Dehqani, on the other hand, took it as an a priori fact that a true revolutionary simply would not break under torture. Thus, for Dehqani, torture was a practice through which militants and their movements were strengthened, not weakened. For Zarkari, the guerrilla movement would have to succeed *despite* pain; for Dehqani, they would succeed *because* of it.

Dehqani's narrative represents the other side of the coin of forced confessions, which were broadcast by a government attempting to stage its own power. Pahlavi interrogators were concerned not only with imprisoning militants like Dehqani but also with making them repent their views in forced confessions. They sought to do so using the same practice that Dehqani believed was transforming her into a stronger revolutionary: torture. After a particularly grueling interrogation, Dehqani recounts, she was left alone with a guard. She writes, "The ropes around my ankles were so tight that my blood couldn't flow and my feet had turned black and blue. The bones in my ankles and my wrists against which the rope was pulling were in extreme pain. . . . I was left like this with one of the guards. The entire time we were together the guard appeared very uncomfortable. I felt limitlessly happy."[114] Pain, finally, is transformed into pleasure, because for Dehqani torture will inevitably produce revolutionary change.

In a sense, Dehqani was right—the centrality of Pahlavi torture in the lead-up to the 1979 revolution was so decisive that the movement has been described by one scholar as "the revolution against torture."[115] This sentiment was channeled by the emergent clerical government into retributive tribunals initially focused on serving revolutionary justice to those with close ties to the Pahlavi policing and security apparatuses. In the first months of the revolution, these tribunals tried and executed several high-ranking SAVAK officials who had overseen the interrogation and torture of hundreds of political prisoners.[116] Militant discourses were instrumental in shaping this image of the shah's prisons as spaces of political violence and in imagining a world without the forces that rendered those prisons ubiquitous. That the postrevolutionary government maintained those prisons and expanded the use of torture and extrajudicial violence should not allow us to lose sight of either the promise of this transformative vision or the painful efforts undertaken to publicize this vision to the world.

Four

THE IRANIAN PRISON GOES GLOBAL
*Iranian Revolutionaries and
the International Human Rights Movement*

IN OCTOBER 1976, MOHAMMAD REZA PAHLAVI SAT DOWN WITH AMERican journalist Mike Wallace of the CBS network's Sunday night news program *60 Minutes* for a wide-ranging if confrontational interview. Citing a study by the International Commission of Jurists that alleged torture in the prisons and interrogation centers of Pahlavi Iran, Wallace inquired about the activities of Iran's notorious intelligence arm, SAVAK, which, he noted frankly to the king, has "a reputation for brutality." The shah repeatedly denied allegations of abuse, claiming that in its interrogations Iran did nothing that European countries didn't also do, though he also noted ominously, if vaguely, that "there are intelligent ways of questioning now."[1] In spite of the shah's public protestations to the contrary, allegations of torture in Pahlavi prisons had by the mid-1970s wormed their way into public conversation even in the United States, where Iran was typically considered a modernizing success and a Cold War ally of the US government.

The growing global outcry against torture in the shah's prisons in this era was not limited to just one journalist or even one country. As the Iranian guerrilla movement gained in public renown and several prominent clerical revolutionaries, including key figures like Ayatollah Hussein Ali Montazeri and Ayatollah Mahmoud Taleghani, were also imprisoned and tortured, condemnation of Iran's penal and judicial policies, particularly the torture and military trials of political prisoners, became increasingly international. In other words, in the second half of the twentieth century, the public life of Iran's prisons went global. While those targeted by Pahlavi intelligence in Iran were largely leftists, outside of Iran, advocacy against Pahlavi torture was taken up by an assorted group of occasionally strange political bedfellows: Marxist-Leninists, Maoists, liberal European and US policymakers, Third Worldists, budding human rights organizations, expatriate student groups, journalists, philosophers, novelists, and religious organizations and activists. These different actors' advocacy overlapped, but their politics, visions for change, and understanding of the nature of torture sometimes did not. Yet this diverse global movement moved public opinion against the shah so much that even British ministers of Parliament and members of United States Congress found themselves publicly condemning SAVAK and demanding to know just what was going on in Iranian prisons.

This chapter is an account of the events, discourses, and prodigious transnational activist efforts that made widespread denunciation of torture in Iran possible on the global stage, transforming the shah's international image from liberal modernizer to "the king of torture."[2] I argue that the growing global prominence of torture in Pahlavi Iran provided both a rallying point for Iranian dissidents and a testing ground for the emergent global human rights movement at a time when this movement had not yet cohered into the industry it is today. It also built a global human rights organizational infrastructure specifically invested in rights abuses in Iran that continues to operate today. As such, this chapter represents an effort to expand and complicate the story we tell about two prominent and much-debated 1970s revolutions. The first is the 1979 revolution in Iran, typically called the Islamic Revolution, which overthrew the Pahlavi monarchy and installed the Islamic Republic of Iran under Ayatollah Ruhollah Khomeini. I argue in this chapter that mounting Iranian awareness of and anger at the Pahlavi state's use of torture played a foundational role in producing a shared language and ethics of anti-Pahlavi sentiment among otherwise disparate opposition groups both inside and outside the country.

Although the revolution succeeded as a mass movement led by Khomeini and linked clerical radicals drawing rhetorical (and institutional) power from Shi'a Islam, the revolution's political language was formed by revolutionaries and citizens of varying backgrounds coming together throughout the 1970s to challenge Pahlavi autocracy, corruption, and—crucially, for this book—torture. Although many of the Iranians active in publicizing Pahlavi torture globally did not play leadership roles in the mass revolutionary groundswell of 1978–79, their advocacy irrevocably transformed Mohammad Reza Pahlavi's global reputation and contributed to the growing conditions of revolutionary possibility in Iran. The public life of the Iranian prison, then, was by the 1970s an increasingly revolutionary life. In order to tell the story of the 1979 revolution in Iran in full, we must tell the story of this global movement against Pahlavi prisons and torture.

The second revolution is one of a different order, and it is one not typically discussed as bearing much relationship to Iran's revolutionary movement. I am referring to the sea change in political thought and international organizing that scholars have called the "human rights revolution" of the 1970s, which has rendered rights talk an omnipresent global political phenomenon ever since.[3] This transformation was undertaken at both the institutional and the rhetorical level, with innumerable organizations, activists, writers, and lawyers dedicated to the defense of human rights emerging or expanding in the second half of the twentieth century. Crucially, this second 1970s "revolution" also initially centered the issue of torture. Amnesty International, the organization most associated with the human rights boom in Europe and the US, made its international name in an early 1970s campaign for the United Nations to adopt a resolution against torture. Historian Barbara Keys notes AI's growing popularity through the 1970s among US-based liberals, particularly in advocating for political prisoners and victims of state torture among states friendly to the US government.[4] It was in this era, during which torture came to be seen as the human rights violation par excellence, that AI's Martin Ennals damningly opined, "No country in the world has a worse human rights record than Iran."[5]

Intervening in what has been the largely Euro- and US-centric historiography of human rights, this chapter aims to contribute to a small but burgeoning wave of critical studies on human rights in the modern and contemporary Middle East.[6] These recent studies have been crucial in outlining the long history of human rights movements in the Middle East and North Africa as well as in critiquing the limits of NGOs and international rights organizations in producing meaningful change or in challenging entrenched structures of neocolonialism, neoliberalism, and authoritarian state power. Following these efforts, decentering Euro/American genealogies in the history of human rights is a crucial aim of this chapter. After all, it was not these nascent Euro/American human rights organizations that initiated the deluge of critiques of the shah's prisons. Torture in Pahlavi Iran was brought to international prominence long before groups like AI's investment in the matter by members of a large Iranian opposition movement, which for years and even decades publicized to anyone who would listen the fact that Iranian prisoners were "exposed to the most horrible conditions" and "continuously tortured in the most inhumane way."[7] Beginning in the 1960s, a formidable segment of this opposition was composed of a large and increasingly revolutionary expatriate student population that publicized Pahlavi torture globally more than any other group outside of the country.

To date, there has been surprisingly little scholarship on the historical emergence of "rights talk" in the Iranian context.[8] While there has been important scholarship on human rights and Iran, the lion's share of this work focuses on human rights efforts in the aftermath of the 1979 revolution, not on the emergence of the language of rights as such.[9] Of course, concern for human rights in the contemporary Islamic Republic is not limited to the scholarly sphere. From its founding, the Islamic Republic's use torture and extrajudicial executions of dissidents has been the topic of major international concern, as policymakers, international and Iranian NGOs, rights watchdog groups, expatriate activists, and scholars alike have worked to "name and shame" the postrevolutionary state for its offenses. The political urgency of contemporary human rights activism against torture and extrajudicial violence in the Islamic Republic has obscured the longer history of global campaigns on behalf of Iranian prisoners. This earlier era saw Iranians taking up the language of human rights in novel and sometimes-contradictory ways, revealing foundational contestations over the meaning, content, and application of such rights. Before the advent of the Islamic Republic or the ascendancy of the human rights industry as we know it today, torture in Iranian prisons became that which brought a large global Iranian dissident movement, liberal journalists, nascent human rights groups, European politicians, world-renowned philosophers, Iranian revolutionaries, and even US policymakers into the same contentious political orbit. It is the history of this now-forgotten global encounter, born of the globalized public life of Iran's modern prisons, that this chapter charts.

HUMAN RIGHTS IN PAHLAVI STATE DISCOURSES AND THE 1968 TEHRAN CONFERENCE

In the aftermath of his downfall, Mohammad Reza Pahlavi understood his government's collapse to be the result of a budding interest in something called "human rights." In a memoir written just before his death, the freshly deposed shah railed against what he believed to be the world's unfair judgment of his rule. Terminally ill with cancer and distressed by his newfound instability, the shah chastised not only the leadership that succeeded his own but also those global critics who censured Pahlavi policies. Writing just after fleeing Iran, the erstwhile shah remarked, "Every day reports come of murder, bloodshed, and summary executions.... All these horrors were part of Khomeini's systematic destruction of the social fabric I had woven for my nation during a 37-year reign. And not a word of protest from American human rights advocates who had been so vocal in denouncing my 'tyrannical' regime!"[10] The shah was particularly embittered by what he felt was cold treatment by President Carter in the aftermath of the revolution. Carter had been in Iran in December 1977 and had, as the shah reminded people in a November 1979 interview, paid him "some very warm compliments."[11] The shah's hurried exit from Iran led to months of travel between Latin America, the US, and finally Egypt, all in an effort both to gain access to medical care for the cancer to which he would soon succumb and to avoid extradition to Iran, where revolutionary forces were demanding his return to stand trial. In the months before his death, Pahlavi complained repeatedly that his former allies had all turned their backs on him while unjustly painting him as a torturer. It was this reputation, Pahlavi surmised, which led to difficulty during his myriad border crossings. The deposed monarch complained, "The United States Consul General in Mexico City waited near the plane to prepare necessary entry documents. I noticed his surprised expression when he saw me.

This is not how he had imagined the Shahanshah, that violator of human rights and oppressor of peoples depicted by the media for so long."[12]

By the time of the shah's ouster in 1979, the notion of "human rights" and its link to torture as the human rights violation par excellence had not only acquired the international traction to be worth mention but had also assumed enough weight to somehow have played a part in the downfall of the Pahlavi government from the point of view of the shah himself. In the aftermath of the revolution, other members of the Pahlavi elite similarly invoked the shah's human rights record and SAVAK's reputation for torture as key to his defeat. In a 1979 interview, Fereydoun Hoveyda, Iranian ambassador to the UN and brother of former prime minister Amir Abbas Hoveyda, claimed that after 1970, "people were becoming more critical and there was more repression. . . . Carter became President and brought up this human rights business, the Iranian Government tried to give a trimming, but a trimming was not enough."[13] Similarly, the former empress Farah Pahlavi later admitted that SAVAK was "quite often heavy-handed," though she tempered criticism of her late husband's intelligence officers by maintaining that this sort of thing "happens in most developing countries."[14]

Despite the shah's apparent disdain for the budding human rights movement, the story of human rights discourses in Iran ironically has some roots with the Pahlavi family itself. In the 1960s, when *human rights* was only starting to be a political buzzword among the international legal community, those employing such rights talk in Iran were often members of the Pahlavi elite. Most prominently, the shah's powerful twin sister Princess Ashraf Pahlavi was a mainstay on several human rights and women's rights bodies, working both at the United Nations and appearing as a delegate at numerous international rights conferences during her brother's reign. The princess served for sixteen years on the UN's Human Rights Commission, including several years as commission chair.[15] Ashraf also spent seven years as head of Iran's delegation to the UN. On doing this work, she claimed, "I felt I had found the natural forum for discussing and solving the problems that concerned me most. The first committee I worked with was the Human Rights Committee, and . . . I believed wholeheartedly that I had become part of a body that could make a difference."[16]

The shah's sister also promoted her reputation as an "itinerant ambassador," meeting with heads of state through her work with the UN.[17] International coverage of the princess often approvingly noted her work on various rights-based projects as well as her glamorous wardrobe and jet-set lifestyle. Two years after the UN dubbed 1968 "International Human Rights Year," a *New York Times* feature on the princess raved, "Given a choice between following the sun or spending February and March in Manhattan and more precisely in meetings 10 hours a day at the United Nations, the Princess says she prefers doing exactly what she is doing: presiding as chairman of the Human Rights Commission."[18] A 1974 *Los Angeles Times* feature on a caviar-laden black-tie party thrown by US film and television executives and attended by the princess told readers that the shah's sister was "a modern kind of princess, which means she's involved," going on to note both Ashraf's UN credentials and designer finery.[19] Others were less sanguine about the princess's globetrotting exploits. One of Farah's former associates later sardonically recalled, "Whenever [Ashraf] attended a conference in New York she would stop off in the south of France to meet a new lover and gamble away millions of pounds at a casino."[20]

The princess made support for women's rights her diplomatic calling card. Asked in 1970 if she considered herself a "militant feminist," she admitted that she wasn't the street demonstration type but nonetheless claimed, "Militant feminist, certainly, in the sense of pursuing the goals of feminine equality and a greater role for women in our socioeconomic life with, I hope, unrelenting perseverance."[21] During her tenure working with the UN, the Iranian government worked to promote the princess's successes in the fields of human and women's rights as markers of the government's modern outlook. In 1975, the UN's "Year of the Woman," the government translated and publicized letters from various heads of state, including Spain's Francisco Franco, the US's Gerald Ford, and Thailand's Bhumibol Adulyadej, all written to the princess and applauding her for her women's rights efforts.[22] For the Pahlavi elite, the language of human rights had nothing to do with what was going on inside of Iran's prisons, as it did for their opposition. Instead, it provided a means through which to broadcast their self-image as enlightened modern rulers. The princess herself often gave credit for her women's and human rights work to her twin brother, claiming that the shah "much more than any other person" had influenced her interest in rights.[23]

Perhaps the most noteworthy conference the princess ever chaired was the UN's first International Conference on Human Rights, an event held in Tehran in 1968 to celebrate the twentieth anniversary of 1948's Universal Declaration of Human Rights.[24] The shah's government agreed to help foot the bill for the conference, using the opportunity to promote their own genealogy of human rights.[25] In his opening remarks, the shah boasted that Iran was the ideal location for a conference. Employing his usual mixture of state-nationalist bluster and rhetorical extravagance, the shah claimed:

> My compatriots . . . are very proud that their country should have been chosen as the site of the first International Conference on Human Rights. Their pride is the more legitimate in that . . . a remarkable coincidence underlies this choice; for I need hardly tell you that the ancestor of the documents recognizing the rights of man was promulgated in this very country by Cyrus the Great about two thousand years ago.[26]

For the shah, "human rights" were best understood as a timeless and essential quality of Iranian political culture in its history as an empire-turned-nation; rights talk was simultaneously evoked to confer modern legitimacy to the Pahlavi government and used to trace the roots of that legitimacy to the earliest years of Persian monarchy and empire.

Members of the Iranian opposition used the occasion of the UN conference to protest Pahlavi prisons and torture. As this book has shown, Pahlavi prisons had long been established as sites to critique; several decades of Iranian dissidents had already written communiqués from and memoirs of their time in prisons and detention centers across Iran. What is novel about this 1960s moment, however, is the increasing use of both the language of and the budding institutions of international human rights in defense of incarcerated Iranian dissidents. During the conference, a group of wives, daughters, and sisters of Iranian political prisoners presented a formal petition to Marc Schreiber, the executive director of the conference and head of the UN's Division of Human Rights. The petition named those being held in "secret police jails" and decried the "inhuman treatment" meted out in SAVAK interrogation centers, particularly Qezel Qal'eh in Tehran, which was located near the site of the conference.[27] Another message, this time in the form of an open letter written by "the political prisoners of Qasr Prison," was also circulated in 1968 and addressed to the Human Rights Commission of the UN. In that letter, prisoners told the Human Rights Commission that they "saw no alternative but to appeal to you.... We appeal to you, who on humanistic grounds, have founded organisations for the defence of Human Rights, to bring pressure to bear on the Iranian regime so that an end could be put to these practices."[28]

These opposition petitions went unremarked on in the state-affiliated Iranian media of the day. Mention of the 1968 UN conference did, however, make it into the first issue of the weekly English-language newsmagazine *Iran Tribune*, published by Iran's primary news publishing company Kayhan for the English-speaking Iranian ultra-elite as well as foreign diplomatic circles. That newsmagazine reported that the conference had been a smash hit, at least insofar as all of the delegates "enjoyed every single night" dancing and carousing until the wee hours. Diplomats and foreigners were assured that the Pahlavi government had taken every precaution during the conference to guard them from unfriendly locals:

> In an effort to protect conference hostesses from any abuse while performing their duty, [the state has] been very strongly reacting to any slight. One hostess, who had to take some delegates shopping, was treated impolitely by a shopkeeper.... Within hours the shopkeeper had been picked up by the police.[29]

The UN conference was not the Pahlavi government's only foray into promoting its state-sanctioned vision of human rights. Later in 1968, the government sponsored a "human rights exhibition" at the national Iran-e Bastan (Ancient Iran) Museum in Tehran, which featured "social realist" paintings of "war, love, strife, racial conflict, etc."[30] In the 1960s, despite mounting unrest among the Iranian opposition and increased scrutiny of their prisons, the Pahlavi elite contentedly deployed the language of human rights as a state-affirming nationalist discourse largely meant to legitimize their rule to friendly heads of state.[31]

Yet despite its best efforts, the Pahlavi state was losing momentum in the international public relations battle, as the ironic location of the UN conference was not only mentioned by Iranian dissidents but also noted by renowned British philosopher Bertrand Russell, who became a vocal critic of Pahlavi prisons in the 1960s. In his 1968 essay "Inside the Shah's Prisons," Russell decries "the new wave of repression that has swept the country, culminating absurdly in the world conference of human rights, held in Teheran from April 22 to celebrate the twentieth anniversary of the Declaration of Human Rights." Echoing the opposition letter quoted above, Russell argues that the proximity of the conference to Qezel Qal'eh and that prison's reputation for torture performed the dubious task of "reminding the world that, after Saigon and Athens, Teheran was the least appropriate choice for such a celebration."[32]

For the next several years, the Bertrand Russell Peace Foundation would continue to publicize Pahlavi carceral violence, including the numbers of Iranian political prisoners—wildly inflated to totals from twenty thousand to one hundred thousand or even more—often promoted by Iranian dissidents.[33] (It would not be until after the revolution that it became clear that the number of dissidents incarcerated in Iran under the shah was never more than a fraction of this total.) Russell's foundation even founded an offshoot exclusively dedicated to Pahlavi torture called the Organisation for the Defence of Human Rights in Iran.[34] Russell did not come to focus on Iranian affairs unaided. Rather, he was influenced by the expatriate Iranian opposition, especially a massive and vociferous Iranian student movement based primarily in Europe and the United States. It is virtually impossible to imagine the global awareness of Pahlavi torture emerging without the ardent efforts of these students, many of whom had earned their political stripes through engagements with earlier Iranian political movements and in some cases directly with the shah's prisons. It is to this opposition movement, which so decisively influenced the global activism of the 1960–70s, that I now turn my attention.

THE IRANIAN OPPOSITION ABROAD

The 1968 UN conference in Tehran was held at the tail end of a decade that saw major changes in Iran. These included the shah's top-down reform program (the White Revolution) as well as the bloody 1963 protests in response to those reforms, which led to the arrests of numerous members of the ulama and brought Ayatollah Ruhollah Khomeini, who was himself arrested and eventually exiled, to the national stage.[35] As shown in previous chapters, the

1960s also witnessed the further expansion of Iran's modern carceral system, with new penitentiaries and prison factories opened in several cities around the country and championed by the Pahlavi elite as progressive institutions of social reform. The 1960s also saw the establishment of an influential student movement outside of Iran, most prominently in Europe and the United States.[36] This movement has fittingly been called "the most active and persistent force of opposition to the shah's regime during the two decades prior to the 1978–79 Revolution."[37] It is primarily due to the tireless efforts of this student movement that knowledge of Iranian political violence and SAVAK torture were brought to the global stage. Without the tenacity of expatriate Iranian dissidents and particularly students in mobilizing widespread global scrutiny of Pahlavi torture and prisons, international activists, intellectuals, and Euro/American legislators are unlikely to have involved themselves in Iranian affairs to the same degree, if at all. The Iranian students organized among a broad range of non-Iranian groups and movements, borrowing both tactical and theoretical approaches from a variety of activists, including Black power, Third Worldist, Maoist, Muslim, liberal, and human rights–seeking groups.[38] The intermingling of these heterogeneous social and political worlds would have a transformative effect on the Iranian opposition abroad, the nascent international human rights movement, and their joint efforts to end torture in the shah's prisons.

Based in Frankfurt, Germany, the Confederation of Iranian Students, National Union (CISNU) formally joined with the United States Iranian Students Association (USISA) and the Organization of Tehran University Students (OSUS) in a 1962 merger, declaring itself the sole representative of Iranian students in Iran and the diaspora. At its inception, CISNU was dominated by nationalist students loyal to Mohammad Mossadeq's National Front and contained a smaller number of students loyal to the communist Tudeh Party, as well as pockets of Islamist members. In its early years, CISNU campaigned against the shah's policies through appeals to the rule of law, not having yet moved to the revolutionary posture that would dominate Iranian opposition politics in the 1970s.[39] In 1971, after a series of successful CISNU campaigns against Pahlavi policies and in the wake of the dramatic emergence of the guerrilla movement, membership in CISNU was banned by the shah. Spurred by this move and radicalized by the actions of the guerrillas, CISNU made increasingly revolutionary demands as the 1970s unfolded.[40] At the same time, while CISNU activism was dominated by revolutionary Marxisms, the student opposition also came to strategically and provocatively employ the evidently un-Marxist language and international institutions of "human rights." Finally, in the late 1970s, immersed in a political atmosphere that it helped create, CISNU experienced two of its greatest public successes: occupying the Iranian consulate in Geneva and revealing it as a SAVAK stronghold in 1976, and disrupting the shah's visit to the White House in 1977.[41]

Unlike some rights talk that expresses concern for rights in abstracted moral terms, when the Iranian opposition abroad used the language of rights in this era, it was as an analytic through which to theorize the *specifics* of the modern Iranian state. In CISNU's theory of state violence, Pahlavi human rights violations were the practical outcome of what was in their view a "comprador capitalist-imperialist" state. Thus, student references to rights abuses, particularly torture, did not signal the end of political (or economic) analysis, let alone revolutionary politics, but rather a means through which to understand the development of autocratic rule in Iran. At the core of this analysis was an examination of SAVAK, the shah's feared intelligence apparatus. Throughout the 1960s and '70s, the Iranian opposition, student and nonstudent alike, published literature on SAVAK in several languages.[42] For Iranian dissidents, this excavation effort had two sometimes-contradictory aims. The first aim was to analyze SAVAK as a historical phenomenon. In a pamphlet devoted to SAVAK, CISNU argued that SAVAK's emergence was a necessary outgrowth of a quasi-fascist state that wielded SAVAK's might as "a tool of imperialism and reaction."[43] That is, for this anonymous author, Pahlavi torture was neither the result of a moral failing (SAVAK is evil) nor was it a vestige of premodern punishment techniques (SAVAK is barbaric). Instead, SAVAK torture was presented as a quintessentially modern technique of governance and a direct outgrowth of an authoritarian state.[44] In this logic, Pahlavi rule was seen as part of the wave, inexorably linked to global capitalism and imperialism, that gave rise to autocratic governments in Atatürk's Turkey, Metaxas's Greece, and fascist Italy and Germany.

The revolutionary turn in student movement politics was inspired and shaped by the new militancy taking root in Iran. As outlined in the previous chapter, the rise of the guerrilla movement in Iran in the early 1970s transformed the terrain of political possibility for Iranian dissidents and would-be revolutionaries. This was no less true for the expatriate student movement, members of which had contacts with or were involved in Iran's budding guerrilla organizations. Just as the Iranian guerrillas publicized details of their imprisonments, interrogations, and courtroom defenses, the expatriate student movement translated and publicized details of these trials, torture, and prisons to audiences abroad. One early guerrilla courtroom defense, that of the Palestine Group's Shokrollah Paknejad in 1970, directly invoked the language of human rights, albeit cast in the revolutionary posture of the day. Appealing to the United Nations on behalf of Iran's political prisoners, Paknejad proclaimed the "human right" to revolution against unjust governments. Paknejad's statement, which was translated into English and circulated by the student movement abroad, suggests that the Iranian dissident movement understood and mobilized the language of human rights less as a matter of liberal legalism than as a natural bedfellow of revolutionary praxis.

Paknejad, who complained of torture during his interrogation, had been arrested with seventeen others while attempting to cross the border into Iraq to join the armed Palestinian resistance. During his trial, Paknejad defended himself by referring to the civil trials of the famous leftist Group of 53 under Reza Shah, arguing that with the post-coup prevalence of military tribunals and the establishment of SAVAK, the human rights situation had deteriorated for political prisoners from this earlier point. Paknejad argued that in the face of SAVAK torture, the Universal Declaration of Human Rights granted Iranians the right to rise up against the state:

> In this situation, in which SAVAK and the authoritarian regime have destroyed even the most basic of people's freedoms and in which there is no trace of the rule of law or of human rights [*huquq-e bashar*], the people of Iran have no choice but to resort to force [*zur*] in defense of their rights [*haq*]. The Universal Declaration of Human Rights has explicitly given all human beings the right, in the face of any government that refuses to provide for the spiritual and bodily security as well as human virtues of its people, to take steps to create a new order in which human dignity is preserved. History has proven in a thousand different ways that justice and rights are always forcibly taken. Rights are not granted freely; rights are taken.[45]

For Paknejad, the Iranian struggles for human rights and against Pahlavi autocracy were not principally to be fought through international law or institutions. Although his defense included an accounting of Iranian constitutional law and international human rights norms that had been jettisoned by the Pahlavi government, Paknejad's understanding of rights was mediated through his commitment to Marxism-Leninism and a revolutionary theory of political change. The student movement made its English-language translations of Paknejad's statements even more blunt in its defense of revolution. Where Paknejad had stated that "the people of Iran have no choice but to resort to force [*zur*]," the students translated the word *zur* as "violence." For the 1970s student movement, as for Paknejad, human rights were ultimately something to be won through the armed revolutionary uprising, not gifted from above.

Expatriate opposition literature also strove to prove that SAVAK was not omnipotent and that despite SAVAK violence, the Pahlavi government was weaker than it appeared.[46] Dissidents argued that SAVAK responded ruthlessly to those taking their first political steps in order to produce a culture of fear in Iran; it is this *culture*, and not SAVAK invincibility, that pushed Iranians toward political quietism. It was the job of the dissident, then, to reveal the "cracked" (*tarak khordeh*) power of the reactionary state.[47] As such, the opposition abroad, with the students as its most vociferous members, remained committed to publicizing its findings on Pahlavi torture, political prisons, and SAVAK to anyone interested, including revolutionary groups like the Black Panthers on the one hand and liberals like Bertrand Russell and human rights organizations like Amnesty International on the other.

In doing so, student literature often challenged the Pahlavi imperial genealogy of rights, such as in the case of a 1973 ISAUS pamphlet that noted sardonically, "The Shah's sister Princess Ashraf . . . was the head of the U.N.'s Human Rights commission. . . . Ironically, not a trace of respect for human rights can be found in Iran."[48] Even as the Carter administration brought the language of human rights into the US political mainstream in the late 1970s, Iranian students in the US continued to partner with allied Third Worldist groups to condemn what they saw as Carter's hypocrisy vis-à-vis prisons and prisoners around the world. Events such as one held at Unite! bookstore in Oakland, California, an offshoot of the US Marxist-Leninist Communist

Party, brought the ISAUS together with the International Association for Filipino Patriots in order to discuss US involvement in torture in Iran, the Philippines, Chile, and Oakland. Evoking police violence across locales, the Iranian students described their work as exposing "the bitter realities of Carter's 'human rights policy,'" particularly as it pertained to torture among Cold War allies and in the US.[49] Here, as elsewhere, the student movement's evocation of human rights was couched in a broader commitment to anti-imperialism and global revolution. Their understanding of the existence of state-sponsored torture, from Iran to Latin America to Southeast Asia to California, was predicated on this shared political rubric.

THE BRITISH LIBERAL LEFT AND IRANIAN PRISONERS' RIGHTS

Adherence to various strands of revolutionary Marxisms or Third Worldism were by no means prerequisites for support of the Iranian anti-torture cause or for global interest in Iran's prisons. The Iranian opposition abroad found some of its most vocal early supporters in the form of some liberal members of the British Parliament, whose public pronouncements against Pahlavi torture were among the first such instances of European statesmen criticizing Iranian state violence. From the earliest stages of the encounter between Iranian dissidents and the European left, the issues that most obviously animated the non-Iranians were those of torture and extralegal punishment tactics. Led by Member of Parliament Stan Newens, British parliamentarians of the Labour Party founded a group called the "British Committee for the Defence of Political Prisoners in Iran" in 1965 and openly stumped for the shah to let outside observers into Iran's courtrooms and prisons.[50] Newens's involvement in Iranian politics came in the wake of a 1965 attempt on the shah's life, the second such attempt during the monarch's reign, in which the would-be assassin killed two guards before being shot.[51] As with the attempted 1949 regicide, the Pahlavi government blamed the attack on the influence of Marxists, in this case a number of British-educated leftist students who had connections to both the Confederation of Iranian Students in Europe and the Maoist Revolutionary Organization of the Tudeh Party.[52] Shortly after the incident, fourteen students were arrested, interrogated, and eventually tried on charges related to the attempted assassination.

These high-profile arrests and trials, backed by Tehran's assertion that the assassination attempt was a "Peking-backed coup . . . planned by Iranian students in Kensington coffee bars," raised the ire of Newens and his Labour Party cohorts.[53] In May 1965, fifty British MPs led by Newens began a letter-writing campaign to Iranian ambassadors, newspapers, parliamentarians, and the prime minister. Their first letter, written on May 7th to Iran's then ambassador in London, Ardeshir Zahedi, and published in *The Times*, claims they have "no wish whatsoever to interfere in the internal affairs of Iran." Still, the MPs demanded that Zahedi "convey our disquiet to your Government" and send "assurances that our fears are groundless." Zahedi, who would later serve as Iran's ambassador to the United States, took "great exception to the manner in which this matter has been handled," insisting that the rumors regarding prisoner abuse were inaccurate.[54] The Pahlavi government responded to this international pressure in a series of editorials in state-run newspaper *Ettela'at* in which the "extreme left wing" MPs were told in no uncertain terms: "Mind Your Own Business!"[55]

Despite Tehran's wishes, however, the British Committee didn't stop there. Over the next months, again led by Newens, letters were sent to the prime minister's office, members of the Iranian Parliament, and eventually to *Ettela'at*. In that final letter, Newens advocates directly for human rights for political prisoners, writing, "If people who stand up for human rights in any country in the world as we are prepared to do, are so denounced in the Iranian Press, our anxieties for the fair press treatment of the graduates who were the subject of our letter are increased enormously."[56] The Pahlavi government would grow so irritated with Newens and company that it would have SAVAK follow and investigate the MPs, going so far as to maintain surveillance on their homes in England.[57] Thanks in part to Newens's efforts, Iran's reputation in Britain suffered so much that by the mid-1970s Pahlavi Iran's last ambassador to London, Parviz Radji, complained that his primary job had become "the defence of the reputation of the country I represent from a constant barrage of attacks on it . . . as a result of the quite needless excesses of Savak."[58] Radji would go on to describe Newens—whom he called "a vocal and extreme anti-Shah left-winger"—as a particular thorn in his side.[59]

At the same time as the 1965 British-led letter-writing campaign, CISNU staged a campaign of its own. In October 1965, members wrote an open letter to the Human Rights Commission of the UN, invoking the Declaration of

Human Rights and demanding UN involvement on behalf of the arrested students:

> Fourteen innocent Iranian patriots ... are being tried before Teheran Military Tribunal ... political trials of this kind held behind closed doors are not only in violation of the fundamental principles of the Iranian Constitution, but also in total disregard of the principles of the Universal Declaration of Human Rights—a document that has been approved and accepted by the Iranian Parliament.[60]

The work of the Iranian students and their British supporters led to unprecedented success on a global scale. Because of the shah's sensitivity about his reputation, the Iranian government eventually lowered the charges against some of the accused, going so far as to commute two death sentences. Several years later, the most well known of those tried, Parviz Nikkhah, who loudly told the world that he had been tortured by SAVAK in 1965, would again make waves by experiencing an evident change of heart while in prison and coming out in support of the shah's White Revolution, which he argued made Maoism "redundant."[61]

Several other forced confessions by CISNU members would soon follow in the Iranian press. Yet the victory of 1965 was not to be forgotten by opponents of the Pahlavi government. In a different essay on Iranian prisoner abuse, Bertrand Russell invokes this success in an effort to cultivate further opposition to Pahlavi repression, reminding readers that "in 1965, following an international outcry at the show trial of various opponents of the regime, at least two people escaped execution. A similar protest must now be mounted around the world to save the men rotting in the shah's prisons."[62] Incredibly, the student opposition and their European supporters had succeeded not only in bringing Iranian legal and carceral policy to global public attention but also in mounting enough pressure on the Pahlavi government to influence its decision-making. As the opposition abroad learned, the language of human rights could be effectively mobilized to advocate internationally for imprisoned dissidents at home. This would be a lesson not soon forgotten.

In the same era, the Iranian opposition abroad also found allies among liberal American human rights activists, despite generally steady support for the Pahlavi government among US policymakers. Even a typically sympathetic mainstream US press found occasion to alter its positive coverage of the Pahlavi monarch. Shift in coverage was coterminous with increasing scrutiny of global torture among global human rights advocates, a trend that provided context to US readers for a critique of Pahlavi rule. In a 1972 feature article in the *New York Times* entitled "Torture as an Institution," James Becket, an American attorney working for Amnesty International, outlines what he classifies as an "eruption" of torture around the globe.[63] Becket argues that despite torture's status as a universally reviled practice, with its most eloquent condemnation coming in the Universal Declaration of Human Rights, its usage had increased rather than disappeared in the twentieth century. He names the shah's Iran as emblematic of this increase:

> One day we read about the burning "metal table" in Iran and the trials where the only evidence are the confessions of those about to be executed; another day it is Uruguay where the recent discovery of a judicious blend of physical torture and "truth drugs" has produced spectacular results, or Northern Ireland where the British army employs the same refined techniques it used in Cyprus or Aden.

As historian Barbara Keys argues, American liberals were increasingly drawn to the language of human rights as a way to recapture the moral high ground in the aftermath of the Vietnam War, focusing largely—unlike their conservative counterparts—on torture perpetrated by Cold War allies of the US.[64] To this end, Becket condemned US involvement in the training of paramilitary torture units, destabilizing the Cold War logic that would lay human rights abuses squarely at the feet of the Soviet bloc. For Becket, US-led support of torturers was among the era's great moral outrages; as a result, he argued, it was precisely this involvement that should be targeted by US-based human rights activists.

Unlike Iranian opposition publications that embedded a theory of torture and political violence in the historical particularities of Iranian history, many liberal human rights activists focused on the problem of torture *as such*. Public attention to torture, which was often described as staging a troubling "reemergence," was drastically expanded by the work of Becket's organization Amnesty International, which had its modest origins in the early 1960s but which influenced the UN into passing a resolution to formally denounce torture in 1973.⁶⁵ That same year, not long after initiating the two-year Campaign for the Abolition of Torture, AI published its first report on torture, with several pages on Iran reporting:

> It is alleged that torture of political prisoners during interrogation has been established practice in Iran for many years. The earliest detailed statement of torture known to Amnesty is dated 23 December 1963 ... opponents of the Iranian regime allege that torture has been taking place since ... 1953.⁶⁶

Another AI report on Iran from the mid-1970s somberly claims that "prisoners are very likely to be ill-treated.... Torture does invariably occur during the period between arrest and trial." In what was rapidly becoming AI's signature style, this report methodically relays information regarding techniques employed by Iranian interrogators, stating that "alleged methods of torture include whipping and beating, electric shocks, the extraction of nails and teeth, boiling water pumped into the rectum, heavy weights hung on the testicles, tying the prisoner to a metal table heated to white heat, inserting a broken bottle into the anus, and rape."⁶⁷ AI focused its attention on political dissidents, though it sometimes downplayed their militancy to better fold them into the rubric of "prisoners of conscience." One such figure was the female revolutionary Vida Hajebi Tabrizi, whose incarceration would become a matter of global concern among figures from feminist activist Kate Millett to the Canadian Sociological Association. In 1973, AI chose to publicize Hajebi Tabrizi's case during its annual Prisoner of Conscience Week, highlighting worries about her health under torture.⁶⁸ AI's work on Hajebi Tabrizi's behalf led to a 1976 mention in *Time* in a cover story on torture, though *Time*—largely following AI's lead—simply referred to Hajebi Tabrizi as a sociologist and not as a revolutionary Marxist.⁶⁹ Following the lead of the Iranian student movement, AI also popularized the notion that there were tens of thousands of political prisoners in Pahlavi Iran, numbers that, after the fall of the shah, would prove to have been exaggerated.

In the late 1960s and early 1970s, damning reports on Pahlavi prisons were increasingly common among other emergent rights watchdog groups in Europe and the US. Several of these groups also sent or attempted to send delegates to Tehran to attend military trials and to take firsthand stock of the conditions in which prisoners were held. A motley assortment of legal experts, activists, politicians, religious leaders and clerics, and intellectuals took part in these fact-finding missions, to varied degrees of success. Again, like Amnesty International, these efforts focused exclusively on incarcerated political dissidents rather than prisoners as such. In 1965, observers from the Italian Committee for the Defense of Political Prisoners were sent to observe political trials in Tehran and produced reports outlining poor treatment and legal inconsistencies in the trials they attended.[70] At the trial of the fourteen dissidents accused of attempted regicide in 1965, a group of Italian and British lawyers and German Amnesty International lawyer Hans Heldmann produced reports of widespread torture.[71] A 1966 observer from the International Association of Democratic Lawyers failed to gain admittance into a trial of fifty-five Islamists accused of crimes against the state.[72] A female American lawyer affiliated with AI was sent to observe the 1968–69 trials of prominent Marxists, including that of guerrilla theorist Bizhan Jazani, who was eventually extrajudicially executed by Pahlavi security forces in prison in 1975 after writing key texts of the guerrilla movement from his prison cell. The AI-sponsored observer reports that confessions "had been extracted … through the intensive use of torture" and that "Jazani had a broken bottle inserted into his anus."[73] These 1968–69 trials were also reported on widely in the international press, with quotes from the accused, including Jazani and future Fadaian leader Farrokh Negahdar, running in newspapers across Europe.[74]

Although SAVAK most aggressively suppressed leftist organizing, seeing communism as the primary threat to Pahlavi rule, militant members of the Shi'a ulama were also routinely imprisoned and tortured. As a result, global religious advocacy groups also endeavored to gain access to Pahlavi trials and prisons in hopes of bearing witness on behalf of Islamist and clerical prisoners in particular. In 1976, the International Association of Democratic Lawyers sent a French lawyer named Jean Michel Braunschweig to Tehran with Father Michel Gest from the Movement of Catholic Intellectuals, Pax Romana in an effort to gain access to imprisoned clerics including Ayatollah Hussein Ali Montazeri, Ayatollah Mahmoud Taleghani, and Ali Akbar Hashemi Rafsanjani—three men who would become household names in Iran during and after the success of the 1979 revolution. Like other such uninvited guests, Gest and Braunschweig were largely met with indifference if not outright obfuscation by Pahlavi officials. According to Braunschweig's frustrated report, Iranian officials did everything to keep the observers from learning any relevant information:

> Concerning those under sentences of death, [the minister of information] confirmed that they would be able to lodge an appeal, but he could not give us any date for their next hearing.... We have since learned that not only were the death sentences upheld ... some 48 hours before we left for France, but that nine out of the ten were executed on Saturday 24 January 1976 [just days after we left Iran].... We are convinced that the trial took place while we were still in Teheran.[75]

Attempts to travel to Tehran were often rejected before the observers could even embark on travel toward Iran.[76] Amnesty International experienced this obstruction firsthand in 1970, when it sent Hans Heldmann back to Tehran alongside Iranian activist and "accredited delegate" of AI Hossein Rezai.[77] The mission went badly, as the German was expelled from Iran, and Rezai was arrested. William Wilson, another key Labor Party parliamentarian involved with the Iranian opposition abroad, applied for a visa to observe this and other political trials in Iran but was denied by the Iranian embassy in London.[78] Two years prior, Wilson had traveled to Iran to observe earlier such trials, writing and speaking widely about his experiences in the country. He also wrote and spoke publicly about his visa denial.[79] AI undertook major efforts to sway the Pahlavi state into granting Rezai his freedom, encouraging its membership to send letters during Rezai's months of detention without trial to Prime Minister Amir Abbas Hoveyda and Minister of Court Asadollah Alam. In a newsletter to members in 1971 during this detention, AI stated:

> Mr. Rezai has not yet been charged or tried, and the Iranian Government has consistently refused to discuss his detention with Amnesty.... Cards should ask for Mr. Rezai's release or public trial, stressing that he has now been under arrest for eight months. In October, Iran celebrates the 2,500 anniversary of the foundation of the Persian Empire by Cyrus the Great. This is an event of great national importance and members should suggest that it is a fitting occasion for clemency.[80]

Rezai was given a prison sentence of ten years once it was discovered that he was a member not only of AI but also of the banned Confederation of Iranian Students. After this debacle, it would be several years before AI was granted access to the inside of Iranian prisons, as the shah finally began to relent to outside pressure in 1976–77.

The work of Harvard-trained American lawyer William J. Butler of the Geneva-based International Commission of Jurists (ICJ), an organization for which Butler served as US chapter president, was crucial in publicizing Pahlavi abuses to global audiences; it was Butler's work that Mike Wallace would reference in his aforementioned interview with Mohammad Reza Shah.[81] In 1976, Butler and his colleague Georges Levasseur were invited to publish reports on human rights abuses and the Iranian legal system. They took what the ICJ avowed was an "apolitical" legalistic approach in their critique. Both US policymakers and Iranian leaders, including the shah himself, found this approach slightly more palatable than the "frontal political tack" of AI, which was seen as biased toward liberal causes.[82] After the publication of Butler and Levasseur's reports, the *New York Times* directly quoted several of the ICJ's more troubling findings. They also published a revealing interview with key SAVAK deputy Parviz Sabeti. In that interview, conducted by the newspaper's Tehran correspondent Eric Pace, Sabeti claimed flatly, "We never torture." Sabeti, whom the article paints as a sinister if mild-mannered figure, also all but admitted that SAVAK maintained a presence in the US surveilling students. "Asked how many agents Savak maintained in the United States," the article explained, "Mr. Sabeti . . . leaned back and said amiably: 'We'd better not talk about this, but we are fully aware of the situation of Iranian students abroad, especially those working in international Communism activities.'"[83] Butler also sent his findings to ranking US senators and in August 1976 testified in front of Congressman Donald Fraser's House Subcommittee on International Organizations.[84] While Butler and the ICJ were instrumental in publicizing Pahlavi wrongdoings to US audiences and legislators, Butler was relatively tempered in his critique of the shah, stating, "I think [the shah is] way down the list of tyrants. He would not even make the A list."[85] As historian Matthew Shannon notes, Butler's testimony to Congress was "measured" though clear-eyed in its reporting on torture and extrajudicial punishment in the shah's Iran.[86]

Eventually, in the face of mounting global and internal pressures, Mohammad Reza Pahlavi finally allowed three international organizations—Amnesty International, the International Red Cross, and Butler's International Commission of Jurists—to enter Iran in 1977 to examine legal, political, and penal conditions in the country. Parviz Radji, Pahlavi Iran's last ambassador to London, wrote in his diaries that he and other members of the Pahlavi diplomatic and security elite had tried to convince the shah to let these organizations visit some prisons for months before the shah relented.[87] Despite Carter's public commitment to human rights, neither Carter nor most US statesmen were prepared to push the shah particularly hard on rights abuses, instead continuing to sell Iran arms and supporting the Pahlavi government as a staunch US ally—a discrepancy mocked by an increasingly radical Iranian student press.[88] Political scientist and CIA operative Richard Cottam largely agreed with this negative assessment of Carter's commitment to human rights principles in Iran, writing in 1980, "Carter's human rights policy as applied to Iran was a doctrine without a strategy. The concern for human rights in Iran was purely abstract. In programmatic development, Carter's policy toward Iran, like that of his immediate predecessors, was one of total and unequivocal support for the Shah's government. Human rights was at most only a distant, hardly discernable counterpoint to the main theme."[89]

Still, Butler's advocacy made an undeniable impact on Iranian affairs. The American lawyer developed a personal relationship with Mohammad Reza Pahlavi during the ICJ's trips to Tehran in October 1977 and Shiraz in 1978; it is in part due to these conversations that the shah agreed to partially reform the Military Justice and Penal Code of the country in an effort to quell mounting dissent.[90] Members of the Iranian opposition saw the shah's willingness to work with Butler and the ICJ as an effort to co-opt the famed human rights body in service of Pahlavi rule. Cottam agreed with the student critiques of the ICJ, calling their 1976 report "unconvincingly mild."[91] In any event, the final years of Pahlavi rule witnessed a significant decrease in the use of the most overt forms of torture that had been synonymous with the shah's interrogation centers, a change that SAVAK director Nematollah Nassiri reportedly bemoaned as being "forced upon them" and another SAVAK official described as being "beyond belief."[92] Of course, painful forms of physical punishment were not eliminated altogether. As former political prisoner and scholar Shahla Talebi has noted sardonically, "As long as one's legs were torn apart not by the heavy strikes of cables on the soles of the feet but by forced standing on them, no torture had occurred."[93] The pain and the punishment remained, albeit in chastened form.

INTERNATIONAL PEN AND GLOBAL LITERARY SOLIDARITIES

By the 1970s, opposing torture in the shah's prisons was no longer merely an Iranian issue; it had become a fully global rallying cry. Pahlavi prisons increasingly attracted the attention of authors, artists, and intellectuals politicized around issues of writer imprisonment and torture. This was especially true among a new generation of US and European literary figures, many of whom were affiliated with International PEN,[94] an anticensorship association founded in 1921 in London that grew in prominence during the human rights boom of the 1960s and '70s. For many members of PEN, this concern was often geared toward those facing repression behind the Iron Curtain. Still, several members of the organization lent their pens to the defense of imprisoned Iranian writers, despite occasional political friction from those whom they championed.

No Iranian writer embodied this politicized intellectual renown better than newly exiled Iranian poet and essayist Reza Baraheni, who had been jailed for 102 days at Tehran's notorious Evin Prison in 1973. After his release from Evin, Baraheni made his way to the US, where despite habitual SAVAK harassment he published two books: 1976's *God's Shadow*, a book of prison poetry, and 1977's *The Crowned Cannibals*, which soon became arguably the best-known text outside of Iran on the subject of Pahlavi prisons and torture.[95] Baraheni's advocacy reached its zenith when he was invited to testify in front of United States Congress in 1976.[96] While in the US, Baraheni also encouraged other writers, artists, and intellectuals to boycott academic and artistic events in Iran, including the Tehran Film and Shiraz Arts Festivals.[97] His work led to vociferous debates about these events by such luminaries as composer John Cage, playwright Eric Bentley, and dancer Merce Cunningham, several of whom chose not to accept invitations to Iran as a result.[98]

While in the US, Baraheni raised the ire of the Pahlavi elite, in particular Iran's ambassador to the US, Ardeshir Zahedi, who worked relentlessly to dampen Baraheni's popularity and to defend his government from the accusations of the dissident poet. When Baraheni appeared on David Susskind's program to discuss torture in Iran, Zahedi enlisted Washington, DC–based legal team Marshall, Leon, Weill, and Mahony to help communicate his displeasure to the television personality. In a letter to Susskind, Zahedi even impugned Baraheni's reputation as a writer. "All Iranians are poets, to some extent," the Iranian ambassador wrote, "but what evidentiary support did he give you for the assertion that he is Iran's 'leading poet'? Did he show you any of his poems published by a responsible publisher? Did he produce any favorable reviews of his poetry, by serious critics? Or did you simply accept him on faith?"[99] At the same time that he wrote prolifically on the issue of repression in Iran, Baraheni joined the US branch of PEN and worked with PEN's Freedom to Write Committee, advocating on behalf of other imprisoned writers. Eventually, after the establishment of Iran's new government in 1979, Baraheni's residence in Canada would be secured in part by the advocacy of PEN Canada on the exiled writer's behalf. Neither PEN's nor Baraheni's investment in Iran ended with the 1979 revolution, as both continued to advocate on behalf of imprisoned Iranians, this time targeting the newly established Islamist state. In 2005, the organization helped release *Strange Times, My Dear*, an anthology of postrevolutionary Iranian writing that included a new poem by Baraheni, whom the volume championed as "still active in trying to promote democratic liberties in his country."[100]

The introduction to Baraheni's *The Crowned Cannibals*, written by bestselling American novelist and fellow PEN member E. L. Doctorow, reveals both the global resonances and ideological dissonances of this Cold War literary anti-torture solidarity. Doctorow's writing strives to contextualize Baraheni's writing in the framework produced by the massive global success of Aleksandr Solzhenitsyn's *The Gulag Archipelago*—a major touchstone for PEN, the Freedom to Write Committee, and many of the new literary coalitions formed in the 1970s in the name of prisoner and human rights.[101] Doctorow doesn't evoke the particulars of Iranian political culture or history, instead granting Baraheni an abstract moral legitimacy afforded to the "kind of writer" typified by Solzhenitsyn who speaks truth to power in the face of torture and imprisonment. He writes:

> There is a kind of writer appearing ... who witnesses the crimes of his own government against himself and his countrymen. He chooses to explore the intimate subject of a human being's relationship to the state. His is the universe of the imprisoned, the tortured, the disfigured, and the doleful authority for the truth of his work is usually his own body. Thus we have Solzhenitsyn's *Gulag Archipelago*, an account of the vast Soviet system of secret police labor camps.[102]

For Doctorow, the significance of writers like Solzhenitsyn and Baraheni is not necessarily in the aesthetic value of their work but in their specific capacity to "bear witness" to otherwise unseen violence. These writers are our eyes and ears in the dark places "to which we have tenuous connection"—and there is no confusion about who "we" are in Doctorow's formulation—which affords such writers a title beyond mere author: "writer-witnesses."

According to Doctorow, these writer-witnesses are creating "a new art, with its own rules, the *Lieder* of victims of the state." But just what is the content of the new *lieder*, the new "song" of these writer-witnesses?

> It sings of regimes so repressive as to be fun-house images of civilization.... It tells of pliers for pulling fingernails, it speaks of electric currents sent into sexual organs, it describes prison cells in which a person can neither stand nor sit down. True, this is a necessarily small range of subject ... but within these strictures the poet is entitled to sing with his or her own voice.[103]

Doctorow tells readers that the writer-witness achieves his or her subject position as such only after experiences of state violence, the content of which is identical across national boundaries and political contexts because torturers perform their sinister craft for the same reasons everywhere. He writes that "torturers all have the same speech, the same rationale" for what they do, which in turn leaves the writer-witness with formal and aesthetic restrictions in what he or she can write. These restrictions are nonetheless freeing precisely because through them the writer-witness is allowed to write in his or her newly achieved "own voice." All torturers torture, Doctorow writes, because they "hate" "the self" and want to destroy it, whereas the writer-witness subverts this attempt to destroy because by writing, he or she restores "the self" to its proper centrality. Doctorow's essay, then, provides a general liberal theory of torture and political violence and the restorative power of writing.

Doctorow wasn't the only well-established Euro/American literary figure to favorably compare Baraheni to Solzhenitsyn. Other PEN members who advocated for Baraheni during his incarceration evoked the renegade Soviet in their defenses of the Iranian writer. Baraheni's *God's Shadow* reprints a letter published during his incarceration written by Jerzy Kosiński (president of PEN America from 1973 to 1975 and Polish American novelist most famous for writing *The Painted Bird*), Joseph Heller (American novelist most famous for writing *Catch-22*), and Dwight Macdonald (American political essayist and editor of the *Partisan Review*). This letter, first published in December 1973 in the *New York Times*, states:

> In September 1973, Reza Baraheni, prominent poet and literary critic, was arrested and imprisoned by the Iranian government. . . . Little of his writing is yet available in the West, but Mr. Baraheni is the author of twenty books. . . . Mr. Baraheni is Iran's Solzhenitsyn—outspoken and independent. As writers, scholars and individuals concerned with the right of free expression everywhere, we protest against the Iranian government's harassment and imprisonment of one of the country's leading authors.[104]

Baraheni cited this advocacy as key in securing his freedom, although ultimately the shah agreed to his release after Baraheni agreed to a publicized "interview" in which he disavowed Marxism.[105] Still, the leftist Baraheni, who also worked with the Trotskyist group CAIFI (Committee for Artistic and Intellectual Freedom in Iran),[106] was discomfited by the comparison to the increasingly conservative Solzhenitsyn: "Mr. Solzhenitsyn is certainly a very great writer, but as soon as he tries to expound his political ideology and historical theory, he becomes so reactionary that I am hard-pressed to find any similarity between my 'independence' and his."[107] Baraheni, whose dedication in *God's Shadow* read like a who's who of radical Iranian intellectuals, places himself in a different literary genealogy. His dedication reads, "Jalal Al-e Ahmad, *friend, killed*; Samad Behrangi, *friend, killed*; Khosrow Golesorkhi, *friend, killed*; Kermat Daneshiyan, *killed*." Despite the occasional dissonance between Baraheni and the movement that adopted him, the Iranian writer saw his international reputation grow with the publication of these books and numerous high-profile articles, along with his testimony to Congress.[108] Even after the revolution, when US audiences were more captivated by the unfolding hostage crisis than by the shah's misdeeds, Baraheni was still reminding readers, "Prerevolutionary Teheran was shown to be a sick city dotted with grisly torture chambers."[109]

Like Doctorow's essay, Baraheni's text also elaborates a theory of political violence. Unlike Doctorow, however, Baraheni is interested in the specific conditions that led to *Iranian* torture, not torture in the abstract. In Baraheni's estimation, torture in Iran is not a modern innovation, though it has taken on new virulence in the twentieth century.[110] Like the abovementioned opposition literature, Baraheni argues that the expansion of torture in Iran was part of the global ascendance of fascism in the early twentieth century and a direct outgrowth of the 1953 CIA-backed coup in Iran. Still, Baraheni argues, while imperial interference helped the shah expand repression in Iran, one should not lay the blame for torture solely at the feet of the global powers. Instead, Baraheni writes, Iranian torture is the result of its "Masculine History"—i.e., the repression of women by men and of ordinary people by the king. Baraheni's gendered theory of violence is an eclectic mix of Orientalist tropes (Iranian kings are "oriental despots"; masculine history has been the normative framework for Iranian politics since the ancient kings), Marxian language if not rigorous theory (the economic structure of masculine history is the "Asiatic mode of production"), and a quasi-feminist critique of patriarchal norms for which he uses Engels's writings on gender.[111] For Baraheni, repression in Iran is the outgrowth of an originary patriarchal violence, which replicates itself in all relationships; this is why on the state level the shah must "emasculate" dissidents by torturing them and why on the quotidian level women live in fear of men, especially their husbands. Overturning 2,500 years of masculine history, Baraheni argues, is the challenge before those invested in ending torture in Iran. Baraheni's commitment to both Marxist materialism and anti-shah polemics caused journalist Richard Sale to lambaste Baraheni's book as nothing more than the "intense and insular prejudices" of a man "full of hatred" in his *New York Times* review of *The Crowned Cannibals*.[112]

Despite his involvement with International PEN, Baraheni nonetheless expresses skepticism about international institutions' ability to meaningfully challenge Pahlavi dictatorship. Recounting a prison conversation in which a fellow detainee hopefully relays a rumor that the UN plans to investigate the conditions at their detention center in the name of human rights, Baraheni wryly responds, "Princess Ashraf was the president of the Human Rights Commission of the UN. . . . No one from that commission will ever set foot in the Komité. The Komité is ours, the lice are ours, the heart attacks are ours, the torture chambers are ours."[113] Baraheni's repetition that the problem of Tehran's notorious Komiteh interrogation center is "ours" (i.e., an Iranian problem that cannot be solved by outside institutions) subverts Doctorow's assertion that Baraheni is primarily serving as writer-witness for a different "us" (i.e., Euro/Americans concerned with human rights violations around the world). For Baraheni, international organizations can only go so far in curing what is essentially an Iranian problem to be solved on Iranian terms.

In order to understand this dissonance, it is necessary to take stock of the self-presentation of *The Crowned Cannibals* as not the work of a rogue "Iranian Solzhenitsyn" but instead as the intellectual inheritor of a wide-ranging corpus of modern Iranian political thought, including modern Iranian prison literature by writers like by Bozorg Alavi, the famed Marxist novelist and cofounder of the Tudeh Party, whom Baraheni translates at length. *The Crowned Cannibals* is deeply citational, making myriad references to major modern Iranian intellectuals, dissidents, and prison writers. Baraheni's most extended engagement is with Jalal Al-e Ahmad, the legendary Marxist-turned-Islamist essayist whose best-known work *Westoxification* is excerpted and translated by Baraheni in the text.[114] Baraheni takes Al-e Ahmad's formulation—that Iranians have been "Westoxified"—and argues that Iranians are not only "Westoxified" but also "doubly alienated." Echoing Al-e Ahmad, he argues that if Westerners are alienated from their labor through capitalist processes, Iranians experience double alienation because "we did not create this technology, this advanced capitalist system and the administrations and the bureaucracies involved, but they make use of us as their raw materials, subjecting us to a process of reification from afar."[115] Baraheni links "double alienation" to "masculine history," claiming, "Our indigenous Masculine History finally turned into a pimp, a comprador pimp, and pandered us all to the West."[116] Baraheni's prescription for this eclectic diagnosis is surprisingly prosaic: he recommends a transformation in the economic base structure of the nation. Baraheni's work is significant because it both directly engages the longer genealogy of Iran's anti-prison discourses and reveals the constitutive tensions in the relationship between the nascent global human rights movement and the Iranian dissidents who worked in and through that idiom.

Doctorow and Baraheni would not be the only writers or members of PEN to write about SAVAK or Iranian prisons. The pervasive influence of the international movement against Pahlavi torture was typified not only in the activism of these literary figures but also in the unexpected ways in which Iranian prisons found their way into cultural and literary works by non-Iranian authors. This now global public life of Iranian prisons was captured in novelist Tim O'Brien's 1978 National Book Award–winning novel *Going after Cacciato*, a text in which Iranian prisons, terrifying SAVAK agents, and gruesome punishments make central if unexpected appearances.[117] Like O'Brien's novel *The Things They Carry*, *Going after Cacciato* is set primarily in Vietnam during the US invasion and war effort. As such, it has largely been read by subsequent scholars through the lens of US Vietnam War literature or American empire.[118] Despite its initial setting in Vietnam, however, the characters in the novel take a long and unlikely detour through the prisons and interrogation centers of Pahlavi Iran, where they are subjected to several incidents of extraordinary and absurd violence. In conjuring a world of SAVAK agents, torture, and extrajudicial violence in Iran, *Going after Cacciato* reveals the extent to which, by the eve of the revolution, Pahlavi prisons signified political violence not only for Iranian dissidents but also for a global reading public typified by readers of critically acclaimed and politically engaged novelists like Doctorow, Kosiński, Heller, and O'Brien.

What are the circumstances in which the characters in *Going after Cacciato* find themselves in Iran, and what does Iran signify in the world of O'Brien's novel? After the eponymous Cacciato goes AWOL early in the story, O'Brien's narrative shifts between chapters in which the narrator Private First Class Paul Berlin recalls the numerous deaths he has witnessed in the war and chapters in which he fantasizes about the squadron leaving

Vietnam in search of Cacciato. It is eventually revealed that the travel chapters outside of Vietnam occur in the imagination of its central character, who daydreams about going after his squad-mate because he is desperate to leave the daily drudgery and extraordinary violence of war behind. Taken on Berlin's imaginary journey, the reader travels through Vietnam, Cambodia, India, Afghanistan, Iran, and Turkey to France in search of the spectral titular character. Most of these imaginary locales get only brief treatment, but the squadron's time in Pahlavi Iran—and especially its prisons and interrogation centers—extends over a number of chapters.

Upon their arrival in Tehran, Paul Berlin and his squadron witness the public beheading of a young man just before they are themselves arrested by Iranian security forces.[119] The troop looks on helplessly as the Tehran police violently disciplines the crowd while contented Iranian officials calmly oversee the gruesome scene:

> On the far side of the platform, police were using clubs to form an aisle through the mob. They would beat their way forward, hitting hard, but then the crowds would swell in again, closing the aisle, and the police would then holler and hit harder. Up on the platform the military officers paid no attention to this. They sat in their chairs and made jokes and sipped sherry.[120]

After their arrest, the American GIs are taken to an interrogation center in Tehran, where they meet Fahyi Rhallon, a man identified as "a captain in His Majesty's Royal Fusiliers. A soldier ... recently transferred to temporary duty with the *Savak*."[121] After Rhallon introduces himself, one of Berlin's companions asks him what SAVAK is, to which Rhallon replies, "Savak ... it is ... how do you say it? Internal security. Terrible duty for a man who would rather be killing Kurds."[122] Berlin is worried; he assumes that his squad's fate will be as bad as that of the beheaded youngster. During questioning, Berlin frets about SAVAK's well-known reputation for torture. The squadron is finally released after this first interrogation, but their freedom doesn't last for long. Another arrest comes days later, after which they are violently interrogated by more sinister members of SAVAK, one of whom tells Berlin that the reason the young man had been beheaded is because he (too) was a deserter and traitor to his country. With this, the squadron's fate is seemingly set, until

Berlin simply decides to fantasize them out of Iran and out of the hands of their SAVAK captors.

Going after Cacciato, of course, is not about Iranian prisons or prisoners in a literal sense, and O'Brien's novel is rightfully understood in US literary studies primarily as an indictment of US involvement in Vietnam. Why is it, then, that in order to *imagine* extraordinary political violence, O'Brien takes his characters out of Vietnam and into SAVAK interrogation centers? *Going after Cacciato*'s unexplained invocation of Iran and SAVAK reveals that, for O'Brien's readership of the late 1970s, Pahlavi Iran was broadly understood as a quintessential space of extralegal violence, prisoner abuse, and torture. O'Brien's novel also emphasizes the proximal relationship of the United States and Iran, both supposed bulwarks against international communism but perpetrators of brutal political violence in their own right.

Through the advocacy of the Iranian opposition abroad, the US-based counterculture press also embraced the image of shah-as-torturer and Iran-as-prison, denouncing those noteworthy figures who, contrary to critical figures like Doctorow and O'Brien, had amiable public relationships with the shah and his global diplomatic entourage. A 1977 article published in the famed New York City alternative weekly the *Village Voice* decried the political legitimacy granted to the shah's government by such luminaries as Liza Minelli, Elizabeth Taylor, and Henry Kissinger, all of whom were spotted in the 1970s at high-profile parties with members of the Pahlavi elite. The essay, entitled "The Beautiful Butchers" and written by Alexander Cockburn, James Ridgeway, and Jan Albert, took particular aim at Iranian ambassador to the US Ardeshir Zahedi, who was romantically involved with Elizabeth Taylor at the time and who was well-known for his star-studded soirees.[123] Andy Warhol, who attended a 1975 White House dinner for Mohammad Reza Shah and who in 1976 and 1977 painted portraits of the Iranian royal family, was also skewered by the *Voice* article for attending the gala. "Torture," the article sardonically started, "... can look better through a champagne glass and taste better after a mouthful of caviar." Zahedi, the article continued:

> has managed to sell the beautiful people on torture by the simple expedient of throwing large parties, amply furnished with caviar. He mastered, you might say, the political economy of Elizabeth Taylor and realized

that one star-studded bash, well-reported in the gossip columns, can do much to offset a couple of Amnesty reports about torture and a few intellectuals detailing exactly how the Shah's secret police ripped out their fingernails.[124]

The rest of the feature was similarly scathing. Glamorous photos of Warhol and Taylor meeting with Zahedi were juxtaposed with headlines touting the inflated number of political prisoners found in Iran circulated by Amnesty International and the Iranian opposition movement abroad. Torture, the article proclaimed, was Iran's "national pastime."

HUMAN RIGHTS IN IRAN ON THE EVE OF REVOLUTION

By the time the popular uprising against the shah was building to its climax in 1977–79, the Iranian students abroad as well as most factions of the Iranian opposition had adopted a wholly revolutionary position. By this point, Ayatollah Ruhollah Khomeini had consolidated his position as leader of a popular groundswell against the Pahlavi state, and the decimated guerrilla movement played a relatively small role in the final victory of the revolutionary masses.[125] For his part, Khomeini spent the late 1970s lambasting Euro/American hypocrisy on human rights and the Universal Declaration. In a speech at Shaykh Ansari Mosque in Najaf, Iraq, in January 1978 after a government-led massacre of protesters in Iran, the revolutionary Ayatollah stated, "All the miseries we have suffered, still suffer, and are about to suffer soon are caused by the heads of those countries that have signed the Declaration of Human Rights, but that all times have denied man his freedom.... As for America, a signatory to the Declaration of Human Rights, it imposed this Shah upon us, a worthy successor to his father.... What crimes that father and this son have committed against the Iranian nation since their appointment by the signatories to the Declaration of Human Rights."[126]

For Khomeini, the language of "human rights" was little more than a hypocritical cudgel wielded by the imperialist powers to further suppress those people under their yoke. At this juncture, Khomeini affirmed the importance of individual rights in the abstract while continuing to critique the hypocrisy of the so-called champions of human rights: "Individual human beings must all be equal before the law, and they must be free. They must be free in their choice of residence and occupation. But we see the Iranian nation, together with many others, suffering at the hands of those states that have signed and ratified the Declaration."[127] After the revolution, Islamic Republic officials often used—and continue to use—the strategy modeled by Khomeini for addressing concerns with rights abuses under their watch: turn the conversation back to rights violations in the United States. In 1984, for instance, amid the deadliest decade in Iranian history in terms of prisoner executions, the future leader of the country, Ali Khamenei, announced the official formation of a committee in Iran for investigating human rights abuses in the United States against African Americans.[128]

In the late 1970s, even in the moment of revolutionary upheaval, despite Khomeini's critiques, the language of human rights nonetheless found its way into further corners of the domestic political conversation. In 1977, the first Iran-based organization to formally link its opposition to the framework of international human rights was established. This organization, the Iranian Committee for the Defense of Freedom and Human Rights (ICDFHR), was founded in Tehran by twenty-nine opposition intellectuals including the soon-to-be first prime minister of the Islamic Republic, Mehdi Bazargan, and the soon-to-be first foreign minister of the Islamic Republic, Ebrahim Yazdi.[129] Abdol-Karim Lahidji, a Tehran University–educated lawyer who had himself been imprisoned twice and who cofounded both the Iranian Association of Jurists and the Progressive Lawyers Group, was named the group's spokesperson.[130] One of ICDFHR's first acts was to write a letter of protest to the secretary-general of the UN regarding the Pahlavi state's prison abuses.

Members of ICDFHR used the brief period of political openness brought about by pressure on the shah in the late 1970s to further pressure the government. Liberal intellectual and ICDFHR member Ali Asghar Javadi wrote two widely circulated open letters to the Pahlavi government bemoaning state corruption, political repression, and torture.[131] In one of these letters, addressed to the shah and the chief of the shah's special bureau, Nosratollah Moinian, Javadi repeatedly invokes the trampled upon "political freedoms" and "human rights" (*huquq-e ensani*) of the people of Iran. While terms like *huquq-e ensan* and *huquq-e bashar*, typically translated as "human rights," were not new to the Persian language, their use in Javadi's letters echoed the new global common sense about human rights.[132] Throughout his letters, Javadi tied his demands to the budding international movement for such rights.[133] These letters were circulated "in xerox copies in [the] hundreds"[134] and called for a series of liberal legal and political reforms that were increasingly out of step with the revolutionary mood in the country: checks and balances between branches of government, an end to Pahlavi corruption, an end to the shah's Rastakhiz (Resurrection) Party, the establishment of legitimate opposition parties, the end of torture, and the immediate release of all political prisoners.

Javadi's writing was circulated outside of Iran by liberal human rights activists and sympathetic Iranian dissidents eager to spread his message. One such organization, the Committee for Human Rights in Iran (Komiteh-ye defaʿ az huquq-e bashar dar Iran), translated and published a Javadi-penned essay that referred to Iran as a "Great Prison" and decried Pahlavi torture in its first communiqué.[135] Javadi's writing was also invoked by British human rights activists as a defining moment in their understanding of the intellectual genealogy of the revolution.[136] During the revolutionary groundswell, members of the ICDFHR would be targeted by security forces. In April 1978, Lahidji's office was bombed and Lahidji himself was attacked by Pahlavi state forces, leading the ICJ's William Butler to visit the Iranian lawyer and rights advocate in the hospital and press for his safety with the shah himself.

Finally, amid the success of the revolution and during the initial establishment of the political formation calling itself the "Islamic Republic," the language of human rights even made its way into some key official discourses. Just after the fall of the shah, the Judicial Organization of the Military of the Islamic Republic (Sazman-e qaza'i-e artesh-e jomhuri-ye eslami) formally granted papers to some prerevolutionary political prisoners stating that those individuals had been imprisoned by the former government because of their efforts "defending freedom and human rights" (*azadi va huquq-e bashar*) in the country.[137]

This chapter outlines a global rise in concern regarding torture, extrajudicial executions, and prison conditions in Mohammad Reza Pahlavi's Iran. This global interest in Pahlavi penal and judicial practices emerged precisely in an era when torture was perceived as a growing global crisis by emergent organizations advocating on behalf of human rights. Yet for Iranian dissidents of various stripes, the plight of political dissidents in Pahlavi prisons was not a new cause. For these dissidents, the language and institutions of human rights came to provide useful tools through which to challenge Pahlavi legitimacy and carceral policy, even when that language didn't define the limits of their politics. In the 1960s, Iranians were joined in their advocacy on behalf of Iran's prisoners by a diverse assortment of international activists, organizers, politicians, and intellectuals alike, often using the language of rights. In taking up the mantle of Iranian prisoners' rights, groups in Europe and the United States found their inspiration—and gained much of their information—from a large expatriate movement of Iranian students. Together, these groups managed to publicize Pahlavi torture and prison abuses to such an extent that the Pahlavi government was pressured into changing its policies.

The notion of human rights in the prerevolutionary era was neither fixed nor stable. For the Iranian expatriate opposition movement, the language of human rights was couched in a political analysis that was, at its core, anti-imperialist, increasingly revolutionary, and inspired by the guerrilla movement in Iran. For the Pahlavi state, human rights were a timeless and essential quality of Iran as an empire-turned-nation. For the European and American liberals who advocated on behalf of Iranian prisoners, human rights were a natural outgrowth of liberal rights in general. For religious activists advocating on behalf of incarcerated clerics, they were an outgrowth of their moral and ethical spiritual commitments. Meanwhile, for Khomeini, "human rights" were little more than a clear example of the hypocrisy of the arrogant and "world-devouring" imperialist powers. In examining the relationship between Iranian dissidents and the emergent global movements for human rights, I argue that these political engagements were not merely the work of an Iranian opposition movement instrumentally mobilizing (or rejecting) an already codified language of human rights in order to further its political agenda. Nor is it accurate to imagine that "rights talk" in Iran's prerevolutionary politics simply reveals a local instantiation of a Euro/American mode of thought that arrived on the Iranian scene fully formed. Instead, human rights as both political language and strategy were produced and transformed through a decades-long interaction with Iranian dissident movements, just as the anti-Pahlavi movement was altered and occasionally propelled by its encounter with the global language of human rights.

In the aftermath of the revolution, several of the international organizations that took up the cause of Iranian prisoners before 1979 would again sound the alarm regarding prisoner abuse in the country. Organizations like Amnesty International immediately used the political infrastructures, languages, and insights of the prerevolutionary era to challenge the carceral violence in the new Islamic Republic. After the fall of the shah, the coalitional lines described above would again be made and remade, and over time the influence of revolutionary Third Worldisms and Marxism-Leninisms would wane in favor of a more entrenched and institutionalized vison of international human rights. In part, this waning was a function of the global changing of political tides that led to human rights emerging as a "last utopia" in place of what were increasingly seen as the flawed utopias of the past. It also was a function of state violence in the Islamic Republic. As the new Islamist government systematically eradicated its revolutionary rivals in the decade after the fall of the shah, nearly an entire generation of Iranian dissidents—and the institutional memory of their impassioned activism—died in Islamic Republic prisons. Those who survived the violence did so as changed people, largely renouncing the incendiary political investments of their youth, even as they continued to publicize the carceral violence of the Islamic government.

Five

MAKING AN EXAMPLE
Carceral Utopianism and Prison Expansion in Revolutionary Iran

ON FEBRUARY 1, 1979, AFTER FIFTEEN YEARS OF FORCED EXILE, AYAtollah Ruhollah Khomeini arrived in Iran as the undisputed leader of a mass revolutionary movement that had just ousted Mohammad Reza Pahlavi from the throne.[1] Having witnessed the seemingly unthinkable scene of the shah and empress fleeing the country just a few weeks prior, approximately three million joyful Iranians poured out onto the streets of Tehran to welcome home the man they had reverently dubbed the Imam. Over the following ten days, which were called the Ten Days of Dawn by the victorious revolutionaries, the final vestiges of Pahlavi rule were defeated, and a provisional revolutionary government was announced.[2] The final battle between the old and new orders began on February 9th with a last-gasp effort by the shah's Imperial Guard to quell a surging mutiny in its ranks. After six hours of fighting between remaining Pahlavi military loyalists and various groups of rank-and-file military deserters and revolutionary guerrillas, the Imperial Guard was forced to withdraw.[3] Over the next several days, Iranians of all stripes took to the streets armed with weapons handed out by the guerrillas to storm police stations, army barracks, SAVAK interrogation centers, military garrisons, and other institutional reminders of the crumbling monarchy. The once-secret files held across these sites were opened and scattered to the winds as the revolutionary movement briefly made radically transparent all that the former government had collected on its citizenry through surveillance.[4] On February 11, 1979, the fighting reached its dramatic conclusion; the revolution was won.

Among other triumphs on that day, revolutionaries occupied Evin Prison, that hated monument to SAVAK torture and political incarceration. The Pars news agency, now in the hands of the revolutionaries, reported the results: "Evin Prison was occupied by the people and fell after several hours of siege.... From the early hours last night, groups of the people's armed units attacked this prison and after several hours [of] battle they succeeded in occupying this last bastion of despotism."[5] Yet the opening of Evin was neither a straightforward nor a lasting victory. As armed revolutionaries were roaming the streets on their way to the prison, some members of the provisional government were not entirely certain that storming Evin, which had already been emptied of virtually all of its prerevolutionary detainees in the previous weeks and months, was the right decision. These reservations were expressed via revolutionary-run media announcements requesting that rebels nearing Evin "maintain their revolutionary order and patience" so as not to "endanger the lives of political prisoners" still housed in the prison.[6] The tone in a later message turned more urgent, pleading with revolutionaries not to open the prison's gates at all, lest new royalist prisoners arrested and incarcerated by the new order use the opportunity to make their way out in the confusion: "Revolutionary forces take note: Evin Prison should not be attacked, since it is possible that elements of the previous regime might be held [there]—elements who would misuse the opportunity and flee."[7]

Despite these warnings, the jubilant mood of the moment won the day and Evin was occupied, though the revolutionaries would not succeed without their own difficulties. Some were flummoxed by the lack of remaining political prisoners, having long believed the anti-shah movement's oft-repeated claims that the shah had imprisoned anywhere from fifty thousand to one hundred thousand dissidents.[8] According to scholar Behrooz Ghamari-Tabrizi, who was among those who stormed and occupied Evin, the occupying revolutionaries searched for but never found the mythic subterranean spaces where the Pahlavi government was said to be keeping those "missing" tens of thousands of prisoners.[9] Others experienced even more urgent complications. Incredibly, just as they were attempting to free any remaining prisoners, "a great many of the people who attacked Evin" accidentally locked *themselves* into the prison "as a result of the shutting of the automatic electric doors on the second floor."[10] Reinforcements had to be sent to help them break their way back out.

Although the trapped rebels didn't know it then, this uncanny moment foreshadowed an ominous future for countless revolutionaries, dissidents, and students in the anti-shah movement who would again come to find themselves incarcerated and tortured, this time by the government they helped bring to power. On February 15th, explosives engineers entered Evin to remove any mines or explosives to make it safe to again operate as a prison, this time under the aegis of the new Khomeini-led government. Exponentially more Iranians would be detained in Evin by the new Islamic Republic than had ever been held there under the shah. Evin's capacity was initially 320 persons when it was built and opened in the early 1970s.[11] Although SAVAK sources of the late 1970s publicly insisted that fewer than 100 persons were then held there, the number of detainees in Evin in 1977 was approximately 1,500—enough to cement its public reputation as among the most brutal of the shah's political prisons.[12] Yet by March 1979, barely three weeks after the revolutionary occupation of Evin, over 7,200 new detainees were held there on charges mounted by the fledgling government.[13] This expansion would only continue in the coming years. Today, Evin remains operational with an official capacity of 15,000 persons, though images leaked in 2021 of detainees sleeping a dozen to a cell reveal that the number of persons held there is likely larger than this official tally.[14] In the public life of Iran's post-1979 prisons, Evin would quickly become "a name synonymous with the system of injustice that prevails" in the Islamic Republic, a one-word reminder of the extraordinary and expansive carceral violence of the revolutionary state.[15] When a massive new round of antigovernment protests broke out in late 2022, one indelible moment from the early months of the uprising occurred on October 15: an unexplained fire broke out at Evin, killing several detainees.[16] As usual, the country's prisons, and Evin in particular, were the firestorm at the center of political life in Iran.

Evin's development reveals the grim irony of Iran's postrevolutionary carceral system: since 1979, Iranians who were once united in their opposition to prisons and torture under the shah have experienced the consolidation of a government that has continued, intensified, and vastly expanded the carceral practices and institutions that so publicly defined the fallen monarchy. This carceral expansion has ensnared political dissidents, religious and ethnic minorities, trade unionists, and common-law detainees alike. I argue that the story of the post-1979 carceral system is one of extraordinary growth similar to carceral expansion in other parts of the world in the same era but marked by the particulars of Islamic revolutionary politics in Iran. This cumulative growth across Iranian jails and prisons has led to the Islamic Republic becoming one of the most heavily carceral states in the world, with a higher total of incarcerated persons than all but seven other countries, the latter a dubious group led (by a vast margin) by the United States.[17]

How should we understand this expansion of the carceral state in the contemporary Islamic Republic of Iran? To what extent is it an outgrowth of the ideological and religious particulars of the Islamic revolutionary government? In contrast, to what extent is it an embedded historical phenomenon with national and global antecedents, including the histories I have examined in this book? In what follows in this chapter, I will analyze the expansion of Iran's prison system in the post-1979 era in two parts: first, as a function of deep institutional, infrastructural, and global continuities with the pre-1979 era, and next, as an outgrowth of the transformative particulars of the Islamic revolutionary government and its ideological proclivities. As I have argued throughout this book, the expansive prison system entrenched in Iran today has been over a century in the making. Upon taking power, the new government used the tools at its disposal—including the preexisting prisons of the Pahlavi era—to consolidate ideological and political authority in a deeply contested social terrain. Although the Islamic revolutionaries won the day promising the eradication of Pahlavi bureaucracy and an end to torture, prisons and carceral violence were nonetheless viewed as mechanisms by which to eradicate Iran of "counterrevolutionary" and un-Islamic influences. Carceral violence was seen as a way to remake Iranian society along a new utopian political and moral horizon. This utopianism, while certainly of a different type than the one that motivated Pahlavi "humanist" prison reformism discussed in earlier chapters, shared with Pahlavi carceral thinking the undergirding belief that at least some forms of criminality or social norm-breaking could be reformed or even eradicated through carceral means. To understand the era of carceral violence and expansion from the success of the revolution in 1979 to the death of Khomeini a decade later, then, is to recognize that for the revolutionaries it was undertaken in service of utopia.

MAKING AN EXAMPLE IN AN ERA OF EXPANSION

Before moving on to the early years after the fall of the shah, a closer accounting of the expansion of Iran's prison system after 1979 is in order. The raw numbers of this expansion paint a stark picture. According to official tallies, the total number of prisoners in the Islamic Republic in 1980 stood at 8,557 in a population of approximately 37 million; by 2016, that number had ballooned by more than twenty-six times to 223,000 prisoners in a population of about 78 million. In certain prisons, the increase in detainee population in that time was as much as 333 percent.[18] According to sociologist, journalist, and reformist political figure Abbas Abdi, one person was incarcerated every two minutes in the years between 1980 and 1986.[19] Young Iranians have borne the brunt of this carceralization, as some 70 percent of all detainees in Iran are under the age of forty.[20] Another recent tally provided by a member of the Islamic Republic parliament puts Iran's total incarcerated persons just before the revolution at 16,000 (or 40 persons per 100,000), compared to the 2020s total of approximately 240,000 (or 300 per 100,000).[21] As in the Pahlavi era, the majority of those incarcerated have been held on drug-related charges. In a 1986 press conference, the first head of the Islamic Republic's Prisons Organization, Hojjat-ol-Eslam Majid Ansari, claimed that approximately 65 percent of the country's incarcerated persons were being held on drug charges.[22] In 1982 a total of 19,160 persons were officially listed as arrested on drug-related charges, and by just 1988 that number had skyrocketed several-fold to 92,046.[23] Class and financial insecurity exacerbated in part by US-led economic sanctions plays a role in contemporary Iran's prison totals. According to official tallies, at least 18,000 individuals are held in debtors' prisons throughout the country—a number slightly in excess of the total number of *all* incarcerated persons in the final months of Pahlavi rule.[24]

In order to deal with this ballooning need for prison space, numerous jails, prisons, and detention centers have been expanded or newly built in the Islamic Republic period, most notably the 15,000-capacity Greater Tehran Central Prison (also known as Fashafouyeh), which opened in the early 2010s to help reduce congestion in other prisons, Evin included.[25] From the earliest years of the Islamic Republic, the need for carceral space has been so great that prisoners have often been held in repurposed and makeshift spaces. One paradigmatic example is the little-known Salehabad Prison, which was opened on the site of a former dairy farm and held both dissidents and common-law prisoners in cow stalls in the mid-1980s.[26] Today, Iran's quarter of a million (official) prisoners are held in 268 jails, prisons, and detention centers initially built to accommodate no more than 88,000 total persons. This means that severe overcrowding remains endemic to the system—a fact readily admitted by Islamic Republic leadership.

It is likely that these official tallies, which are provided by the Prisons Organization, undercount the total detainee population as well as the total number of carceral sites across the country. This is in part because the Prisons Organization, formally in charge of Iran's prisons since its 1986 founding, under the aegis of the judiciary, isn't granted jurisdiction over the interrogation, detention centers, and prison wards run by the Islamic Revolutionary Guard Corps (IRGC) or the Ministry of Intelligence and Security.[27] As such, access to official information and statistics on detainees held by these security organs—such as Evin's notorious Ward 209—is limited at best.[28] This means that the prisoners who typically elicit the greatest public concern and international outcry are today rarely formally addressed by the leaders of the country's major prison institution. Recent directors of the Prisons Organization have often avowed their lack of jurisdiction in such facilities, claiming that it is not in the organization's power to interfere with the actions of the country's security forces, even as they pertain to incarceration, torture, or prison deaths.[29] This jurisdictional distinction was not initially the plan. When the Prisons Organization was first founded in 1986, the Supreme Judicial Council set regulations whereby "the Ministry of Intelligence, the Islamic Revolutionary Guard Corps, the Islamic Revolution Committees, the

Armed Forces of the Islamic Republic of Iran, and other organizations and revolutionary bodies" were rendered "dutybound to hand over their detention centers to that organization."[30] Yet this centralization under the Prisons Organization never fully took root, and parallel jurisdictions continue to exist in Iran's prison system today.

The reach of contemporary Iran's carceral system is not limited to traditional jails and prisons. The above numbers don't include those captured in a swelling network of probation, parole, or house arrest—a significant component of those who live along the carceral continuum in Iran, and to whom I will return in the following chapter.[31] They also don't include other vulnerable populations captured in the Islamic Republic's expanded carceral dragnet, such as, for instance, the growing population of largely Iraqi and Afghan refugees held in migrant detention camps. These camps are not prisons as such, but they reveal the extent to which the carceral imaginary—that is, the belief that social problems from private debt to border crossing to drug use to political opposition should be addressed by mass surveillance, detention, and social sequestering—dominates the contemporary Islamic Republic's political horizon.[32] Following an insight from philosopher Omid Tofighian, I include migrant camps in this conversation to remind us of the extent to which modern incarceration is *always* a "bordering practice," limiting human mobility and delimiting and defining social boundaries.[33]

The reappropriation of the shah's prisons mirrored the Islamic Republic's broader approach to the bureaucratic organs of the Pahlavi state. Despite their promise to abolish the much-maligned bureaucracy, the Islamic revolutionaries simply "took over the previous state intact, merely purging the top echelons, and then gradually but steadily expanded its ranks."[34] Prisons were a major part of this state-expanding effort. Upon taking power, the embryonic Islamic government commandeered Pahlavi Iran's prisons, frenziedly expanding their capacity to account for a flood of new detainees captured by revolutionary militias. The new government inaugurated a system of ad hoc revolutionary tribunals (*dadgah-e enqelab*), which in Tehran quickly set up shop in Qasr and Evin Prisons, institutions that had just seen their cells emptied by revolutionaries fighting for a new world.[35] Within just a few days of the revolution's success, Qasr was, according to one observer, newly "full of persons arrested by the revolutionary militia."[36] Within months, Qasr's total detainee population grew by at least four times the 1978 number.[37] Evin, as mentioned above, was similarly overwhelmed with new detainees. Other prerevolutionary prisons near Tehran such as Qezel Hesar and Gohar Dasht (today officially known as Rajaishahr Prison) were also appropriated and, in the latter's case, extensively expanded by construction completed in 1982.[38] Outside of Tehran, in cities including Tabriz, Isfahan, Mashhad, Shiraz, Hamadan, Sanandaj, and Kermanshah, new prisoners were also "herded into the existing city prisons" by revolutionaries.[39] Both political dissidents and common-law prisoners experienced these carceral continuities. The regulatory code promulgated in 1982 on the administration of the Islamic Republic's prisons was eerily similar to the 1975 code first enacted by the Pahlavi government—its regulations for how detainees should be made to spend their days also advised vocational training, education, and exercise, although Islamic studies were now added to the list.[40]

That the triumphant Islamic revolutionaries would immediately inhabit and vastly expand the carceral machinery of the shah's fallen government would perhaps not have seemed a given to hopeful onlookers on the eve of the revolution. In the first place, there was the thorny issue of the clear-cut public consensus against Pahlavi prisons and torture in the lead-up to the monarchy's collapse. There was also the fact that imprisonment is not typically a form of punishment found in classical Islamic law.[41] Indeed, in certain of Khomeini's public statements on Islamic justice, modern incarceration was presented as a symptom of the bureaucratic modern state that true Islamic governance would eradicate altogether. That modern prisons appear in the arsenal of the contemporary Islamic Republic is a fact legally massaged by the use of *ta'zir*—that is, punishments at the discretion of the Islamic judge. In Shi'a Islamic law, and thus in the Islamic Republic of Iran, *ta'zir* stands in distinction from *hudud*, or those punishments that are specifically outlined in sharia, as well as *qisas*, or retaliatory punishments, and *diyat*, or punishment by blood money.

Modern prisons, according to at least some of Khomeini's statements, could be rendered unnecessary under a truly just Islamic system. "If a member of the clergy wishes to inflict a penalty on someone," Khomeini argued, "he must do so publicly, according to established practice, and lash him the specific number of times, without insulting him or slapping him *or imprisoning him even for a single day*" (emphasis added).[42] According to Khomeini, transforming Iran's legal system into a sharia-based order would quickly bring about a breezy and utopian form of Islamic justice, in contradistinction to sluggish, bureaucratic, and "childish" forms of Western legality:

> Islamic justice is based on simplicity and ease. It settles all criminal or civil complaints in the most convenient, elementary, and expeditious way possible. All that is required is for an Islamic judge, with a pen and inkwell and two or three enforcers, to go into a town, come to his verdict on any kind of case, and have it immediately carried out. Look at the present cost in time and money in Western society with all its judicial procedures surrounding any judgement, in the name of principles alien to Islam.... If the punitive laws of Islam were applied for only one year, all the devastating injustices and immoralities would be uprooted. Misdeeds must be punished by the law of retaliation: cut off the hands of the thief; kill the murderer instead of putting him in prison; flog the adulterous woman or man. Your concerns, your "humanitarian" scruples are more childish than reasonable.[43]

Despite this seeming mandate to rethink the nature of punishment in a revolutionary Islamic state, and despite the government's self-conscious—if fitful and incomplete—effort to govern and legislate by sharia, at no point was any serious effort made by the revolutionary government to avoid or even reduce reliance on the prisons built and cultivated under the Pahlavi monarchs.

International human rights organizations immediately noted this carceral continuity. In the summer of 1980, Amnesty International explained to its followers that many of those being incarcerated in Iran "had been foremost in the opposition to the government of the Shah and had suffered imprisonment at that time for their political beliefs."[44] AI further lamented the fact that the torture techniques preferred by the new government "were similar to abuses committed under the Shah before the 1979 revolution."[45] Incarcerated dissidents also noted these disturbing similarities, dispiritedly noting the continued use of the bastinado and other forms of prerevolutionary torture. As one detainee wrote in 1982, "They [the interrogators of the Islamic Republic] use another form of torture developed by Savak under the

Shah: after whipping the soles of the feet, a booted guard stands on them until the swelling is gone. Then he forces the prisoner to walk around or sit and stand repeatedly. One man was forced to sit and stand 1,120 times before he collapsed into unconsciousness."[46] Still another opposition organization lamented, "Three years ago, no one expected that the old Savak apparatus would be revived so soon or that the Pahlavi dungeons would become Islamic torture chambers. No one knew that those patriots who survived the Shah would now be facing Khomeini's death squads."[47]

Among the most remarkable examples of Iran's modern carceral continuity is the infamous Tehran detention center known in the late Pahlavi period as the Komiteh-ye Moshtarek-e Zedd-e Kharabkar, or Joint Anti-Sabotage Committee, often known in those years simply as the Komiteh. True to its name, the Komiteh opened as such after the 1970s inauguration of the guerrilla movement and represented an effort by the Pahlavi government to consolidate the work of SAVAK, the gendarmerie, the military, and the National Police Force—organizations that had otherwise spent years clashing over matters of jurisdiction in cases related to political dissidents. Like Evin, the Komiteh became synonymous with the escalated use of torture and forced confessions in the 1970s. After 1979, this infamous site was taken over by the new government, renamed the Komiteh-ye Towhid (Oneness of God Committee), and reopened as a political detention and interrogation center in service of the Islamic Republic. This institutional continuity goes even further back to the very first years of the modern carceral system in Iran. The late Pahlavi government had itself repurposed earlier prison space to open the Komiteh, inaugurating the interrogation center on the site of a prison built in the 1930s with input from German engineers and opened in 1937 under Reza Shah.[48] The public life of the modern prison in Iran has drawn from deep infrastructural roots, even across profound political upheaval.

The story of this carceral site doesn't end here. Towhid Prison, by then run by the Ministry of Intelligence, finally closed its doors as a prison in 2000 amid complaints of torture after a wave of student protests in the summer of 1999. It soon reopened its doors as a new type of institution: a prison museum now known as 'Ebrat (Example) Museum. Even the name 'Ebrat has a remarkable resonance with the pre-1979 public life of the prison. In the mid-1950s, SAVAK helped produce a magazine also called 'Ebrat, in which "repentant" incarcerated members of the communist Tudeh Party championed Pahlavi policies and wrote screeds against their now-abandoned Marxist political beliefs. 'Ebrat magazine largely focused on dissuading other leftists and would-be leftists from joining the Tudeh by featuring long-form histories of Tudeh malfeasance, Soviet (and particularly Stalinist) treachery, depictions of prison life, and letters from former party members renouncing their abandoned leftist worldviews.[49] The journal also translated writing by the CIA-funded journal the *Problems of Communism*.[50] As these various "examples" show, the prison, both before and after 1979, has been imagined by subsequent Iranian governments as a pedagogical space through which dissidents and ordinary citizens alike could be trained into views more friendly to the preferred ideology of the state. Nor is the discourse of carceral example limited to "soft" culture like museums or journals; the secretive IRGC-run basement ward in which dissident wrestling champion Navid Afkari was held before his execution in fall 2020 in Central Shiraz Prison, also known as Adelabad Prison, is also called 'Ebrat.[51]

'Ebrat Museum, like Qasr Prison Museum, is a monument to the Islamic Republic's authorized historical framing of both the Pahlavi era and the revolution that ended it. In presenting a sanitized version of prison history, 'Ebrat mobilizes a selective memory of Iran's carceral spaces to stage and reinscribe Islamic Republic legitimacy vis-à-vis the monarchist government it overthrew. When I visited the museum in 2014, I was led on a mandatory guided tour alongside several school-age children as we were regaled with emotionally charged stories of SAVAK cruelty and ulama heroism in the face of torture. The tour guide took particular note of the experiences of Ayatollah Ali Khamenei—now leader of the Islamic Republic—who was imprisoned and tortured in the Komiteh. The life of the interrogation center as the Towhid Committee under the Islamic Republic is erased from this official story. The experiences of leftists and members of ethnic liberation movements imprisoned before 1979 are also effaced in favor of an Islamist narrative. Anthropologist Shahla Talebi, a formerly incarcerated leftist, outlines these erasures in her prison memoir, in which she movingly describes visiting 'Ebrat years after her own incarceration and torture:

The bitter taste in my mouth from witnessing the nearly absolute erasure of the history of the leftists' resistance and suffering . . . and an exaggerated predominance of religious clergy presented in this museum became unbearable when [my friend] recalled the different spots where she had been interrogated and beaten [during the Islamic Republic era]. . . . Now here we were, walking around in this prison-museum, whose opening to the public felt like a slap in the face, considering that [we] had lived through the torture chambers of this regime.[52]

Although there is some prisoner graffiti visible on 'Ebrat's walls, these markers have also largely been scrubbed. Xavier Gaillard argues that what remains of 'Ebrat's graffiti is possibly inauthentic, insofar as it appears too clean—both physically and ideologically—to represent the thoughts of those ever actually imprisoned there.[53]

In the office of the former head of the Komiteh, there is now an organizational flow chart displayed featuring headshots and information on Pahlavi intelligence and prison officials, with Mohammad Reza Pahlavi at the top of the organizational chain. In fact, the former shah's image, along with images of the former empress and crown prince, adorn many of 'Ebrat's exhibition rooms. Today, those curious about 'Ebrat's selective staging of history are no longer required to visit the museum to experience it, as it is now possible to take a virtual tour of the facility on 'Ebrat's official website.[54] This virtual tour begins with a short clip of the famed interview conducted by Mike Wallace with Mohammad Reza Pahlavi discussed in the last chapter, in which Wallace presses the shah on his government's use of torture. The tour continues by allowing the virtual visitor to click through all of the rooms currently on exhibit at 'Ebrat with a soundtrack of mournful music to further set the somber emotional tone.

UTOPIAN TERROR AFTER 1979

Despite the official account promoted in prison museums like 'Ebrat, the aftermath of Iran's February 1979 revolution and the phase of state consolidation that took place through Khomeini's June 1989 death was in fact the deadliest period of carceral violence in Iran's modern history to date. If the Islamic Republic has come to be synonymous with prisons, torture, forced confessions, and executions in the eyes of its political adversaries and many of its citizens, it was during this first decade that the revolutionary government first cemented this macabre reputation. The victorious Islamic revolutionaries used carceral means, including mass arrests, incarceration, trials, forced confessions, and executions, to push Iranian society toward their utopian political and moral horizon and to consolidate the *nezam* (system) of supreme clerical rule through the *velayat-e faqih*, or guardianship of the jurist. (In this system, an unelected Shi'a cleric—first Khomeini and then Ali Khamenei—sits at the top of the decision-making hierarchy of the state in all matters.) Initially, the revolutionary coalition largely and most publicly set its retributive sights on royalists and high-ranking members of the shah's intelligence and military organizations, including SAVAK, but the shrinking inner circle of revolutionary Islamists and clerics would soon come to capture Islamic liberals, Islamic leftists, secular nationalists, Marxist-Leninists, Maoists, eclectic leftists, members of ethnic independence movements (such as the Kurdish people's movement), students, Muslim iconoclasts, and other would-be ideological adversaries in its expanding carceral crosshairs.

The wave of terror that began in 1979 and culminated with the mass executions of thousands of imprisoned dissidents in 1988 quickly earned the nascent government critics both inside and outside of the country. These activists noted the bitter irony of a government that came to power opposing extrajudicial violence and torture so quickly and so brutally adopting similar practices toward its own opponents. For revolutionary stalwarts however, this paroxysm of carceral violence did not happen *despite* the revolution's early utopian promises but rather as a foundational method of enacting those promises. In fact, the victorious revolutionaries explicitly linked carceral violence to the utopian political horizon of the revolutionary movement. Khomeini himself promised that their government would do nothing less than "cleanse society of the putrefied vestiges of the tyrannical regime" and eradicate un-Islamic, criminal, and counterrevolutionary influences from Iran altogether.[55] In the months after the fall of the shah, revolutionaries promoted widespread incarceration, punishment, and executions as necessary components of a revolutionary telos in which carceral violence would directly lead to the establishment of a truly just and revolutionary Islamic polity.

To say that the first decade after the success of the revolution was marked by revolutionary utopianism and the promise of Islamic justice is not to say that the process of judicial and legal consolidation was not chaotic, deeply contested, and at times remarkably ad hoc. At the level of state structure and constitutional law, contestations between opposed factions over the content and meaning of formalizing an "Islamic Republic" roiled the fragile revolutionary coalition from Khomeini's February 1979 return to Iran.[56] Upon his arrival in Iran, Khomeini founded the revolutionary tribunals, which he tasked with meting out justice and bringing judicial and legal institutions into clerical hands and into compliance with sharia. The first tribunal was conducted at Khomeini's temporary headquarters in Tehran's Refah School, and the first executions were carried out on February 16th by Sadeq Khalkhali, the so-called hanging judge of the revolution.[57] The tribunals also served a practical function insofar as they worked to "preserve some semblance of law and order since the whole judiciary, especially the law enforcement system, was in complete disarray."[58] The messy and labored process of marrying sharia norms and sympathetic clerical personnel to the already existing legal, judicial, and policing institutions of the modern Iranian state and bureaucracy while simultaneously endeavoring to rid Iran of "counterrevolutionary" forces and those "at war with God" would be key efforts for the new government for several years to come.

As Khomeini insisted, these tribunals were not simply a matter of retribution—although they were that—but were also a matter of "social justice" (*'adalat-e ejtema'i*). Khomeini explicitly put these efforts in both Islamic *and* carceral terms, regularly referring to the fallen shah and his associates as both "idolators" (*taghuti*) and "criminals" (*jenayatkar*). Khomeini and his allies argued that these punishments were not only a matter of Islamic justice but also a matter of that all-important Iranian desire: the rule of law. Pahlavi cronies had committed crimes by any meaningful legal standard, Khomeini argued, and thus they had to be punished in accordance with the law. The revolutionaries also demanded the extradition to Iran of the man whom they claimed was the biggest criminal of all: the former shah, Mohammad Reza Pahlavi, who fled Iran in January 1979 and eventually died in Anwar Sadat's Egypt in mid-1980. Pahlavi-era torture and imprisonments of political dissidents, particularly militant clerics, were hailed as among the most serious of the Pahlavi government's criminal acts and the most in need of public revolutionary redress. As Khomeini explained, Pahlavi-era political imprisonments were criminal not merely because they were unjust but because they deprived the Iranian nation of the crucial manpower and intellectual resources of religious intellectuals and the leading ulama. On February 2, one day after his return to Iran from his final exilic home in Neauphle-le-Château, France, Khomeini expounded on his view of Pahlavi criminality to a group of followers at the Alavi School in Tehran, evoking themes of loss, endurance, and struggle so central to his revolutionary rhetoric:

> I see that the black-bearded friends I had left behind [while in forced exile outside of Iran] now all have white beards. We had people in prison who, when they were imprisoned, were healthy and strong, who when they were released from prison—those who made it out alive—they had become weak, they had become old men. These human resources [*niru-ha-ye ensani*] whom we lost, this was the most important thing. Of all of the crimes of the Pahlavi dynasty this may well have been the greatest crime of all, that all of our active human resources were either destroyed or their activities neutralized for great lengths of time. Those people who should have been working in service of this country, such as the ulama and other intellectually minded people, they took them to prison. They put them in prison for ten years, fifteen years, five years . . . they wasted all of these people.[59]

Revolutionaries promised swift justice for these Pahlavi crimes. The tribunals worked quickly and processed large numbers of cases with little attention to procedural or legal detail. By July 1979, Tehran's public prosecutor general, Ayatollah Abolfazl Shahshahani, claimed that the revolutionary courts had processed an astonishing ten thousand cases.[60] By this point, Shahshahani was so worried about overcrowding in the capital city's prisons that he issued a short-lived order for revolutionary law enforcement to cease all arrests.[61] (Shahshahani, allied with the Islamic liberals in government, would only serve in the role as public prosecutor until October and would in 1990 be imprisoned for his own political opposition to Islamic Republic policies.)[62] The orders of these tribunals were enacted by the Komiteh-ye Enqelab, or Revolutionary Committees—ad hoc groups of revolutionary foot soldiers who served law enforcement and other para-state functions.[63] The Revolutionary Committees first emerged in late 1978 as an autonomous means to organize protests and strikes and distribute resources, but by spring of 1979, they were used increasingly as de facto law enforcement.[64]

Front-page stories in the Iranian press outlining trials and executions were commonplace throughout the first months after the revolution, though as historian Ervand Abrahamian notes, the heavily publicized forced confessions that would become a hallmark of the Islamic Republic's carceral practices did not take off until 1981.[65] While many of the leftist, liberal, and non-Khomeinist Islamist organizations of the anti-shah coalition remained at least nominally committed to Khomeini's efforts through the relatively open period of 1979 and in some cases beyond, some in the opposition challenged Khomeini's efforts more quickly, leading to renewed political incarceration among revolutionaries and dissidents. This in turn gave rise to the rapid reestablishment of pre-1979 prisoner protest methods, such as when newly incarcerated leftist prisoners launched prison hunger strikes in the summer of 1979.[66]

Meanwhile, the international human rights organizations that had so recently critiqued the shah's carceral practices turned their sights toward the summary violence endemic to the revolutionary tribunals and committees. From April 12 to May 1, 1979, Amnesty International sent representatives to Tehran in hopes of "[conducting] research into the jurisdiction and function of the Revolutionary Tribunal," but those representatives were disallowed from attending any trials in person.[67] As AI reported in 1980, the Revolutionary Committees were often composed of unofficial members with no experience or authorization beyond their devotion to the cause:

> The local revolutionary Komitehs took on certain responsibilities at the time of the revolution's success. Groups of people assumed a de facto jurisdiction over a local area and exercised a security function by, for example, patrolling the streets during the hours of darkness. The Komitehs acted independently of government and were often made up of people with no previous experience of law enforcement.[68]

Certain members of the ulama were also circumspect, taking aim at the rough and ready nature of these proceedings; rather than using the human rights language now completely entrenched among the international NGOs, they challenged the legitimacy of the revolutionary courts on grounds of Islamic legality. Ayatollah Tabatabai-Qomi from Mashhad, who had notably "stayed aloof" from the Khomeinist coalition, told the press in March 1979 that the tribunals contravened Islamic principles and were rife with "unwarranted expropriations, unwarranted jailings, unwarranted judicial decisions, unwarranted killings, unwarranted whippings."[69] Grand Ayatollah Mohammad Kazem Shariatmadari, a critic of Khomeini's theory of guardianship of the jurist who would eventually be arrested, tortured, and forced into making a public confession of his own, spoke out against the violence enacted by the committees:

> Armed... individuals forcefully enter houses to arrest what they call the criminals of the former regime thus causing fright and inconvenience among the families. Such individuals are warned once again that the majority of the former government's employees are decent citizens and that the punishment of those responsible for the past crimes, torture, and plundering of public funds falls exclusively under the jurisdiction of the provisional Islamic government.[70]

Members of revolutionary leadership also expressed certain doubts about the tribunals and the relative autonomy of the committees—or at least some desire to rein in their most public and unsupervised excesses. Ayatollah Ali Qoddusi, who was named attorney general by Khomeini, admitted soon after taking office that the revolutionary tribunals did not bear "the least resemblance" to true Islamic courts.[71] Criticism of the tribunals and committees was particularly common among liberal members of the Islamic provisional government, including Prime Minister Mehdi Bazargan, who was appointed by Khomeini on February 4th and resigned amid the US embassy crisis on November 4th, having lost the struggle with the militant Islamist faction over the nature of Iran's new constitution and power-sharing structures.[72] While still in positions of power, Bazargan and his allies often complained about the violence endemic to the tribunals. In early March 1979, Deputy Prime Minister Abbas Amir-Entezam, who would be arrested in December 1979 and remain imprisoned for the better part of three decades, lamented the "very poor" state of law and order in the country, admitting that until the government could bring the committees under its full management, "it could do little to improve the situation." In October, just weeks before his resignation, Bazargan stated his position in an interview with the *International Herald Tribune* in even harsher terms, exasperatedly claiming, "I have already explained to you that the revolutionary tribunals are not subject to the government, they do not act in accordance with the government, they are completely outside my control. In a message to the nation, I denounced their abuses, their lack of witnesses and of proper inquiry. I have quite expressed my rejection of them and my disdain. What else do you want me to add?"[73]

Khomeini and his militant allies largely supported the violence meted out by the committees, repeatedly extolling both their revolutionary and Islamic bona fides. Still, they were anxious to bring any seemingly legitimate use of revolutionary violence under the centralized control of the new state. On March 8, 1979, the same day as the historic International Women's Day protests in Tehran,[74] Ayatollah Mohammad Reza Mahdavi Kani, a member of Khomeini's Revolutionary Council appointed to serve as chief of the Central Provisional Committee, issued a set of official directives aimed at curtailing unregulated decision-making by the committees.[75] Among the provisions in Mahdavi Kani's order were a demand for full compliance with any directive from Khomeini and an imperative to report any activities directly to the Central Provisional Committee.[76] Khomeini personally tried several times to encourage the committees to do their work through centralized formal channels rather than by taking matters or important decisions into their own hands. On February 18, the ayatollah addressed the rank-and-file members of the committees and other citizen-revolutionaries in no uncertain terms: "You must identify the criminals to the provisional Islamic government so that steps can be taken for their arrest and trial. This is an Islamic order and acting contrary to it is not permissible."[77] Despite these rejoinders, ad hoc structures and inconsistent rulings continued to percolate.

Even into 1983, the lack of consistency in legal rulings plagued the Islamicizing judiciary. In part, this was due to a lack of personnel: there weren't enough trained clerics ready to take every open position in a system cleansed of the secular jurists groomed to run the judiciary since Reza Shah's time.[78] It also took several years before the country's prisons were fully centralized.

In September 1979, with Bazargan's signature as prime minister, the provisional government promulgated the Islamic Republic's first law related to its prisons, putting all matters of prison administration, including budgeting and policy, under the aegis of the new Ministry of Justice. Before the founding of the Prisons Organization, prison management was placed under the Prisons, Security, and Corrective Measures Managerial Council comprised of three members of the ulama.[79] Finally, in 1986 the Prisons Organization was inaugurated with the mandate to further centralize management of the country's prisons and to move away from the chaotic conditions of the first years after the revolution. In a 1986 press conference, the first head of the Prisons Organization, Hojjat ol-Islam Majid Ansari, announced that the Prisons Organization had indeed taken over "most" prisons from the police and the Revolutionary Committees across the various provinces of the country.[80]

Although some human rights organizations were already sounding the alarms about the actions of the revolutionary tribunals, there was little enthusiasm among most of the broad revolutionary coalition, leftists and Islamists alike, for liberal proceduralism. As political scientist James A. Bill has noted, the violence of these early months was just as often driven by the indignant masses as by the leadership of the new government. When the government tried to slow down the pace of executions and hold more standardized trials, "the masses demanded retribution. . . . In Isfahan, for example, a large mob took over the central prison and massacred several high-ranking members of the former regime who were being held there. In mid-May 1979, a large delegation (including members of the revolutionary tribunals and militias) visited Ayatollah Khomeini and demanded that either the executions continue or they would take matters into their own hands and execute all those held in the various prisons."[81] Members of the early Islamic government also scoffed at the notion that international organizations should have any say in how the Islamic Republic conducted its business, critiquing the international community's formerly cozy relationship with the shah. The first appearance of an Islamic Republic official in the US is emblematic of both this disdain and the continued importance of torture before 1979 in Iran's revolutionary ethos. In the fall of 1980, the first prime minister of the Islamic Republic, Mohammad 'Ali Raja'i, spoke at a meeting of the United Nations Security Council in New York. Raja'i, who was raised in conditions of poverty in Qazvin, had spent years incarcerated and tortured in Pahlavi prisons, having first been imprisoned at the age of fourteen.[82] At the UN, Raja'i stunned onlookers by revealing the sole of his right foot, scarred and deformed from evident torture in the shah's prisons. As the *Washington Post* reported, "It was a bizarre tableau: Iran's Prime Minister sitting back, tieless and stubble-bearded, with his bare foot propped up on an elegant conference table against the background of the U.N. symbol on the pleated, powder-blue draperies.... [At the U.N.] Rajai asked, where were those who worry about these conventions when the shah's secret police were torturing Iranian dissidents, himself included?"[83]

The revolutionaries undertaking the retributive violence of these early tribunals routinely named their widespread abhorrence of Pahlavi torture as a major driving force of their efforts. In May 1979, in an interview with Iran Radio, the newly minted minister of foreign affairs, Ebrahim Yazdi, echoed the popular view of the day among the revolutionary coalition: "These people were criminals. They tortured people, they killed and massacred people."[84] (Yazdi, an Islamic liberal, would fall afoul of the Islamic government himself and eventually be imprisoned at Evin in 1997.) The tribunals quickly tried and executed the three surviving directors of SAVAK—Hassan Pakravan,[85] Nematollah Nassiri, and Nasser Moghaddam; other high-ranking members of the shah's intelligence, law enforcement, and military forces; and former prime minister Amir Abbas Hoveyda—all figures whom the Islamic Republic's first *hakem-e shar'* (chief sharia-based state prosecutor), Sadeq Khalkhali, later called the "first-degree criminals" of the Pahlavi government.[86]

Statements from the SAVAK leadership tribunals were published in newspapers and publicized widely, further cementing the new government's revolutionary bona fides.[87] One such tribunal was that of infamous SAVAK interrogator Bahram Naderpour, alias "Tehrani," whose role in the torture and deaths of several high-profile revolutionaries made him a favorite target of anti-Pahlavi Iranians across the political spectrum. In his tribunal statement, Naderpour claimed to see the error of his former ways and pleaded for an opportunity to serve the new Islamic Republic. Naderpour's statement was published in newspapers and reprinted and circulated in revolutionary pamphlets and other ephemera, including one featuring an anonymous broadside against the former SAVAK interrogator. The anonymous author excoriated the former SAVAK official for his hand in torturing and executing Iranian dissidents, as well as for his efforts to join the revolutionary government. "How simpleminded we would have to be," the author exclaimed, "to believe the man who cruelly murdered nine people's *mojahed*s and revolutionary fighters in the hills of Evin . . . and who until yesterday, with full awareness, used all of his talents and abilities in service of the suppression of our Muslim people, is now worried about Islam, the Islamic revolution, and the Islamic Republic!!!"[88] Khalkhali similarly mocked the efforts made by the last director of SAVAK, general Nematollah Nassiri, to disavow knowledge of torture during his tribunal. "What kind of a person would believe," Khalkhali later wrote, "that he could have had no knowledge of all these goings-on? He was the source of the corruption and the cause of the wickedness. All of the arrests and torture and executions and annihilation [*sar beh nist kardan*] were directly ordered by SAVAK under Nassiri's direction."[89] For the anonymous author critiquing Naderpour, as for Khalkhali, the actions of the tribunals against known torturers were not human rights violations at all but rather the rightful result of revolutionary justice.

In his field-shaping work on the history of torture and forced confessions in Iran, Ervand Abrahamian explicitly divides the categories of those arrested and later executed by the revolutionary government in the 1980s and 1990s into "political" and "nonpolitical" categories, with drug-related charges making up the largest number of those in the latter category. The "nonpolitical" category also includes gendered and sexual offenses such as adultery. I posit here, however, that Iran's carceral history renders any clear distinction between political and nonpolitical offenses difficult to maintain. For all of their early focus on SAVAK interrogators and Pahlavi loyalists, members of Khomeini's coalition defined the nebulous concept of "counterrevolutionary activity" far beyond just those who collaborated with the Pahlavi state or those whose political commitments challenged the emerging clerical order. According to the Islamic militants, counterrevolutionary crimes could be anything from supporting a royalist coup to drug dealing to bazaar price gouging. In an interview with *Bamdad* newspaper in May 1979, Sadeq Qotbzadeh, then managing director of National Iranian Radio and Television (NIRT) and a onetime translator for Khomeini, proclaimed, "The merchant who charges a high price is a counter-revolutionary. Similarly, those who stole money from people on the day the arms were seized, those who smuggle heroin and other narcotic drugs and those who indulge in sabotage and espionage are counter-revolutionaries and must not be given a chance."[90] (Qotbzadeh himself would be arrested and executed in 1982 for allegedly organizing a plot to overthrow the government.)[91] According to this logic, many evidently "nonpolitical" detainees, or those who, like price-gouging merchants, were perceived as doing unjust things, were understood as just as significant a threat to the utopian political imaginary of the post-revolutionary state as royalists and SAVAK agents.

This ethos, at once punitive and utopian, took drug users and drug abuse as particular targets of its revolutionary crosshairs.[92] So important were illicit drugs in the moral imaginary of the revolution and so total were the revolutionaries' promises to rid Iran of drug abuse that after Khomeini's death in 1989, one of his supporters argued that "the Imam ... carried out the most successful campaign against drug addiction, and came nearer than anyone else to eradicating the drug culture in Iran."[93] Yet more than Khomeini himself, the figure most associated with the violence of the revolutionary tribunals in general, including against drug users, was the aforementioned Sadeq Khalkhali, who was appointed *hakem-e shar'* in Tehran by Khomeini on February 24, 1979, and soon after tapped by President Abolhassan Bani-Sadr, with whom he would come into open conflict, to head the country's antinarcotics efforts. Like so many other members of the Islamic Republic leadership, Khalkhali's first experience with Iranian prisons was during his own arrest, incarceration, and internal exile under the shah during the 1963 Khomeini-led protests of the White Revolution.[94] By the end of the summer of 1979 alone, Khalkhali's orders led to the execution of approximately two hundred people on alleged drug-related charges.[95]

For Khalkhali, the fervent drive to eradicate drugs in the country was intimately linked with the utopian moral and political horizon of the revolution. As Maziyar Ghiabi has shown, charges against political adversaries of the Islamic Republic, such as members of the Marxist Fadaian guerrillas, were often trumped up with drug charges—in this case, "harboring massive amounts of opium (20 tons), heroin (435 kg), and hashish (2742 kg)."[96] Khalkhali argued that the influx of drugs into the country, particularly opium and heroin, simply represented a different tactic in the arsenal of the imperialist powers in their efforts to drag Iran's youth toward moral "degeneration" and spiritual decline. In response to a 1980 interview question asking him to justify the drug-related executions he ordered, Khalkhali defiantly responded, "The drug dealers' activities brought two million young people to nothingness, thousands of couples to separation, thousands of children to a miserable life, the entire country to destruction. . . . A month ago hundreds of drug addicts lined the streets of the Jamshid Quarter. After three public executions of dealers, almost all of them have disappeared now. *I've* stopped all that. Killing makes people think. And I kill only those who are harmful to our society."[97] For Khalkhali, these were not simply crimes but rather efforts egged on by global imperialists aimed at destroying the fabric of the Islamic Republic that would only stop with a show of mortal extrajudicial force.[98]

Despite the similarities Islamic Republic policies had with other locales waging wars on drugs in the 1980s, including the United States, Khalkhali waged his drug war in what he believed was a fight for establishing a revolutionary Islamic society and for the very concept of Islamic justice itself. Critiques of the violence of the Revolutionary Committees and tribunals were brushed off in just such maximalist terms. In November 1980, when the Islamic Republic's first president, Abolhassan Bani-Sadr, then embroiled in a power struggle against the militant ulama and their supporters, "accused his enemies in the conservative Islamic clergy yesterday of committing abuses reminiscent of the late shah and suggested that the mullahs are continuing torture of political prisoners,"[99] Khalkhali defended himself by declaring that his critics "know nothing about Islamic justice." For Khalkhali, carceral violence was a both a revolutionary and an Islamic necessity, and anything less than what he prescribed would, in his view, have been the truly immoral practice. "When I instructed that someone be whipped 50 times," Khalkhali boasted, "I supervised myself so they wouldn't beat him softly."[100] Yet in the immediate aftermath of the shah's fall, it was not only clerical militants who promoted the notion that mass arrests and executions were a necessary step in the making of a postrevolutionary utopia. Even those in the initial revolutionary coalition who would come to critique the Islamic Republic's actions toward its prisoners as "SAVAK-like," as President Bani-Sadr routinely did throughout 1980–81, initially insisted that the nascent state's carceral violence was a necessary step toward consolidating a truly just polity.[101]

All told, 757 individuals were executed by the revolutionary government between January 1979 and May 1981.[102] This wave of terror would escalate in June 1981, in the aftermath of a Mojahedin-e Khalq attempt to overthrow the Khomeini-led government, when the revolutionary state redoubled its efforts in culling Iran's remaining political opposition, especially among members of the Mojahedin and various leftist groups. From that point to June 1985, another 12,500 were arrested and executed. The intensity of this violence was such that one prison saw upward of 75 percent of its prisoners executed in 1981–82 alone.[103] It was in also this era that the Islamic Republic begin to implement and expand the use of torture and forced confessions, which were first inaugurated in the post-coup era by the shah and were dramatically magnified in use, intensity, and publicity in the Islamic Republic period. Throughout the 1980s, a parade of well-known dissidents—from Tudeh Party leaders like Noureddin Kianuri to former Khomeini allies like Sadeq Qotbzadeh to numerous members of the Mojahedin and many more—appeared on television and in newspapers to denounce their organizations and movements, often to the surprise and despair of their remaining comrades. The most notorious event in the Islamic Republic's carceral history took place at the end of the decade, when several thousand long-incarcerated political dissidents were furtively executed on Khomeini's order upon the end of the Iran-Iraq war in 1988.[104] In this same bloody moment, the Islamic Republic also established a national Drug Control Headquarters (Markaz-e mobarezah ba mavad-e mokhadar) and similarly undertook the incarceration and execution of drug offenders with renewed fervor. As in the earlier period, the widespread execution of political dissidents and the eradication of drug users were championed as part of the same revolutionary political process, again linking the fates of ostensibly "nonpolitical" detainees to the vicissitudes of political decision-making in Iran.

As I have argued here, the carceral practices established in postrevolutionary Iran represented a utopian vision that yielded a profoundly dystopian reality. Despite Khomeini's promise that with a system of Islamic justice no one would have to be imprisoned for even a day, Khomeinist revolutionaries used the infrastructural tools they inherited from the Pahlavi government—including Pahlavi-built prisons and interrogation centers—to consolidate power over their ideological adversaries. This carceral utopianism took in its crosshairs both active political rivals (royalists, Marxists, rival Islamists) alongside socially vulnerable persons (drug users, sex workers) in an expansive effort to cleanse Iran of counterrevolutionaries, un-Islamic elements, and those "spreading corruption on earth." The technocratic language of the "humanist prison," established during the Pahlavi era, gave way to an ideological fervor that presented itself as capable of eradicating sin, vice, and political error from Iran through extrajudicial violence and carceral means. It would not be until the late 1980s that technocratic logics and languages of prison management would return, although—like the Pahlavi government before it—the Islamic Republic would graft those technocratic logics with political suppression and the use of torture going forward. It is to that story that I now turn.

Six

CARCERALITY BEYOND PRISONS?
The Politics of Punishment in the Contemporary Islamic Republic

IN 1995, THE MEDICAL DEPARTMENT OF THE PRISONS ORGANIZATION of the Islamic Republic held a two-day academic workshop inside Evin Prison.[1] At the workshop, which was organized in conjunction with the Psychiatry Institute of Tehran, university professors and mental health professionals presented papers on prisoner mental health and best practices for preventing crime and recidivism. Asadollah Lajaverdi, the head of the Prisons Organization, delivered the keynote address. Lajaverdi stated that the primary goal of the Prisons Organization was to boost the morale of prisoners so they could learn to lead decent and crime-free lives. Education was key to this process. "To achieve this goal," Lajaverdi averred, the Prisons Organization has "made literacy and physical exercises obligatory for prisoners."[2] Lajaverdi was no stranger to Evin Prison. He was incarcerated there under the shah and returned to serve as its warden from 1980 to 1984, earning the moniker "the Butcher of Evin."[3] Stories of Lajaverdi's cruelty to imprisoned dissidents—whom he referred to as his "guests" and whom he *also* claimed to be "educating"—are legion.[4] Former political prisoner Monira Baradaran recounts an example of Lajaverdi's pedagogy in the institution that dissidents called "Evin University." In 1981, Baradaran and her fellow prisoners were made to view the bodies of executed political prisoners in the prison courtyard. She writes:

> We were all taken to the holding area. Meanwhile, it was announced from the loudspeaker that those persons interested should proceed outside in order to look at corpses. Amazed, I saw that a number of people quickly put on their *chadors* and blindfolds and proceeded outside.... That night, they showed the scene on the prison televisions. Bodies were covered in cloth and stacked next to one another. Their faces were still visible.[5]

As prisoners viewed the corpses, rumors circulated that well-known leaders of the Mojahedin-e Khalq were among the dead. Baradaran spotted one of those opposition leaders among the bodies. Moments later, Lajaverdi appeared on prison televisions, holding the infant child of one of the dead militants and grinning. In Lajaverdi's years as Evin's warden, prisoner "education" was a matter of breaking down incarcerated dissidents until they gave forced confessions, recanting their political views and swearing allegiance to the Islamic Republic. Years later, in his role as head of the Prisons Organization, this legacy of prisoner "education" haunted the technocratic language the institution attempted to adopt.

The Prisons Organization has described its mission in terms of education and rehabilitation since its 1986 founding, framing its efforts as a commitment to Islamic values and the Islamic Republic's constitution. Like the supervisory clerical council of three that the Prisons Organization superseded, the first head of the organization was a member of the ulama: Hojjat ol-Eslam Majid Ansari, who had earlier served as a Majles deputy and would later sit on the Assembly of Experts.[6] In a 1986 interview, Ansari described the organization's work in terms of education and rehabilitation as opposed to punishment for punishment's sake, couching these ideas as derived from Islamic principles:

> The most important aim of this organization is to correct and re-educate offenders. This is because in Islam the aim is not just to punish the criminal. The constitution has specified that one of the duties of the judicial branch is to prevent crime. Therefore, when criminals are gathered

in one place, one cannot hope only to keep them there. They must be corrected and re-educated so that they can return to society as useful human beings.[7]

Over the coming years, even as stories of torture continued to dominate public conversations about incarceration in Iran, the Prisons Organization further attempted to routinize and professionalize prison management, entrenching itself as a key part of Iran's expanding state bureaucracy. In 1988, the year of the notorious massacre of thousands of imprisoned dissidents, the organization sent dozens of trainees and staff members to a program at Islamic Azad University in Tehran with the goal of systematizing staff training. In 1993, it established a new center tasked with conducting prison-related research and training personnel. Reviving the criminological discourses of the prerevolutionary era, this center—the Prisons Organization Research and Education Center (Markaz-e amuzesh va pajuheshi-ye sazman-e zendanha)—promoted its work as an effort to cure offenders of their "social diseases" through the "most up-to-date knowledge" of "jail-keeping sciences."[8] The center also launched a series of training courses in fields including social work, law, and corrections and security methods. Although the training program started modestly, with eighty trainees participating in three center-led courses in 1993–94, that number jumped to nearly eight hundred by 1997–98. By 1999, training courses included psychology, criminology, statistics, penal law, health care, first aid, mental health, counseling, prisoner reform, computer sciences, foreign languages, humanities research methods, prison management, social work, and the care and education of children. While most of this list would not have looked out of place in a criminology textbook of the Pahlavi era, classes in Islamic ethics stood as a distinctly Islamic Republic addition.[9] Today, the reformist myth at the heart of the modern prison—that prisons are for reforming and rehabilitating wayward people and preparing them for life as law-abiding citizens—is completely embedded in the story that the Prisons Organization promotes about its work. "Social rehabilitation is the central principle of prison administration," the organization proudly proclaims.[10]

The professionalization of the Prisons Organization anticipated technocratic and reformist changes that were on the horizon in the postwar Islamic Republic. The center fostered relationships with universities and research centers and started an archive and library. In 1993, two center-based research groups were founded, the first focusing on criminal law and criminology and the second on psychology. "In addition to doing field research," the Prisons Organization explained, these groups "have been observing research activities" in prisons across Iran.[11] The center also began a publishing wing, beginning with a 1995 collection of papers on youth delinquency and continuing with a monthly magazine launched in 1997 with articles in "judicial and social sciences, psychology, and jail-keeping experiences."[12] In 1999, the same year that a popular student-led protest movement was violently suppressed by Iran's security forces, leading to the mass arrest and imprisonment of a new generation of Iranians, the Prisons Organization promoted its expert bona fides by publishing a list of research conducted by scholars

FIGURE 15. Logo of the Islamic Republic's Organization of Prisons and National Security Measures (Sazman-e zendanha va eghdamat-e ta'mini va tarbiyati-e keshvar). Source: Photograph by Golnar Nikpour, 2023

affiliated with the center. Topics ranged from long-standing criminological favorites like juvenile delinquency and female criminality to two subjects that had begun to dominate official conversations about Iran's prisons: the health of incarcerated drug users and methods to reduce the overall prison population.

Indeed, by the 1990s, the prison expansion and rising prisoner totals of the prior decade would come to be seen as urgent problems in need of official intervention and solutions. Members of the Islamic Republic's governing elite and prison leadership began to publicly fret over the country's ever-swelling incarceration rates, expressing concern about rising rates of drug-related incarceration among younger Iranians in particular. The elevated number of drug-related detainees had by 2000 become "so alarming" that the head of the Prisons Organization publicly requested the country's police force "not to refer . . . arrested addicts to the prisons.'"[13] Although myriad law enforcement and government officials championed the building of new prisons as a solution for prison overcrowding, these new prisons would not be enough to keep up with demand for carceral space. Eventually, the leadership of the Prisons Organization, with the backing of the judiciary and Khamenei himself, publicly vowed to reduce Iran's number of incarcerated persons altogether, citing the cost—social, moral, and economic—of Iran's bulging prisoner totals. In the 2010s, Islamic Republic leadership increasingly promoted a move away from the conventional prison and toward new carceral technologies such as ankle monitors and biotechnological surveillance both to try to stem the tide of prison growth and to more closely surveil "problem" populations.

In what follows in this chapter, I examine two key crises of the postwar era that were directly linked to the emergency of prison overcrowding: the crisis of disease and the crisis of dissent. The first crisis derived from the realization that mass incarceration and prison overcrowding were directly responsible for the spread of serious infectious diseases in Iran, including HIV/AIDS (and more recently, COVID-19). The second was a crisis of a different sort, sparked by continued dissent in the country, whether in the form of political protest, hijab law protests, ethnic nationalist movements, labor activism, or human rights work. Both of these crises facilitated the adoption of new technocratic languages and logics alongside cutting-edge global carceral technologies in response. The use of these technologies has revealed the extent to which the Islamic Republic has absorbed global carceral practices to manage the particular social and political issues that have arisen in the country. This chapter analyzes these transformations, showing that even as the Iranian government has shown flexibility in adapting some of its methods of social control, the carceral network has only further expanded its reach into Iranian lives. I end the chapter by showing that efforts to reduce the number of incarcerated persons in Iran have represented not a retreat of the carceral system but rather its continued proliferation and expansion by other means.

TECHNOCRACY, REFORM, AND THE CRISIS OF HIV/AIDS IN IRAN'S PRISONS

The dawn of the 1990s was a time of transformation in the Islamic Republic. The Iran-Iraq war, which had devastated both countries for eight grueling years, ended in a stalemate on August 20, 1988, when Ayatollah Ruhollah Khomeini grudgingly accepted UN Security Council Resolution 598, likening it to drinking from a "poisoned chalice." Within a year, on June 3, 1989, the man that many Iranians continued to reverently call the Imam died at the age of eighty-nine, leading millions to pour into the streets in mourning.[14] Before his death, with his health ailing, Khomeini made several decisions seemingly aimed at institutionalizing the ideological fervor of the prior decade. Among these was a covert order to enact a brutal act of carceral violence: the 1988 execution of several thousand incarcerated dissidents, many of whom belonged to or were onetime sympathizers of the Mojahedin-e Khalq Organization.[15] As if anticipating the dissent that would result from this five-month-long cloak-and-dagger effort, Khomeini's edict asserted, "To hesitate in the judicial process of revolutionary Islam is to ignore the pure and clean blood of the martyrs."[16] Upon Khomeini's death, amid controversy, contestation, and an amended constitution, the then president Ali Khamenei was made the *vali-e faqih* (ruling jurist; commonly called "supreme leader"), despite not having the Islamic learning, personal charisma, or mass political following of his predecessor.[17] The 1988 prison massacre was indirectly responsible for Khamenei's surprising eleventh-hour rise as Khomeini's successor. Ayatollah Hussein Ali Montazeri, the revolutionary cleric long seen as Khomeini's heir apparent, fell out with Khomeini, his decades-long ally, in part because of the former's resolute opposition to the prison executions initiated by the latter.[18]

This series of events would prove pivotal. As the 1990s began, the war that had so dominated Iranian lives was over, Khomeini was dead, Montazeri was out of the official picture, and most of the Islamic Republic's early political adversaries were eliminated. With the revolutionary struggle seemingly won by the ruling Khomeinists, a general amnesty was announced for Iran's remaining imprisoned dissidents. Prisoners were released, many for the first time in a decade, into a totally changed political atmosphere. The government also suspended televised recantations and allowed the UN special representative on human rights, Reynaldo Gallindo Pohl, to visit the country's prisons three times, the first such visits allowed to a UN official since the fall of the shah.[19] However, this seeming pivot was short lived. It would not take long for reports of torture to resurface and forced confessions to make their return, and Pohl, having found widespread evidence of prisoner abuse, was barred from returning to Iran after his third visit.[20] Still, the 1990s marked the end of the inaugural era for the Islamic Republic. A decade of war and ideological struggle under Khomeini's watchful eye gave way to postwar reconstruction efforts, fitful efforts at political pragmatism, economic liberalization, and, in the absence of Khomeini's mediating gravitas, factional struggles between the left and right wings of a fraying ruling coalition that could no longer be ended with a deciding word from the Imam.

If the first decade of Islamic Republic rule was typified by ideological ardor and the all-consuming war effort, subsequent years brought a certain degree of adaptability into the government's approach. Sociologist Nazanin Shahrokni expounds on this dynamic, aptly describing the history of the Islamic Republic as one of change from a "revolutionary ideological construct to a postrevolutionary, problem-solving machine."[21] This shift has been a function of the practical (if contested) work of governing a modern bureaucratic state with a large and diverse citizenry as opposed to winning a utopian political revolution. If the Islamic Republic had to become a problem-solving machine, the country's overcrowded prisons would emerge as a key problem site as the revolutionary government moved into its second decade. The crisis of disease would be among the first to test the postwar, post-Khomeini government.

Arriving quietly amid the war was an urgent worldwide crisis: the HIV/AIDS epidemic. The first known case of the virus in Iran was in 1986, when a boy with hemophilia was diagnosed with the disease. In 1989, the first known case of HIV in Iran linked to intravenous drugs was identified. That year, Iran began screening blood supplies across the country in its effort to curtail the spread of the virus.[22] That the first official step toward limiting the reach of the virus was linked to blood transfusion reveals the ideological and social limits governing the Islamic Republic's early response to the crisis. Early on, Iran's governing elite paid little attention to the virus, except to dismiss its danger to Iranians and paint it as a problem afflicting only Western countries. Imported blood, rather than unprotected sex or drug use, was singled out for blame for the virus's presence in Iran.[23] It would take the epidemic reaching crisis proportions and its spread being linked to the country's prisons for this hands-off posture to move toward proactive policy. In the section that follows, I analyze the epidemic of HIV/AIDS in Islamic Republic prisons, tracing the contested means by which the Prisons Organization, pushed by civil society medical experts and advocates, incorporated new forms of medical expertise in order to combat the spread of the virus.

Iran's response to HIV/AIDS was shaped by the fluctuating political terrain of the postwar era, which included not only the rise of Ali Khamenei as Khomeini's successor but also changes at the highest levels of elected government. (As Eskandar Sadeghi-Boroujerdi notes, the Islamic Republic government is composed of "dictatorial, oligarchic, and formally 'democratic' institutions," with the elected elements subordinate to the unelected elements.)[24] The first postwar presidency was that of powerful Islamic Republic stalwart Hojjat ol-Eslam Ali Akbar Hashemi Rafsanjani, who served for two terms from 1989 to 1997. Rafsanjani was instrumental in elevating Khamenei to the office of *vali-e faqih*, cementing a key post-Khomeini allyship with the new leader.[25] Rafsanjani's presidency was also key in bringing technocratic ideas and private sector investment into postwar reconstruction efforts, signaling a willingness to move Iran away from the ideological and economic populism of the 1980s. After a decade during which professional expertise was shunned in favor of Islamic revolutionary commitment, a "new technocratic class gained legitimacy and asserted the right to manage the challenging environment of post-war Iran."[26] It was in this context that medical expertise and technocratic ideas were invited into the fold of the Prisons Organization. This newfound embrace of expertise would also help shape the terrain in which the prison HIV/AIDS crisis was addressed.

Rafsanjani downplayed the threat of the virus well into the 1990s. At a 1993 press conference, he used the well-worn tactic of painting the virus as a uniquely Western problem, deriding the "serious difficulties ... that Western youth are entangled in ... families who have no bread winners, children without responsible mothers or fathers, helpless women without husbands, and issues such as AIDS."[27] These were the sorts of problems, Rafsanjani assured listeners, that the faithful Muslims of Iran didn't face. That same year, a scathing assessment of the George Bush presidency published by the state-run Islamic Republic News Agency (IRNA) boasted of the imminent "self-destruction" of the United States due to homosexuality and the spread of HIV/AIDS. "Sodomists and homosexuals are another symbol of fast-disintegrating American society," the report crowed, adding, "about one million persons are infected with the HIV virus ... many of them are to die soon like did Rock Hudson, Bush's favorite movie star."[28]

As the viral case count increased, however, officials would be forced to take a more realistic posture. Although the number of verified cases of HIV/AIDS between 1986 and 2002 in Iran was low in relative terms compared to some global locales—4,424 total cases according to the official tallies of the country's National AIDS Prevention Committee—its spread rendered it impossible to ignore the disease.[29] The first known outbreak of HIV/AIDS in an Iranian prison began in 1995 in Kermanshah, the country's largest majority Kurdish-speaking city. Drug-related incarceration in Kermanshah, like other western provinces of Iran devastated by the war, saw spikes in the postwar era.[30] By 1996, the number of confirmed cases of HIV-positive prisoners in Kermanshah had risen to 58. By 1998, it had reached 407.[31] In 1997, an official study across three provincial prisons including Kermanshah's Dizel Abad Prison showed alarming results: nearly every imprisoned intravenous drug-user tested was HIV positive. As anthropologist Orkideh Behrouzan has shown, the initial response to this study was uneven, as officials first attempted to segregate Kermanshah's HIV-positive population and to transfer the HIV-positive detainees from the other sites.[32] These half measures proved ineffective. According to a 2004 report published by the Regional

Office for the Eastern Mediterranean of the World Health Organization (WHO/EMRO), the city of Kermanshah reported 1,228 cases of HIV from 1995 to 2001, the majority of which were linked to Dizel Abad.[33] A decade after the first known HIV case in Iran, the virus had become a full-blown crisis in the country's prisons.

A note on the history of Dizel Abad Prison, also known as the Central Kermanshah prison, is in order here. The main prison in Kermanshah Province, Dizel Abad was built in 1975 in the last years of Pahlavi rule. Like virtually all modern Iranian prisons, Dizel Abad has suffered systemic overcrowding since its opening. Today, the prison is estimated to house over six thousand detainees, though it is meant to hold only half that number. Male and female detainees are housed in nine cellblocks for adults and one for juveniles, with hundreds estimated to be held in solitary confinement.[34] Although most of Dizel Abad's detainees are common-law prisoners, the prison has earned a particularly brutal reputation among Kurdish political activists and rights organizations due to the high number of Kurdish activists, writers, and individuals incarcerated, tortured, and executed there.[35] Rebin Rahmani, a former Kurdish prisoner, described the facility in damning terms: "This is the last station in the world, this is where humanity fades, this is Dizel Abad in Kermanshah."[36] Dizel Abad has also been a key site in the story of public health policy in Iran. According to Behrouzan, outbreaks of HIV in prisons like Dizel Abad "catalysed a paradigm shift that led to new policy approaches and public perceptions" of a disease that was "sexually transmitted and drug-related."[37]

Prison outbreaks were Iran's wake-up call regarding HIV/AIDS. The sheer scope of the crisis soon forced Islamic Republic officials—impelled by medical professionals, infectious disease specialists, and patient advocates—toward proactive measures to curtail the virus's spread. Yet official intransigence was not the only barrier to effectively treating the virus. Advocates were also stymied by social stigma and misinformation surrounding HIV/AIDS among the general populace, which rendered treatment in provincial cities like Kermanshah particularly challenging. The doctors most associated with promoting harm reduction measures in Kermanshah, brothers Kamiar and Arash Alaei, "requested an unmarked office in the city's main university clinic . . . deliberately avoiding any public association with HIV and AIDS." When the Alaeis attempted to follow up with HIV-positive prisoners in Dizel Abad soon after the 1997 study, they found that 176 of them had already died, many of apparent suicide, a testament to both the social opprobrium and uncertainty facing those who had tested positive.[38] More recent accounts of Iran's HIV-positive prisoners corroborate the continued sense of social stigma associated with the disease. In recounting her interactions with a female HIV-positive prisoner, for instance, formerly incarcerated journalist Maryam Hosseinkhah explains that this woman begged her not to tell anyone about her condition, lest she be further marginalized in the prison. "For God's sake [*toro khodah*]," the woman pleaded, "don't tell anyone I have AIDS."[39]

The Alaeis first came to HIV/AIDS research as medical students in Isfahan in the 1990s, when their father shared a news clipping with them about the high rates of the virus in Kermanshah's prison.[40] They eventually started a nonprofit clinic in Kermanshah in 1999, integrating health care, counseling, and social support for those living with the disease.[41] The Alaeis were also key in researching the epidemiological links between rates of incarceration, intravenous drug use, and the spread of infectious diseases in the country. In a 2002 study, the brothers, in tandem with Dr. Davood Mansoori of the National Research Institute of Tuberculosis and Lung Disease at Shahid Beheshti University of Medical Sciences, found that rates of tuberculosis were higher among Kermanshah's HIV-positive population due to the prevalence of both among the prison's drug users.[42] A year later, Mansoori and the Alaeis published a study analyzing the effects of the hepatitis B vaccine on HIV-positive patients, concluding that intravenous drug use limited the vaccine's effectiveness—an issue in prisons with high rates of all of the above.[43] The upshot was clear: the spread of infectious diseases in Iran was inexorably linked to intravenous drug use and to incarceration.

The Kermanshah prison outbreak happened on the eve of a political sea change in the Islamic Republic: the 1997 election of reformist Mohammad Khatami to the presidency. Khatami's landslide victory was a shock to the power brokers of Iran's Islamic *nezam* (system), Khamenei included. During his campaign, Khatami canvassed Iran's ethnic minorities, students, and women's organizations, and his candidacy electrified these marginalized constituencies. Ultimately, Khatami won handily because his message of change also persuaded segments of the Islamic Republic base, including members of the IRGC and war veterans who had grown dispirited with the corruption seemingly endemic to the system.[44] Khatami's election offered a stunning rebuke to his opponent's powerful allies, eliciting hope that the limited democratic elements in Iran's Constitutional order could push back against the autocratic elite to broker social change. After 1997, hostility from powerful conservatives led by Khamenei and the IRGC alongside timidity from the reformist camp conspired to systematically disempower the reformist movement. Still, despite this, various strands of reformism—economic, political, social, intellectual, and religious—have shaped the contemporary landscape in Iran.

As Ghiabi notes, the possibilities opened by the reformist victory manifested in Iranian drug policies in the late 1990s. Under the guidance of former prison official Mohammad Fellah, the Drug Control Headquarters "pushed tactically towards the medicalisation of 'addiction'" in an effort to de-emphasize the long-standing "crime-oriented weight of the drug laws."[45] This was a big shift in rhetoric from the late 1980s, when acting head of the Revolutionary Committees Mokhtar Kalantari proclaimed in an interview in *Kayhan* that Iranians in fact wanted a return to the ruthless tactics toward drug users exemplified by Sadeq Khalkhali, arguing, "Today, our society hungers for decisive decisions from our numerous officials. In a general assessment concerning narcotics [we] concluded that 80 percent of the people want Mr. Khalkhali to come back to fight."[46] Remarkably, the move away from zero tolerance won the day, at least in this case, as the Khamenei-appointed Expediency Council ruled in 1997 "that addiction is not a crime and could be therefore treated without punishment."[47]

In 1999, Khatami's Ministry of Health and the State Welfare Organization collaborated with the UN's International Drug Control Programme to produce a report on drug use in Iran.[48] The report featured several insights on drug use in the country's prisons. Although at the time, opium remained the most widespread drug of abuse in Iran, the report indicated that intravenous heroin use was on the rise. The authors also reported that "despite strong security and control measures," intravenous drugs were used inside of Iran's prisons. Hypodermic needles, droppers, and handmade needles known as "pomps" were named as the main methods of injection.[49] Needle sharing was commonplace, with one incarcerated interview subject explaining that "there is no choice inside the prison than to use the same syringes and needles." This person further explained that new prisoners, family members, and prison guards were the main methods of entry for drugs into prisons.[50] Later events corroborated the report's assertion that heroin use was rising, as within a few years heroin seizures by Iranian law enforcement far surpassed those of other opioids.[51] Opioid trafficking further increased in Iran after the 2001 United States occupation of Afghanistan and the onset of the US-led "global war on terror."[52] According to the UN, Afghan farmers produced 3,400 tons of opium in 2002, a massive increase from the 185 tons produced the year prior.[53] A significant portion of this production was trafficked through Iran, in turn feeding the Iranian opioid crisis.

Pushed by the advocacy of health-care professionals and spurred on by troubling trends in drug use and infectious diseases, the Prisons Organization appealed to the Alaei brothers to help institutionalize harm reduction programs in prisons in the late 1990s. As the Alaeis explained at an event in New York in 2003, they had been reticent to ask the Prisons Organization directly to initiate such programs. Because of the brothers' efforts to meet directly with clerical, community, and prison leaders, the organization itself eventually approached the brothers, asking them to lend their expertise toward efforts to curtail the spread of infectious diseases.[54] By the early 2000s, Iranian infectious diseases experts and state officials were routinely working with the World Health Organization, the Joint UN Programme on HIV/AIDS, and the UN Office on Drugs and Crime (UNODC) to institute harm reduction programs for drug users. The Prisons Organization adopted key programs including methadone maintenance therapy (also known as opioid substitution therapy), HIV/AIDs sentinel surveillance sites, and programs referred to as "triangular clinics" (*klinik-e mosalesi*), which include counseling and harm reduction training as well as the treatment of sexually transmitted infections and other related illnesses. These efforts, unthinkable in the zero-tolerance context of the 1980s, won international acclaim in 2004 when the World Health Organization granted Iran's Alaei-led harm reduction clinic its "best practice certification."[55]

Despite these successes, the road for Iran's harm reduction programs was not entirely smooth. On the one hand, harm reduction programs grew across the country throughout the late 1990s and 2000s, and important figures among the country's political and judicial leadership, clerics included, promoted harm reduction logics. In 2005, the judiciary announced its support of needle exchange programs and warned skeptical members of law enforcement against interference. That same year, Justice Minister Ayatollah Mohammad Esmail Shooshtari wrote a directive to prosecutors telling them to "defer to the Health Ministry in order to counter the spread of HIV/AIDS and hepatitis" in the country.[56] On the other hand, zero-tolerance thinking never really disappeared from the public conversation, as law enforcement officials often pointed to high levels of heroin trafficking and law enforcement deaths and injuries in order to champion harsher policies toward drug offenders.[57] The international acclaim public health practitioners received globally also raised some conservative and factional hackles. In 2005, after two terms for the reformist Khatami, conservative populist Mahmoud Ahmadinejad was elected president. As Kamiar Alaei stated plainly during Ahmadinejad's second term, "President Ahmadinejad doesn't support these [harm reduction] clinics."[58] These contradictions came to a head when the Alaeis were arrested in 2008 and held in solitary confinement in Evin, having been accused of "communication with an enemy government" and "trying to overthrow the government."[59]

The legacy of public health practitioners' dogged advocacy for prison harm reduction programs can be seen in reports from later Dizel Abad prisoners who noted the continued use of methadone maintenance therapy in that prison.[60] Iran's prisons were transformed by civil society efforts and by the adaptability of the Prisons Organization, and the crisis of HIV/AIDS in prison was at least partly abated by the adoption of new harm reduction practices. The first HIV/AIDs sentinel surveillance sites—that is, testing programs tasked with identifying trends related to the virus among the incarcerated—opened in 1999 under the aegis of the Prisons Organization.[61] The sentinel program began modestly, with 11 testing sites opened in prisons in 1999 and 3,334 persons tested, a reported 52 of whom tested positive for HIV.[62] Between 1999 and 2011, a total of 551 prison sentinel sites opened across the country, testing 212,475 detainees for HIV/AIDS in that period.[63] Methadone maintenance therapy also expanded over the same period, such that by 2019, "among 187,373 prisoners, 62,743 received opioid substitution therapy" at Prisons Organization–run prison methadone clinics. By December 2019, two decades into the program, "more than 62,000 inmates were receiving methadone maintenance treatment."[64] Prison-based safe sex programs, which faced more pushback than drug-related programs, also grew in this era. Beginning in the 2000s, condoms were made available in some conjugal visit rooms, although the notion of sex *between* (same-sex) prisoners remained largely a taboo.[65] Still, according to a 2016 survey, 26.5 percent of those who had a history of sex in prison used condoms during their last sexual contact. The study also showed that 34 percent claimed to have in-prison access to condoms.[66] While none of these practices ultimately addressed the root causes of expanding prisoner totals or increasing intravenous drug use in the country, they nonetheless endeavored to address the crisis of disease in Iran's prisons through novel ways, moving prison crisis management from the ideological posture of the 1980s into a more flexible technocratic terrain.

CARCERALITY BEYOND PRISONS?

The Islamic Republic has faced another carceral crisis in the postwar period—the crisis of dissent. As with its adoption of harm reduction practices in response to the spread of HIV/AIDS, the government has adapted to new and changing crises of dissent in part through using new cutting-edge carceral technologies, many of which resonate with global trends in controlling "trouble" populations. In recent years, the Iranian government's carceral approach to managing prisoners has moved forward on two seemingly incongruous but, I argue, ultimately linked tracks. On the first track, the government has further carceralized its responses to mass protests and civil society organizing in the wake of the Green Movement of 2009, during which millions of Iranians crowded the streets to protest the contested reelection of Mahmoud Ahmadinejad. After 2009, the Islamic Republic both intensified and diversified its use of carceral methods, using old and new tactics including increased digital and conventional surveillance, internet blackouts, mass arrests, police and prison violence, and forced confessions in its effort to suppress public dissent and social organizing. In response to the Woman, Life, Freedom uprising that began in fall 2022, security forces have again escalated this carceral crackdown, arresting tens of thousands and staging public executions of protesters.

On another track, high-ranking members of the judiciary, with approval from Khamenei, have avowed that a central goal of Iran's government is to significantly *reduce* the number of detainees in Iran's prison system—in part as a result of the crisis of disease outlined above. It is not only those in the reformist camp who have suggested the need for significant changes to Iran's penal and judicial systems. In fact, it has often been those members of the Islamic Republic elite most closely linked with prison violence who have suggested—though rarely followed through with—the most significant carceral reforms. One such figure is the country's current president, Ebrahim Raisi, who is well known for his role in the mass executions of 1988. In 2019, just before his rise to the presidency, Khamenei tasked Raisi with reforming Iran's much-maligned judiciary. Raisi's stewardship of that institution included an eyebrow-raising 2020 promise, so far unfulfilled, to eradicate torture and forced confessions from Iran's carceral arsenal.[67]

How do we understand these seemingly divergent approaches—or at least divergent rhetorics—toward carcerality in the contemporary Islamic Republic? Have any of the suggested reforms significantly reduced Iran's prisoner total? Have any of these efforts led to a meaningful shrinking of the carceral state? A key starting point for these current contestations is the 2009–2010 Green Movement. Like Khatami's 1997 election to the presidency, the Green Movement represented a watershed in Islamic Republic politics. Upon Ahmadinejad's reelection, which many Iranians viewed as illegitimate and even falsified, protesters rallied around the question "Where is my vote?" Protests continued for months and grew more urgent in tone, in some instances eventually calling for Khamenei's ouster or death. Security forces responded by attacking protesters, killing dozens, and arresting and imprisoning thousands more.[68] Mir Hossein Mousavi and Mehdi Karroubi, the reformist presidential candidates around whom protesters rallied, were placed under house arrest, where they and members of their families remain as of 2023. Security forces were unable to quell the unrest for months, and the government couldn't control the outpouring of global publicity that the demonstrations elicited. Images and videos of rallies and of security forces' crackdown on protesters spread in real time on social media, generating viral hashtags that circulated the world over.[69] The protests were not solely the province of those constituencies typically aligned with the reformist movement. As Narges Bajoghli has shown, many long-standing members of the IRGC and war veterans also sympathized with the movement, voted for the reformist candidates, and disapproved of the government's violent response.[70]

Through 2009–2010, Iran's prisons again became central to public life in Iran, as stories of the detention and torture of protesters circulated widely. One detainee described the archetypal combination of physical and psychological abuse in disturbing detail, stating, "In one of the interrogation sessions they showed me footage of my son in one of the streets of Tehran. I was told by the interrogator that they had my son in custody and would rape him if I didn't confess . . . I lost control and started screaming. I begged them not to harm my son. I was then beaten by baton until I fainted."[71] Some detainees were detained for years or sentenced to prison terms of decades. Others, including several student activists, were sent into internal exile to prisons or detention camps in provincial parts of Iran.[72] One carceral site became particularly synonymous in the public imagination with the crackdown: Kahrizak Detention Center (Bazdashtdgah-e Kahrizak), in the southern part of Tehran Province, just outside of Behesht-e Zahra cemetery. During the protest movement, Kahrizak went from a largely unknown entity to a terrifying household name. Reports and images from the facility of overcrowding, violence, torture, rape, and death circulated widely.

Kahrizak was a relatively new site, having opened without fanfare in the early 2000s and used by the then chief of police (and future Tehran mayor) Mohammad Baqer Qalibaf to quietly house detainees from campaigns to "cleanse" (*pak sazi*) impoverished Tehran neighborhoods. The most notable of these *pak sazi* efforts was an intensive raid on the Khak-e Sefid neighborhood. Although these earliest Kahrizak detainees were not considered political prisoners as such, their imprisonment was nonetheless a function of the criminalization of poverty and the policing of working-class urban spaces in Iranian cities. Kahrizak's early history also reveals the extent to which tactics used on political dissidents—including sweeps, mass roundups, and new carceral sites—have often first been used against other vulnerable populations. During the raid, unhoused people, vagrants, drug users and sellers, and others whom law enforcement officials referred to as "thugs" were arrested en masse in an effort to "rejuvenate" the working-class Tehran neighborhood.[73] Law enforcement raids on working-class neighborhoods such as the one on Khak-e Sefid were common in this era and, as Ghiabi notes, did lasting damage to harm reduction programs serving those disenfranchised neighborhoods.[74] Indeed, despite the recent success of harm reduction programs, carceral methods like the raid of Khak-e Sefid still often won the day among law enforcement agencies, particularly in policing Iran's poorest populations. Family members of these early detainees and dedicated rights activists attempted to sound the alarm regarding the facility long before 2009. They worked to publicize what they described as "inhumane" conditions, noting that the detention center was subterranean and that detainees were held in dank and dark spaces and disallowed from going outside.[75]

In an August 2009 letter to the then speaker of the parliament Ali Larijani, reformist presidential candidate Mehdi Karroubi demanded the opportunity to present evidence of systemic torture and rape at Kahrizak to members of the country's leadership, including Speaker Larijani, President Mahmoud Ahmadinejad, and Chief Justice Ayatollah Sadeq Amoli Larijani, among others. Karroubi's letter stated he had physical evidence of his claims; Speaker Larijani responded by dismissing the allegations as "baseless."[76] Drawing from his typical playbook, Khamenei disparaged the protests as the work of hostile governments and foreign-sponsored agents provocateurs, though initially he refrained from accusing Mousavi or Karroubi of having direct knowledge of any alleged foreign machinations. Still, the apparent violence at Kahrizak was so extensive and the public outcry so vociferous that Khamenei was forced in July to order the prison, which he merely referred to as "sub-standard," closed.[77]

Three detainees died in Kahrizak during the height of the movement, including two young men named Mohammad Kamrani and Amir Javadifar. The most widely publicized of these deaths was that of Mohsen Rouholamini, the son of prominent scientist and conservative political figure Abdolhossein Rouholamini, head of Iran's Louis Pasteur Institute and senior advisor to former IRGC chief and presidential candidate Mohsen Rezai. The younger Rouholamini was arrested and taken to Kahrizak on July 9, 2009, after which he was moved to Evin and then to the hospital, where he died a week later. Rouholamini's death not only sparked an outcry from protesters, but also elicited concern in government circles due to its ham-fisted brutality and his father's renown; it is likely that it was publicity from this death that led Khamenei to order the prison's closure. Tehran prosecutor general Saeed Mortazevi reluctantly responded to the controversy by announcing that he would appoint a special judge to investigate the Kahrizak deaths.[78] Mortazavi had initially attempted to downplay the matter by claiming that deaths were the result of a meningitis outbreak in the detention center. Rouholamini's father, however, insisted that his son's cause of death was physical abuse, emphasizing that when was allowed to view his son's dead body, "severe facial injuries" were visible.[79]

The Green Movement protests revealed splits between factions of Iran's ruling elite. While allies of Ahmadinejad called for more arrests, repression, and executions, numerous members of Majles, including some prominent conservatives, critiqued the cavalier attitudes of Ahmadinejad's camp. These divisions spilled into the Rouholamini affair, and in January 2010 a parliamentary committee formally made Mortazavi, an Ahmadinejad ally, into the bad apple that could explain the spoiled situation at Kahrizak. This parliamentary report was the first official admission by any Iranian officials that abuse had transpired during the protests. The report rejected Mortazavi's earlier claims of a meningitis outbreak, instead stating that "limitation of space, poor sanitary conditions, inappropriate nutrition, heat, lack of ventilation" played a part in the deaths, which were also "a result of physical attacks." The report also stated that on Mortazavi's orders, 147 detainees were held in a seventy-square-meter room for four days, though it also unequivocally denied that rape had taken place in the facility, against myriad detainee accounts to the contrary.[80] In 2013, Mortazavi was put on trial behind closed doors, although some claimed that the trial was little more than a matter of settling scores with Ahmadinejad, who by that point had ruffled many high-ranking feathers.[81] This affair would not be the last Iranians heard of Kahrizak. Despite Khamenei's 2009 promise to close the facility, Kahrizak again became a site of Iranian and international outcry in 2022 when, during the early weeks of the Women, Life, Freedom uprising, teenage protester Nika Shakarami was found dead in the facility's morgue after her arrest by security forces days prior.[82]

Since 2009, the reformist dream of a democratic public sphere in Iran achieved from within the *nezam* (system) has all but withered and died on the vine. The conservative elite and linked security forces used 2009 as a learning moment, choosing as their lesson the need for increased surveillance and punishment across Iran's civil sphere, as well as the need for more control over the digital sphere. This has led to suffocating responses to all forms of public protest, from water protests in southern Iran to labor unrest to environmental activism to the Woman, Life, Freedom protests that began in late 2022.[83] The government's response to the protests that broke out on November 15, 2019, against an announced hike in fuel prices is instructive in this regard. Iran's security apparatus took a two-pronged approach to this working-class revolt: violent suppression of the protests by security forces and the complete control of the digital sphere in the form of an unprecedented internet shutdown, the first of its kind in Iran. On November 16, one day into the protests, Interior Minister Abdolreza Rahmani Fazli announced that riot police would no longer display "tolerance" and "self-control" toward protesters and would instead "fulfill their duty to restore calm." The next day, Khamenei went a step further, calling the protesters "evil-doers, hate-mongers, and unscrupulous people" and calling on security forces to put an end to the protests once and for all.[84] Amnesty International later reported that it was able to verify the deaths of at least 304 protesters, but because of the internet shutdown, images and videos of the protests didn't circulate as widely as in 2009. Tellingly, the total death toll in 2019 was somewhere between four and eight times that of the protests of 2009, despite being significantly shorter in duration and seemingly smaller in participation. The lesson of 2009 for the governing elite and security forces seemed to be to act quickly and powerfully and to manipulate digital technologies for the government's benefit rather than its global embarrassment.[85]

Yet in this same era of increased securitization, another carceral strategy has taken root in the Islamic Republic. As security forces have worked to stamp out virtually all forms of civil organizing and public dissent through carceral means, many government officials, including the leadership of the judiciary and the Prisons Organization, have also come to loudly call for the *reduction* of Iran's total number of detainees. The Prisons Organization had long promised that its prisons are "human-making universities" (*danesh-gah-e ensan sazi*) that would reform bad criminals into honorable Muslim citizens through vocational and religious education, but ever-escalating numbers of detainees led even those criminologists working with the government to worry, as did their Pahlavi predecessors, that Iranian prisons were doing little more than hardening detainees into career recidivists.[86] Official statistics backed these concerns, as the number of prisoners in Iran only continued to trend upward, pushing nearly three times beyond stated prison capacity in the country by late in the 2000s. In 2008, the Iranian judiciary put the total number of detainees in the country at 156,000. A year later, the total was announced at 170,000. In 2010, amid the Green Movement, the total had jumped to 220,000.[87]

From the 1990s, the judiciary and the Prisons Organization typically addressed the issue of overcrowding by calling for new and more "state-of-the-art" prisons. Resultantly, the number of official prisons in the Islamic Republic increased from 227 in 2006 to 242 in 2011, and again to 268 by 2020.[88] Plans for new facilities remained a major official response to prison overcrowding well into the 2010s, with the then head of the Prisons Organization Gholamhosseim Esmaili expressing the position that overcrowding required new and more "modernized" carceral facilities. Among the outcomes of this push was the official opening of the Greater Tehran Penitentiary, also known as Fashafouyeh, approximately twenty miles south of Tehran. Construction on Fashafouyeh had originally begun in 2000 but languished until 2009, when the government renewed its efforts to fund the new facility. When the prison opened its doors over a decade after its initial planning, several thousand incarcerated persons, largely held on drug charges, were transferred from Evin and other older sites to the new facility.[89] Esmaili announced plans for further prison expansion during a January 2014 press conference in Shahr-e Kord, promising new temporary detention centers in cities with populations larger than twenty thousand as well as new prison facilities outside of the major cities. Esmaili also indicated that the organization planned to hire at least two thousand more trained prison personnel, championing these hires as central to the rehabilitative function of the prison system. Echoing the rehabilitative rhetoric that was by then reflexive for the Prisons Organization, Esmaili claimed, "Our efforts are such that if an individual commits a crime and the judiciary decides on a prison sentence, those prisons or camps [*ordugah*] are managed in such a way that educational, reform-oriented, corrective, and disciplinary classes are available for that individual." After all, he reasoned, these reforms and expansions were not simply practical matters but rather matters of "Islamic and human rights" (*huquq-e Islami va ensani*).⁹⁰ Today, prisons continue to be planned and built, as concerns about dilapidated and crumbling older prisons, particularly in provinces away from major cities, continue to drive officials toward building new carceral spaces.⁹¹

During the 2014 press conference, Esmaili signaled a key shift in rhetoric regarding prisons and prisoners in Iran. Alongside the organization's perennial devotion to building more detention centers, Esmaili announced another commitment: reducing the number of prisoners in Iran altogether. "As custodian of the prisoners in this country's prisons," Esmaili stated, "I will work to decrease the numbers" of those incarcerated across the country.⁹² Esmaili explained that this goal was a judiciary directive and championed by Ayatollah Khamenei himself. While Esmaili continued to emphasize the need for new prisons as well as upkeep on existing facilities, he announced that the Prisons Organization was also investing in cutting-edge surveillance technologies such as electronic ankle monitors and body scanners for use in its prisons and jails. These technologies, Esmaili claimed, would allow Iran to shift its approach to punishment in line with contemporary global norms and significantly reduce its number of incarcerated persons.⁹³

In January 2015, the Prisons Organization again announced that its priority would be the reduction of the prisoner population.⁹⁴ Asghar Jahangir, who replaced Ebrahimi as head of the organization after the latter figure was removed amid a prison violence scandal at Evin, lamented the fact that over the past year alone, the country's prisoner population had increased by 5 percent.⁹⁵ Particularly worrisome, Jahangir acknowledged, was the decreasing average age of detainees. Still, Jahangir stood by the Prisons Organization's work, arguing that increasing rates of incarceration couldn't be blamed on the organization alone. Instead, he insisted, economic issues, widespread unemployment, and a lack of investment in youth activities played pivotal roles in these rates.⁹⁶ In his outgoing message as organization head in summer 2020, amid a widescale prisoner furlough prompted by the COVID-19 crisis, Jahangir claimed that his efforts had been a success and that the number of incarcerated persons in the country had decreased by 6 percent in his six-year tenure.⁹⁷ The COVID-19 furloughs—approved by Khamenei with the aim of reducing the spread of the virus in prisons—brought together several issues outlined in this chapter: harm reduction logics used in the management of infectious diseases in prison, an official desire to reduce prisoner totals, evidence of dilapidated provincial prisons, and political action among Iran's nominally nonpolitical prisoners, in this case revolts led by common-law prisoners during the early months of the pandemic born of apparent worry about the spread of illness in carceral facilities.[98]

Ebrahimi, Jahangir, and the Prisons Organization were part of a broader judiciary effort to reduce Iran's detainee population in the 2010s. This included judicial plans to reduce the types of charges levied against arrestees and to reduce the length of sentences. In September 2016, Iran's then chief justice Ayatollah Sadeq Amoli Larijani—a former member of the Guardian Council appointed to the head judicial post by Khamenei in 2009 and the man whose office oversaw the prison system—issued a remarkable thirty-three-point directive with instructions for the country's judiciary on sentencing, bail, prosecutorial norms, and more, many of which were aimed at reducing Iran's bloated prisoner total. Larijani's directive was emblematic of the flexible approach to punishment in the contemporary Islamic Republic, insofar as it included measures for which liberal reformists around the world have advocated—including limiting cases in which arrestees could be detained over nonpayment of bail, reducing some forms of temporary and pretrial detention, mitigation measures for the detention of juveniles, and drug treatment options for drug offenders—alongside the promotion of forms of corporal punishment long used in the Islamic Republic but frowned upon by human rights organizations, such as flogging and the death penalty.[99] A year later the parliament, with the approval of the twelve-member Guardian Council, further modified Iran's approach to punishment, amending the country's strict drug smuggling laws such that fewer persons would face the death penalty in cases of drug possession, opening the door for the Larijani-mandated commutation of prior death sentences shortly thereafter.[100]

Despite their seeming contradictions, this shift toward more lenient sentencing and reduced prisoner totals on the one hand and the expanded surveillance and rigorous carceralization of public dissent on the other are linked by an undergirding logic of carceral expansion. Official efforts to reduce prisoner totals have not ushered in an end to or even a meaningful shrinking of the carceral state in Iran so much as a modification of its preferred methods of social control. As the judiciary signaled a desire to move away from mass imprisonment, its efforts to do so have been enacted alongside the adoption of new carceral technologies. Most of these changes have amounted to an escalation of surveillance and policing in everyday people's lives. To this end, Iran has increasingly incorporated new and internationally popular surveillance and monitoring technologies such as ankle monitors, facial recognition software, and various forms of biotechnology—what scholars have elsewhere critiqued as "prison by any other name"[101]—in its carceral toolkit. It is in part through these new technologies that the Islamic Republic has hinted at an approach in which fewer people are held in traditional jails and prisons but *more* people are surveilled, monitored, and tracked.[102]

In 2016, Khamenei called on Iranian law enforcement agencies to update their technological capabilities in keeping with global standards and norms of policing and punishment.[103] Reforms and new carceral technologies of this sort, Maya Schenwar and Victoria Law argue in a different context, "focus on decreasing prison populations, not on releasing more people from state control altogether." In the words of anti-prison activist Mariame Kaba, these reform efforts amount to little more than a drive to find a new "Somewhere Else" not calling itself prison but nonetheless meant to hide away criminalized populations under heightened state control.[104] These new carceral technologies and high-tech surveillance are not limited to use on those charged of crimes, rendering the "somewhere else" of surveillance and punishment the whole of Iran's public sphere. Jahangir linked the Prisons Organization's success in reducing Iranian prisoner totals to their adoption of new monitoring technologies, the foremost of which were electronic ankle monitors. In summer 2020, these monitors weren't only used on those released from prison—some eight hundred detainees were also monitored by electronic ankle devices full time while still incarcerated.[105] As is the case in other countries (such as the US), where the use of ankle monitors has ballooned in recent years, the monitors used in the Islamic Republic are a financial burden for those court-ordered to wear them: those released on the condition of ankle monitoring are charged a daily fee. In 2017, that fee was approximately 100,000 rials (then about three US dollars) per day.[106]

Although much of the technology the Iranian government has adopted is popular all over the world, used by liberal and illiberal governments (and private companies) alike, Islamic Republic law enforcement agencies have adopted these new surveillance methods in novel ways linked to the country's particular political anxieties and preoccupations. Two examples might help better illustrate this dynamic interplay between global tech and the localized needs of the carceral state in Iran. In 2019, Tehran chief of police general Hossein Rahimi announced via the Tasnim News Agency that several areas known for unauthorized currency exchange in downtown Tehran were newly being monitored with state-of-the-art facial recognition cameras.[107] In this case, the use of this globally ubiquitous surveillance equipment was both a sign of the Islamic Republic's adoption of new carceral technologies *and* a function of its sanctions-addled economy, in which hyperinflation, currency black markets, and the devaluation of the rial are common features of an economy in many ways cut off from the normal flows of global capital.[108] Iranian law enforcement agencies have adopted a form of surveillance tech that is now practically universal around the world in order to surveil and ultimately punish persons in a political economic context particular to the Islamic Republic.

Another example of this interplay between the local and the global is recent innovations in the use of traffic enforcement cameras, which have come to be used not only to issue citations for traffic violations but also to enforce hijab rules.[109] Beginning in 2020, amid the height of the COVID-19 pandemic, first-time offenders received text messages with a summons to report to the Guidance Police office within ten days to sign affidavits promising not to break hijab rules again. If drivers ignored the texts, or if they repeated the violation, they were in danger of having their cars impounded. Cars represent a liminal space in the moral geography of the Islamic Republic—not quite private and not quite public—and as a result, the question of whether people are legally entitled to some privacy from state intrusion in their cars has become a matter of legal, theological, and political dispute. Ayatollah Mohsen Gharavian, a religious scholar at Qom Seminary, argued in 2017 that the issue of privacy in personal cars was one that required more serious research by Shi'a scholars.[110] Gharavian, citing another leading Qom seminarian, Ayatollah Mousa Shobiri Zanjani, asserted that Shi'a sources of emulation believed cars to be private spaces, and as such they were not subject to the laws policing public appearance. Referencing the issue of clothing norms, however, Gharavian averred that cars take on a different status when moving through crowded roads in plain sight of the public. In such cases, the cleric argued, surveillance would be permissible. "Sometimes while inside of a car," Gharavian argued, "a woman might take off her scarf. If this violates a norm and is against the law, the government may enter the car." Gharavian conceded, however, that the question of the state's reach into people's private spaces, cars especially, remained uncertain. He continued, "There might occasionally be roads on which no one else is traveling or are deserted [*biabani ast*], and the individual takes off her scarf due to the heat when a police car happens to drive by; it is an open question whether this is a matter of norm-breaking."[111]

Social media, sometimes seen as a site of democratic information-sharing for Iranians looking for news beyond official channels, has also emerged as a site of mass surveillance and state-encouraged digital snitching. In 2019, Mohammad Mehdi Haj Mohammadi—a recent head of the country's Prisons Organization, previously at the helm of the Guidance Prosecutor's office (*dadsara-ye ershad*) in Tehran—announced that his office had set up social media channels including an Instagram page that would allow Iranians to report their fellow citizens for violations of the country's morality laws. Haj Mohammadi encouraged "compassionate" (*delsuz*) and "ethical" (*akhlaq madar*) citizens to report, with pictures and other identifying information, "norm-breaking" behaviors—the holding of mixed-gender parties and dances, the drinking or serving of alcoholic beverages, improper hijab—to the relevant authorities. For Haj Mohammadi, the new social media campaign was a means to "accelerate responses to norm-breaking by using the capacities of concerned citizens."[112] Peer-to-peer surveillance tactics like these digital snitching apps replicate the interpolation of citizens into the work of law enforcement enacted during the revolutionary era, especially in the earliest and most chaotic days of the Revolutionary Committees. Such programs will also be familiar to people outside of Iran as marking a particularly twenty-first century form of global carceral thinking that asks individuals to perform what Mark Andrejevic calls "lateral surveillance" on peers, friends, and fellow citizens.[113] Again, as in the earlier example, policing institutions in the Islamic Republic have adopted globally popular technologies and surveillance tactics—including ubiquitous peer-to-peer surveillance—in ways and for reasons particular to the political context of the Islamic Republic. These new approaches for moral policing fully burst into the public eye during the Woman, Life, Freedom protests that began in 2022, when Islamic Republic officials suggested that the Morality Police would be disbanded but that morality policing would continue unimpeded through the increased use of new surveillance technologies.[114]

This chapter has analyzed several key moments in the recent history of the Islamic Republic, arguing that since the end of the Iran-Iraq war and the death of Ayatollah Ruhollah Khomeini, the Iranian government has shown significant adaptability in the way it has managed its prisons. In particular, the government had to address crises born out of the massive prison expansion of the immediate postrevolution period, including the crisis of disease and the crisis of dissent. This flexibility has taken the form of new programs (such as harm reduction programs), new technologies (including ankle monitors), new digital practices (such as shutting down the internet during protests and peer-to-peer surveillance networks), and new strategies for sentencing certain offenders. Despite repeated promises to decrease the numbers of incarcerated persons in the country, this flexibility has largely not amounted to a radical shrinking of the carceral system in Iran but rather to its continued expansion. At times, this expansion has meant new prisons or even new bureaucratic institutions (such as prison research centers or sentinel surveillance sites); more recently, it has also included the adoption of new global technologies of surveillance and punishment. Although Iranian prisons have undergone significant reforms in the contemporary period, the institutions of policing and punishment—that constellation of interlinked entities that compose the carceral state—have become a ubiquitous part of daily life in Iran not only for detainees but also for those Iranians who are nominally "free."

Conclusion

POLITICS AND PRISONS BEYOND REFORM

ACROSS ERAS, GOVERNMENTS, AND POLITICAL DIVIDES, THE MODERN prison system established just over a century ago in Iran has remained a constant and ever-expanding reality. The dizzying growth of prisons and prisoners in this time has left an indelible mark on life in Iran, so much so that most Iranians—much like most people around the world—don't often consider how historically novel and radical the modern prison system is *in its form*, not simply in its current application. This book has been an effort to address this forgetting and, through archival excavation and historical analysis, to denaturalize modern prisons and the carceral imaginaries so recently built with them. To say that the history of the modern prison in Iran needs historical excavation is not to say that prisons are absent in the public conversation among Iranians—to the contrary, as this book has also endeavored to show. Prisons are a constant presence in the public and political culture of the contemporary Islamic Republic, just as they were under the Pahlavi monarchs before them. They remain very much at the forefront of Iranian political conversations across the political and social spectrum, both inside and outside of the country.

Recently, a new people's movement in Iran has emerged in response to an incident of deadly police force in Tehran, again bringing carceral violence in Iran into the public spotlight. On September 13, 2022, Tehran's so-called Guidance Police, a religious vice squad often referred to as the "morality police," arrested twenty-two-year-old Kurdish Iranian Jina Mahsa Amini for an apparent violation of the country's dress code for women. Just two hours later, as Amini's brother waited for her outside of the police station where his sister was taken for a compulsory moral education session, officials delivered a comatose Amini to the hospital, where she died three days later. The official coroner's report blamed "underlying diseases" for Amini's death, while officials claimed that she had collapsed and died of natural causes while in custody. Eyewitness reports surfaced, however, of Amini being badly beaten by police.[1] As images of a comatose Amini and the news of her death circulated, protests erupted in virtually every city and province in the country, including the seminary city of Qom.[2] The popular uprising instantly captured Iranian and global imaginations with images of protesters chanting "Death to the dictator!" and facing down armed police and security forces. The government's response was swift and vicious: within weeks, many thousands had been arrested, and by early 2023, over five hundred protesters had been killed.[3] Among those arrested, reports of torture and prison rape surfaced immediately,[4] and journalists offered damning new evidence of secret detention centers, including off-the-grid sites, where detainees were exposed to seemingly "unfettered cruelty" during violent interrogations.[5] Once again, the Islamic Republic's prisons and interrogation centers were the subject of widespread scrutiny, eliciting a deep well of public anger toward the government that relies on them for its survival.

Rallying around the Kurdish movement cry "Woman, Life, Freedom," this mass protest movement—led by women, young people, and ethnic minorities—has adopted a revolutionary posture toward the *nezam* (system) of absolute clerical rule. What the long-term future holds for this movement, as well as for Iran's prisons and prisoners, is not yet clear. Although the protest movement has been leaderless to date, there have been several efforts to outline its contours and demands. On February 4, 2023, Mir Hossein Mousavi, the man whose 2009 electoral loss set off the Green Movement, broke with other prominent reformists and argued (while still under house arrest) that it was time for a new constitution and truly democratic elective bodies.[6] Other reformists, including former president Mohammad Khatami, disagreed, cautioning against transformative change lest the country fall into chaos or war. Still, even Khatami admitted that the reform movement had all but hit a dead end.[7] Days later, a group of feminist, labor, student, and environmental unions and organizations in Iran issued a charter of minimum demands, including, among others things, calls for full gender equality, unconditional freedom of belief, wage increases and stable jobs for all workers, and—of course—the release of all political prisoners and the immediate end to torture and the death penalty.[8] As labor historian Peyman Jafari has argued, the statement stands as a "potent reminder that radical change [in Iran] will come from inside and from below."[9]

Meanwhile, in certain pockets of the Iranian diaspora, voices of the those once deposed by the Islamic revolutionaries—including Reza Pahlavi, the son of Mohammad Reza Shah—have reemerged into conversations on Iran's future, buoyed by support from those using the interventionist language of "regime change." In January 2023, actor Ehsan Karimi started an online petition seeking to give the erstwhile crown prince "power of attorney" to lead Iran in a transition to a secular state.[10] To virtually no one's insistence, some US lawmakers formally championed the long-discredited Mojahedin-e Khalq, which over years in exile has become an authoritarian cult of personality.[11] At the same time, the looming cloud of a potential US- and Israeli-led war of aggression in Iran has emerged yet again as a serious threat.[12]

Other even more shocking faces associated with the fallen monarchy, as well as its carceral and security apparatus, have also reappeared on the public stage. On February 12, 2023, the daughter of infamous SAVAK deputy director Parviz Sabeti posted a photo of her long-secretive father posing openly with his family at an Iran solidarity rally in the US. Before the fall of the shah, Sabeti led SAVAK's much-feared Third Division, the branch of the intelligence organization charged with internal security and thus responsible for the treatment of imprisoned dissidents. Responses to Sabeti's surprising public appearance revealed deep fissures in the public view of SAVAK's legacy. Diasporic monarchists and Pahlavi allies responded positively, calling Sabeti a "living legend" and thanking him for fighting "terrorism" in the 1970s. At a rally in Munich, one such group carried a picture of Sabeti on a placard, along with a message promising that he would be "the nightmare of future terrorists" (*kabus-e teroristha-ye ayandeh*).[13] Many others responded with a mix of outrage and disbelief. Longtime dissident activist Mahdieh Golrou summed up this sentiment succinctly, stating, "Torture is a crime regardless of who committed it."[14] Some on social media further noted that the Islamic Republic, like Sabeti and his supporters, also uses the language of "anti-terrorism" to justify its use of carceral violence and mass arrests.[15] In response to Sabeti's appearance, a group of shah-era political prisoners published an open letter outlining their experiences with torture before 1979, calling Sabeti "shameless" for appearing at a pro-democracy rally and demanding that he be held legally accountable for his past actions. "Let's not praise a murderer," the open letter demanded. "Let's not speak of the revival of SAVAK!"[16]

The current uprising in Iran is a trenchant reminder that torture, mass arrests, and extrajudicial executions remain central to political life in Iran, as they continue to be wielded by the government against dissent. Sabeti's vexed reappearance on the public stage is also a reminder, albeit one of a different sort. It is a reminder of the unhealed wounds and sedimented traumas of the longer history of carceral violence in Iran's modern history, much of which—whether from before or after 1979—has not received the moral or historical reckoning so needed among all Iranians. Among the most disquieting examples of this will to forget is the political success of current president Ebrahim Raisi, who as deputy prosecutor general played a key role in carrying out the 1988 prison massacre. Raisi, like most of the Islamic Republic elite, has studiously avoided public conversations on the killings. It has been the tireless work of groups like the Mothers of Khavaran, comprising mothers and family members of those killed in 1988, that has kept the Iranian government from erasing this carceral bloodletting from the history books. These erasures and fissures serve as a sobering reminder that, even should today's protesters achieve their highest revolutionary aspirations in the face of both internal repression and imperialist aggression, there will be more work to be done to address the long-standing violence of Iran's entrenched carceral state.

This book has been an effort to understand the making of this carceral state. I have argued that carcerality has shaped notions of citizenship, rights, and political belonging in Iran—key aspects of what I have termed the public life of the modern prison. The public life of the prison has most visibly been a political life. Virtually all of modern Iran's most well-known political and intellectual figures have counted themselves among the country's legendary political prisoners or infamous prison wardens, jurists, and torturers. Some, depressingly, have been both. Politically active—or merely politically curious—Iranians have had their work surveilled, their lives upended, and their families and livelihoods threatened by looming exile or incarceration. Members of numerous dissident political parties either formed or elaborated their positions while incarcerated. In the years leading up to the 1979 revolution, political movements with disparate aims and worldviews—from armed guerrillas to diasporic human rights groups to oppositional ayatollahs—nonetheless all agreed on the centrality of prisons to their critique of the Pahlavi government. In the years after the revolution, prisons and torture again dominated political conversations in Iran as the revolutionary government only expanded and further entrenched the carceral state. To live a political life in Iran, from the late nineteenth century until today, has been to experience the inside of some of the country's most notorious political prisons, from the dingy Anbar-e Shahi of the late Qajar era to the shah's Komiteh interrogation center to the infamous Ward 209 of Evin, still operational today. The public life of the prison, however, is not something only experienced by dissidents. Modern carcerality has meant that *everyone* in Iran has had to navigate the thin line between nominal freedom and formal unfreedom, albeit with greater or lesser degrees of vulnerability. Carcerality has shaped and produced the very notion of the public, delimiting and policing the fuzzy space between healthy citizenship and social deviancy, the surveilled border between nationalized inclusion and criminalized exclusion. The process of criminalization in Iran has rendered certain acts akin to social diseases, necessitating modern prisons for the cure.

The behaviors necessitating the rehabilitation of policing and imprisonment in Iran have, at various points, included acts like drug use, sex work, the reading of political pamphlets, and certain forms of gendered dress. I have argued that regardless of whether these are typically considered political acts, the process of mass criminalization and carceralization has been a fundamentally political project from the outset. As I have noted, the lion's share of incarcerated persons in modern Iran's history have been those held for evidently "nonpolitical" crimes, particularly those held on drug-related charges. I have argued against the strict policing of the line between "political" and "nonpolitical" crimes and prisoners, making the case instead that the criminalization of certain behaviors in Iran has been a political process regardless of who is ensnared. To imagine that only some prisoners are political is to accept the historically radical idea that the imprisonment of tens of millions of people around the world is a natural occurrence rather than a contingent and contested historical process. It is also to reify the myth undergirding liberalism that political prisoners only exist "over there" in places like the Islamic Republic of Iran and to imagine that Iran's prisons are a historical exception to the otherwise humane story of modern carcerality. Yet as I have also shown, Iran's prisons do not represent aberrant strands of carcerality in which recalcitrant forms of primordial Oriental despotism or Islamic barbarity have habitually disallowed "real" modern reforms from taking root; they share architectures, economies, tactics, and profound failures with prisons all over the world.

I want to conclude here by arguing that prisoner and anti-police violence movements all over the world can learn from the current uprising in Iran, which has now largely rejected the rubric of "reform" as a possibility in facing down the violence of the carceral state. In the face of the police killing of Jina Amini, Iranians aren't demanding police body cameras or better police training, although the government has suggested precisely that using modern surveillance technologies will help reduce the chance of violence in similar encounters. Instead, protesters are demanding fundamental change. The Islamic Republic's recent prison reform efforts, aimed at reducing prisoner totals while nonetheless expanding the reach of the carceral state, reveal a remarkable if ominous truth about prison reformism throughout modern Iranian history. That is, in every era since prisons were first built in Iran, the promise of reform has only served as a catalyst for the expansion of the carceral system.[17] Since the first modern prisons in Iran, the prison system has been buttressed by the modernist logic of reform. In the late Qajar era, prisons were themselves imagined as reformist institutions, capable of transforming lawless Persia into a progressive and modern nation-state. Later carceral modernists and carceral Islamists have since routinely claimed that prisons could make Iran safer, fairer, less lawless, less colonial, more civilized, more progressive, more educated, more modern, more ethical, even more Islamic. Pahlavi statesmen and Islamic Republic clerics alike have claimed that modern carceral methods could reform and rehabilitate those people locked away behind prison bars, or at least inoculate Iranians against their contagious presence. Despite the reformist promise at the heart of the modern prison in Iran, the exponential rise in incarcerated Iranians over the past century has long given lie to the notion that prisons can be a cure-all for social issues. And as Iranians too well know, the intrusive forms of surveillance, policing, and punishment at the heart of the carceral state have instead all too often been linked to the project of social repression and autocratic forms of political power. But despite their omnipresence today, prisons were not a historical inevitability in Iran or anywhere else in the world. This book is thus undergirded by a belief that to understand the historical origins of the modern prison in Iran is to be able to imagine a world beyond the prison as well. It is toward that horizon of freedom that this book is oriented.

Notes

Epigraph

All translations in this book, including the translation of this poem, are my own unless otherwise noted. Mehdi Akhavan-Sales, *Seh Ketab* [Three books] (Tehran: Zemestan, 1385/2006), 19–24.

Introduction

1. Tara Sepehri Far, "Why Nasrin Sotoudeh Is on Hunger Strike to Protest Iran's Dire Prison Conditions," *Human Rights Watch*, September 10, 2020, https://www.hrw.org/news/2020/09/10/why-nasrin-sotoudeh-hunger-strike-protest-irans-dire-prison-conditions.

2. Anna Schaverian, "Trial Is Postponed of British-Iranian Woman Held in Iran," *New York Times*, September 13, 2020, https://www.nytimes.com/2020/09/13/world/middleeast/nazanin-zaghari-ratcliffe-iran-delay.html.

3. Farnaz Fassihi and Marjorie Olster, "Iran Executes Wrestler Accused of Murder after He Took Part in 2018 Protests," *New York Times*, September 12, 2020, https://www.nytimes.com/2020/09/12/world/middleeast/iran-wrestler-navid-afkari.html.

4. Haleh Esfandiari, *My Prison, My Home: One Woman's Story of Captivity in Iran* (New York: Harper Collins, 2009); Marina Nemat, *Prisoner of Tehran: A Memoir* (New York: Simon & Schuster, 2008); and Marziyeh Amirzadeh and Maryam Rostampour, *Captive in Iran: A Remarkable True Story of Hope and Triumph amid the Horror of Tehran's Brutal Evin Prison* (Atlanta: Tyndale Momentum, 2013). There has been controversy surrounding Nemat's book. In 2007, a group of women led by Monira Baradaran, all of whom were once imprisoned in Evin Prison, signed a letter of protest to Penguin, the book's publisher, writing,

For us who have spent many dark years in the prison, the publication of any book that would shed light on the unknown facts of the prisons of the Islamic Republic, particularly during the 1980s, is a source of hope.... Unfortunately we have to say that the publication of Ms. Nemat's book outraged us. The scenes and atmosphere described in the book not only fail to bring to light the reality of the prison experience but it also distorts the truth.... The atmosphere and scenes are fictional.... We ... have spent years inside the Islamic Republic's Prison, and are familiar with the methods used for interrogation ... and the behaviour of the interrogators and prison guards towards the prisoners and the scenes of execution.... We consider the publication of this book of distortions and fiction, an insult to ourselves and the thousands of political prisoners that were executed in prisons of the Islamic Republic.

Nemat has her supporters, however, including novelist Shahrnush Parsipur, who has also written a prison memoir recounting her experiences in Islamic Republic prisons in roughly the same era. For the letter, see Monira Baradaran and Golroch Jahangiri, "Letter to Penguin Publishers regarding Marina Nemat's *Prisoner of Tehran*," July 25, 2007, http://sites.utoronto.ca/prisonmemoirs/Protest.pdf. For Parsipur's prison writing, see Shahrnush Parsipur, *Khaterat-e zendan* [Prison memoir] (Stockholm: Baran Press, 2000). For the English translation, see Shahrnush Parsipur, *Kissing the Sword: A Prison Memoir*, trans. Sara Khalili (New York: The Feminist Press, 2013).

5. From Amnesty International's 2016/2017 report on Iran. See Amnesty International, *Amnesty International Report 2016/17—Iran*, February 22, 2017, https://www.refworld.org/docid/58b033ef13.html.

6. Organization of Iranian People's Fadai Guerrillas (OIPFG), "A Prisoner's Report from Evin Prison," *Kar* no. 14 (October 1984): 24.

7. For just a few examples in Persian, see Parvaneh Alizadeh, *Khub negah konid, rastaki ast* [Look closely, it's real] (Paris: Khavaran Press, 1366/1987); and Monira Baradaran, *Haqiqat-e sadeh* [Plain truth], 2nd ed. (Lindenallee, Germany: Nima Verlag, 1379/2000). There are also numerous English-language Iranian prison memoirs. See, for instance, Jason Rezaian, *Prisoner: My 544 in an Iranian Prison* (Ecco: New York, 2018); Zarah Ghahramani, *My Life as a Traitor: An Iranian Memoir* (New York: Farrar, Straus & Giroux, 2008); Maziar Bahari, *Then They Came for Me: A Family's Story of Love, Captivity, and Survival* (New York: Random House, 2011); Jila Baniuyaghoob, *Women of Evin: Ward 209* (Bloomington, IN: Xlibris, 2013); Ramin Jahanbegloo, *Time Will Say Nothing: A Philosopher Survives an Iranian Prison* (Saskatchewan: University of Regina Press, 2014); and Narges Mohammadi, *White Torture: Interviews with Iranian Women Prisoners*, trans. Amir Rezanezhad (New York: Oneworld, 2022).

8. Nasser Mohajer, *Voices of a Massacre: Untold Stories of Life and Death in Iran, 1988* (New York: Oneworld, 2020).

9. There have been letter-writing campaigns representing a wide range of political worldviews on behalf of Iranian prisoners from all corners of the Iranian diaspora. The former crown prince Reza Pahlavi has engaged in several of these campaigns, many of which are documented on his website: http://en.rezapahlavi.org.

10. See, for example, Saʿid Ghiasian, ed., *Khaterat-e zendan: Gazideh az nagofteha-ye zendanian-e siyasi-ye rezhim-e shah* [Prison memoirs: A selection of untold stories by the political prisoners of the shah's regime] (Tehran: Sureh Mehr, 1390/2011). Sureh Mehr is a publishing house connected to the state-affiliated Howzeh-Ye Honari (Department of Arts) of the Organization for Islamic Propaganda. See also Saʿid Samdipur, *Shekanjeh dar rezhim-e shah* [Torture in the shah's regime] (Tehran: Markaz-e Asnad-e Enghelab-e Eslami [Center for the Documentation of the Islamic Revolution], 1386/2007). For an example of the Islamic Republic's selective reporting on torture outside of Iran, see a report published by IRNA (the Islamic Republic News Agency) on the torture of Palestinians in Israeli prisons: "Zendanhaye Zionisti: Makhuf va makhfi" [Zionist prisons: Horrific and secretive], IRNA, Farvardin 11, 1392/March 31, 2013, irna .ir / news / 80597859/-زندان-هاي-صهيونيستي-مخوف-و-مخفي.

11. "Moruri bar khaterat-e Ayatollah Khamenei dar zendanha-ye setamshahi" [A review of Ayatollah Khamenei's memoirs from the prisons of the oppressive shah], *Khamenei.ir*, Bahman 21, 2017/February 9, 2017, https://farsi.khamenei.ir/memory-content?id=35645.

12. On legal centralization, see Hadi Enayat, *Law, State, and Society in Modern Iran: Constitutionalism, Autocracy, and Legal Reform, 1906–1941* (New York: Palgrave Macmillan, 2013).

13. Ahmad Rahraw Khuajah and Nasser Rubayʿi, *Tarikh-e zendan dar ʿasr-e Qajar va Pahlavi* [The history of prison in the Qajar and Pahlavi eras] (Tehran: Entesharat-e Qoqnus, 1390/2011), 104. For more on Hooman, see Parviz Saney, "Iran," in *International Developments in Criminology*, ed. E. H. Johnson (Westport, CT: Greenwood, 1983), 2:357–69.

14. "Modir-e tarahi-ye bagh, muzeh-ye zendan-e qasr," ISNA, 9 Tir 1385/June 30, 2006, https://www.isna.ir/news/8504-03527/مدير-طراحي-باغ-موزه-ي-زندان-قصر-پلان-اصلي-باغ-تاريخي-مبناي-.

15. The construction of the radio masts was announced in *Ettelaʿat Monthly*. Quoted in Mohammad Javad Moradiniya, *Hekayat-e Qasr: Az Qajar ta Pahlavi* (Tehran: Entesharat-e Negah, 1397/2018), 39.

16. Grainy video of the liberation of these prisoners has continued to circulate

online, reminding contemporary viewers of the highest original aspirations of the revolutionary movement. See Televizion-e Rah-e Kargar Dar YouTube, "Azadi zendanian-e siasi beh dast-e mardom," February 9, 2013, YouTube video, 1:58, https://www.youtube.com/watch?v=1uAQhJN2RYI.

17. In 1935, Reza Shah announced to the world that the nation over which he presided, known internationally as Persia, would from that point forward be known externally, as it already was internally, as Iran. In this book, I often use the term Iran to refer to the region both before 1935 and after, for ease of reference and because switching back and forth can be clunky for nonspecialist readers. Yet the act of calling the region in question one name across time and space raises a thorny historiographical and philosophical issue, insofar as the nation-state of "Iran" is decidedly a modern construction even if some version of Iranzamin (the Land of Iran) is not. I endeavor to write against the grain of nationalist understandings of an essential and timeless Iran, but because I must call it something, Iran it usually is. In the post-1979 period, Iran once again formally changed its name, this time to the Islamic Republic of Iran. For the post-1979 era, I use Iran and the Islamic Republic interchangeably.

18. Fazlollah Bahrami, then head of Reza Shah's department of prisons, lists the number of prisoners held in Tehran in 1927 on the eve of legal centralization at four hundred. See Fazlollah Bahrami, *Majaleh-ye polis*, no. 17 (Azar 1306/December 1927).

19. "Iran: 333% Increase of Prison Populace in 30 Years," *Prison Insider*, May 25, 2017, https://www.prison-insider.com/en/articles/iran-333-increase-of-prison-populace-in-30-years. This number is likely an undercount, for reasons I explain in chapter 5. Jahangir, whose tenure as head of the prison system ended in 2020, routinely cited the number of Iran's prisoners at about a quarter million. See also "Iran's Overcrowded Prisons Hold a Quarter of a Million People, Says Chief Warden," *Radio Farda*, May 12, 2018, https://en.radiofarda.com/a/iran-s-overcrowded-prisons-hold-a-quarter-of-a-million-people-says-chief-warden-/29222716.html.

20. Michel Foucault, *Discipline and Punish: The Birth of the Prison*, trans. Alan Sheridan, 2nd ed. (New York: Pantheon Books, 1977; New York: Vintage Books, 1995). Citations refer to the Vintage edition. In *Discipline and Punish*, Foucault introduces the notion of the carceral continuum or carceral network—that is, linked institutions including prison, policing, and judicial systems.

21. Donne Raffat, *The Prison Papers of Bozorg Alavi* (Syracuse, NY: Syracuse University Press, 1985), 49.

22. Fadaian-e Islam, "Communiqué from a Group of Visitors to Hazrat Navab Safavi Written to the Brave Muslims of Iran and the World," n.d., file no. 5-26-256, the Institute for the Study of Contemporary Iranian History Archives, Tehran.

23. For an example of work Jazani produced while imprisoned, see Bizhan

Jazani, *Tarh-e jama'eh shenasi va mabani-ye esteratezhi-ye jonbesh-e enqelabi-ye Iran* (Tehran: Maziyar Press, 1979).

24. For instance, see the digital map of Evin Prison produced by former political prisoners: "Evin Prison," comp. and ed. by Xavier Greenwood and Basia Cummings, *Tortoise Media*, September 7, 2020, https://members.tortoisemedia.com/2020/09/07/evin-prison-iran-interactive-map/content.html.

25. Bongah-e Ta'avun va Sana'i-e Zendanian [Institute for the Cooperation and Industry of Prisoners], *Fa'aliyat-e seh saleh-ye Bongah-e Ta'avun va Sana'i-e Zendanian* [Three years of activity of the Institution for the Cooperation and Industry of Prisoners] (Tehran: n.p., 1344/1965), 10.

26. Bongah-e Ta'avun va Sana'i-e Zendanian, *Gozaresh-e az zendanha* [A report from the prisons] (Tehran: Edareh-e Kol-e Zendanha va Chapgah-e Bongah-e Ta'avun va Sana'i-e Zendanian, 1347/1968), 24.

27. On similar processes in Latin America, see Carlos Aguirre and Ricardo D. Salvatore, eds., *The Birth of the Penitentiary in Latin America: Essays on Criminology, Prison Reform, and Social Control: 1830–1940* (Austin: University of Texas Press, 1996)

28. "Haj Mohammadi: Baraye tabdil-e zendan beh amuzeshgah-e nikiha, niazmand-e amuzgaran-e tarbiati hastim," ISNA, 26 Farvardin 1400/April 15, 2021, www.isna.ir/news/1400012615147/حاج-محمدی-برای-تبدیل-زندان-به-آموزشگاه-نیکی-ها-نیازمند-آموزگاران.

29. Rohollah Faghihi, "Enough Is Enough: Iranians Frustrated over Police Drive to Enforce Hijab-Wearing in Cars," *Middle East Eye*, October 25, 2020, https://www.middleeasteye.net/news/iran-morality-police-enforce-hijab-cars.

30. "Sotangu-ye setad-e amr be ma'ruf: gasht-e amniyat-e akhlaqi tamam shod; dar charchub-e novintar erae'h mishavad," *Radio Farda*, 15 Azar 1401/December 6, 2022, https://www.radiofarda.com/a/iran-s-propagation-of-virtue-and-the-prevention-of-vice-spokesperson-on-morality-police/32162978.html.

31. Ardeshir Avanessian, *Yaddashtha-ye zendan: Salha-ye 1928–1942* [Prison writing: The years 1928–1942] (Stockholm: Hezb-e Tudeh, 1979).

32. Angela Davis, foreword to Mojaher, *Voices of a Massacre*, xv.

33. Quoted in Manijeh Moradian, *This Flame Within: Iranian Revolutionaries in the United States* (Duke University Press, 2022), 150.

34. "U.S. Imposes Visa Restrictions on 14 Iranians over Human Rights Violations," Reuters, August 21, 2020, https://www.reuters.com/article/us-usa-iran-designations/u-s-imposes-visa-restrictions-on-14-iranians-over-human-rights-violations-idUSKBN25H2AL.

35. Ian Talley, "U.S. Sanctions Iran's Evin Prison, Broadcasting Chief, and Others, Alleging Human Rights Abuses," *Wall Street Journal*, May 30, 2018, https://www

.wsj.com/articles/u-s-sanctions-irans-evin-prison-broadcasting-chief-and-others-alleging-human-rights-abuses-1527705343#comments_sector.

36. My argument here is influenced by that of political theorist Darius Rejali, who has written on torture in Iran and in the world. Darius Rejali, *Torture and Democracy*, Princeton, NJ: Princeton University Press, 2007.

37. Bozorg Alavi, *Panjah va seh nafar* [The Fifty-three] (Tehran: Amir Kabir, 1357/1978).

38. Ervand Abrahamian, *The Coup: 1953, the CIA, and the Roots of Modern U.S.-Iranian Relations* (New York: The New Press, 2015).

39. *Iran Human Rights Monitor*, for instance, refers to Evin's "medieval equipment for torture." This is one in countless examples of such language. "A Glimpse of Evin Prison, Iran's Most Notorious Jail," *Iran Human Rights Monitor*, October 28, 2018, https://iran-hrm.com/index.php/2018/10/28/iran-evin-prison-irans-most-notorious-jail.

40. The term "prisoner of conscience" was coined by Amnesty International's founder, Peter Benenson, who first used the phrase in a 1961 article. Peter Benenson, "The Forgotten Prisoners," *Observer* (London), May 28, 1961. Amnesty International includes the full text of the article on its website: https://www.amnesty.org.uk/files/info_sheet_3.pdf.

41. On political incarceration, see Afshin Matin-Asgari, "Twentieth Century Iran's Political Prisoners," *Middle Eastern Studies* 42, no. 5 (September 2006): 689–707. For an account of Iranian torture, see Darius Rejali, *Torture and Modernity: Self, Society, and State in Modern Iran* (Boulder, CO: Westview Press, 1994).

42. Shahla Talebi, *Ghosts of Revolution: Rekindled Memories of Imprisonment in Iran* (Stanford: Stanford University Press, 2011); Behrooz Ghamari, *Remembering Akbar: Inside the Iranian Revolution* (New York: O/R Books, 2016).

43. Monira Baradaran, *Ravanshenasi-ye shekanjeh* [The psychology of torture] (Spånga, Sweden: Baran, 1380/2001).

44. See, for instance, Mohajer, *Voices of a Massacre*.

45. Ervand Abrahamian, *Tortured Confessions: Prisons and Recantation in Modern Iran* (Los Angeles: University of California Press, 1999).

46. Moradiniya, *Hekayat-e Qasr*; Khuajah and Rubayʿi, *Tarikh-e zendan dar ʿasr-e Qajar va Pahlavi*; Yaʿqub Khazaʾi, *Farayand-e sakhtyabi-ye nehad-e zendan* (Tehran: Agah, 1395/2016).

47. For "sex-related crimes" in the Iranian archive, see Jairan Gahan and Reyhaneh Javadi, "Sex, Law, and the Archives: A History from Below Using the National Archives of Iran," *Jadaliyya*, August 10, 2021, https://www.jadaliyya.com/Details/43193/Sex,-Law,-and-the-Archives-A-History-from-Below-Using-the-National-Archives-of-Iran.

48. There are myriad examples of this practice. For one, see the memoir of Abbas Samakar, who was sent to a provincial prison as punishment for organizing a hunger strike in Qasr in the 1970s. Abbas Samakar, *Man yek shureshi hastam: Khaterat-e zendan va yadbud-e khosrow Golsorkhi va Kermat Daneshian* [I am a rebel: Prison memoirs and reminiscences of Khosrow Golsorkhi and Kermat Daneshian] (Los Angeles: Ketab, 2001).

49. See, for instance, the cases of Yasaman Ariyani, Monireh Arabshahi, and Nasrin Sotoudeh, who were moved from the "security" ward in Evin to provincial prisons with common-law prisoners as punishment. "Iran Moving Women Political Prisoners to Jails with Common Criminals," Center for Human Rights in Iran, October 23, 2020, https://iranhumanrights.org/2020/10/iran-moving-women-political-prisoners-to-jails-with-common-criminals.

50. Larijani claimed that there were no political prisoners in Iran but rather those who had breached national security. "No Political Prisoners in Iran, Claims Judiciary Chief," *Radio Farda*, February 5, 2019, https://en.radiofarda.com/a/iran-judiciary-claims-no-political-prisoners-in-iran/29753080.html.

51. AI stripped Mandela of the title of "prisoner of conscience" because he contravened AI's belief that such prisoners should not "use or advocate violence." For a brief history of this affair, see "Nelson Mandela and Amnesty International," Amnesty International UK, May 18, 2020, https://www.amnesty.org.uk/nelson-mandela-and-amnesty-international.

52. Iran Human Rights Documentation Center, *Rights Disregarded: Prisons in the Islamic Republic of Iran* (New Haven, CT: IHRDC, 2015), 3.

53. Dissidents occasionally balk at the notion that they should be thought of in the same terms as "real" criminals who ostensibly deserve punishment. In presenting my argument in a talk before a group of former Iranian political prisoners, one gentleman got agitated at my call to expand the definition of political incarceration. He argued that while there is something noble about being incarcerated for one's beliefs, there is nothing noble about selling drugs or thieving. My argument hinges not on the question of the ethics of the action undertaken by the detainee, however, but the ethics, politics, and history of throwing people into cages at all.

54. The GIP's membership included both incarcerated and non-incarcerated persons. Michel Foucault and the Prisons Information Group, *Intolerable: Writings from Michel Foucault and the Prisons Information Group (1970–1980)*, ed. Kevin Thompson and Perry Zurn, trans. Perry Zurn and Erik Beranek (Minneapolis: University of Minnesota Press, 2021), 157.

55. Michelle Alexander, *The New Jim Crow: Mass Incarceration in the Age of Colorblindness* (New York: The New Press, 2012).

56. Maziyar Ghiabi, "Drugs and Revolution in Iran: Islamic Devotion, Revolu-

tionary Zeal and Republican Means," *Iranian Studies* 48, no. 2 (2015): 139–63, https://doi.org/10.1080/00210862.2013.830877; Golnar Nikpour, "Drugs and Drug Policy in the Islamic Republic of Iran," *Brandeis University Crown Center for Middle East Studies Middle East Brief*, no. 119 (June 2018): 1–7.

57. The torture and forced confessions of over two hundred men in Chicago, Illinois, between 1972 and 1991 is one recent confirmed example of systemic torture in the US. See Flint Taylor, *The Torture Machine: Racism and Police Violence in Chicago* (Chicago: Haymarket Books, 2019). For activist efforts to win reparations for the survivors of this violence, see Mariame Kaba, "Police Torture, Reparations, and Lessons in Struggle and Justice from Chicago," in *We Do This 'Til We Free Us* (Chicago: Haymarket Books, 2021), 104–9.

58. Abu-Jamal has been extraordinarily prolific in writing about his own case and in defense of other prisoners. See Mumia Abu-Jamal, *Live from Death Row* (New York: Harper Perennial, 1996); and Abu-Jamal, *Writing on the Wall: Selected Prison Writings* (San Francisco: City Lights, 2015). As of this writing in 2023, Abu-Jamal has been in prison for nearly four decades.

59. US-based movements have long used the language of political imprisonment, despite the popular conception that political incarceration is nonexistent in the US. For a collection of documents on these movements, see Matt Meyer, ed., *Let Freedom Ring: A Collection of Documents from the Movements to Free U.S. Political Prisoners* (Oakland, CA: PM Press, 2008). See also Dan Berger, *The Struggle Within: Prisons, Political Prisoners, and Mass Movements in the United States* (Oakland, CA: PM Press, 2014).

60. Stuart Hall, *Essential Essays*, 2 vols. (Durham, NC: Duke University Press, 2018).

61. Angela Davis, *Are Prisons Obsolete?* (New York: Seven Stories Press, 2003). See also Davis, *Abolition Democracy: Beyond Empire, Prisons, and Torture* (New York: Seven Stories Press, 2005).

62. Ruth Wilson Gilmore, *Golden Gulag: Prisons, Surplus, Crisis, and Opposition in Globalizing California* (Berkeley, CA: University of California Press, 2007); Ruth Wilson Gilmore, *Abolition Geography: Essays towards Liberation*. New York: Verso Books, 2022).

63. Kaba, *We Do This 'Til We Free Us*. See also Kaba's work with organizations such as Project NIA and Survived and Punished.

64. This literature is now extensive. Jackie Wang examines the predatory political economy of incarceration in the US in *Carceral Capitalism* (South Pasadena, CA: Semiotext(e), 2018); Naomi Murakawa reveals the constitutive link between the history of mass incarceration and political liberalism in the US in *The First Civil Right: How Liberals Built Prison America* (New York: Oxford University Press, 2014);

Micol Siegel argues that we must see police as "violence workers" in *Violence Work: State Power and the Limits of Policing* (Durham, NC: Duke University Press, 2018); and A. Naomi Paik establishes the link between racist taxonomies of the global war on terror and earlier modes of racialized incarceration in *Rightlessness: Testimony and Redress in U.S. Prison Camps since World War II* (Chapel Hill: University of North Carolina Press, 2016).

65. See Davis's 2015 speech, "Transnational Solidarities," delivered in Turkey at Boğaziçi University and published in Angela Davis, *Freedom Is a Constant Struggle: Ferguson, Palestine, and the Foundations of a Movement* (Chicago: Haymarket Books, 2016), 129–46.

66. Alex Vitale, *The End of Policing* (New York: Verso, 2018). For a critique of the language of policing, see David Correia and Tyler Wall, *Police: A Field Guide* (New York: Verso, 2018). For a text that uncovers the material links between policing in the US and US-trained counterinsurgency policing around the world, see Stuart Schrader, *Badges without Borders: How Global Counterinsurgency Transformed American Policing* (Berkeley, CA: University of California Press, 2018).

67. Mohajer, *Voices of a Massacre*.

68. Anahita Rahmani, "Summer 1988," in Mohajer, *Voices of a Massacre*, 34.

69. Frank Dikötter, *Crime, Prison, and Punishment in Modern China* (New York: Columbia University Press, 2001), 2.

70. Dikötter, 2–3.

71. Clive Emsley, *Crime, Police, and Penal Policy: European Experiences 1750–1940* (New York: Oxford University Press, 2006), 3. See also Clive Emsley and Louis A. Knafla, eds., *Crime Histories and Histories of Crime: Studies in the Historiography of Crime and Criminal Justice in Modern History* (Westport, CT: Greenwood Press, 1996).

72. Emsley, *Crime, Police, and Penal Policy*, 3.

73. My work builds on that of scholars of modern prisons who have also noted the reformist logic, humanist pretense, and colonial division of power informing the spread of this institution. See Bruce Adams, *The Politics of Punishment: Prison Reform in Russia, 1863–1917* (Dekalb: Northern Illinois University Press, 1996); Carlos Aguirre, *The Criminals of Lima and Their Worlds: The Prison Experience, 1850–1935* (Durham, NC: Duke University Press, 2006); Aguirre and Salvatore, eds., *The Birth of the Penitentiary in Latin America*.

74. Dikötter, *Crime, Prison, and Punishment*, 5.

75. With the exception of a series of articles written for the newspaper *Rheinische Zeitung*, which he edited, as well as a discussion on the sometimes-criminal underclass in *Capital* and the *Grundrisse*, Marx wrote little about crime or punishment. The field of "Marxist criminology" was inaugurated in the early twentieth century by a treatise titled *Criminality and Economic Conditions* by Willem Adriaan Bonger,

who was influenced by Karl Kautsky, the Austrian best known for his opposition to the October Revolution. In this work, which became influential among Marxist criminologists in his day, Bonger argued for a rigidly causal link between class conditions and criminal behaviors. While later Marxist criminologists have agreed that crime is a social and not biological issue, most have rejected the vulgar causality that Bonger advocated. See Willem Adriaan Bonger, *Criminality and Economic Conditions*, trans. H. Horton (Boston: Little, Brown, 1916). For more, see Paul Phillips, *Marx and Engels on Law and Laws* (Oxford: Martin Robertson Press, 1980). See also Karl Marx, *Capital*, vol. 1, *A Critique of Political Economy*, trans. Ben Fowkes (New York: Penguin, 1992); and Karl Marx, *The Grundrisse: Foundations of the Critique of Political Economy*, trans. Martin Nicolaus (New York: Penguin, 1993). Early Marxist criminologists, such as Otto Kirchheimer and Georg Rusche, argued that prison reforms inaugurated by figures like Bentham were not instigated by humanitarian concerns but rather by the needs of the European ruling classes. See Emsley, *Crime, Police, and Penal Policy*, 5.

76. Kent Schull's work on Ottoman prisons challenges this trend. Kent Schull, *Prisons in the Late Ottoman Empire: Microcosms of Modernity* (Edinburgh: Edinburgh University Press, 2014).

77. Mary Gibson, "Global Perspectives on the Birth of the Prison," *American Historical Review* 116, no. 4 (2011): 1040–63, http://www.jstor.org/stable/23307878.

78. This work includes several studies on the history of punishment across the global south. The best of these works includes Anupama Rao and Steven Pierce's work on colonial discipline, *Discipline and the Other Body: Correction, Corporeality, Colonialism* (Durham, NC: Duke University Press, 2006); Anoma Pieris's scholarship on forced labor and ethnic segregation in the prisons of colonial Singapore, *Hidden Hands and Divided Landscapes: A Penal History of Singapore's Plural Society* (Honolulu: University of Hawaii Press, 2009); Anand Yang's work on colonial policing in India, *Crime and Criminality in British India* (Tucson: University of Arizona Press, 1985); Samera Esmeir's text on the category of "the human" in the colonial Egyptian legal order, *Juridical Humanity: A Colonial History* (Stanford: Stanford University Press, 2012); Florence Bernault's work on convict labor in Africa, "The Politics of Enclosure in Colonial and Post-colonial Africa" in *A History of Prison and Confinement in Africa*, ed. Florence Bernault (Portsmouth, NH: Heinemann, 2003), 1–53; and Peter Zinoman's study of imprisonment in Vietnam, *The Colonial Bastille: A History of Imprisonment in Vietnam, 1862–1940* (Berkeley: University of California Press, 2001). In the Middle East context, the work of Anthony Gorman, *Prison, Punishment and Society in the Middle East, 1800–1950* (Edinburgh: Edinburgh University Press, 2023) and Laleh Khalili and Jill Schwedler's volume on prisons and policing, *Policing and*

Prisons in the Middle East: Formations of Coercion (New York: Columbia University Press, 2010), have been particularly instructive.

79. Paik, *Rightlessness*, 8.

80. Abrahamian, *Tortured Confessions*.

81. Mohammadi, *White Torture*.

82. Rejali, *Torture and Democracy*.

83. Foucault is much more interested in the lives and communities of imprisoned people in his political work as a member of the Prisons Information Group. See Foucault and the Prisons Information Group, *Intolerable*.

84. The volumes of *Book of the Street* were published over decades. Between 1979 and 1981, when Khomeini ordered the project stopped, Shamlu published five volumes. Some excerpts of this compendium, including the entry on prison slang, were published in *Ketab-e jom'eh* (Friday book), a literary journal founded by Shamlu in 1979. He would again take up the project from exile in the 1990s, where he periodically published volumes in collaboration with his wife, Ayda, until his death in 2000. As Leonardo Alishan notes, *Book of the Street* was the result of Shamlu's "love affair" with everyday language. See Leonardo Alishan, "Ahmad Shamlu: The Rebel Poet in Search of an Audience," *Iranian Studies* 18, nos. 2–4(1985): 375–422. For a reading of *Book of the Street* that links Shamlu's vernacular poetics to the work of constitutionalist writer Ali Akbar Dehkhoda, see Hamid Dabashi, *Iran: A People Interrupted* (New York: New Press, 2007), 97–98. For a piece on translating Shamlu's lexicography, see Solmaz Sharif, "Trying to Conjugate Displacement," *Kenyon Review*, December 30, 2013, www.kenyonreview.org/2013/12/trying-conjugate-displacement. I take my translation of "Ketab-e kucheh" as "Book of the Street" rather than the more literal (and common) "Book of the Alley" from Sharif's insight that the meaning of *kucheh* is better captured by the English word "street," because it represents a street poetics that the English word "alley" doesn't convey. My sincere thanks to Arash Davari for both alerting me to Shamlu's prison slang text and for finding me a copy and to Solmaz Sharif for critical conversations regarding this work.

85. Ahmad Shamlu, "Farhang-e zendan" [Prison dictionary], *Ketab-e jom'eh*, 11 Murdad 1358/August 2, 1979, 159–61.

86. Antonio Gramsci, *Selections from the Prison Notebooks*, New York: International Publishers, 1971.

Chapter One

1. Nasser al-Din Shah was king from 1848 to 1896. For more on his reign, see Abbas Amanat, *The Pivot of the Universe: Nasir al-Din Shah and the Iranian Monarchy, 1831–1896* (New York: I.B. Taurus, 2008).

2. Sir M. Durand to the Marquess of Salisbury, confidential telegram no. 51, August 14, 1896, Gulhek, inclosure in no. 1, *Statement of Mr. Tanfield*, India Office Records and Private Papers, British Library, London.

3. The company would become unpopular among both Iranians and even Brits for its poor business and labor practices. Shahbaz Shahnavaz, *Britain and South-West Persia 1880–1914: A Study in Imperialism and Economic Dependence* (New York: Routledge, 2005).

4. Abbas Amanat, *Iran: A Modern History* (New Haven, CT: Yale University Press, 2017), 129–39, 315–89; Nikki Keddie, *Qajar Iran and the Rise of Reza Khan, 1796–1925* (Costa Mesa, CA: Mazda, 2012).

5. Durand to the Marquess of Salisbury, telegram no. 51.

6. Durand to the Marquess of Salisbury, telegram no. 51.

7. Samuel Gottlieb Gmelin, *Travels through Northern Persia 1770–1774*, trans. Willem Floor (Washington, DC: Mage, 2007), 305.

8. Gottlieb Gmelin, 77.

9. Mr. Grant Duff to Sir Edward Grey, confidential telegram no. 171, received June 30, 1906, L/PS/10/100, India Office Records and Private Papers, British Library, London.

10. Firoozeh Kashani-Sabet, *Frontier Fictions: Shaping the Iranian Nation, 1804–1946* (Princeton, NJ: Princeton University Press, 1999), 80.

11. Enayat, *Law, State, and Society*, 52. See also Cyrus Schayegh, *Who Is Knowledgeable Is Strong: Science, Class, and the Formation of Modern Iranian Society* (Berkeley: University of California Press, 2009).

12. For an overview of the Tanzimat, see M. Şükrü Hanioğlu, *A Brief History of the Late Ottoman Empire* (Princeton, NJ: Princeton University Press, 2010), 72–150. For Qajar reforms compared to the Tanzimat, see Enayat, *Law, State, and Society*, 38–48.

13. Ervand Abrahamian, *A History of Modern Iran* (New York: Cambridge University Press, 2008), 9.

14. Enayat, *Law, State, and Society*, 24.

15. Abrahamian paraphrasing the memoir of Abdallah Mostowfi, a leading accountant of the Qajar era in Abrahamian, *A History of Modern Iran*, 12.

16. Reza Sheikholeslami argues that although Qajar power was decentralized, it is simplistic to call Qajar rule "arbitrary." See Reza A. Sheikholeslami, *The Structure of Central Authority in Qajar Iran, 1871–1896* (Costa Mesa, CA: Mazda, 1996). Darius Rejali makes a similar point regarding the apparently "arbitrary" nature of Qajar punishment. See Rejali, *Torture and Modernity*, 18.

17. Enayat, *Law, State, and Society*, 24. The form sharia took in Qajar Persia was that of Twelver Shi'ism—the state religion in Persia from the time the Safavid Empire introduced it as such beginning in the sixteenth century.

18. Rudolph Peters, *Crime and Punishment in Islamic Law: Theory and Practice from the Sixteenth to the Twenty-First Century* (Cambridge: Cambridge University Press, 2005), 7.

19. Rahraw Khuajah and Rubay'i, *Tarikh-e zendan*, 18–19; Abrahamian, *Tortured Confessions*, 18.

20. Fariba Zarinebaf, *Crime and Punishment in Istanbul: 1700–1800* (Berkeley: University of California Press, 2011).

21. Enayat, *Law, State, and Society*, 28.

22. Hallaq, *An Introduction to Islamic Law*, 108.

23. Hallaq, 95.

24. Abrahamian, *Tortured Confessions*, 18.

25. S. G. Wilson, *Persian Life and Customs: With Scenes and Incidents of Residence and Travel in the Land of the Lion and the Sun* (New York: Fleming H. Revel, 1895), 66.

26. C. J. Wills, *Persia as It Is* (London: S. Low, Marston, Searle & Rivington, 1886), 49–50.

27. Wills, 43.

28. Rahraw Khuajah and Rubay'i, 20–21.

29. Gottlieb Gmelin, *Travels through Northern Persia*, 77.

30. Wilson, *Persian Life and Customs*, 67.

31. Emphases in original. For this quote, see "Mr. Perkins, Missionary to Persia," *Liberator*, April 7, 1837, 58. Perkins also published a book based on his journals recounting his experiences during his eight years in Persia. See Justin Perkins, *Residence of Eight Years in Persia among Nestorian Christians: With the Notices of the Muhammedans* (Andover, MA: Allen, Morrill, and Wardwell, 1843).

32. Joseph Knanishu, *About Persia and Its People* (Rock Island, IL: Lutheran Augustana Book Concern Printers, 1899), 177–78.

33. "The Land of the Lion and the Sun: Curios Types and Customs of Persia," *Detroit Free Press*, August 17, 1902.

34. Sir John Chardin, *Travels in Persia 1673–77* (New York: Dover, 1988), 53.

35. Gottlieb Gmelin, *Travels through Northern Persia*, 39.

36. Gottlieb Gmelin, 77.

37. Wills, *Persia as It Is*, 190.

38. Ja'far Shahri, *Tehran-e qadim* [Old Tehran] (Tehran: Entesharat-e Mo'in, 1369/1997), 368–90.

39. Abrahamian, *Tortured Confessions*, 19.

40. Knanishu, *About Persia and Its People*, 172.

41. Wills, *Persia as It Is*, 12.

42. Wills, 192.

43. Wills, 11.

44. Khaza'i, *Farayand-e sakhtyabi-ye nehad-e zendan* (Tehran: Agah, 1395/2016), 76–122.

45. Ella Constance Sykes, *Persia and Its People* (New York: The Macmillan Company, 1910), 62.

46. Amanat, *Iran: A Modern History*, 241–43.

47. Abrahamian, *Tortured Confessions*, 18.

48. Wills, *Persia as It Is*, 183–84.

49. Carla Serena, *Hommes et choses en Perse* (Paris: Charpentier, 1883).

50. George N. Curzon, *Persia and the Persian Question* (London: Longmans, Green, 1892), 1:457.

51. "Penalties in Persia: Cruel but Effectual Modes of Dealing with Criminals," *The Globe*, August 24, 1885. Interestingly, much of this article is directly drawn from Wills's travelogue, *Persia as It Is*, even though it is not cited as such.

52. Wills, *Persia as It Is*, 187.

53. Wills, 188.

54. Samuel Greene Wheeler Benjamin, *Persia and the Persians* (London: J. Murray, 1887), 455–56.

55. Wills, *Persia as It Is*, 186.

56. Curzon, *Persia and the Persian Question*, 458.

57. Benjamin, *Persia and the Persians*, 405.

58. Alavi, *Varaq pareh ha-ye zendan*, 51–84.

59. See the Constitution of the Islamic Republic of Iran, https://www.wipo.int/edocs/lexdocs/laws/en/ir/ir001en.pdf.

60. Khaza'i, *Farayand-e sakhtyabi-ye nehad-e zendan*, 115.

61. Abrahamian, *Tortured Confessions*, 25.

62. *Encyclopaedia Iranica*, s.v. "Ḥājj Sayyāḥ," by Ali Ferdowsi, last modified March 1, 2012, http://www.iranicaonline.org/articles/hajj-sayyah.

63. Muhammad Ali Sayyah Mahallati, *Khaterat-e Hajj Sayyah: Dowreh-ye khawf va vahshat* (Tehran: Amir Kabir, 1977), 342–421. My sincere thanks to Naveed Mansoori for helping me locate this source.

64. Mahallati, 346.

65. Ahmad Kasravi, *Tarikh-e mashruteh-ye Iran* [The history of the Constitutional Revolution in Iran] (Tehran: Amir Kabir, 1930/1951).

66. Nazem al-Islam Kermani, *Tarikh-e bidari-ye Iranian: Jeld-e aval* [The history of the awakening of the Iranians: Volume 1] (Tehran: Amir Kabir, 1384/2005), 346–47.

67. Shahri publishes some of these in his social history, explaining that most are likely from the Constitutional period. See Shahri, *Tehran-e qadim*, 383–90.

68. W. M. Floor, "The Police in Qajar Persia," *Zeitschrift der Deutschen Morgenländischen Gesellschaft* 123, no. 2 (1973): 293–315. See also Nobuaki Kondo, *Islamic Law and Society in Iran: A Social History of Qajar Tehran* (New York: Routledge, 2017).

69. Rahraw Khuajah and Rubay'i, *Tarikh-e zendan*, 40–42.

70. Morteza Sayfi Fami Tafreshi, *Polis-e khofiyeh-ye Iran 1299–1320: Mururi bar rukhdadha-ye siyasi va tarikhcheh-ye shahrbani* (Tehran: Entesharat-e Qoqnus, 1367/1988), 66–67.

71. Edward Stack, *Six Months in Persia* (London: S. Low, Marston, Searle & Rivington, 1882), 166–67.

72. Ahmad Hooman, *Zendan va zendanian* [Prisons and prisoners] (Tehran: Chapkhaneh Daneshgah, 1339/1960), 229.

73. Arthur Arnold, *Through Persia by Caravan* (London: Tinsley Brothers, 1877), 1:221.

74. Arnold, 1:73–74.

75. E. Crawshay Williams, *Across Persia* (London: E. Arnold, 1907), 21.

76. Williams, 23.

77. "Persia & Seistan Disturbances and Consular Guard," telegram, March 29, 1906, L/PS/10/100, India Office Records and Private Papers, British Library, London.

78. "Persia & Seistan Disturbances and Consular Guard," telegram, April 1, 1906, L/PS/10/100, India Office Records and Private Papers, British Library, London.

79. "Persia & Seistan Disturbances and Consular Guard," telegram, April 1, 1906.

80. Mr. Grant Duft to Sir Edward Grey, telegram no. 118, "Persia & Seistan Disturbances and Consular Guard," telegram, April 22, 1906, L/PS/10/100, India Office Records and Private Papers, British Library, London.

81. Memorandum #35681 to the Persian chargé d'affaires, "Persia & Seistan Disturbances and Consular Guard," October 30, 1906, L/PS/10/100, India Office Records and Private Papers, British Library, London.

82. No. 174-C (Confidential), May 22, 1908, L/PS/10/100, India Office Records and Private Papers, British Library, London.

83. *Encyclopaedia Iranica*, s.v. "Gendarmerie," by Stephanie Cronin, last modified February 7, 2012, https://www.iranicaonline.org/articles/gendarmerie.

84. *Encyclopaedia Iranica*, s.v. "Gendarmerie."

85. "Penalty Severe for Theft in Persia," *Boston Daily Globe*, November 2, 1926.

86. Elahe Helbig, "Performing Violence, Displaying Evidence: Photographs of Criminals and Political Inmates in Qajar Iran (1860s–1910s)," *History of Photography* 45, no. 3–4 (2021): 264–77.

87. John Gilmour, *Report on an Investigation into the Sanitary Conditions in Persia Undertaken on Behalf of the Health Committee of the League of Nations at the Request*

of the Persian Government (Geneva: League of Nations Health Organisation, 1925), 32.

88. "Persia: An Execution in Teheran," *The Times*, January 28, 1910, 5.

89. Longtime SAVAK official Mansur Rafizadeh describes one such local public execution from his childhood in his memoir. See Mansur Rafizadeh, *Witness: From the Shah to the Secret Arms Deal, An Insider's Account of U.S. Involvement in Iran*. New York: William Morrow & Co., 1987.

90. Tafreshi, *Polis-e khofiyeh-ye Iran*, 106–7. See also Khaza'i, *Farayand-e sakhty-abi-ye nehad-e zendan*, 206–7.

91. Gilmour, *Report on an Investigation*, 32.

92. Hooman, *Zendan va zendanian*, 230. See also the entry on the Swedish officers in *Encyclopaedia Iranica*, which examines Swedish sources on the matter: *Encyclopaedia Iranica*, s.v. "Swedish Officers in Iran 1911–1915," by Mohammad Fazlhashemi, last modified August 15, 2006, http://www.iranicaonline.org/articles/sweden-ii.

Chapter Two

An earlier version of this chapter appeared in *Global 1979*, edited by Arang Keshavarzian and Ali Mirsepassi. See Golnar Nikpour, "The Criminal is the Patient, the Prison Will Be the Cure: Building the Carceral Imaginary in Modern Iran," in *Global 1979: Geographies and Histories of the Iranian Revolution*, ed. Arang Keshavarzian and Ali Mirsepassi (Cambridge: Cambridge University Press, 2021), 297–327.

1. Enayat, *Law, State, and Society*, 52. On the importance of Ottoman and Russian political thought in Iran, see Afshin Matin-Asgari, *Both Eastern and Western: An Intellectual History of Iranian Modernity* (New York: Cambridge University Press, 2018), 15–42.

2. Enayat, *Law, State, and Society*, 49–81; Janet Afary, *The Iranian Constitutional Revolution, 1906–1911: Grassroots Democracy, Social Democracy, and the Origins of Feminism* (New York: Columbia University Press, 1996).

3. Maziyar Ghiabi, *Drugs Politics: Managing Disorder in the Islamic Republic of Iran* (New York: Cambridge University Press, 2019), 40.

4. For a table of legal reform between May 1911 and June 1940, see Enayat, *Law, State, and Society*, 193–97.

5. Stephanie Cronin, ed., *The Making of Modern Iran: State and Society under Riza Shah 1921–1941* (New York: Routledge, 2007).

6. From an article written by M. Kazemi in the first issue of *Farangestan* journal in 1924. Quoted in Ervand Abrahamian, *Iran between Two Revolutions* (Princeton, NJ: Princeton University Press, 1982), 124.

7. Enayat, *Law, State, and Society*, 115–16.

8. For details on Davar, see *Encyclopaedia Iranica*, s.v. "Dāvar, ʿAlī Akbar," by Baqer ʿĀqelī, last modified November 18, 2011, http://www.iranicaonline.org/articles/davar-ali-akbar.

9. Enayat, *Law, State, and Society*, 113–44.

10. Avanessian, *Yaddashtha-ye zendan*, 7.

11. Avanessian, 7.

12. Ali Dashti, *Ayyam-e mahbas* [Prison days] (Essen: Nashr-e Nima, 2003), 8.

13. Dashti, 7.

14. "Former Minister Rahnama Reported Under Arrest," August 10, 1980, NC101220, Paris AFP, Foreign Broadcast Information Service (FBIS), South Asia Daily Report (FBIS-SAS-80-157).

15. Dashti, *Ayyam-e mahbas*.

16. Maryam Hosseini, "Zendan va zendani dar Iran" [Prisons and imprisonment in Iran], *Ganjineh* 1, no. 3–4: 44.

17. These numbers are compiled from Vezarat-e Keshvar Document # فلا12062— —ش4, National Library and Archives of Iran.

18. Hosseini, "Zendan va Zendani dar Iran," 44.

19. For a discussion of this linguistic history, see Khazaʾi, *Farayand-e sakhtyabi-ye nehad-e zendan*, 79–80.

20. *Encyclopaedia Iranica*, s.v. "Farhangestān," by M. A. Jazyeri, last modified December 15, 1999, https://iranicaonline.org/articles/farhangestan. For information on the etymology of the word *zendan* and its popularization in modern Persian, see the entry for the word in the famed Dehkhoda dictionary, accessed May 23, 2021, https://www.vajehyab.com/dehkhoda/-زندان3.

21. Tafreshi, *Polis-e khofiyeh-ye Iran*, 105.

22. Negley Teeters, *Deliberations of the International Penal and Penitentiary Congresses, Questions and Answers, 1872–1935* (Philadelphia: Temple University Bookstore, 1949), 42.

23. Evelyn Ruggles-Brise, *Prison Reform at Home and Abroad: A Short History of the International Movement since the London Conference, 1872* (London: Macmillan, 1924), 1.

24. Ruggles-Brise, 3.

25. Ruggles-Brise, 6.

26. Tarde and Durkheim presented rival sociological views. As Andrew Barry and Nigel Thrift note, "Whereas his [Tarde's] contemporary and intellectual opponent Émile Durkheim strenuously sought to demarcate the realm of 'society' from the realm of the psychological and geographical, Tarde's conception of sociology ap-

pears more generous in its scope, pointing towards the possibility of connections between the work of sociologists, psychologists and researchers in the natural sciences and humanities." Andrew Barry and Nigel Thrift, "Gabriel Tarde: Imitation, Invention and Economy," *Economy and Society* 36, no. 4 (2007): 509–25.

27. Ruggles-Brise, *Prison Reform*, 6.

28. For Markov's contribution to architecture, see Victor Daniel, Bijan Shafei, and Sohrab Soroushiani, *Nikolai Markov: Architecture of Changing Times in Iran* (Tehran: Did, 2004). For a mention of Markov's time in the Cossacks, as well as a picture of him with Reza Khan, see Stephanie Cronin, "Deserters, Convicts, Cossacks, and Revolutionaries: Russians in Iranian Military Service, 1800–1920," in *Iranian-Russian Encounters: Empires and Revolutions Since 1800*, ed. Stephanie Cronin (New York: Routledge, 2013), 143–86.

29. Tafreshi, *Polis-e khofiyeh-ye Iran*, 105–7.

30. In 2008, Qasr was turned into a museum. When first visiting the museum in 2014, I saw that signs around the grounds continued to refer to the site as *zendan-e Markov*, or "Markov's prison."

31. Abrahamian writes: "A large, tall building perched prominently on the hilltops next to an army barracks, Qasr became a symbol of both the new Pahlavi state and the modern judicial system." Abrahamian, *Tortured Confessions*, 27.

32. Rahraw Khuajah and Rubayʿi, *Tarikh-e zendan*, 104–30. For more on Dargahi, see the entry on his life in *Encyclopedia Iranica*. *Encyclopaedia Iranica*, s.v. "Dargāhī, Moḥammad," by Baqer ʿĀqelī, last modified November 17, 2011, http://www.iranicaonline.org/articles/dargahi.

33. Tafreshi, *Polis-e khofiyeh-ye Iran*, 105.

34. Bahrami, *Majaleh-ye polis*, no. 17.

35. For more on Bahrami's career, in which he held posts including mayor of Tehran, governor of several provinces, and cabinet member, see Baqer ʿAqeli, *Sharh-e hal-e rajal-e siasi va nezami-ye moʿaser-e Iran* (Tehran: Nashr Goftar, 1380/2001), 344–45. After retiring from public life in his twilight years, Bahrami traveled to Europe to study law.

36. Bahrami, *Majaleh-ye polis*, no. 17.

37. J. Rives Childs, American chargé d'affaires to the United States Secretary of State, telegram, 1935. My sincere thanks to Firoozeh Kashani-Sabet for generously sharing this source from her private archive with me.

38. Richard Halliburton, *The Flying Carpet: America's Most Dashing 1920s Adventurer Conquers the Air* (n.p.: The Long Rider's Guild, 2002), 221.

39. For a photo of the Lawrence of Arabia room at Qasr, see Pontia, "A Palace Turned Prison: A Look inside Tehran's Qasr Prison Museum," *My Persian Corner*

(blog), July 21, 2018, https://www.mypersiancorner.com/qasr-prison-museum-tehran.

40. Iranians were regaled with the exploits of characters like "Sheikh 'Ali the Murderer." See "Maktub-e Sheikh 'Ali ghatel az zendan" [Sheikh Ali the Murderer's writings from prison], *Ettela'at*, 8 Mordad 1309/July 30, 1930, 1.

41. For one instance of political writing from Qasr, see the 1952 communiqués (*elamiyeh*) from the Fadaian-e Islam regarding their imprisoned leader, Sayyid Mojtaba Navab Safavi. One of these communiqués is written by a member of the group who had gone to Qasr and claimed they would stay there "until the final hour Hazrat Navab Safavi spends in Qasr Prison." Fadaian-e Islam, "Communiqué from a Group of Visitors to Hazrat Navab Safavi Written to the Brave Muslims of Iran and the World," file no. 5-26-256, the Institute for the Study of Contemporary Iranian History Archives, Tehran.

42. For exemplary such works from this era, see Alavi, *Varaq pareh ha-ye zendan* and Alavi, *Panjah va seh nafar*. For more on Alavi's prison texts, see Abrahamian, *Tortured Confessions*, 48–72.

43. D. Amini, *Polis dar Iran* (Tehran: n.p., 1325/1946), 9.

44. Hedayatollah Hakim-Elahi, *Ba man beh zendan biyaid* [Come with me to prison] (Tehran: Sherkat-e Sehami, 1325/1946). Although Hakim-Elahi wrote numerous articles and books from the 1940s to the 1960s, there has been little scholarly notice of his work. The most in-depth engagement with Hakim-Elahi's writing, in this case with his writing on the red-light district, can be found in Jairan Gahan's recent dissertation on prostitution in Iran. See Jairan Gahan, "Red-Light Tehran: Prostitution, Intimately Public Islam, and the Rule of the Sovereign, 1910–1980" (PhD diss., University of Toronto, 2017), 165–77.

45. Hakim-Elahi, *Ba man beh zendan biyaid*, 1–2.

46. Gahan, "Red-Light Tehran," 165.

47. Hakim-Elahi, *Ba man beh zendan biyaid*, 4–5.

48. Hakim-Elahi, 74.

49. Firuz Nosrat al-Dowleh, *Majmuah-e makatibat asnad khaterat va asar-e firuz mirza firuz (Nosrat al-Dowleh)* (Tehran: Nashr-e Tarikh-e Iran, 1990).

50. Hakim-Elahi, *Ba man beh zendan biyaid*, 42.

51. Halliburton, *The Flying Carpet*, 221.

52. Hooman, *Zendan va Zendanian*, 238.

53. Hakim-Elahi, *Ba man beh zendan biyaid*, 7.

54. Rahraw Khuijah and Rubay'i, *Tarikh-e zendan*, 104–18; Hakim-Elahi, 9.

55. Dargahi's efforts are recounted in *Iran* newspaper in 1922, quoted in Tafreshi, *Polis-e khofiyeh-ye Iran*, 109.

56. Hakim-Elahi, *Ba man beh zendan biyaid*, 8–10.

57. For reference to this issue by an incarcerated militant, see Cherikha-ye Fadai-ye Khalq [The People's Fadai Guerrillas], "Zendanha-ye rezhim va zendanian-e siyasi" [The regime's prisons and political prisoners] *'Asr-e 'amal*, no. 4 (1973): 29.

58. Hakim-Elahi, *Ba man beh zendan biyaid*, 3

59. In August 1930, a writer named Abul Fath Irani wrote to *Ettela'at* with ideas for helping Iran's judges decrease their case load. See Abul Fath Irani, "Pishnehad beh vazir-e 'adliyeh" [Suggestions to the head of the judiciary], *Ettela'at*, 13 Mordad 1309/August 4, 1930.

60. Bongah-e Ta'avun va Sana'i-e Zendanian, *Fa'aliyat-e seh saleh*, 18–20.

61. Hakim-Elahi, *Ba man beh zendan biyaid*, 65.

62. Shirdel's 1960s films depict life in Tehran in gritty, noir-ish detail not unlike that of Elahi's text. Unsurprisingly, his films were not well received by the state institutions that funded them. See *Women's Penitentiary*, directed by Kamran Shirdel (1965), film. For more on Shirdel and Iran's state-funded documentary cinema, see Hamid Naficy, *A Social History of Iranian Cinema*, vol. 2, *The Industrializing Years, 1941–1978* (Durham, NC: Duke University Press, 2011), 49–146. For a feminist reading of Shirdel, see Niki Akhavan, "Nonfiction Form and the 'Truth' about Muslim Women in Iranian Documentary," *Feminist Media Histories* 1, no. 1 (Winter 2015): 89–111. For more on Iranian cinema generally, see Hamid Dabashi, *Close Up: Iranian Cinema, Past, Present, and Future* (New York: Verso Press, 2001); and Dabashi, *Masters and Masterpieces of Iranian Cinema* (Washington, DC: Mage, 2007).

63. On patriotic motherhood, see Afsaneh Najmabadi, *Women with Mustaches and Men without Beards: Gender and Sexual Anxieties of Iranian Modernity* (Los Angeles: University of California Press, 2005), 181–206. For a discussion of nationalist maternalism in Iran, see Firoozeh Kashani-Sabet, *Conceiving Citizens: Women and the Politics of Motherhood in Iran* (New York: Oxford University Press, 2011).

64. As this essay explains, "Imprisoned women and mothers constitute a significant portion of the political prisoner population . . . under the Islamic Republic." Monira Baradaran, "Children of Prison," in *Torture in The Age of Fear*, ed. Ezat Mossallanejed (Hamilton, Canada: Serephim Editions, 2005), 109.

65. "Mohemtarin khabarha-ye keshvar va jahan" [The most important news from the country and the world], *Khandaniha* 9, no. 212 (1946): 213–14. The editor of *Khandaniha*, 'Ali Asghar Amirani, was executed in 1981 despite attempting to change allegiance from the monarchy to the new clerical order. *Khandaniha* was published from September 1940 to August 1979.

66. "Mohemtarin khabarha-ye keshvar va jahan," 214.

67. Hakim-Elahi, *Ba man beh zendan biyaid*, 3

68. This interview, which aired May 9, 1968 (2 Ordibehesht 1347), is reprinted

in the literature of the state-run Institute for the Cooperation and Industry of Prisoners. See Bongah-e Taʿavun va Sanaʿi- e Zendanian, *Gozaresh az zendanha*, 36–37.

69. Hakim-Elahi, *Ba man beh zendan biyaid*, 5.

70. Hakim-Elahi, 59.

71. Hakim-Elahi, 58.

72. Ali Akbar Mahdi and Abdolali Lahsaeizadeh, *Sociology in Iran* (Bethesda, MD: Jahan, 1992), 6. For the leftist intellectual lineage of this research institute, see Matin-Asgari, *Both Eastern and Western*, 194–96.

73. *Encyclopaedia Iranica*, s.v. "Institute of Social Studies and Research," by Kazem Izadi, last modified March 29, 2012, http://www.iranicaonline.org/articles/institute-of-social-studies-and-research.

74. Ehsan Naraqi, *From Palace to Prison: Inside the Iranian Revolution* (Chicago: Ivan R. Dee, 1993).

75. Mahdi and Lahsaeizadeh, *Sociology in Iran*, 6–7.

76. Schayegh, *Who Is Knowledgeable Is Strong*, 7.

77. Iranian criminologist Parviz Saney mentions Iran's participation in his essay on criminology in the country, though he marks the date of the conference as 1951. See Saney, "Iran," 366. For the numbers on international participation, see the essay by Dennis Carroll, the London-based president of the International Society for Criminology: "International Society of Criminology," *British Journal of Delinquency* 2, no. 2 (October 1951): 162–64.

78. Khanbaba Mushar, ed., *Fehrest-e ketabha-ye chapi-e farsi* (Tehran: University of Tehran Press, 1958).

79. Abolhasan Behpur, "Zendan va zendanha" (PhD diss., University of Tehran, College of Law, Political Science, and the Economy, 1336/1957).

80. Behpur, 2.

81. Behpur, 4.

82. Behpur, 5–6.

83. Behpur, 6.

84. Behpur, 8.

85. Behpur, 10–11.

86. Behpur, 9.

87. Behpur, 12.

88. Mahmud Qahremani, "Barresi-ye qavanin-e Iran: Masuliyat az lehaz-e ravanpezeshki" [A study of Iranian laws: Responsibility from the perspective of psychoanalysis], (PhD diss., University of Tehran, 1338/1959), 1–5.

89. Qahremani, 6.

90. Ahmad Hooman, "Bimariha-ye ravani dar dadgahha-yeh keyfari-ye Iran"

[Psychological disorders in Iran's criminal courts, *Kanun-e vokala*, no. 95, Ordibehesht 1344/April 1965): 18–24.

91. Ahmad Hooman, *Zendan va zendanian*, i.

92. Hooman, iii–iv.

93. Hooman, v.

94. Taj Zaman Danesh, *Usul-e elm-e zendanha* [The fundamentals of prison science] (Tehran: University of Tehran Press, 1353/1973). See also Taj Zaman Danesh, *Keyfarshenasi va huquq-e zendanha* [Criminology and prison Law] (Tehran: University of Tehran, 1352/1973).

95. For the police academy publication of Danesh's scholarship, see Taj Zaman Danesh, *Kefarshinasi va elm-e zendanha* (Tehran: Entesharat-e Daneshgah-e Polis, Shumareh 21 [Police Academy Publishing, Number 21], n.d.).

96. Saney, "Iran," 367.

97. Mohsen Mobasser, "National Police of Iran," *International Police Academy Review* 2, no. 1 (January 1968): 13. My sincere thanks to Stuart Schrader for sharing this and other important sources revealing the links between Iranian law enforcement, particularly Mobasser, and the US State Department. See also Schrader's scholarship on the broader influence of US police and military on global policing practices. Schrader, *Badges without Borders*.

98. My argument here draws on Foucault's theory of the biopolitical. Michel Foucault, *Society Must Be Defended: Lectures at the College de France*, trans. David Macey (New York: Picador, 2003).

99. Bongah-e Ta'avun va Sana'i-e Zendanian, *Fa'aliyat-e seh saleh*, 8.

100. Bongah-e Ta'avun va Sana'i-e Zendanian, 20.

101. Bongah-e Ta'avun va Sana'i-e Zendanian, 23.

102. Bongah-e Ta'avun va Sana'i-e Zendanian, 12.

103. As Siavush Randjbar-Daemi writes, "The White Revolution was . . . carried out almost entirely within the confines of the Pahlavi elite and was significantly shaped by the latter's increasing interaction with American economic advisers." Siavush Randjbar-Daemi, "The Tudeh Party of Iran and the Land Reform Initiatives of the Pahlavi State, 1958–1964," *Middle Eastern Studies* 58, no. 4 (2022): 617–35. For more on the Ford Foundation and land reform, see Afsaneh Najmabadi, *Land Reform and Social Change in Iran* (Salt Lake City: University of Utah Press, 1988). See also Ali M. Ansari, "The Myth of the White Revolution: Mohammad Reza Shah, 'Modernization,' and the Consolidation of Power," *Middle Eastern Studies* 37, no. 3 (2001): 1–24.

104. Mobasser, "National Police of Iran," *International Police Academy Review* 2, no. 1, 11–13.

105. Bongah-e Ta'avun va Sana'i-e Zendanian. *Fa'aliyat-e seh saleh*, 5.

106. For an overview on dialectics in pre-Marxist and Marxist philosophy, see Leszek Kolakowski, *Main Currents of Marxism: Its Rise, Growth, and Dissolution*, vol. 1, *The Founders*, trans. P. S. Falla (New York: Oxford University Press, 1981).

107. Mobasser's speech is reprinted in part in the April 1967 issue of *International Police Academy Review*. See "Excerpts from Speech of Major General Mohsen Mobasser," *International Police Academy Review* 1, no. 2 (April 1967): 10.

108. Abrahamian briefly discusses this agency in his overview of the dismantling of the Tudeh Party. See Abrahamian, *Tortured Confessions*, 74.

109. From an oral history interview with Mobasser by Habib Lajavardi for the Harvard Iranian Oral History Project. Habib Lajavardi, ed., *The Memoirs of Lieutenant General Mohsen Mobasser, National Chief of Police (1343–1349)* (Tehran: Safhe-ye Sefid, 1390/2011), 16–17.

110. For a recent work contextualizing Arani's significance to Iranian political thought, see Ali Mirsepassi, *The Discovery of Iran: Taghi Arani, A Radical Cosmopolitan* (Stanford, CA: Stanford University Press, 2021).

111. Lajavardi, 17.

112. Siavash Saffari, "Taqi Erani, Bizhan Jazani, and a Marxian Framework for the Critique of Religion in Twentieth Century Iranian Political Thought," *Iranian Studies* 54, no. 5–6 (2018): 859–77.

113. Reza M. Ghods, "The Iranian Communist Movement under Reza Shah," *Middle Eastern Studies* 26, no. 4 (October 1990): 506–13.

114. Matin-Asgari, *Both Eastern and Western*, 144–89.

115. Abrahamian, *Tortured Confessions*, 89.

116. For an overview of the CIA presence in Iran, see *Encyclopaedia Iranica*, s.v. "Central Intelligence Agency (CIA) in Persia," by Mark J. Gasiorowski, last modified October 10, 2011, https://iranicaonline.org/articles/central-intelligence-agency-cia-in-persia. According to Gasiorowski, "By the time the CIA team was withdrawn [in 1960], it had trained virtually all of the first generation of SAVAK personnel. After the five-man team left Persia the CIA continued to provide specialized training to SAVAK officers on a routine though limited basis, both in Persia and in the United States.... A team of instructors from the Israeli intelligence agency Mossad replaced the five-man CIA team when it left Persia and remained until 1344 Š./1965, after which SAVAK's own instructors provided basic training to all new SAVAK recruits."

117. Ghiabi, *Drugs Politics*, 56.

118. Ghiabi, 57.

119. Mobasser, "National Police of Iran," *International Police Academy Review* 2, no. 1, 12.

120. See the Confidential End of Tour Report from Colonel Charles Maclean

Peake in which he describes his time reforming the Iranian police and gendarmerie as chief of mission, May 1959–July 1963. National Archives and Records Administration (NARA), Agency for International Development [AID], Records of the Operations Division, Records of the Africa (Near East) and South Asia Branch, subject file 1956–1972, 1–11.

121. Peake, Confidential End of Tour Report, 2.

122. Mobasser, "National Police of Iran," 12.

123. Peake, Confidential End of Tour Report, 2.

124. Peake, Confidential End of Tour Report, 3.

125. Bongah-e Taʿavun va Sanaʿi-e Zendanian, *Faʿaliyat-e seh saleh*, 6–7.

126. Bongah-e Taʿavun va Sanaʿi-e Zendanian, 6.

127. *Kayhan*, Tehran, October 23, 1967.

128. Bongah-e Taʿavun va Sanaʿi-e Zendanian, *Gozaresh az zendanha*, 1.

129. Bongah-e Taʿavun va Sanaʿi-e Zendanian, 17.

130. Richard Savin, *Vakil Abad Iran: A Survivor's Story* (Edinburgh: Canongate, 1979), 88.

131. Savin, 83.

132. Bongah-e Taʿavun va Sanaʿi-e Zendanian, *Gozaresh az zendanha*, 2.

133. Bongah-e Taʿavun va Sanaʿi-e Zendanian, 9–10.

134. For the 1975 regulatory code, see "A'in Nameh-ye Zendanha," accessed July 9, 2023, https://www.solh.ir/regulation/7/4955.

135. The government was, of course, interested in its expenditures in its prisons. See budgetary reports from the 1960s: *Qanun-e bujeh-ye sal-e 1345 kol-e keshvar* [The budget laws for 1345] (Tehran: Majles-e Shura-ye Melli, 1345/1961); *Qanun-e bujeh-ye sal-e 1346 kol-e keshvar* [The budget laws for 1346] (Tehran: Majles-e Shura-ye Melli, 1346/1962).

136. Bongah-e Taʿavun va Sanaʿi-e Zendanian, *Faʿaliyat-e seh saleh*, 10.

137. Bongah-e Taʿavun va Sanaʿi-e Zendanian, 21.

138. Bongah-e Taʿavun va Sanaʿi-e Zendanian, 23.

139. "Qezel hesar," *Mahnameh-ye shahrbani* [Monthly police journal], no. 407 (July–August 1969): 30.

140. Bongah-e Taʿavun va Sanaʿi-e Zendanian, *Faʿaliyat-e seh saleh*, 11.

141. See Newbold's introduction in Stephen C. Richards, ed., *The Marion Experiment: Long Term Solitary Confinement and the Supermax Movement* (Carbondale: Southern Illinois University Press, 2015), vii–ix. See also Stephen C. Richards, "USP Marion: The First Federal Supermax," *Prison Journal* 88, no. 1 (March 2008): 6–22.

142. Plan and Budget Organization, Statistical Centre of Iran, *Statistical Yearbook of Iran: 1352 (March 1973–March 1974)* (Tehran: Plan and Budget Organization, 1976), 162.

143. Lisa Cacho, *Social Death: Racialized Rightlessness and the Criminalization of the Unprotected* (New York: New York University Press, 2012).

Chapter Three

1. Hamid Ashraf, "An Analysis of One Year of Urban and Guerrilla Warfare: How Did the Siahkal Insurrection Begin?" trans. A. Keshavarzi (n.p., c.a. 1970s), https://www.marxists.org/archive/hamid-ashraf/works/urban-mountain.htm.

2. Yusef Zarkari, *Khaterat-e yek cherik dar zendan: Neveshteh-i az cherik-e fadai-ye khalq* (N.p.: Sazmanha-ye Jebheh-ye Melli-ye Iran dar Kharej az Keshvar [Bakhsh-e Khavar Miyaneh], 1352/1973; London: Cherikha-yi Fadai-yi Khalq Iran, 1391/2013). This citation refers to the 1973 edition; all other citations are to the 2013 edition.

3. For the argument that the mass movement of 1978–79 was mobilized around Khomeini, see Behrooz Ghamari-Tabrizi, *Foucault in Iran: Islamic Revolution after the Enlightenment* (Minneapolis: University of Minnesota Press, 2016).

4. Though less scholarly attention has been paid to the Iranian guerrillas than to their famed counterparts in Latin America or East Asia, key recent work has begun to address this lacuna. On the Marxist Fadaian, see Touraj Atabaki and Nasser Mohajer, eds., *Rahi digar: Ravayatha dar bud va bash-e cherikha-ye fada'i-ye khalq-e Iran* [Another Path: Narratives on the life and times of the Iranian Fada'i Guerrillas], 2 vols (Cedex, France: Noghteh, 2018; Ali Rahnema, *Call to Arms: Iran's Marxist Revolutionaries—Formation and Evolution of the Fada'is, 1964–1976* (London: Oneworld Press, 2021); Peyman Vahabzadeh, *A Guerrilla Odyssey: Modernization, Secularism, Democracy, and the Fadai Period of National Liberation in Iran, 1971–1979* (Syracuse, NY: Syracuse University Press, 2010). For a work on Iranian leftist movements, including the guerrilla groups, see Maziar Behrooz, *Rebels with a Cause: The Failure of the Left in Iran* (New York: I.B. Taurus, 1999). For a study of a key leftist guerrilla theorist, see Peyman Vahabzadeh, *A Rebel's Journey: Mostafa Sho'aiyan and Revolutionary Theory in Iran* (London: Oneworld, 2019). For a study of the leftist-Islamist strand in the guerrilla movement, see Ervand Abrahamian, *The Iranian Mojahedin* (New Haven, CT: Yale University Press, 1989).

5. In some cases, this stems from a postrevolutionary desire to answer the question of "what went wrong" for Iranian left and liberal movements. See, for instance, Behrooz, *Rebels with a Cause*. See also Ali Mirsepassi, "The Tragedy of the Iranian Left," in *Reformers and Revolutionaries in Modern Iran: New Perspectives on the Iranian Left*, ed. Stephanie Cronin (New York: Routledge, 2004), 229–49.

6. My argument draws from Naghmeh Sohrabi's insightful essay examining the historiography of Iran's 1979 revolution. Sohrabi notes that the Persian-language historiography of the revolution published in Iran (either supported by the state or

otherwise limited by the climate of censorship) and the English-language scholarship published outside of the country have traveled different paths. Whereas the scholarship published in Iran narrativizes events around the triumph of the Khomeinist movement with scant attention to leftist, liberal, or left-Islamist actors who may have influenced politics on the ground, "'tragedy' remains the main emplotment of the revolution's story" in the English-language historiography. Sohrabi notes the generational component to this diasporic trend, observing that "many of the scholars who created the canon of revolutionary scholarship were active in the revolution either in Iran or outside, were members of left or nationalist organizations or sympathized with it, or at the very least belong to the generation that observed the revolution in real time." Naghmeh Sohrabi, "The 'Problem Space' of the Historiography of the 1979 Iranian Revolution," *History Compass* 16, no. 11 (2018): e12500.

7. Ghamari-Tabrizi, *Foucault in Iran*, 7.

8. Adom Getachew, *Worldmaking after Empire: The Rise and Fall of Self-Determination* (Princeton, NJ: Princeton University Press, 2019).

9. At various points the OIPFG went by abbreviated versions of the name—People's Fadai Guerrillas, or Iranian Fadai Guerrillas. There have also been schisms and splinter groups of the group, including an acrimonious split in the postrevolutionary era, which saw the group divide into "majority" and "minority" factions. I use the terms OIPFG and Fadaian (the Persian plural of the singular noun Fadai) to refer to iterations of the group as it existed until 1979. Much of the literature on the group leaves the term Fadai untranslated because there is no one word in English capacious enough to fit the term's meaning or etymology. Fadai is translated literally as "those who sacrifice themselves," but has often been translated as "freedom fighters."

10. Vahabzadeh, *A Guerrilla Odyssey*, 22–23.

11. Abrahamian, *Iran between Two Revolutions*, 480–96.

12. On the theory of armed propaganda, see Vahabzadeh, *A Guerrilla Odyssey*, 38–41.

13. Michel Foucault, *Discipline and Punish*.

14. Abrahamian, *Tortured Confessions*, 112–23.

15. Vahabzadeh, *A Guerrilla Odyssey*, 29.

16. Abrahamian, *The Iranian Mojahedin*, 128.

17. "Official Charges," *Ettela'at*, February 14, 1972.

18. Moslem Students Society (U.S.A), *The Defenses of Martyred Mojahed Mehdi Rezai* (Washington DC: International Relations Bureau of Moslem Students Society [U.S.A]), 1980), 13.

19. For Sadeq's defense, see *Matn-e defa'iyeh-e mojahed shahid Naser Sadeq* [The

text of the defense of martyred mojahed Naser Sadeq] (n.p., n.d.). For Sadeq and Masoud Rajavi's statements, see *Akharin defa'at-e du nafar az sazman-e Mojahedin-e Khalq-e Iran* [Final testimonies of two members of the People's Mojahedin Organization of Iran] (n.p., 1972). For an account of this trial, see Abrahamian, *The Iranian Mojahedin*, 128–35.

20. For Taregol's defense, see Confederation of Iranian Students, National Union, *The Legacy of a Revolutionary: Targol* (Frankfurt: CISNU, 1974). See also Fan Group of the Organization of People's Fadai Guerrillas [Goruh-e havadar-e sazman-e cherikha-ye fadai khalq], *Matn-e defa'iyeh-e mobarez shahid houshang taregol goruh-e javed-e arman-e khalq,* (n.p., 1357/1978). For Paknejad's defense, see Iranian Students Association, *Paknejad: Text of Defence Speech of S. Paknejad, a Member of the 'Palestine Group' in Military Tribunal No. 3 of Tehran Dec. 1970*. (Houston, TX: ISAUS, 1976). For a postrevolution publication featuring Paknejad's defense and further writing, see National Democratic Front of Iran, *Daftar haye azadi: Beh yad-e Shokrollah Paknejad* [Freedom notebooks: In memory of Shokrollah Paknejad] (Paris: NDFI, 1985). For more on the Palestine Group, see Naghmeh Sohrabi, "Remembering the Palestine Group: Global Activism, Friendship, and the Iranian Revolution," *International Journal of Middle East Studies* 51, no. 2 (May 2019): 281–300.

21. For instance, see the biographical essay in Fan Group of the Organization of People's Fadai Guerrillas, *Matn-e defa'iyeh-e mobarez shahid houshang taregol*.

22. "Around the World: Iran Confirms Executing an Opposition Leader," *New York Times*, January 16, 1982.

23. For an insightful analysis of Taregol's and Paknejad's courtroom statements, see Arash Davari, "Indeterminate Governmentality: Neoliberal Politics in Revolutionary Iran, 1968–1979" (PhD diss., UCLA, 2016), 209–10.

24. Houshang Taregol, *Sepideh dar hal-e damidan ast: Akharin defa-ye taregol az goruh-e javed-e Arman-e Khalq dar dadgah-e nezami* (Rome: Sazman-e Enqelabi-ye Hezb-e Tudeh-ye Iran Dar Kharej az Keshvar, 1973), 8.

25. Bongah-e Ta'avun va Sana'i-e Zendanian, *Gozaresh az zendanha*, 1.

26. For an account of the trial of the Group of Twelve, see the memoir of Abbas Samakar, one of those group members given a life sentence: Samakar, *Man yek shureshi hastam*. For a brief historical account of the trial, see Behrooz, *Rebels with a Cause*, 69–70.

27. Behrooz, 69.

28. For more on Golsorkhi's statement and its resonances with Shi'a iconography, see Hamid Dabashi, *Shi'ism: A Religion of Protest* (Cambridge: Harvard University Press, 2011), 73–99.

29. For a transcript of Golsorkhi's defense, see Khosrow Golsorkhi, "Defa'iat-e

Khosrow Golsorkhi" [The defense of Khosrow Golsorkhi], reprinted in *Nazm-e novin* (New York), no. 7 (Shahrivar 1364/August–September 1985).

30. See the translation of Mojahed Mehdi Rezai's 1972 court defense, published in the US in 1980. Moslem Students Society (U.S.A), *The Defenses of Martyred Mojahed Mehdi Rezai* (Washington DC: International Relations Bureau of Moslem Students Society [U.S.A], 1980).

31. Abrahamian, *Tortured Confessions*, 103.

32. Samakar, *Man yek shureshi hastam*, 284.

33. Abrahamian, *Tortured Confessions*, 105.

34. Cherikha-ye Fadai-ye Khalq, "Zendanha-ye rezhim va zendanian-e siyasi," 30.

35. Samakar, *Man yek shureshi hastam*, 364–65

36. Hakim-Elahi, *Ba man beh zendan biyaid*, 12.

37. Sadeq Khalkhali, *Khaterat-e Ayatollah Sadeq Khalkhali* [The memoirs of Ayatollah Sadeq Khalkhali], (Tehran: Nashr-e Sayeh, 1379/2000), 179–238. Khalkhali was exiled after his involvement with the 1963 Khomeini-led protests against the shah's White Revolution.

38. Monaghah also designed several factories, university buildings, and hospitals, among other institutions. For more information on Monaghah's career in architecture, see the artist's website: http://www.monaghah.com/.

39. Abrahamian, *Tortured Confessions*, 105. See also Shekast Napazir, *Yaddashtha-e az Zendan-e Evin* [Notes from Evin Prison] (Springfield, MO: Nehzat-e Azadi-ye Iran [Kharej az Keshvar], 1355/1976), 3.

40. Zarkari, *Khaterat-e yek cherik dar zendan*, 59.

41. Jalal Rafi', *Az daneshgah-e Tehran ta shekanjehgah-e SAVAK: Goftegu ba Jalal Rafi'* [From the University of Tehran to SAVAK's Torture Chambers] (Tehran: 'Ebrat Museum, 1382/2003), 24.

42. For a moving account of the terrifying reputation the Komiteh had acquired among young dissidents in the late '70s, see Talebi, *Ghosts of Revolution*, 7.

43. Napazir, *Yaddashtha az Zendan-e Evin*, 3. For a reference to Qezel Qal'eh as the "Red Castle," see Mahmud Rezvian, ed., *Naghmehha va ash'ar-i zendanian dar band-e SAVAK* [Prison songs and poetry from SAVAK's cells] (Tehran: 'Ebrat Museum, 1388/2009), 13.

44. Hooman, *Zendan va zendanian*, 241.

45. Rafi', *Az daneshgah-e Tehran ta shekanjehgah-e SAVAK*, 33.

46. Savin, *Vakil Abad*, 88.

47. An *aftabeh* is a spouted watering can or wall hose with which Iranians cleanse themselves after answering the call of nature.

48. Samakar, *Man yek shureshi hastam*, 352.

49. Hakim-Elahi, *Ba man beh zendan biyaid*, 35.

50. Cherikha-ye Fadai-ye Khalq, "Zendanha-ye rezhim va zendanian-e siyasi," 29.

51. Anonymous, "Yaddashtha-ye zendan," in *'Asr-e 'amal*, no. 5, 85–87. See also Napazir, *Yaddashtha az Zendan-e Evin*.

52. Anonymous, "Yaddashtha-ye zendan, 30.

53. Anonymous, 30.

54. Samakar, *Man yek shureshi hastam*, 293. For a reference to Salakhanian, see Behrooz, *Rebels with a Cause*, 11.

55. For a brief reference to this poem in the context of mythologizing rank-and-file Tudeh resistance to Pahlavi torture, see Behrooz, 11–12.

56. This pamphlet was written in 1971 and published in 1972. Sazman-e Mojahedin-e Khalq, *Hushyari-ye enqelabi: vazifeh-ye yek mobarez asir dar zendan* [Revolutionary consciousness: Responsibilities of an imprisoned militant in prison] (Tehran: Sazman-e Mojahedin-e Khalq, 1972), 27.

57. Rafi', *Az daneshgah-e Tehran ta shekanjehgah-e SAVAK*, 36.

58. Sazman-e Mojahedin-e Khalq, *Hushyari-ye enqelabi*, 27.

59. Zarkari, *Khaterat-e yek cherik dar zendan*, 124.

60. For an account of discussing Shari'ati's writings in prison by a former Mojahedin prisoner, see Rafi', *Az daneshgah-e Tehran ta shekanjehgah-e SAVAK*. For more on Shari'ati's life, including his time in prison, see Ali Rahnema, *An Islamic Utopian: A Political Biography of Ali Shari'ati* (New York: I.B. Taurus, 1999).

61. Anonymous, "Yaddashtha-ye zendan." See also Samdipur, *Shekanjeh dar rezhim-e shah*.

62. Rafi', *Az daneshgah-e Tehran ta shekanjehgah-e SAVAK*, 35.

63. Quoted in Sussan Siavoshi, *Montazeri: The Life and Thought of Iran's Revolutionary Ayatollah* (Cambridge: Cambridge University Press, 2017), 81.

64. Siavoshi, 77–78.

65. Samakar, *Man yek shureshi hastam*, 291–92.

66. Zarkari, *Khaterat-e yek cherik dar zendan*, 145.

67. Personal communication with former leftist political prisoner, November 23, 2014.

68. Personal communication with former leftist political prisoner, November 19, 2014.

69. Talebi, *Ghosts of Revolution*, 6–7.

70. For more on revolutionary media, particularly Khomeini's famous cassettes, see Annabelle Sreberny Mohammadi and Ali Mohammadi, *Small Media, Big Revo-*

lution: Communication, Culture, and the Iranian Revolution (Minneapolis: University of Minnesota, 1994).

71. For a key text on the poster art of the revolution, see Peter Chelkowski and Hamid Dabashi, *Staging a Revolution: The Art of Persuasion in the Islamic Republic of Iran* (New York: New York University Press, 1999). For a more recent work, see also Hamid Dabashi, *In Search of Lost Causes: Fragmented Allegories of an Iranian Revolution* (Asheville, NC: Black Mountain Press, 2014).

72. For Marxist influences on the White Revolution, also known as the Shah–People Revolution, see Matin-Asgari, *Both Eastern and Western*, 144–89.

73. Samakar, *Man yek shureshi hastam*, 281.

74. Rezvian, *Naghmehha va ash'ar-e zendanian dar band-e SAVAK*, 39–43.

75. OIPFG, *Beh aftabkaran: Ghazalsorudeha az band* [To the sunplanters: The songs of the cell] (Tehran: [publisher unknown, n.d.). See also OIPFG, *Daftarha-ye she'r-e zendan* [Prison poetry notebooks] (n.p.: Entesharat-e Rafiq Hassan Zia Zarifi Dar Khedmat-e Cherikha-ye Fadai-e Khalq-e Iran, n.d.). See also a book of revolutionary songs popularized by religious prisoners: Mahmud Rezvian, ed., *Naghmehha va ash'ar-e zendanian dar band-e SAVAK*. Rezvian's book, like others published by institutions of the Islamic Republic, focuses only on certain prisoners at the expense of those who would become enemies of the post-1979 government but is nonetheless a useful document of revolutionary culture.

76. For a study of this movement, see Cosroe Chaqueri, *The Soviet Socialist Republic of Iran 1920–1921: Birth of the Trauma* (Pittsburgh: University of Pittsburgh Press, 1995). See also Pezhmann Dailami, "The First Congress of Peoples of the East and the Iranian Soviet Republic of Iran," in Cronin, *Reformers and Revolutionaries*, 85–117. For an appraisal of the historiography of the movement, see Janet Afary, "The Contentious Historiography of the Gilan Republic in Iran: A Critical Exploration," *Iranian Studies* 28, no. 1–2 (1995): 3–24.

77. Rasmus Christian Elling, " 'In a Forest of Humans': The Urban Cartographies of Theory and Action in 1970s Iranian Revolutionary Socialism," in Keshavarzian and Ali Mirsepassi, *Global 1979*, 145.

78. Ellis notes the importance of Brazilian revolutionary guerrilla Carlos Marighella to the Fadai theorization of the urban. Ellis, "In a forest of humans."

79. From a poem entitled "Atash" [Fire]. See OIPFG, *Beh aftabkaran*.

80. Chorgroup Munich, *Solh va danesh*, Confederation of Iranian Students, National Union 1354, n.d., 7" EP.

81. Chorgroup 1973 CISNU, *Long Live the Antiimperialistic Solidarity of the Nations of the World*, Confederation of Iranian Students, National Union 1506, 1973, LP.

82. This vinyl album was produced by CISNU in collaboration with the Indian People's Association of North America, the Committee of Democratic Kampuchean

Patriots in Canada, the Third-World People's Anti-Imperialist Committee, the Organization to Fight for the Rights of Immigrants, and the Canadian Communist League. See *Long Live International Solidarity!–Vive La Solidarité Internationale!*, Confederation of Iranian Students (National Union) et al., CF 002, 1979, LP.

83. Sazman-e Mojahedin-e Khalq, *Sazmandahi va taktikha* (Aden, Yemen: PMOI, 1353/1974).

84. These maps were often hand drawn and appeared in guerrilla publications such as '*Asr-e 'amal*, a short-lived militant publication produced in part by the Star Group (*goruh-e setareh*), the forerunner of the Organization of Communist Unity (Sazman-e Vahdat-e Kommunisti). For a reference to the provenance of this journal, see Cosroe Chaqueri, "The Iranian Left in the Twentieth Century: A Critical Appraisal of Its Historiography," *Revolutionary History* 10, no. 3 (2011): 318 f29. For an appraisal of the history of the Organization of Communist Unity, see Eskandar Sadeghi-Boroujerdi, "The Origins of Communist Unity: Anti-colonialism and Revolution in Iran's Tri-continental Moment," *British Journal of Middle Eastern Studies* 45, no. 5 (2018): 796–822.

85. Sazman-e Mojahedin-e Khalq, *Hushyari-ye enqelabi*, 4.

86. Abrahamian also notes that during the guerrilla era, unlike in the earlier torture of Tudeh members, torture was also used to elicit forced recantations and break down guerrilla psyches. Abrahamian, *Tortured Confessions*, 114–15.

87. Sazman-e Mojahedin-e Khalq, *Hushyari-ye enqelabi*, 9–10.

88. Sazman-e Mojahedin-e Khalq, 23.

89. Sazman-e Mojahedin-e Khalq, 24.

90. Sazman-e Mojahedin-e Khalq, 25.

91. Yusef Zarkari, *Khaterat-e yek cherik dar zendan*. Zarkari's memoir has recently been reprinted for the first time since its original release by members of the 1970s Fadai guerrillas who still operate in some form under that name, including most prominently Ashraf Dehqani. For this edition, see Yusef Zarkari, *Khaterat-e yek cherik dar zendan: Neveshteh-i az cherik-e fadai-ye khalq yusef zarkari*, 2nd ed. (London: Cherik-e Fadai-ye Khalq-e Iran, 1391/2013). For a reference to Zarkari's contemporaneous influence, see Anonymous, "Yaddashtha-ye zendan," 78–93.

92. Ashraf Dehqani, *Hamaseh-e moqavemat* [Epic of resistance] (Tehran: Nashr-e Mardom, 1353/1974).

93. Ashraf Dehqani, introduction to Zarkari, *Khaterat-e yek cherik dar zendan*, 23. In some texts, including the one quoted here, Yusef Zarkari's name is written as "Zarkar" instead of "Zarkari," but it is typically spelled "Zarkari."

94. Autobiographical information taken from Ashraf Dehqani's 2013 introduction to Zarkari's text, *Khaterat-e yek cherik dar zendan*, 9–27.

95. Zarkari, 33.

96. Zarkari, 45n3.

97. Zarkari, 53.

98. Zarkari, 79–82.

99. Sazman-e Mojahedin-e Khalq, *Hushyari-ye enqelabi*.

100. Personal correspondence with former leftist student activist, February 15, 2014.

101. Personal correspondence with former leftist student activist, February 15, 2014.

102. Talebi, *Ghosts of Revolution*, 7.

103. Personal correspondence with former leftist student activist, August 15, 2015. Zarkari uses the moniker "Café Saqi" in *Khaterat-e yek cherik dar zendan*, 51. He also sarcastically calls it "bashgah Sahghi," or in other words, "Saqi's flophouse."

104. Personal correspondence by the author with former leftist student, November 20, 2019.

105. Saba Mahmood, *The Politics of Piety: The Islamic Revival and the Feminist Subject* (Princeton, NJ: Princeton University Press, 2005).

106. For an English translation, see Ashraf Dehqani, *Torture and Resistance in Iran: Memoirs of the Woman Guerrilla Ashraf Dehqani* (N.p.: The Iran Committee, 1978). For a French translation, see Ashraf Dehqani, *Camarade, n'oublie pas le vol, l'oiseau est mortel: Souvenirs d'une révolutionnaire évadée de la prison du chah d'Iran* (N.p.: Commission Conjointe des Peuples Iraniens et Palestinien, n.d.). See also Gulf Committee, *Political Prisoners in the Oil States: Bahrain, Iran, Oman, Saudi Arabia* (London: Gulf Committee, 1974). This pamphlet has a section dedicated to Dehqani and her escape from prison, briefly quoting *Epic of Resistance*. For another Iranian guerrilla text that references Dehqani, see Anonymous, "Yaddashtha-ye zendan."

107. Sazman-e Mojahedin-e Khalq, *Hushyari-ye enqelabi*, 54.

108. For further biographical information on Dehqani, see her current website: www.ashrafdehghani.com. Accessed November 13, 2021.

109. Her brother was not so lucky, as he was killed in prison.

110. For one such myth-making repetition of the story, see Ashraf Dehqani, "Farar az zendan" [Escape from prison], *Tehran-e musavar*, no. 5 (1978): 54–57.

111. Abrahamian mentions the text in passing to note that it is the first prison memoir in Iran written by a woman. Abrahamian, *Tortured Confessions*, 103–4. Vahabzadeh discusses Dehqani's political career in some detail, outlining the important role she played in guerrilla history, but doesn't examine *Epic of Resistance* as a text. Vahabzadeh, *A Guerrilla Odyssey*.

112. Vahabzadeh, *A Guerrilla Odyssey*.

113. Dehqani, *Hamaseh-ye moqavemat*, 15.

114. Dehqani, 144.

115. Scott Horton, "Six Questions for Darius Rejali," *Harper's Magazine*, February 2008.

116. Abrahamian, *Tortured Confessions*, 125.

Chapter Four

An earlier version of this chapter appeared in *Humanity: An International Journal of Human Rights, Humanitarianism, and Development*. See Golnar Nikpour, "Claiming Human Rights: Iranian Political Prisoners and the Making of a Transnational Movement, 1963–1979," *Humanity: An International Journal of Human Rights, Humanitarianism, and Development* 9, no. 3 (Winter 2018): 363–88.

1. "The Shah on Israel, Corruption, Torture, And . . . ," *New York Times*, October 22, 1976, https://www.nytimes.com/1976/10/22/archives/the-shah-on-israel-corruption-torture-and.html. The shah was unhappy with the interview and tried to stop its airing through Ardeshir Zahedi, the Iranian ambassador in the US. In a telegram to Zahedi from Minister of Court Asadollah Alam conveying the shah's wishes, Alam wrote, "Many of the questions submitted by [Wallace] were of an impertinent unfriendly and provocative nature. In view of this as far as we are concerned we would prefer that this interview not be televised or given any publicity. I should be grateful if you would kindly take up this matter with competent authorities." Abbas Milani, ed., *A Window into Modern Iran: The Ardeshir Zahedi Papers at the Hoover Institution Library and Archives* (Stanford, CA: Hoover Institution Press, 2019), 266–69.

2. "Mr. Human Rights Meets King Torture," *Resistance* 5, no. 1 (December 1977): 1–2.

3. Akira Iriye, Petra Goedde, and William I. Hitchcock, eds., *The Human Rights Revolution: An International History* (New York: Oxford University Press, 2012); and Barbara Keys, *Reclaiming American Virtue: The Human Rights Revolution of the 1970s* (Cambridge, MA: Harvard University Press, 2014). In the wake of the human rights boom, much of the rhetoric surrounding human rights has painted these rights as universal, timeless, and inevitable, if differentially available in different national contexts. In the past several years, however, the field of human rights history has rethought this convention, contextualizing human rights as a phenomenon of the latter half of the twentieth century. The scholar most identified with the rethinking is Samuel Moyn, who in his book *The Last Utopia* argues that "human rights" are distinct from nationally bounded calls for rights such as the rights of man and citizen. For Moyn, human rights as a language arrived "stillborn" in the aftermath of World War II, only to be more seriously taken up in the 1970s in the context of the collapse of earlier forms of political utopianism, including revolutionary Marxisms

and Third Worldism. See Samuel Moyn, *The Last Utopia: Human Rights in History* (Cambridge, MA: Harvard University Press, 2010). This chapter takes Moyn's work as a key jumping-off point, although the Iranian story complicates his timeline by arguing that the Iranian case cannot be neatly folded into a periodization that imagines "rights talk" as representing a clean break with earlier political utopias. As this chapter shows, the history of rights talk in the Iranian case has been entangled in disparate political languages—Pahlavism, socialism, nationalism, liberalism, Islamism, communism—in historically contingent ways. For an earlier version of this argument, see Nikpour, "Claiming Human Rights."

4. Keys, *Reclaiming American Virtue*.

5. Quoted in Ahmad Faroughy, "Repression and Iran," *Index on Censorship* 3, no. 4 (Winter 1974): 9–18.

6. See, for instance, the roundtable "Problematics of Human Rights and Humanitarianism" featuring Lori Allen, Keith David Watenpaugh, Samera Esmeir, and Ilana Feldman, among others: "Problematics of Human Rights and Humanitarianism," *International Journal of Middle East Studies* 48, no. 2 (May 2016): 357–86. See also work on the human rights industry and Palestine: Ilana Feldman, *Life Lived in Relief: Humanitarian Predicaments and Palestinian Refugee Politics* (Oakland: University of California Press, 2018); and Lori Allen, *The Rise and Fall of Human Rights: Cynicism and Politics in Occupied Palestine* (Stanford, CA: Stanford University Press, 2013). For the politics of human rights in Turkey, see Elif M. Babül, *Bureaucratic Intimacies: Translating Human Rights in Turkey* (Stanford, CA: Stanford University Press, 2017).

7. Iranian Students Association, "The Shah of Iran Visits His U.S. Imperialist Bosses!," *Daneshju* [The collegian] (October 1969): 1–3.

8. One exception is the work of Matthew K. Shannon, whose chapter "The Reckoning: Human Rights, Iran, and the World" in *Losing Hearts and Minds* examines human rights in the context of Iranian student influence on US-Iran relations. While Shannon's work examines the Iranian student movement in the context of the history of education and US-Iran foreign relations, my work is more specifically invested in the longer Iranian political genealogies of rights talk and political prisoner movements. See Matthew K. Shannon, *Losing Hearts and Minds: American-Iranian Relations and International Education during the Cold War* (Ithaca, NY: Cornell University Press, 2017).

9. Reza Afshari, *Human Rights in Iran: The Abuse of Cultural Relativism* (Philadelphia: University of Pennsylvania Press, 2011).

10. Mohammad Reza Pahlavi, *Answer to History*, trans. Michael Joseph (New York: Stein and Day, 1980), 12.

11. "Shah Reportedly Bitter at Carter in Interview," *New York Times*, November 18, 1979.

12. Pahlavi, *Answer to History*, 12.

13. Fereydoun Hoveyda, interview by Frederick Peterson Jessup, 1979, transcript 30, Columbia University Oral History Collection.

14. Farah Pahlavi, *An Enduring Love* (New York: Hyperion, 2004).

15. For more on Ashraf and the elite women's movement, see Parvin Paidar, *Women and the Political Process in Twentieth-Century Iran* (New York: Cambridge University Press, 1995), 149–50.

16. Ashraf Pahlavi, *Faces in a Mirror: Memoirs from Exile* (Englewood Cliffs, NJ: Prentice Hall, 1980), 173.

17. Pahlavi, 149.

18. Kathleen Teltsch, "She May Be a Princess, but the Shah's Twin Is More Interested in Equal Rights," *New York Times*, March 22, 1970.

19. Jody Jacobs, "Party Trimmings Fit for a Princess," *Los Angeles Times*, November 10, 1974.

20. Minou Reeves, *Behind the Peacock Throne* (London: Sidgwick & Jackson, 1986), 49.

21. "Sister of Shah Hits Race Bias," *Los Angeles Times*, March 26, 1970.

22. Women's Organization of Iran, *Vali Hazrat Shahdokht Ashraf Pahlavi dar barayeh huquq-e zanan* [Her Royal Majesty Princess Ashraf Pahlavi on women's rights] (Tehran: Women's Organization of Iran, 1354/1975). For more on Princess Ashraf and the issue of women's rights, see Paidar, *Women and the Political Process*.

23. "Sister of Shah Hits Race Bias," *Los Angeles Times*.

24. For more on the conference, see Roland Burke, "From Individual Rights to National Development: The First UN International Conference on Human Rights, Tehran 1968," *Journal of World History* 19, no. 3 (2008): 275–96; Roland Burke, *Decolonization and the Evolution of International Human Rights* (Philadelphia: University of Pennsylvania, 2010), 92–111. Burke stresses that the Pahlavis used the conference to claim the importance of economic development over that of political rights and to mark out reservations with the Universal Declaration. Burke makes a compelling case for a non-Western genealogy of rights, although his accounting remains entirely grounded in the history of state leaders and the UN. I argue, on the contrary, that the language of rights has been mobilized by disparate actors in ways that the diplomatic elite could not have anticipated at the time of the 1968 conference. The groups most responsible for bringing the Third Worldist ethos to bear on the language of rights in an Iranian context were opponents of the Pahlavi state, not the Pahlavis themselves.

25. Kathleen Teltsch, "U.N. Opens Year on Human Rights," *New York Times*, January 1, 1968.

26. See UN Doc. A/Conf.32/SR.1–13 (1968), United Nations Archives, New York,

for conference proceedings. The 1968 conference was not the only time the shah would invoke the legacy of Cyrus, as he was fond of putting his government in the same symbolic universe as the kings of ancient Persia in order to elevate Iranian myth-history over Islamic (and Marxian) tropes. In 1971, at the extravagant state celebration of 2,500 years of Persian empire, the shah stood before Cyrus's tomb and declared, "Rest in peace Cyrus, for we are awake and will always stay awake." Afshin Marashi, *Nationalizing Iran: Culture, Power, and the State, 1870–1940* (Seattle: University of Washington Press, 2008), 3. For more on Pahlavi uses of Iranian myth-history, see Hamid Dabashi, *Theology of Discontent: The Ideological Foundation of the Islamic Revolution in Iran*, 2nd ed. (Edison, NJ: Transaction, 2005).

27. Quoted in Confederation of Iranian Students, National Union, *Documents on the Pahlavi Reign of Terror: Eyewitness Reports and Newspaper Articles* (Frankfurt: Documentation Centre of Confederation of Iranian Students, National Union, n.d.), 153.

28. Confederation of Iranian Students, National Union, 148–49.

29. "Tribune Tattler," *Iran Tribune* 1, no. 1 (1968): 24.

30. "Human Rights Exhibition Opens at Iran Bastan Museum," *Iran Tribune* 1, no. 1 (1968): 32.

31. These events complicate Roland Burke's argument that the Pahlavis had Third Worldist reservations about the language of human rights due to concerns regarding national self-determination. The Pahlavis were no champions of Third Worldism and were, as I show, perfectly content to use the language of rights in order to legitimize the shah's rule when expedient. The shah's use of rights talk and reference to ancient Persian kings must be understood in the context of the Pahlavi state's particular brand of decidedly non-Third Worldist nationalism.

32. Bertrand Russell, "Inside the Shah's Prisons" (Iranian Students Association of the United States, 1973), 1–4.

33. Nasrim Pakizegi, "The Shah and His Great University with a Little Help from His Friends," *Harvard Crimson*, May 25, 1976.

34. For a reference to this organization, see the August 13, 1970, article of the *Guardian* entitled "Two Killed in Iranian Prisons" reprinted in Confederation of Iranian Students, National Union, *Documents on the Pahlavi Reign of Terror*, 198.

35. Abrahamian, *Iran between Two Revolutions*, 419–95.

36. There is surprisingly little scholarship on the Iranian student movement of the 1960s to 1970s. The major historical work is a field-shaping monograph by Afshin Matin-Asgari. See Afshin Matin-Asgari, *Iranian Student Opposition to the Shah* (Costa Mesa, CA: Mazda, 2002). A new study on the US Iranian Student Association by Manijeh Moradian charts the world of students as they struggled not only for freedom in Iran but also made connections with revolutionary causes in the US,

including the Black Panthers and the Palestinian freedom movement. See Manijeh Moradian, *This Flame Within: Iranian Revolutionaries in the United States* (Durham, NC: Duke University Press, 2022). See also the work of Matthew K. Shannon, "'Contacts with the Opposition': American Foreign Relations, the Iranian Student Movement, and the Global Sixties," *The Sixties: A Journal of History, Politics, and Culture* 4, no. 1 (2011).

37. Matin-Asgari, *Iranian Student Opposition to the Shah*, 1.

38. For Iranian solidarity with Third Worldist and Black power movements, see Moradian, *This Flame Within*, 128–75.

39. Matin-Asgari, *Iranian Student Opposition to the Shah*, 58.

40. CISNU was plagued by sectarianism, with splits between Maoists, Marxist-Leninists, Islamists, nationalists, and those professing eclectic mixtures of the above. For these splits, see *Encyclopaedia Iranica*, s.v. "Confederation of Iranian Students, National Union," by Afshin Matin-Asgari, last modified October 28, 2011, www.iranicaonline.org/articles/confederation-of-iranian-students.

41. *Encyclopaedia Iranica*, s.v. "Confederation of Iranian Students, National Union."

42. Tudeh Party, *SAVAK: Police secrète du chah* (Paris: Comité Central du Parti Toudeh d'Iran, 1976); Nasser Kanani, *SAVAK: Der Iranische Geheimdienst Eine Dokumentation* (Münster: Periferia Verlag, 1979); Confederation of Iranian Students, National Union, *Kampf der Tätigkeit des SAVAK in der BRD: Dokumentation: Wie die Bundesregierung die Tätigkeit der Mörderbande des Faschistischen Schah-Regimes SAVAK in der BRD und Westberlin Duldet und Unterstützt* (Darmstadt: Föderation Iranischer Studenten, 1977).

43. Confederation of Iranian Students, National Union, *Dar barayeh SAVAK* [About SAVAK] (N.p.: Confederation of Iranian Students, National Union, n.d.), 3–4.

44. Confederation of Iranian Students, National Union, 3–4.

45. National Democratic Front of Iran, *Daftar haye azadi*.

46. Confederation of Iranian Students, National Union, *Dar barayeh SAVAK*, 3–5. See also National Front, *Pareh-i az asrar-e sazman-e "amniyat" (SAVAK)* (N.p.: Jebheh-ye Melli [Kharej Az Keshvar], 1350/1971).

47. Confederation of Iranian Students, National Union, *Dar barayeh SAVAK*, 5.

48. Iranian Students Association in the US, *Defend the 41*, ISAUS, 1973, 1.

49. Unite! Bookstore, "Support the Iran Revolution, Expose Carter's 'Human Rights' Policy!," flyer for event with ISAUS and the International Association for Filipino Patriots (Oakland, CA, n.d.)

50. For several references to Newens and the British Committee for the Defense of Political Prisoners, see numerous sources collected in Confederation of Iranian Students, National Union, *Documents on the Pahlavi Reign of Terror*.

51. Two attempts were made on the shah's life, first in 1949 and then in 1965.

These attempts were of major consequence for the Iranian political landscape. The shah blamed the 1949 attempt on the Tudeh Party, leading to the systematic suppression of the party. Similarly, the 1965 attempt was linked to leftist student activism in Europe.

52. Abrahamian, *Tortured Confessions*, 114.

53. Confederation of Iranian Students, National Union, *Documents on the Pahlavi Reign of Terror*, 46.

54. Confederation of Iranian Students, National Union, 81.

55. An *Ettela'at* editorial also implies that some of the MPs are secretly homosexuals. Confederation of Iranian Students, National Union, 92.

56. Confederation of Iranian Students, National Union, 100.

57. "Secret Message from Simon to Bristol," SAVAK #332–1274, 6 Shahrivar 1354 / 28 August 1975. A photocopy of this SAVAK archival source was shared with me by a former prisoner. My sincere thanks to that generous individual for sharing this valuable source with me.

58. Parviz C. Radji, *In the Service of the Peacock Throne: The Diaries of the Shah's Last Ambassador to London* (London: Hamish Hamilton, 1983), 85.

59. Radji, 85.

60. Confederation of Iranian Students, National Union, *Documents on the Pahlavi Reign of Terror*, 65–69.

61. Abrahamian, *Tortured Confessions*, 114.

62. Russell, "Inside the Shah's Prisons," 4.

63. James Becket, "Torture as an Institution," *New York Times*, August 4, 1972.

64. Keys, *Reclaiming American Virtue*.

65. As AI reported: "The first year of the campaign was successful in publicizing the widespread use of torture, in collecting more than a million signatures from all over the world in support of an anti-torture resolution in the United Nations, and in obtaining the unanimous passage of that resolution, General Assembly Resolution 3059 (XX–VIII), which calls on all governments 'to become parties to existing international instruments which contain provisions relating to the prohibition of torture and other inhuman or degrading treatment or punishment.'" Amnesty International, *Amnesty International Report on Torture* (New York: Farrar, Straus & Giroux, 1975), 7.

66. Amnesty International, 228.

67. Amnesty International, *Iran: An Amnesty International Briefing* (London: Amnesty International, 1976), 8.

68. Hajebi Tabrizi was an important, dedicated, and complex revolutionary figure whose life—which took her from Tehran to Venezuela to Algeria to Paris—deserves serious appraisal in the broader context of Iranian revolutionary Marxism.

Later in her life, Hajebi Tabrizi wrote extensively about her prison and political experiences. For her collected oral histories of the incarcerated female dissidents she met in the 1970s, see Vida Hajebi Tabrizi, *Dad va bidad: Nakhostin zendan-e zanan-e siasi* (Tehran: Entesharat-e Baztabnegar), 2004. See also her memoir, *Yadha* (Koln: Forough Books 1389/2010). For a brief analysis of Hajebi Tabrizi's life written by an scholar and socialist who advocated on her behalf in the 1970s, see Kamran Nayeri, "Vida Hadjebi Tabrizi: Her Life and Times," *Our Place in the World, a Journal of Ecosocialism*, March 25, 2017, http://forhumanliberation.blogspot.com/2017/03/2585-vida-hadjebi-tabrizi-her-life-and.html.

69. "Human Rights: Torture and Policy: The Network of Evil," *Time Magazine*, August 16, 1976.

70. William J. Butler and Georges Levasseur, *Human Rights and the Legal System in Iran: Two Reports* (Geneva: International Commission of Jurists, 1976), 9.

71. Butler and Levasseur, *Human Rights and the Legal System in Iran*, 10. For more on Heldmann's activism on Iranian prisons in Germany, see Quinn Slobodian, *Foreign Front: Third World Politics in 1960s West Germany* (Durham, NC: Duke University Press, 2012). Slobodian argues that German activists were mobilized by radical third-world students, including Iranians, on German campuses.

72. Butler and Levasseur, *Human Rights and the Legal System in Iran*, 10–11.

73. Butler and Levasseur, 11.

74. In *The Times*, Negahdar defended his actions by saying, "I knew I was doing something illegal which could have landed me in gaol, but I nevertheless carried on with my plans for I firmly believe in the principle of the National Front." "From Our Correspondent: Confessions Alleged over Iran plot," *The Times*, January 3, 1969, 4.

75. *Irandefence: News Bulletin of the Organisation for the Defence of Human Rights in Iran* 6, no. I (1976): 8.

76. Butler and Levasseur, *Human Rights and the Legal System in Iran*, 12–14.

77. "Hossein Rezai: Iran," *Amnesty International Newsletter* 1, no. 7 (July 1971): 3.

78. Confederation of Iranian Students, National Union, *Documents on the Pahlavi Reign of Terror*, 220

79. See the letter written by Wilson to the *Guardian* on the matter in April 1971, reprinted in full in Confederation of Iranian Students, National Union, *Documents on the Pahlavi Reign of Terror*, 241

80. "Hossein Rezai: Iran,", 3. For a brief mention of the Rezai case, see Jonathan Power, *Like Water on Stone: The Story of Amnesty International* (Boston, MA: Northeastern University, 2001), 144. At this same trial, Iran allowed an observer from the International Federation of Human Rights to attend. See Butler and Levasseur, *Human Rights and the Legal System in Iran*, 13.

81. Aside from Iran, Butler's activism also focused on places including Burundi,

South Africa, and the Philippines. For an account of Butler's engagement with Iran, see James A. Bill, *The Eagle and the Lion: The Tragedy of American-Iranian Relations* (New Haven, CT: Yale University Press, 1988). Bill is himself an important figure, as he had a crucial role in educating US policy circles on the shah's Iran. Bill, along with fellow Iran expert Martin Zonis, attempted to outline what they saw as the shah's shaky footing in several reports to the State Department.

82. Bill, *The Eagle and the Lion*, 246. For more on AI's preference for liberal causes, see Keys, *Reclaiming American Virtue*, 75–102.

83. Victor A. Lusinchi and Eric Pace, "Torture and Denials of Rights Laid to Iran by Jurists' Group," *New York Times*, May 29, 1976.

84. For more on Fraser's subcommittee, see Keys, *Reclaiming American Virtue*. For more on Fraser, Butler, and Iran, see Shannon, *Losing Hearts and Minds*, 128–29.

85. Quoted in Robert C. De Camara, "The Shah as Tyrant: A Look at the Record," *Washington Post*, March 23, 1980. De Camara's op-ed was initially published in the conservative journal the *National Review* and reprinted in the *Washington Post*. Like others who wrote for the *National Review*, De Camara believed reports of Pahlavi violence were overblown.

86. Shannon, *Losing Hearts and Minds*, 130.

87. Radji, *In the Service of the Peacock Throne*, 20.

88. See, for instance, the front-page polemic sardonically entitled "Mr. Human Rights Meets King Torture" in a 1977 issue of *Resistance*, the newspaper of the ISAUS.

89. Richard W. Cottam, "Human Rights in Iran under the Shah," *Case Western Reserve Journal of International Law*, no. 121 (1980): 121–36.

90. Bill, *The Eagle and the Lion*, 223.

91. Cottam, "Human Rights in Iran," 134.

92. Radji, *In the Service of the Peacock Throne*, 84–85.

93. Talebi, *Ghosts of Revolution*, 7.

94. The organization is now known as PEN International.

95. Despite his celebrity, Baraheni's prison texts have gone largely unnoted by scholars. One exception is Darius Rejali's *Torture and Modernity*, which argues that Baraheni is among the Iranian intellectuals—alongside Jalal al-e Ahmad and Gholam Hossein Saedi—who try to answer the question of how Iranians came to be torturers. See Rejali, *Torture and Modernity*, 143.

96. Baraheni testified before the Subcommittee on International Organizations, House Committee on International Relations on October 28, 1976. For more on his testimony, see Shannon, *Losing Hearts and Minds*, 130–31.

97. See, for instance, Baraheni's exchange in the *New York Review of Books* in 1976 with Gregg E. Gorton, then the associate editor of *Praxis*, a journal for leftist

views on the arts. Baraheni and Gorton agreed on the need for artists, writers, and intellectuals to engage in an "active boycott" of Iranian events, while Baraheni outlined efforts he had made to date in convincing artists to engage in such boycotts, including events held in the US but paid for in part or in full by the shah's government. Reza Baraheni and Gregg E. Gorton, "Iran Boycott; An Exchange," *New York Review of Books*, November 25, 1976, https://www.nybooks.com/articles/1976/11/25/iran-boycott-an-exchange.

98. Negar Azimi, "Good Intentions," *Frieze*, March 11, 2011, https://www.frieze.com/magazines/frieze-magazine/issue-137. For some of these debates, see Victor S. Navasky, "Boycott: The Moral Question, the Political Question, the Practical Question," *New York Times*, August 15, 1976.

99. For a reproduction of this letter, and the letter from Marshall, Leon, Weill, and Mahony to Zahedi, see Milani, ed., *A Window into Modern Iran*, 284–91.

100. Mozaffari Nahid, ed., *Strange Times, My Dear: The PEN Anthology of Contemporary Iranian Literature* (New York: Arcade, 2005), 416.

101. Solzhenitsyn's opus was championed by anticommunists the world over and derided by those who were pro-Soviet. Yet the *Gulag Archipelago* was also an important text for those Marxist intellectuals who did not share Solzhenitsyn's emergent conservative nationalist romanticism but were nonetheless critical of the gulag. See the review by anti-Stalinist Marxist Roy Medvedev, first published in English in 1974. Roy Medvedev, "On Solzhenitsyn's 'Gulag Archipelago,' " *Index on Censorship* 3, no. 2 (1974), https://doi.org/10.1080/030642274085323. See also Boris Frankel, "The 'Gulag Archipelago' and the Left," *Theory and Society* 1, no. 4 (Winter 1974): 477–95. Frankel makes the bold if now forgotten claim that "the only audience which can have a critically meaningful relationship to Solzhenitsyn's document is the Marxist Left" (478).

102. Doctorow, introduction to *The Crowned Cannibals: Writing on Repression in Iran*, by Reza Baraheni (New York: Random House, 1977, ix.

103. Doctorow, xi.

104. Quoted in Reza Baraheni, *God's Shadow: Prison Poems* (Bloomington, IN: Indiana University Press, 1976), 25.

105. In his writing, Baraheni doesn't mention this forced confession, which was played on radio and published in newspapers in Iran. He only references the international advocacy on his behalf: "I am grateful to all the American writers and poets who made my release possible. Their efforts were led by Jerzy Kosiński, president of the US chapter of PEN, and eventually were taken up by my Iranian friends in CAIFI." Baraheni, 10. For Baraheni's confession, see Abrahamian, *Tortured Confessions*, 116.

106. For an example of CAIFI's influence among US intellectuals, see Kate Millett's Iran travelogue, in which she calls her work with CAIFI "one of the most important things I've done": Kate Millett, *Going to Iran* (New York: Coward, McCann & Geoghegan, 1982), 4. For more on Millett, Baraheni, and CAIFI's work together, see Patricia Steulke, *The Ruse of Repair: US Neoliberal Empire and the Turn from Critique* (Durham, NC: Duke University Press, 2021), 44. Steulke notes that there was mistrust between the Iranian student movement abroad and Baraheni. Indeed, there was sectarian antagonism between Marxist-Leninist and Stalinist factions of the student movement and the Trotskyist CAIFI. For a mention of CAIFI and Iranian Trotskyism in the context of global Trotskyism, see Robert Jackson Alexander, *International Trotskyism, 1929–1985: A Documented Analysis of the Movement.* (Durham, NC: Duke University Press, 1991), 558–66.

107. Baraheni, *God's Shadow*, 25.

108. Reza Baraheni, "Terror in Iran," *New York Review of Books,* October 28, 1976; Reza Baraheni, "Torture in Iran: 'It Is a Hell Made for One Man by Another Man,'" *New York Times*, April 21, 1976.

109. Reza Baraheni, "The SAVAK Documents," *The Nation*, February 23, 1980, 198–202.

110. Baraheni, *The Crowned Cannibals: Writing on Repression in Iran* (New York: Random House, 1977), 12.

111. Baraheni, 26.

112. Richard Sale, "Baraheni: An Angry Voice From Iran," *New York Times*, September 4, 1977.

113. Baraheni, *The Crowned Cannibals*, 164. The Komiteh, or Komiteh-ye Moshtarek-e Zedd-e Kharabkar (Joint Anti-Sabotage Committee), was among the most notorious interrogation centers in Tehran in the prerevolutionary era. For more on its history, see chapter 5.

114. Al-e Ahmad is among the most widely read twentieth-century Iranian intellectuals. The scholarship on his most well-known work, *Westoxification*, is vast, in part because Al-e Ahmad has been championed by the Islamic Republic as a theorist of the revolution. As such, he has often been read as a nativist. See Mehrzad Boroujerdi, *Iranian Intellectuals and the West: The Tormented Triumph of Nativism* (Syracuse, NY: Syracuse University Press, 1996); and Ali Mirsepassi, *Political Islam, Iran, and the Enlightenment: Philosophies of Hope and Despair* (New York: Cambridge University Press, 2010). For a more generous reading of the entirety of Al-e Ahmad's oeuvre, see Dabashi, *Theology of Discontent*, 39–101. See also Hamid Dabashi, *The Last Muslim Intellectual: The Life and Legacy of Jalal Al-e Ahmad* (Edinburgh: Edinburgh University Press, 2022). For a key rethinking of *Gharbzadegi* in the context of

the global color line and capitalist colonialism, see Eskandar Sadeghi-Boroujerdi, "Gharbzadegi, Colonial Capitalism, and the Racial State in Iran," *Postcolonial Studies* 24 (2020): 173–94.

115. Baraheni, *The Crowned Cannibals*, 82.

116. Baraheni, 83–84.

117. Tim O'Brien, *Going after Cacciato* (1978; reprint, New York: Broadway Books, 1999).

118. John M. Jakaitis, "Two Versions of an Unfinished War: 'Dispatches' and 'Going after Cacciato,'" in "American Representations of Vietnam," special issue, *Cultural Critique*, no. 3 (Spring 1986): 191–210; Katherine Kinney, "American Exceptionalism and Empire in Tim O'Brien's 'Going after Cacciato,'" *American Literary History* 7, no. 4 (Winter 1995): 633–53.

119. Public executions had been abandoned in Iran by which point O'Brien was writing in late 1970s, though they would reappear during the 1979 revolution.

120. O'Brien, *Going after Cacciato*, 189.

121. O'Brien, 185.

122. O'Brien, 190.

123. Warhol confidante Bob Colacello notes the affair in his memoir. Bob Colacello, *Holy Terror: Andy Warhol Up Close* (New York: Vintage, 2014).

124. Alexander Cockburn, James Ridgeway, and Jan Albert, "The Beautiful Butchers: The Shah Serves Up Caviar and Torture," *Village Voice*, November 14, 1977.

125. Ghamari-Tabrizi, *Foucault in Iran*, 19–53.

126. Ruhollah Khomeini, *Islam and Revolution: Writings and Declarations of Imam Khomeini*, trans. Hamid Algar (Berkeley, CA: Mizan Press, 1981), 213–15.

127. Khomeini, *Islam and Revolution*, 213.

128. "Paper Urges Ties with Dispossessed," *Kayhan International*, May 5, 1990, trans. Foreign Broadcast Information Service (FBIS), Middle East and North Africa Daily Report (FBIS-NES-01-097), 45.

129. For a reference to this group, see Abrahamian, *Iran between Two Revolutions*, 503. Unsurprisingly, given Bazargan's political roots in the National Front, the ICDFHR was predominantly liberal-nationalist, including some Islamic liberals like Bazargan. See Cottam, "Human Rights in Iran," 134.

130. See Lahidji's biography on his personal webpage for the International Federation of Human Rights, "Abdol-Karim Lahidji, President of FIDH – International Federation for Human Rights," https://www.fidh.org/IMG/pdf/bio_karim_long_en.pdf.

131. Ali Asghar Javadi, *Nameh-ha* [Letters] (Tehran: Tandur, 1357/1978).

132. Firoozeh Kashani-Sabet notes the use of terms like *huquq-e ensan* and

huquq-e bashar in discourses of the 1905–11 Constitutional era. See Kashani-Sabet, *Conceiving Citizens*, 109–10.

133. Javadi, *Nameh-ha*, 2–3.

134. Index on Censorship,: *The News Bulletins of the Committee for the Defence of Political Prisoners in Iran* (London: Index on Censorship, 1979), v.

135. Committee for Human Rights in Iran, *Letters from the Great Prison: An Eyewitness Account of Human and Social Conditions in Iran* (Washington, DC: CHRI, 1978).

136. An Index on Censorship pamphlet claims, "The first open dissent came from people like Ali Asqar Javadi.... Soon there followed a flood of protest literature from individuals and groups." Index on Censorship, *The Iranian Bulletins*, v.

137. Doc. 1278411, "Sazman-e ghaza'i-ye artesh-e jomhuri-ye islame (dadsetani), 3/12/1358" (6/2/1979). In an earlier version of this chapter, I linked this source both to the nascent Islamic Republic government and to the ICDFHR. In fact, this source was not linked to the latter organization. The original document is from the private collection of a former political prisoner who was imprisoned for several years in the late Pahlavi era. I would like to express my sincere gratitude to this generous individual for showing me this personal material.

Chapter Five

1. There is a vast literature on the revolution. For some key texts, see Charles Kurzman, *The Unthinkable Revolution in Iran* (Cambridge, MA: Harvard University Press, 2005); Ervand Abrahamian, *Iran between Two Revolutions*; Nikki Keddie, *Modern Iran: Roots and Results of Revolution* (New Haven, CT: Yale University Press, 2003); Said Amir Arjomand, *The Turban for the Crown: The Islamic Revolution in Iran* (New York: Oxford University, 1989); Roy Mottahadeh, *The Mantle of the Prophet: Religion and Politics in Iran* (New York: Oneworld, 1985); Asef Bayat, *Workers and Revolution in Iran* (London: Zed, 1987); Misagh Parsa, *Social Origins of the Iranian Revolution* (New Brunswick, NJ: Rutgers University Press, 1989); and Dabashi, *Theology of Discontent*.

2. Michael Axworthy, *Revolutionary Iran: A History of the Islamic Republic* (New York: Oxford University Press, 2013), 1–14.

3. Abrahamian, *Iran between Two Revolutions*, 526.

4. For a revealing meditation on the archive of the revolution through an analysis of a photo of scattered files after the takeover of a police station in February 1979, see Naghmeh Sohrabi, "In Search of Iran's Revolutionary Archives," *Jadaliyya*, October 4, 2021, https://www.jadaliyya.com/Details/43281/In-Search-of-Iran%E2%80%99s-Revolutionary-Archives.

5. "Forces Occupy Evin Prison," February 12, 1979, LD120505 Tehran Domestic

Service in Persian, trans. Foreign Broadcast Information Service (FBIS), Middle East and North Africa Daily Report (FBIS-MEA-79–030), R33.

6. "Group Heading to Evin Prison," February 11, 1979, LD112108, Iran: Tehran Reports Incidents, Events of 11 February, trans. Foreign Broadcast Information Service (FBIS), Middle East and North Africa Daily Report (FBIS-MEA-79-030), R26.

7. "Evin Prison," February 12, 1979, LD120254 Tehran Domestic Service in Persian, trans. Foreign Broadcast Information Service, Middle East and North Africa Daily Report (FBIS-MEA-70-030), R31.

8. After the first amnesties of incarcerated dissidents in 1976–77, which were the result of the global pressure on the Pahlavi government detailed in the previous chapter, about three thousand incarcerated dissidents remained in Pahlavi prisons. See Abrahamian, *Tortured Confessions*, 120.

9. Behrooz Ghamari Tabrizi, personal correspondence with the author, February 11, 2023.

10. This Pars news report then requested that anyone with welding know-how "go immediately to the prison together with acetylene welding equipment" to help the trapped revolutionaries. "Report on Evin Prison," February 12, 1979, LD120820 Tehran Domestic Service in Persian, trans. Foreign Broadcast Information Service, Middle East and North Africa Daily Report (FBIS-MEA-70-030), R37.

11. Richard T. Sale, "SAVAK: A Feared and Pervasive Force," *Washington Post*, May 9, 1977, https://www.washingtonpost.com/archive/politics/1977/05/09/savak-a-feared-and-pervasive-force/ad609959-d47b-4b7f-8c8d-b388116df90c.

12. About one hundred of these detainees were held in solitary confinement. See Abrahamian, *Tortured Confessions*, 105.

13. Shaul Bakhash, *The Reign of the Ayatollahs: Iran and the Islamic Revolution* (New York: Basic, 1985), 102.

14. Radio Farda, "Exclusive: Leaked Documents from Iran's Notorious Evin Prison Reveal Plight of Inmates," *Radio Free Europe/Radio Liberty*, November 3, 2021, https://www.rferl.org/a/iran-evin-prison-leaked-documents/31544336.html.

15. Ann Harrison, "A Birthday in Evin Prison: An Opportunity to Remember Iran's Prisoners," Amnesty International, June 10, 2010, https://www.amnestyusa.org/a-birthday-in-evin-prison-an-opportunity-to-remember-irans-prisoners.

16. "Evin Prison Fire: Several Dead after Fire at Iran's Notorious Detention Center," *BBC News*, October 16, 2022, https://www.bbc.com/news/world-asia-63271817.

17. Countries with higher totals of incarcerated persons are, in order, the US, China, Russia, Brazil, India, Thailand, and Mexico. The US remains an outlier both in total number of detainees and in per-capita rates of incarceration. See Roy Walsmsley, *World Prison Population List*," 11th ed., Institute for Criminal Policy Research,

2015, www.prisonstudies.org/sites/default/files/resources/downloads/world_prison_population_list_11th_edition_0.pdf.

18. "Iran: 333% Increase of Prison Populace in 30 Years," *Prison Insider*.

19. Abbas Abdi, *Tasir-e zendan bar zendani: Asibshenasi-ye ejtema'i* (Tehran: Nur, 1387/2008).

20. "Iran: 333% Increase of Prison Populace in 30 Years," *Prison Insider*.

21. "Ghabl az enqelab 16 hezar zendani dashteh-im ama aknun 240 hezar zendani darim" [Before the revolution we had 16 thousand prisoners but now we have 240 thousand prisoners], *E'temad Online*, accessed July 10, 2023, https://etemadonline.com/content/516808/قبل-از-انقلاب-16--هزار-زندانی-داشته-ایم-اما-اکنون-240-هزار-زندانی-داریم-که-وضعیت-اسف-باری-است-بوروکرا.

22. "Head of Prison Service Holds News Conference," December 23, 1986, PM061633, Tehran Keyhan in Persian, trans. Foreign Broadcast Information Service (FBIS), South Asia Daily Report (FBIS-SAS-87-004).

23. Ghiabi, *Drugs Politics*, 80.

24. Iran Human Rights Documentation Center, *Imprisonment for Debt*, 3, accessed August 14, 2021, https://tbinternet.ohchr.org/Treaties/CCPR/Shared%20Documents/IRN/INT_CCPR_ICS_IRN_42314_E.pdf. Iran's debtors' prisons were dramatized in Oscar-winning filmmaker Asghar Farhadi's drama *A Hero*.

25. "Zendan bozorg Tehran pazirai-ye 15 hezar nafar mi shavad," 12 Ordibehesht 1395/May 1, 2016, https://www.khabaronline.ir/news/148249/زندان-بزرگ-تهران-پذیرای-15--هزار-زندانی-می-شود.

26. "Saleh Abad: Former Inmates Say They Were Held in Cow Stalls," *Amnesty International Newsletter* 13, no. 2 (February 1983): 5; Amnesty International, *Torture in the Eighties* (London: Amnesty International, 1984), 231.

27. For the body of the bill changing prison administration in 1986, see "Qanun-e tabdil shura-ye sarparasti zendanha," accessed July 9, 2023, http://www.dastour.ir/brows/?lid=124750.

28. Carl Anthony Wege, "Iranian Counterintelligence," *International Journal of Intelligence and Counterintelligence* 32, no. 2 (2019): 272–94.

29. "Chairman of Prisons Organization Hopes to Prevent Death under Torture in Prisons," *Iran International*, November 25, 2019, https://iranintl.com/en/iran/chairman-prisons-organization-hopes-prevent-death-under-torture-prisons.

30. "Supreme Judicial Council on Detention Centers," November 2, 1987, LD022035, Tehran Domestic Service in Persian, trans. Foreign Broadcast Information Service (FBIS), Near East and South Asia Daily Report (FBIS-NES-87-212), 63.

31. For Iran's criminal code of procedure, which includes bail and parole processes, see "English Translation of the Islamic Republic of Iran's Criminal Code of Procedure

for Public and Revolutionary Courts," Iran Human Rights Documentation Center, December 22, 2011, https://iranhrdc.org/english-translation-of-the-islamic-republic-of-irans-criminal-code-of-procedure-for-public-and-revolutionary-courts/.

32. Not all migrants in Iran live in camps. There are millions of refugees in the country, many of whom have documentation and who are integrated into Iranian communities and economies. See Xavier Creach and Jack Redde, "Iraqi Refugees Heed Call of Home over Comforts of Camp," United Nations Refugee Agency, May 2003, https://www.unhcr.org/en-us/news/latest/2003/5/3ec7532a2/iraqi-refugees-heed-call-home-comforts-camp-iran.html.

33. Arash Davari, Naveed Mansoori, Golnar Nikpour, and Omid Tofighian, "Is Abolition Global? Iran, Iranians, and Prison Politics (Part I)," *Jadaliyya*, September 2, 2020, https://www.jadaliyya.com/Details/41658.

34. Abrahamian, *A History of Modern Iran*, 169.

35. Amnesty International, *Law and Human Rights in the Islamic Republic of Iran: A Report Covering Events within the Seven Month Period Following the Revolution of February 1979* (Amnesty International: London, 1980), 7; Abrahamian, *Tortured Confessions*, 125.

36. Amnesty International, *Law and Human Rights*, 18.

37. Abrahamian, *Tortured Confessions*, 133–36.

38. "Gohardasht Prison or Rajaishahr Prison," *Radio Zamaneh*, March 28, 2022, https://en.radiozamaneh.com/31996; Ziba Yari, "Behind Prison Walls: Inmates on Execution Wednesdays at Rajaei Shahr Prison," *Iran Wire*, August 19, 2022, https://iranwire.com/en/prisoners/106767-behind-prison-walls-iranian-inmates-on-execution-wednesdays-at-rajaei-shahr-prison; Abrahamian, *Tortured Confessions*, 135.

39. Abrahamian, *Tortured Confessions*, 135.

40. For these regulations, see "A'in nameh-ye omur-e zendanha va eghdamat-e ta'mini va tarbiati-ye keshvar-e jomhuri-ye eslami-ye Iran," accessed July 11, 2023, http://www.dastour.ir/brows/?lid=112628.

41. Irene Schneider, "Imprisonment in Pre-classical and Classical Islamic Law," *Islamic Law and Society* 2, no. 2 (1995): 157–73.

42. Ruhollah Khomeini, *The Little Green Book: Selected Fatawah and Sayings*, trans. Harold Salemson (New York: Bantam Books, 1985).

43. Khomeini, *The Little Green Book*.

44. "Iran: Wave of Executions—290 Die," *Amnesty International Newsletter* 10, no. 10 (October 1980): 6.

45. Quoted from an AI press release from February 1982, reprinted in the International Solidarity Front for the Defense of the Iranian People's Democratic Rights (ISF-IRAN), *The Crimes of Khomeini's Regime* (N.p., 1982), 119.

46. ISF-IRAN, 14.

47. ISF-IRAN, vi.

48. 'Ebrat's official website has much of this basic information: https://ebrat museum.ir/.

49. *'Ebrat* journal published seventeen issues in 1956 and 1957.

50. Abrahamian, *Tortured Confessions*, 98; *Encyclopaedia Iranica*, s.v. "'Ebrat," last modified December 8, 2011, https://www.iranicaonline.org/articles/ebrat.

51. "'Ebrat' Ward, Medieval Torture Chamber in Adelabad Prison of Shiraz," *Iran Human Rights Monitor*, September 22, 2020, https://iran-hrm.com/2020/09/22/ebrat-ward-adelabad-prison-of-shiraz. See also Iran Kargar, "Band-e 'ebrat ya shekanjehgah-e makhuf-e zendan-e 'adel abad-e shiraz: Gozareshi az mahal-e negahdari-ye navid afkhari," accessed January 11, 2023, https://irankargar.com/بند-گاه-مخوف-زندان-عادلC8%80%E2%-عبرت-یا-شکنجه.

52. Talebi, *Ghosts of Revolution*, 9–10.

53. Xavier Gaillard, "The Museumification of Prisons in Tehran and Suleymaniyeh: Power, Collective Memory, and Hegemony" (PhD diss., Middle East Technical University, 2019), 115.

54. "Tour-e mojazi-ye Muzeh-ye Ebrat-e Iran," accessed July 9, 2023, tour.ebrat museum.com.

55. Ruhollah Khomeini, quoted in Abrahamian, *Tortured Confessions*, 124.

56. Asghar Schirazi, *The Constitution of Iran: Politics and the State in the Islamic Republic*, trans. John O'Kane (New York: I.B. Tauris, 1997); Behrooz Ghamari-Tabrizi, *Islam and Dissent in Postrevolutionary Iran: Abdolkarim Soroush, Religious Politics, and Democratic Reform* (New York: I.B. Taurus, 2008), 36–88.

57. Bakhash, *Reign of the Ayatollahs*, 59–61.

58. Abrahamian, *Tortured Confessions*, 124.

59. Ruhollah Khomeini, *Sahife-ye imam: Majmu'eh asar-e imam khomeini, jeld-e shishom* (Tehran: Moassaseh-ye Tanzim Va Nashr-e Asar-e Imam Khomeini, 1379/2000), 24.

60. This number is taken from a report in *Ayandegan* newspaper and reproduced in Amnesty International, *Law and Human Rights*, 8.

61. "Iran: The Unknown Ayatullah Khomeini," *Time*, July 16, 1979, https://content.time.com/time/subscriber/article/0,33009,920508-1,00.html.

62. "Imprisonment, Torture, and Execution of Political Opponents," Amnesty International, January 1, 1992, https://www.amnesty.org/en/documents/mde13/001/1992/en.

63. Bakhash, *Reign of the Ayatollahs*, 100–124.

64. Bakhash, 57–58.

65. Abrahamian, *Tortured Confessions*, 127.

66. "E'tesab ghaza-ye 14 ozv-e zendani-ye 'Kargaran-e Sosialist' edameh darad" [Hunger strike for fourteen imprisoned members of 'The Socialist Workers Group' continues], *Ayandegan*, 16 Tir 1358/July 7, 1979.

67. Amnesty International, *Law and Human Rights*, 7.

68. Amnesty International, 18.

69. From a statement to *Bamdad* newspaper, quoted in Bakhash, *Reign of the Ayatollahs*, 102.

70. Quoted in Amnesty International, *Law and Human Rights*, 19.

71. Bakhash, *Reign of the Ayatollahs*, 102.

72. Schirazi, *The Constitution of Iran*, 45–85.

73. Quoted in Amnesty International, *Law and Human Rights*, 14.

74. Negar Mottahedeh, *Whisper Tapes: Kate Millett in Iran* (Stanford, CA: Stanford University Press, 2019). See also Moradian, *This Flame Within*.

75. Like many members of the revolutionary coalition, Mahdavi Kani had experienced incarceration under the shah. Dilip Hiro, *Iran under the Ayatollahs* (Routledge: New York, 1987), 194.

76. For a translated text of the order, see Amnesty International, *Law and Human Rights*, 18–20.

77. Quoted in Amnesty International, 18.

78. Maziar Behrooz, "Reflections on Iran's Prison System during the Montazeri Years (1985–1988)," *Iran Analysis Quarterly* 2, no. 3 (Winter 2005): 11–23.

79. Organization of Prisons and National Security Measures, "Darbareh-ye Ma" [About us], accessed July 9, 2023, https://www.prisons.ir/news/47/.

80. "Head of Prison Service Holds News Conference," December 23, 1986, PM061633, Tehran Keyhan in Persian, trans. Foreign Broadcast Information Service (FBIS), South Asia Daily Report (FBIS-SAS-87-004).

81. Bill, *The Eagle and the Lion*, 261–62.

82. Peter Kihss, "Obituary: Mohammad Ali Rajai, Iran's President," *New York Times*, September 1, 1981, https://www.nytimes.com/1981/09/01/obituaries/mohammad-ali-rajai-iran-s-president.html.

83. Edward Cody, "Iranian Officials Shun the Diplomacy of U.N.'s Pin-striped World," *Washington Post*, October 21, 1980.

84. Amnesty International, *Law and Human Rights*, 57.

85. For an account by the wife of Hassan Pakravan, the SAVAK director from 1961 to 1966, see Fatemeh Pakravan, *Khaterat-e Fatemeh Pakravan* [The memoirs of Fatemeh Pakravan] (Tehran: Mehrandish, 1378/1999). See also Abrahamian, *Tortured Confessions*, 125.

86. Sadeq Khalkhali, *Khaterat-e Ayatollah Sadeq Khalkhali*, 352.

87. *Matn-e kamel-e nameh-ye tute'eh amiz "Tehrani" dazhkhim va shekanjehgar-e SAVAK* [The complete text of conspiratorial letter of Tehrani, executioner and torturer of SAVAK] (N.p., 1979), 5.

88. *Matn-e kamel-e nameh-ye tute'eh amiz "Tehrani."*

89. Khalkhali, *Khaterat-e Ayatollah Khalkhali*, 359.

90. Amnesty International, *Law and Human Rights*, 14.

91. "Qotbzadeh, Ex-Foreign Minister, Executed in Iran," *New York Times*, September 16, 1982.

92. "Khomeini Is Reported to Put Ban on Consumption of Drugs in Iran," *New York Times*, June 27, 1979, https://www.nytimes.com/1979/06/27/archives/khomeini-is-reported-to-put-ban-on-consumption-of-drugs-in-iran.html.

93. S. A. A. Razwy, "Khomeini Upheld the Ideals and Values of Islam," *New York Times*, June 8, 1989.

94. Khalkhali, *Khaterat-e Ayatollah Khalkhali*, 165–238.

95. Bakhash, *Reign of the Ayatollahs*, 111.

96. Ghiabi, *Drugs Politics*, 74.

97. Emphasis in original. Sadeq Khalkhali, "All Those Who Oppose the Revolution Must Die," *MERIP Reports*, no. 104 (March–April 1982): 31.

98. AP Archive, "Unused 11 3 81 Ayatollah Khalkhali Speaking at a Press Conference in Tehran," filmed March 11, 1981, YouTube video, 8:38, https://www.youtube.com/watch?v=FIjprtFarBE.

99. Edward Cody, "Bani-Sadr Says Abuse Continues under Mullahs: Iranian Leader Assails Clergy for Abuses Reminiscent of Shah," *Washington Post*, November 20, 1980.

100. "Iranian Judge Quits in Torture Scandal," *New York Times*, December 8, 1980.

101. Abolhassan Bani Sadr, who, like many other revolutionaries, had been imprisoned under the shah, challenged clerical militants on the issue of torture through 1981, before his ouster from power. Just months before, however, Bani-Sadr had defended the government's approach toward other opponents as a revolutionary necessity. See Alan Berger, "An Old Struggle with New Terms," *Boston Globe*, August 24, 1980, and Ned Temko, "Bani-Sadr Strives to Rein in Iran's Revolutionary Guard," *Christian Science Monitor*, June 20, 1980, 4. For an insightful account of the Bani-Sadr presidency, see Siavush Randjbar-Daemi, *The Quest for Authority in Iran: A History of the Presidency from Revolution to Rouhani* (New York: I.B. Taurus, 2017), 18–36.

102. Abrahamian, *Tortured Confessions*, 124.

103. From a 1982 issue of the IRGC journal *Payam-e Enqelab*. Quoted in Ghamari-Tabrizi, *Islam and Dissent in Postrevolutionary Iran*, 1.

104. The Islamic Republic has never formally admitted to this prison massacre, and the exact number of detainees killed is not known. Activists and scholars believe that it is somewhere between 2,500 and 5,000 executions. Mohajer, *Voices of a Massacre*.

Chapter Six

1. "Prisons Organization Holds Meeting," January 25, 1995, LD2501150195, Tehran IRNA, trans. Foreign Broadcast Information Service (FBIS), Near East and South Asia Daily Report (FBIS_NES-95-018).

2. "Prisons Organization Holds Meeting," January 25, 1995. Lajaverdi served as head of the Prisons Organization from 1989 to 1997.

3. Lajaverdi served three separate prison sentences under the shah. He was dismissed from his role as warden of Evin in 1984 by the High Council of the Judiciary and assassinated in 1998 by a member of the Mojahedin-e Khalq. Mehrzad Boroujerdi and Kourosh Rahimkhani, *Postrevolutionary Iran: A Political Handbook* (Syracuse, NY: Syracuse University Press, 2018), 564. See also Matin-Asgari, "Twentieth Century Iran's Political Prisoners," 701.

4. Abrahamian, *Tortured Confessions*, 5.

5. Baradaran, *Haqiqat-e sadeh*, 51–52.

6. Boroujerdi and Rahimkhani, *Postrevolutionary Iran*, 388–89.

7. "Head of Prison Service Holds News Conference," December 23, 1986, PM061633, Tehran Keyhan in Persian, trans. Foreign Broadcast Information Service (FBIS), South Asia Daily Report (FBIS-SAS-87-004).

8. Organization of Prisons and National Security Measures, *Familiarity with Research and Educational Centre of Prisons Organization* (Tehran: Islamic Republic of Iran Publishing, 1999), 1.

9. Organization of Prisons and National Security Measures, *Familiarity with Research and Educational Centre of Prisons Organization*, 7–14.

10. This quote is taken from the official website of the Prisons Organization: https://www.prisons.ir/.

11. Organization of Prisons and National Security Measures, *Familiarity with Research and Educational Centre of Prisons Organization*, 8.

12. Markaz-e Amuzesh Va Pajuheshi-ye Sazman-e Zendanha, *Shenakht-e vizhegi-ha-ye atfal-e bazahkar* (Tehran: Markaz-e Amuzesh Va Pajuheshi-ye Sazman-e Zendanha, 1374/1995). For more on the monthly magazine, see Organization of Prisons and National Security Measures, *Familiarity with Research and Educational Centre of Prisons Organization*, 13.

13. Ghiabi, *Drugs Politics*, 108. NAJA (Disciplinary Force of the Islamic Republic of

Iran, or Niru-ye entezami-ye jomhuri-ye islami) is the sixty-thousand-strong police force in the Islamic Republic. NAJA was formed in 1992 by combining the Shahrbani (police), the Gendarmarie, and the Revolutionary Committees into one centralized force. Today, NAJA also includes Iran's border police and narcotics police and has been used for crowd control during protests. On policing in the Islamic Republic, see Saeid Golkar, "The Evolution of Iran's Police Force and Social Control in the Islamic Republic," *Brandeis University Crown Center for Middle East Studies Middle East Brief*, no. 120 (July 2018): 1–9.

14. Axworthy, *Revolutionary Iran*, 304.

15. One possible reason for the prison massacre was the recent activities of the exiled Mojahedin-e Khalq, which had relocated its base of operations to Iraq and undertaken attacks on Iran alongside the Iraqi military. Of course, the incarcerated dissidents had no foreknowledge of these actions.

16. Mohajer, *Voices of a Massacre*, 362–63.

17. Iran's constitution had to be amended to allow Khamenei, who had not risen to the rank of *marja'i taqlid* (source of emulation), to ascend to power as the ruling *faqih* (jurist) in the country's system of supreme rule of the Shi'a jurist (*velayat-e faqih*).

18. Montazeri, a revolutionary of the highest clerical rank, was long expected to be Khomeini's successor. In 1986, this expectation was solidified when Montazeri was nominated for the role by Iran's Assembly of Experts. Dilip Hiro, "Montazeri, Longtime Khomeini Ally, Seen as Successor," *Washington Post*, February 13, 1986, https://www.washingtonpost.com/archive/politics/1986/02/13/montazeri-longtime-khomeini-ally-seen-likely-successor/65c6d881-eb36-4b04-a824-9c678e833007. Before their break, Montazeri irritated Khomeini by critiquing Islamic Republic policies, championing the cause of political prisoners, and pleading for an end to torture. Siavoshi, *Montazeri*, 103–94.

19. Paul Lewis, "Iran Agrees to Allow Visit by U.N. Rights Inspector," *New York Times*, December 3, 1989, https://www.nytimes.com/1989/12/03/world/iran-agrees-to-allow-visit-by-un-rights-inspector.html.

20. For Pohl's time in Iran, see Afshari, *Human Rights in Iran*, 175–84.

21. Nazanin Shahrokni, *Women in Place: The Politics of Gender Segregation in Iran* (Los Angeles: University of California Press, 2020), 116.

22. SeyedAhmad Seyedalinaghi et al., "HIV in Iran: Onset, Responses, and Future Directions," *AIDS* 35, no. 4 (March 15, 2021): 529–42.

23. Orkideh Behrouzan, "An Epidemic of Meanings: HIV and AIDS in Iran and the Significance of History, Language, and Gender," in *The Fourth Wave: Violence, Gender, Culture and HIV in the 21st Century*, ed. Jennifer F. Klot and Vinh-Kim Nguyen (Paris: UNESCO, 2009), 319–46.

24. Eskandar Sadeghi-Boroujerdi, "Iran's Uprisings for Women, Life, Freedom: Overdetermination, Crisis, and the Lineages of Revolt," *Politics* (forthcoming), published ahead of print, January 27, 2023, https://doi.org/10.1177/02633957231159351.

25. In a piece written on Rafsanjani's 2017 death, Eskandar Sadeghi-Boroujerdi and Siavush Randjbar-Daemi write,

> Khomeini's death came after a period of incapacitation, but it nevertheless caught senior state figures unprepared. As a result, the Assembly of Experts, the clerical body in charge of selecting and supervising the guardian jurist (*vali-ye faqih*), had to decide how best to handle the succession. Rafsanjani took to the podium and declared that Khomeini had stated his preference for Khamenei, despite his lack of clerical rank and authority. The latter was not an Ayatollah, let alone a *marja' al-taqlid* (source of emulation or Grand Ayatollah). Khamenei's accession unfolded in tandem with major constitutional amendments and changes in the revolutionary state's institutional structure. The position of *vali-ye faqih* . . . was radically revised. No longer was his capacity to act as a source of emulation for the faithful, namely the criterion of *marja'iyyat* a prerequisite for the office. Instead, Khamenei had an 'absolute mandate' to rule. At the same time, the office of prime minister was abolished, leaving a directly elected president, which Rafsanjani promptly assumed. These moves quickly consolidated power between the longstanding allies.

Eskandar Sadeghi-Boroujerdi and Siavush Randjbar-Daemi, "Serving the Leviathan," *Jacobin*, January 18, 2017, https://www.jacobinmag.com/2017/01/iran-rafsanjani-ahmadinejad-khamenei-reform.

26. Ghiabi, *Drugs Politics*, 97.

27. "Relay of President's 31 January News Conference," Tehran IRIB Television First News Program, Foreign Broadcast Information Service (FBIS), Near East and South Asia Daily Report (FBIS-NES-93-021), February 3, 1993.

28. "Commentary Assesses Bush Presidency," Tehran IRNA, Foreign Broadcast Information Service (FBIS), Near East and South Asia Daily Report, (FBIS-NES-93-007), January 11, 1993.

29. World Health Organization (WHO), Regional Office for the Eastern Mediterranean, *Best Practice in HIV/AIDS Prevention and Care for Injecting Drug Abusers: The Triangular Clinic in Kermanshah, Islamic Republic of Iran* (Cairo: World Health Organization, 2004), https://www.who.int/hiv/pub/idu/idu_emro_iran_2004.pdf.

30. Ali Akbar Haghdoost et al., "HIV Trend among Iranian Prisoners in 1990s and 2000s: Analysis of Aggregated Data from HIV Sentinel Sero-Surveys," *Harm Reduction Journal* 10, no. 32 (2013): 1–2; Ghiabi, *Drugs Politics*, 110.

31. Haghdoost et al., 1–5.

32. The other prisons included in the study were Ab-e Hayat in Kerman and Adelabad in Shiraz. See Behrouzan, "An Epidemic of Meaning," 325.

33. World Health Organization (WHO), Regional Office for the Eastern Mediterranean, *Best Practice,* 17–20.

34. These numbers are taken from US-based NGO United for Iran's Iran Prison Atlas: "Zendan-e Kermanshah," Iran Prison Atlas, accessed July 9, 2023, https://ipa.united4iran.org/fa/prison/21/. See also "A Brief Report about Diesel Abad Prison of Kermanshah," Human Rights Activists News Agency, May 8, 2016, https://www.en-hrana.org/brief-report-diesel-abad-prison-kermanshah.

35. "Dizel Abad Prison Archives," Kurdistan Human Rights Network, https://kurdistanhumanrights.org/en/tag/dizel-abad-prison.

36. Mahmoud Hakam, "Iran: Who Is Hedayat Farzadi?," *Iran News Update,* February 11, 2022, https://irannewsupdate.com/news/human-rights/iran-who-is-hedayat-farzadi. According to Rahmani, the head of security at Dizel Abad during the 2000s was a former member of the Mojahedin-e Khalq who was imprisoned at the site, became a *tavvab* (a "repentant" prisoner who collaborates with the state), and was eventually granted a prison security position. Rebin Rahmani, "Witness Statement of Rebin Rahmani: A Kurdish Activist," interview by Iran Human Rights Documentation Center Staff, Iran Human Rights Documentation Center, January 16, 2012, https://iranhrdc.org/witness-statement-of-rebin-rahmani-a-kurdish-activist.

37. Behrouzan, "An Epidemic of Meaning," 320. Seyedalinaghi et al. similarly emphasize the importance of these 1990s prison outbreaks on the country's approach to HIV/AIDS more broadly. Seyedalinaghi et al., "HIV in Iran," 533.

38. Behrouzan, "An Epidemic of Meaning," 325–26.

39. Maryam Hosseinkhah, *Zanan-e faramush shodeh: Gheseh-ye zendanian-e band-e nesvan* (Montreal: Asoo Publishers, 1397/2018), 106.

40. Yudhijit Bhattacharjee, "Iran's Alaei Brothers to Continue AIDS Work after Release from Prison," *Science* 334, no. 6055 (October 28, 2011): 444.

41. Bhattacharjee, 444.

42. Davood Mansoori, Kamiar Alaei, and Arash Alaei, "Prevalence of Clinical Tuberculosis in HIV Infected Patients from Kermanshah Province, Iran," *Tanaffos* 1, no. 2 (2002): 27–33.

43. Davood Mansoori, Kamiar Alaei, and Arash Alaei, "The Response to Hepatitis Virus Vaccine in HIV-Infected Patients," *Archives of Iranian Medicine* 6, no. 4 (October 2003): 269–72.

44. Axworthy, *Revolutionary Iran,* 324–69.

45. Ghiabi, *Drugs Politics,* 93.

46. "Kalantari on Disciplinary Forces, Cleanup," November 22, 1988, WA0912 141588, Tehran Keyhan in Persian, trans. Foreign Broadcast Information Service (FBIS), Near East and South Asia Daily Report (FBIS-NES-88-237), 51.

47. Ghiabi, *Drugs Politics*, 94.

48. Emran M. Razzaghi et al., "Rapid Assessment (RSA) of Drug Abuse in Iran (1998–1999)," United Nations International Drug Control Programme, the Ministry of Health, Islamic Republic of Iran, and the Prevention Department, State Welfare Department, Islamic Republic of Iran, 1999, https://www.unodc.org/documents/islamicrepublicofiran/publications/RSA2000SUMMARY.pdf

49. Razzaghi et al., "Rapid Assessment of Drug Abuse in Iran," 22.

50. See the charts in Ghiabi, *Drugs Politics*, 103–5.

51. Ghiabi, 103–5.

52. Mahmood Mamdani, *Good Muslim, Bad Muslim: America, the Cold War, and the Roots of Terror* (New York: Random House, 2005).

53. UNODC, *The Opium Economy in Afghanistan: An International Problem* (New York: United Nations, 2003).

54. Kaveh Khosnood et al., "In Iran, a New Fight against AIDS" (panel discussion transcript), Asia Society, New York, October 3, 2003, https://asiasociety.org/iran-new-fight-against-aids.

55. Behrouzan, *An Epidemic of Meanings*, 319.

56. John Calabrese, "Drugs and Counter-drug Policies in Iran: A Brief Historical Excursion," Middle East Institute, December 1, 2007, https://www.mei.edu/publications/irans-war-drugs-holding-line#sdfootnote66sym.

57. Nikpour, "Drugs and Drug Policy in the Islamic Republic of Iran," 5.

58. Sara Smelka, "In or Out of Prison, Iranian Doctors Find a Way to Help," AIDS Foundation Chicago, November 16, 2012, https://www.aidschicago.org/page/news/inside-story/in-or-out-of-prison-iranian-doctors-find-way-to-help.

59. Smelka, "In or Out of Prison."

60. Rahmani, "Witness Statement of Rebin Rahmani."

61. Sentinel sites are, in the words of Sandra Roush of the US Center for Disease Control, research nodes that work with "a limited number of recruited participants, such as healthcare providers or hospitals, who report specified health events that may be generalizable to the whole population." Sandra Roush, "Chapter 19: Enhancing Surveillance" in *Manual for the Surveillance of Vaccine-Preventable Diseases*, ed. Sandra W. Roush, Linda M. Baldy, Mary Ann Kirkconnell Hall, National Center for Immunization and Respiratory Diseases, Center for Disease Control, last modified November 17, 2017, https://www.cdc.gov/vaccines/pubs/surv-manual/chpt19-enhancing-surv.html.

62. Joint United Nations Programme on HIV/AIDS, *Country Progress Report: Iran* (Joint United Nations Programme on HIV/AIDS, 2020), 3.

63. Mohammad Shahbazi et al., "Trend of HIV/AIDS Prevalence and Related Interventions Administered in Prisons of Iran—13 Years' Experience," *Iran Journal of Public Health* 43, no. 4 (April 2014): 473.

64. Joint United Nations Programme on HIV/AIDS, *Country Progress Report: Iran*, 8–9.

65. Joint United Nations Programme on HIV/AIDS, 7.

66. Joint United Nations Programme on HIV/AIDS, 8–9.

67. "Iran's Judicial Authority Moves to Ban Torture and Forced Confessions," *Bourse and Bazaar*, October 15, 2020, https://www.bourseandbazaar.com/news-1/2020/10/15/irans-judicial-authority-moves-to-ban-torture-and-force-confessions.

68. Pouya Alimagham, *Contesting the Iranian Revolution: The Green Uprisings* (New York: Cambridge University Press, 2020).

69. Negar Mottahedeh, *#iranelection: Hashtag Solidarity and the Transformation of Online Life* (Stanford, CA: Stanford University Press, 2015).

70. Narges Bajoghli, *Iran Reframed: Anxieties of Power in the Islamic Republic* (Stanford, CA: Stanford University Press, 2019).

71. "Post-election Iran Violations Some of the Worst in 20 Years," Amnesty International, December 10, 2009, https://www.amnesty.org/en/latest/news/2009/12/post-election-iran-violations-some-worst-20-years-20091210.

72. Amnesty International, *Silenced, Expelled, Imprisoned: Repression of Students and Academics in Iran* (London: Amnesty International LTD, 2014), 47–57.

73. Tasnim News reported that, because little investment was made in the neighborhood after the raid, it remained impoverished and rife with drug use fifteen years later. Tasnim News Agency, "Khak-e Sefid: 15 sal bad," Mehr 27, 1395/October 18, 2016, https://www.tasnimnews.com/fa/news/1395/07/27/1215482/خاک-سفید-۱۵-سال-بعد.

74. Ghiabi, *Drugs Politics*.

75. Committee of Human Rights Reporters, "Gozaresh-e tekan dahandeh az barkhordha-ye surat gerefteh ba motahamin ba onvan-e 'arazel va owbash,'" Mordad 9, 1386/July 31, 2007, https://web.archive.org/web/20100612073006/http://schrr.net/spip.php?article302.

76. "Iran Reformer Says He Wants to Present Rape Evidence," Reuters, August 19, 2009, https://www.reuters.com/article/Iran/idUSDAH93169320090819.

77. "Amnesty Urges Iran to Allow Observers into Trials," Reuters, August 12, 2009, https://www.reuters.com/article/us-iran-amnesty/amnesty-urges-iran-to-allow-observers-into-trials-idUSTRE57B28L20090812.

78. Nazila Fathi and Robert F. Worth, "Strong Words from Iran's Opposition," *New*

York Times, July 27, 2009, https://www.nytimes.com/2009/07/28/world/middleeast/28iran.html.

79. Amnesty International, *Silenced, Expelled, Imprisoned*, 34.

80. Robert Tait, "Iran's Parliament Exposes Abuse of Opposition Prisoners at Tehran Jail," *The Guardian*, January 10, 2010, https://www.theguardian.com/world/2010/jan/10/iran-prisoners-abuse-jail.

81. Golnaz Esfandiari and Mohammad Zarghami, "In Iran, Trials That Are Just for Show," *The Atlantic*, February 27, 2013, https://www.theatlantic.com/international/archive/2013/02/in-iran-trials-that-are-just-for-show/273570.

82. "Pas az 10 ruz bi khabari, khanevadeh-ye Nika Shakarami ba peykar-e bi-janesh dar kahrizak ruberu shod," *BBC Persian*, Mehr 8, 1401/September 30, 2022, www.bbc.com/persian/articles/c3gwqw4xk5po.

83. For more on labor unrest, see M. Ali Kadivar and Peyman Jafari, "Labor Organizing on the Rise among Iranian Oil Workers," MERIP, August 25, 2021, https://merip.org/2021/08/labor-organizing-on-the-rise-among-iranian-oil-workers.

84. "A Web of Impunity: The Killings Iran's Internet Shutdown Hid," Amnesty International, last modified November 16, 2021, https://iran-shutdown.amnesty.org.

85. "Parvandehha-ye bi farjam-e koshteh shodegan-e entekhabat-e 1388" [Unresolved cases of those killed during the 2009 election], *BBC Persian*, June 9, 2012, https://www.bbc.com/persian/iran/2012/06/120607_l39_killed_post-election_alinejad.

86. "Zendan mahal-e tarbiyat va parvaresh-e akhlaq ast," Fars News Agency, Esfand 21, 1399/March 11, 2021, https://www-farsnews-ir.translate.goog/kordestan/news/13991221000156/زندان-محل-تربیت-و-پرورش-اخلاق-است.

87. See *BBC Persian* on Esmaili's statement: "1389: Payan-e daneshgah-e ensan sazi, aghaz-e nehzat-e zendan sazi" [1389: The end of the human-making university, the start of the prison-making movement"], March 19, 2011, https://www.bbc.com/persian/iran/2011/03/110319_l13_89_iran_jails.

88. This total is quoted in Shahbazi et al., "Trend of HIV/AIDS Prevalence," 473.

89. "Haft hezar nafar beh zendan jadid-e Tehran dar fashafouyeh montaqel shodand," *BBC Persian*, Shahrivar 24, 1391/September 14, 2012, https://www.bbc.com/persian/rolling_news/2012/09/120914_rln_prison_fashafoye.

90. "Taqaza-ye 2 hezar pasdar bara-ye zendanha-ye keshvar," Tasnim News Agency, 25 Dey 1392/January 15, 2014, https://www.tasnimnews.com/fa/news/1392/10/20/245032/تقاضای-2-هزار-پاسدار-برای-زندان-های-کشور.

91. "Bish az 14 milliard toman baraye sakht-e zendan-e jadid-e Aligodarz lehaz shod" Tasnim News Agency, Khordad 28, 1398/June 18, 2019, https://www.tasnimnews.com/fa/news/1398/03/28/2035130/لرستان-بیش-از-14-میلیارد-تومان-برای-ساخت-زندان-جدید-الیگودرز-لحاظ-شد.

92. Bish az 14 milliard toman," Tasnim News Agency

93. "Taqaza-ye 2 hezar pasdar," Tasnim News Agency.

94. "Kahesh jam'iat-e keyfari avaliyat-e sazman-e zendanha ast," Young Journalists Club (YJC), 13 Dey 1393/January 3, 2015, https://www.yjc.ir/fa/news/5089166 / کاهش-جمعیت-کیفری-اولویت-سازمان-ها-زندان-ها-استضرورت-استفاده-از-ظرفیت-های-قانون- مجازات-اسلامی.

95. "Rais-e sazman-e zendanha: Afzayesh-e zendanian va kahesh sen-e anha beh amalkard hameh dastgah-ha baz migardad," Human Rights Activists News Agency, 22 Tir 1394/July 15, 2015, https://www.hra-news.org/2015/hranews/a-861/.

96. Interview with Asghar Jahangir, "Bedun-e Taarof," IRIB News Agency, October 2019, https://www.youtube.com/watch?v=Hh3i0aRRf04.

97. "Asghar Jahangir: 211 hezar zendani dar keshvar darim," ISNA, Khordad 24, 1399/June 13, 2020, https://www.isna.ir/news/99032414685/ ۲۱۱-هزار-اصغر-جهانگیر-زندانی-در-کشور-داریم.

98. Some prisoners in these revolts briefly escaped. These included uprisings and escapes in Parsilon Prison in the city of Khorramabad in the province of Loresetan and in Aligodarz Prison, also in Lorestan. Golnar Nikpour, "All Prisoners Are Political Prisoners: Rethinking the Campaign to #FreeThemAll Beyond Borders and Beyond COVID-19," *Jadaliyya*, March 25, 2020, https://www.jadaliyya.com/Details/40865.

99. "Bakhshnameh-ye samandehi zendanian va kahesh jam'iat-e keyfari-ye zendanha sader shod," *Mashreq News*, 27 Shahrivar, 1395/September 17, 2016, https://www.mashreghnews.ir/news/632044/ بخشنامه-ساماندهی-زندانیان-و-کاهش-جمعیت-کیفری-زندانها-صادر-شد.

100. The IRI has among the highest global rates of the death penalty. See Nikpour, "Drugs and Drug Policy," 1.

101. For the devastating effects of these technologies in the US, see Maya Schenwar and Victoria Law, *Prison by Any Other Name: The Harmful Consequences of Popular Reforms* (New York: The New Press, 2020).

102. "Paband-e elektronik jaygozin-e habs mishavad" [Electronic ankle monitors to be used instead of imprisonment,] *Hamshahri Online*, 4 Farvardin 1400/March 24, 2021, https://www.hamshahrionline.ir/news/591756/ پابند-الکترونیکی-جایگزین-حبس-می-شود.

103. Tasnim News Agency, "Iran: Police Using Facial Recognition Cameras against Illegal Currency Dealers," *Eurasia Review*, June 26, 2019, https://www.eurasiareview.com/26062019-iran-police-using-facial-recognition-cameras-against-illegal-currency-dealers.

104. Schenwar and Law, *Prison by Any Other Name*, 17.

105. "Asghar Jahangir," ISNA.

106. "Iranian Inmates to Wear Ankle Monitors and Go Free," *Tehran Times*, June 15, 2017, tehrantimes.com/news/414288/Iranian-inmates-to-wear-ankle-monitors-and-go-free.

107. "Iranian Inmates," *Tehran Times*.

108. "Iranian Rial Slides to New Low as Coronavirus, Sanctions Weigh," Reuters, July 4, 2020, https://www.reuters.com/article/us-iran-economy-rial/iran-rial-slides-to-new-low-as-coronavirus-sanctions-weigh-idUSKBN2450NL.

109. Faghihi, "Enough Is Enough.".

110. "Ayatollah gharavian: Mozuʿ harim khosusi dakhel-e khodroha barresi bishtar darad," IRNA, 19 Tir 1396/July 10, 2017, https://www.irna.ir/news/82593185/آیت-الله-غرویان-موضوع-حریم-خصوصی-داخل-خودروها-نیاز-به-بررسی-بیشتر.

111. "Ayatollah gharavian," IRNA.

112. "Kanal 'dadsara-ye ershad' baraye daryaft gozareshhaye henjarshekani rah andazi shod," 15 Tir 1398/July 6, 2019, Tasnim News Agency, www.tasnimnews.com/fa/news/1398/04/15/2047454/کانال-دادسرای-ارشاد-برای-دریافت-گزارش-های-هنجارشکنی-راه-اندازی-شد.

113. Mark Andrejevic, "The Work of Watching One Another: Lateral Surveillance, Risk, and Governance," *Surveillance and Society* 2, no. 4 (2004): 479–97.

114. "Sotangu-ye setad-e amr be maʿruf," *Radio Farda*.

Conclusion

1. "Iranian Coroner Denies Mahsa Amini Died from Blows to Body," *Al-Jazeera*, October 7, 2022, https://www.aljazeera.com/news/2022/10/7/iranian-coroner-denies-mahsa-amini-died-from-blows-to-body.

2. Cora Engelbrecht and Farnaz Fassihi, "Protests Intensify in Iran over Woman Who Died in Custody," *New York Times*, September 21, 2023, https://www.nytimes.com/2022/09/21/world/middleeast/iran-protests-mahsa-amini.html; Jomana Karadsheh and Tamara Qiblawi, "A Barrier of Fear Has Been Broken in Iran," *CNN World*, October 5, 2022, https://www.cnn.com/2022/10/05/middleeast/iran-protests-regime-intl.

3. @HRANAEnglish, "Daily Statistics on Iran Protests," Twitter, February 20, 2023, 6:18 p.m., https://twitter.com/HRANA_English/status/1627809833293344769.

4. Deepa Parent and Ghoncheh Habibzadeh, "They Used Our Hijabs to Gag Us: Iran Protesters Tell of Rapes, Beatings, and Torture by the Police," *The Guardian*, February 6, 2023, https://www.theguardian.com/global-development/2023/feb/06/iran-protesters-police-rapes-beatings-and-torture.

5. CNN International Investigative Unit, "How Iran Used a Network of Secret Torture Centers to Crush an Uprising," *CNN*, February 21, 2023, https://www.cnn

.com/interactive/2023/02/middleeast/iran-torture-jails-black-sites-mahsa-amini-protests-cmd-intl/.

6. "Mir hossein mousavi khahan-e qanun-e assasi-ye jadid va tashkil-e majles-e moassan 'baraye nejat-e Iran' shod," *BBC Persian*, 15 Bahman 1401/February 4, 2023, https://www.bbc.com/persian/iran-64522691.

7. Middle East Eye Correspondent, "Iran: A Detained PM Issues a Plan to 'Save' the Country and Gains New Prominence," *Middle East Eye*, February 26, 2023, https://www.middleeasteye.net/news/iran-detained-ex-pm-plan-save-new-prominence.

8. @AzadEttehad, "Zan, zendegi, azadi, montasher motalebat hadaqali," Twitter, February 14, 2023, 3:03 p.m., https://twitter.com/AzadEttehad/status/1625586467299811343.

9. Golnaz Esfandiari, "'Radical Change Will Come': Iranians Propose New Political System after Months of Anti-regime Protests," *Radio Free Europe/Radio Liberty*, February 17, 2023, https://www.rferl.org/a/iran-new-political-system/32276451.html.

10. As of early spring 2023, this petition had just about half a million signatures. "Prince Reza Pahlavi Is My Representative," Change.org, January 17, 2023, https://www.change.org/p/prince-reza-pahlavi-is-my-representative-c0fab7a1-2d92-4e8d-93c2-5f894a6e439b.

11. Akela Lacy and Murtaza Hussein, "Amid Ongoing Protests, Congress Boosts Cultish MEK Exile Group," *The Intercept*, February 11, 2023, https://theintercept.com/2023/02/11/iran-protests-mek-congress-maryam-rajavi/. For more on the cult-like atmosphere in the MEK today, see Murtaza Hussein and Matthew Cole, "Defectors Tell of Torture and Forced Sterilization in Militant Iranian Cult," *The Intercept*, March 22, 2020, https://theintercept.com/2020/03/22/mek-mojahedin-e-khalq-iran/.

12. Murtaza Hussein, "Hawkish Israel Is Pulling U.S. into War with Iran," *The Intercept*, March 1, 2023, https://theintercept.com/2023/03/01/us-israel-iran-war/.

13. The image of the placard circulated widely on social media. See, for one example, @farbodmah, "Today (19.02.2023) at the Women, Life, Freedom protest in Munich supporters of Reza Pahlavi raised a picture of SAVAK-torturer Parviz Sabeti," Twitter, February 19, 2023, 10:47 a.m., https://twitter.com/farbodmah/status/1627334021767127044.

14. Golnaz Esfandiari, "'Hands Are Stained with Blood': Iranians Outraged after Shah-Era Secret-Police Official Attends U.S. Rally," *Radio Free Europe/Radio Liberty*, February 15, 2023, https://www.rferl.org/a/iran-sabeti-us-protest-savak/32271395.html.

15. For a reference to protesters as terrorists by the Islamic Republic, see Maziar Motamedi, "Iran's Khamenei Blames Israel, US in First Comments on Protests," *Aljazeera*, October 3, 2022, https://www.aljazeera.com/news/2022/10/3/irans-khamenei-blames-israel-us-in-first-comments-on-protests.

16. "Dadkhahi goruhi az zendanian-e siyasi-ye doran-e shah; parviz sabeti ghatel ast; bayad dar barabar dadgah gharar girad," *Radio Zamaneh*, 26 Bahman 1401/February 15, 2023, https://www.radiozamaneh.com/753513/.

17. My argument here is inspired by the foundational thinking of Angela Davis, who has argued, "Those of us who identify as prison abolitionists, as opposed to prison reformers, make the point that oftentimes reforms create situations where mass incarceration becomes even more entrenched; and so, therefore, we have to think about what in the long run will produce decarceration, fewer people behind bars, and hopefully, eventually, in the future, the possibility of imagining a landscape without prisons." "Angela Davis on Prison Abolition, the War on Drugs and Why Social Movements Shouldn't Wait on Obama," *Democracy Now*, March 6, 2011, https://www.democracynow.org/2014/3/6/angela_davis_on_prison_abolition_the, quoted in Françoise Vergès, *A Feminist Theory of Violence: A Decolonial Perspective* (London: Pluto Press, 2022), 83.

Bibliography

Archival Sources
Foreign Broadcast Information Service
    Middle East and North Africa Daily Report (FBIS-NES-01-097)
    Middle East and North Africa Daily Report (FBIS-MEA-70-030)
    Middle East and North Africa Daily Report (FBIS-MEA-79-030)
    Near East and South Asia Daily Report (FBIS-NES-87-212)
    Near East and South Asia Daily Report (FBIS-NES-88-237)
    Near East and South Asia Daily Report, (FBIS-NES-93-007)
    Near East and South Asia Daily Report (FBIS-NES-93-021)
    Near East and South Asia Daily Report (FBIS_NES-95-018)
    South Asia Daily Report (FBIS-SAS-80-157)
    South Asia Daily Report (FBIS-SAS-87-004)
Hoveyda, Fereydoun. Interview by Frederick Peterson Jessup, 1979. Transcript 30, Columbia University Oral History Collection.
India Office Records and Private Papers. British Library Archives, London.
Institute for the Study of Contemporary Iranian History Archives, Tehran.
International Institute of Social History Archive, Amsterdam, Holland.
Peake, Charles Maclean. Confidential End of Tour Report, May 1959–July 1963. Subject file 1956–1972, 1–11. Agency for International Development [AID], Records of the Operations Division, Records of the Africa (Near East) and South Asia Branch. National Archives and Records Administration (NARA), Washington, DC.

UN Doc. A/Conf.32/SR.1–13 (1968). United Nations Archives, New York.

Vezarat-e Keshvar Document # 4—ش—12062فلا. National Library and Archives of Iran, Tehran.

Books, Articles, and Essays

Abdi, Abbas. *Tasir-e zendan bar zendani: Asibshenasi-ye ejtema'i*. Tehran: Nur, 1387/2008.

Abrahamian, Ervand. *The Coup: 1953, the CIA, and the Roots of Modern U.S.-Iranian Relations*. New York: The New Press, 2015.

———. *A History of Modern Iran*. New York: Cambridge University Press, 2008.

———. *Iran between Two Revolutions*. Princeton, NJ: Princeton University Press, 1982.

———. *The Iranian Mojahedin*. New Haven, CT: Yale University Press, 1989.

———. *Tortured Confessions: Prisons and Recantation in Modern Iran*. Los Angeles: University of California Press, 1999.

Abu-Jamal, Mumia. *Live from Death Row*. New York: Harper Perennial, 1996.

———. *Writing on the Wall: Selected Prison Writings*. San Francisco: City Lights, 2015.

Abul Fath Irani. "Pishnehad beh vazir-e 'adliyeh" [Suggestions to the head of the judiciary]. *Ettela'at*, 13 Mordad 1309/August 4, 1930.

Adams, Bruce. *The Politics of Punishment: Prison Reform in Russia, 1863–1917*. Dekalb: Northern Illinois University Press, 1996.

Afary, Janet. "The Contentious Historiography of the Gilan Republic in Iran: A Critical Exploration." *Iranian Studies* 28, no. 1–2 (1995): 3–24.

———. *The Iranian Constitutional Revolution, 1906–1911: Grassroots Democracy, Social Democracy, and the Origins of Feminism*. New York: Columbia University Press, 1996.

Afshari, Reza. *Human Rights in Iran: The Abuse of Cultural Relativism*. Philadelphia: University of Pennsylvania Press, 2011.

Aguirre, Carlos. *The Criminals of Lima and Their Worlds: The Prison Experience, 1850–1935*. Durham, NC: Duke University Press, 2006.

Aguirre, Carlos, and Ricardo D. Salvatore, eds. *The Birth of the Penitentiary in Latin America: Essays on Criminology, Prison Reform, and Social Control: 1830–1940*. Austin: University of Texas Press, 1996.

Akharin defa'at-e du nafar az sazman-e Mojahedin-e Khalq-e Iran [Final testimonies of two members of the People's Mojahedin Organization of Iran]. N.p., 1972.

Akhavan, Niki. "Nonfiction Form and the 'Truth' about Muslim Women in Iranian Documentary." *Feminist Media Histories* 1, no. 1 (Winter 2015): 89–111.

Akhavan-Sales, Mehdi. *Seh ketab*. [Three books] Tehran: Zemestan, 1385/2006.

Alavi, Bozorg. *Panjah va seh nafar* [The Fifty-three]. Tehran: Amir Kabir, 1357/1978.

———. *Varaq pareh ha-ye zendan* [Scrap papers from prison]. Tehran: Amir Kabir, 1357/1978.
Alexander, Michelle. *The New Jim Crow: Mass Incarceration in the Age of Colorblindness*. New York: The New Press, 2012.
Alexander, Robert Jackson. *International Trotskyism, 1929–1985: A Documented Analysis of the Movement*. Durham, NC: Duke University Press, 1991.
Al-Jazeera. "Iranian Coroner Denies Mahsa Amini Died from Blows to Body." October 7, 2022. https://www.aljazeera.com/news/2022/10/7/iranian-coroner-denies-mahsa-amini-died-from-blows-to-body.
Allen, Lori. *The Rise and Fall of Human Rights: Cynicism and Politics in Occupied Palestine*. Stanford, CA: Stanford University Press, 2013.
Allen, Lori, Keith David Watenpaugh, Samera Esmeir, and Ilana Feldman. "Problematics of Human Rights and Humanitarianism." *International Journal of Middle East Studies* 48, no. 2 (May 2016): 357–86.
Alimagham, Pouya. *Contesting the Iranian Revolution: The Green Uprisings*. New York: Cambridge University Press, 2020.
Alishan, Leonardo. "Ahmad Shamlu: The Rebel Poet in Search of an Audience." *Iranian Studies* 18, nos. 2–4 (1985): 375–422.
Alizadeh, Parvaneh. *Khub negah konid, rastaki ast* [Look closely, it's real]. Paris: Khavaran Press, 1366/1987.
Amanat, Abbas. *Iran: A Modern History*. New Haven, CT: Yale University Press, 2017.
———. *The Pivot of the Universe: Nasir al-Din Shah and the Iranian Monarchy, 1831–1896*. New York: I.B. Taurus, 2008.
Amini, D. *Polis dar Iran*. Tehran, 1325/1946.
Amirzadeh, Marziyeh, and Maryam Rostampour. *Captive in Iran: A Remarkable True Story of Hope and Triumph amid the Horror of Tehran's Brutal Evin Prison*. Atlanta: Tyndale Momentum, 2013.
Amnesty International. *Amnesty International Report on Torture*. New York: Farrar, Straus & Giroux, 1975.
———. *Amnesty International Report 2016/17—Iran*. February 22, 2017. https://www.refworld.org/docid/58b033ef13.html.
———. "Hossein Rezai: Iran." *Amnesty International Newsletter* 1, no. 7 (July 1971).
———. "Imprisonment, Torture, and Execution of Political Opponents." January 1, 1992. https://www.amnesty.org/en/documents/mde13/001/1992/en.
———. *Iran: An Amnesty International Briefing*. London: Amnesty International, 1976.
———. "Iran: Wave of Executions—290 Die." *Amnesty International Newsletter* 10, no. 10 (October 1980): 6.

———. *Law and Human Rights in the Islamic Republic of Iran: A Report Covering Events within the Seven Month Period Following the Revolution of February 1979*. Amnesty International: London, 1980.

———. "Post-election Iran Violations Some of the Worst in 20 Years." December 10, 2009. https://www.amnesty.org/en/latest/news/2009/12/post-election-iran-violations-some-worst-20-years-20091210.

———. "Saleh Abad: Former Inmates Say They Were Held in Cow Stalls." *Amnesty International Newsletter* 13, no. 2 (February 1983): 5.

———. *Silenced, Expelled, Imprisoned: Repression of Students and Academics in Iran*. London: Amnesty International LTD, 2014.

———. *Torture in the Eighties*. London: Amnesty International, 1984.

———. "A Web of Impunity: The Killings Iran's Internet Shutdown Hid." Last modified November 16, 2021. https://iran-shutdown.amnesty.org.

Amnesty International UK. "Nelson Mandela and Amnesty International." May 18, 2020. https://www.amnesty.org.uk/nelson-mandela-and-amnesty-international.

Andrejevic, Mark. "The Work of Watching One Another: Lateral Surveillance, Risk, and Governance." *Surveillance and Society* 2, no. 4 (2004): 479–97.

Anonymous. *Taqut nameh*. n.p., n.d.

Ansari, Ali M. "The Myth of the White Revolution: Mohammad Reza Shah, 'Modernization,' and the Consolidation of Power." *Middle Eastern Studies* 37, no. 3 (2001): 1–24.

AP Archive. "Unused 11 3 81 Ayatollah Khalkhali Speaking at a Press Conference in Tehran." Filmed March 11, 1981. YouTube video, 8:38. https://www.youtube.com/watch?v=FIjprtFarBE.

'Aqeli, Baqer. *Sharh-e hal-e rajal-e siasi va nezami-ye mo'aser-e Iran*. Tehran: Nashr Goftar, 1380/2001.

Arjomand, Said Amir. *The Turban for the Crown: The Islamic Revolution in Iran*. New York: Oxford University, 1989.

Arnold, Arthur. *Through Persia by Caravan*, vol.1. London: Tinsley Brothers, 1877.

Ashraf, Hamid. "An Analysis of One Year of Urban and Guerrilla Warfare: How Did the Siahkal Insurrection Begin?" Translated by A. Keshavarzi. N.p., ca. 1970s. https://www.marxists.org/archive/hamid-ashraf/works/urban-mountain.htm.

Atabaki, Touraj, and Nasser Mohajer, eds. *Rahi digar: Ravayatha dar bud va bash-e cherikha-ye fada'i-ye khalq-e Iran* [Another Path: Narratives on the life and times of the Iranian Fada'i Guerrillas]. 2 vols. Cedex, France: Noghteh, 2018.

Avanessian, Ardeshir *Yaddashtha-ye zendan: Salha-ye 1928–1942* [Prison writing: The years 1928–1942]. Stockholm: Hezb-e Tudeh, 1979.

Axworthy, Michael. *Revolutionary Iran: A History of the Islamic Republic*. New York: Oxford University Press, 2013.

Ayandegan. "E'tesab ghaza-ye 14 ozv-e zendani-ye 'Kargaran-e Sosialist' edameh darad" [Hunger strike for fourteen imprisoned members of the 'Socialist Workers Group' continues]. *Ayandegan*, 16 Tir 1358/July 7, 1979.

Azimi, Negar. "Good Intentions." *Frieze*, March 11, 2011. https://www.frieze.com/magazines/frieze-magazine/issue-137.

Babül, Elif M. *Bureaucratic Intimacies: Translating Human Rights in Turkey*. Stanford, CA: Stanford University Press, 2017.

Bahari, Maziar. *Then They Came for Me: A Family's Story of Love, Captivity, and Survival*. New York: Random House, 2011.

Bahrami, Fazlollah. *Majaleh-ye polis*, no. 17 (Azar 1306/December 1927).

Bajoghli, Narges. *Iran Reframed: Anxieties of Power in the Islamic Republic*. Stanford, CA: Stanford University Press, 2019.

Bakhash, Shaul. *The Reign of the Ayatollahs: Iran and the Islamic Revolution*. New York: Basic Books, 1985.

Baniuyaghoob, Jila. *Women of Evin: Ward 209*. Bloomington, IN: Xlibris, 2013.

Baradaran, Monira. "Children of Prison." In *Torture in the Age of Fear*, edited by Ezat Mossallanejed, 99–112. Hamilton, Canada: Serephim Editions, 2005

———. *Haqiqat-e sadeh* [Plain truth]. 2nd ed. Lindenallee, Germany: Nima Verlag, 1379/2000.

———. *Ravanshenasi-ye shekanjeh* [The psychology of torture]. Spånga, Sweden: Baran 1380/2001.

Baradaran, Monira, and Golroch Jahangiri. "Letter to Penguin Publishers Regarding Marina Nemat's *Prisoner of Tehran*." July 25, 2007. http://sites.utoronto.ca/prisonmemoirs/Protest.pdf.

Baraheni, Reza. *The Crowned Cannibals: Writing on Repression in Iran*. With introduction by E. L. Doctorow. New York: Random House, 1977.

———. *God's Shadow: Prison Poems*. Bloomington: Indiana University Press, 1976.

———. "The SAVAK Documents." *The Nation*, February 23, 1980, 198–202.

———. "Terror in Iran." *New York Review of Books*, October 28, 1976.

———. "Torture in Iran: 'It Is a Hell Made for One Man by Another Man.' " *New York Times*, April 21, 1976.

Baraheni, Reza, and Gregg E. Gorton. "Iran Boycott; An Exchange." *New York Review of Books*, November 25, 1976. https://www.nybooks.com/articles/1976/11/25/iran-boycott-an-exchange.

Barry, Andrew, and Nigel Thrift. "Gabriel Tarde: Imitation, Invention and Economy." *Economy and Society* 36, no. 4 (2007): 509–25.

Bayat, Asef. *Workers and Revolution in Iran*. London: Zed, 1987.
BBC News. "Evin Prison Fire: Several Dead after Fire at Iran's Notorious Detention Center." October 16, 2022. https://www.bbc.com/news/world-asia-63271817.
BBC Persian. "Haft hezar nafar beh zendan jadid-e Tehran dar fashafuyeh montaqel shodand." Shahrivar 24, 1391/September 14, 2012, https://www.bbc.com/persian/rolling_news/2012/09/120914_rln_prison_fashafoye.
———. "Mir Hossein Mousavi khahan-e qanun-e assasi-ye jadid va tashkil-e majles-e moassan 'baraye nejat-e Iran' shod." 15 Bahman 1401/February 4, 2023. https://www.bbc.com/persian/iran-64522691.
———. "Parvandehha-ye bi farjam-e koshteh shodegan-e entekhabat-e 1388" [Unresolved cases of those killed during the 2009 election]. June 9, 2012, https://www.bbc.com/persian/iran/2012/06/120607_l39_killed_post-election_alinejad.
———. "Pas az 10 ruz bi khabari, khanevadeh-ye Nika Shakarami ba peykar-e bijanesh dar kahrizak ruberu shod." Mehr 8, 1401/September 30, 2022, www.bbc.com/persian/articles/c3gwqw4xk5po.
———. "1389: Payan-e daneshgah-e ensan sazi, aghaz-e nehzat-e zendan sazi" [1389: The end of the human-making university, the start of the prison-making movement"]. March 19, 2011, https://www.bbc.com/persian/iran/2011/03/110319_l13_89_iran_jails.
Becket, James. "Torture as an Institution." *New York Times*, August 4, 1972.
Behpur, Abolhasan. "Zendan va zendanha." PhD diss., University of Tehran, College of Law, Political Science, and the Economy, 1336/1957.
Behrooz, Maziar. *Rebels with a Cause: The Failure of the Left in Iran*. New York: I.B. Taurus, 1999.
———. "Reflections on Iran's Prison System during the Montazeri Years (1985–1988)." *Iran Analysis Quarterly* 2, no. 3 (Winter 2005): 11–23.
Behrouzan, Orkideh. "An Epidemic of Meanings: HIV and AIDS in Iran and the Significance of History, Language, and Gender." In *The Fourth Wave: Violence, Gender, Culture and HIV in the 21st Century*, edited by Jennifer F. Klot and Vinh-Kim Nguyen, 319–46. Paris: UNESCO, 2009.
Benenson, Peter. "The Forgotten Prisoners." *Observer* (London), May 28, 1961.
Benjamin, Samuel Greene Wheeler. *Persia and the Persians*. London: J. Murray, 1887.
Berger, Alan. "An Old Struggle with New Terms." *Boston Globe*, August 24, 1980.
Berger, Dan. *The Struggle Within: Prisons, Political Prisoners, and Mass Movements in the United States*. Oakland, CA: PM Press, 2014.
Bernault, Florence. "The Politics of Enclosure in Colonial and Post-colonial Africa." In *A History of Prison and Confinement in Africa*, edited by Florence Bernault, 1–53. Portsmouth, NH: Heinemann, 2003.

Bhattacharjee, Yudhijit. "Iran's Alaei Brothers to Continue AIDS Work after Release from Prison." *Science* 334, no. 6055 (October 28, 2011): 444.
Bill, James A. *The Eagle and the Lion: The Tragedy of American-Iranian Relations*. New Haven, CT: Yale University Press, 1988.
Bongah-e Taʿavun va Sanaʿi-e Zendanian [Institute for the Cooperation and Industry of Prisoners]. *Faʿaliyat-e seh saleh-ye Bongah-e Taʿavun va Sanaʿi-e Zendanian* [Three years of activity of the Institution for the Cooperation and Industry of Prisoners]. Tehran: Edareh-e Kol-e Zendanha va Chapgah-e Bongah-e Taʿavun va Sanaʿi-e Zendanian, 1344/1965.
———. *Gozaresh az zendanha* [A report from the prisons]. Tehran: Edareh-e Kol-e Zendanha va Chapgah-e Bongah-e Taʿavun va Sanaʿi-e Zendanian, 1347/1968.
Bonger, Willem Adriaan. *Criminality and Economic Conditions*. Translated by H. Horton. Boston: Little, Brown, 1916.
Boroujerdi, Mehrzad. *Iranian Intellectuals and the West: The Tormented Triumph of Nativism*. Syracuse, NY: Syracuse University Press, 1996.
Boroujerdi, Mehrzad, and Kourosh Rahimkhani. *Postrevolutionary Iran: A Political Handbook*. Syracuse, NY: Syracuse University Press, 2018.
Boston Daily Globe. "Penalty Severe for Theft in Persia." November 2, 1926.
Bourse and Bazaar. "Iran's Judicial Authority Moves to Ban Torture and Forced Confessions." October 15, 2020. https://www.bourseandbazaar.com/news-1/2020/10/15/irans-judicial-authority-moves-to-ban-torture-and-force-confessions.
Burke, Roland. *Decolonization and the Evolution of International Human Rights*. Philadelphia: University of Pennsylvania, 2010.
———. "From Individual Rights to National Development: The First UN International Conference on Human Rights, Tehran 1968." *Journal of World History* 19, no. 3 (2008): 275–96.
Butler, William J., and Georges Levasseur. *Human Rights and the Legal System in Iran: Two Reports*. Geneva: International Commission of Jurists, 1976.
Cacho, Lisa. *Social Death: Racialized Rightlessness and the Criminalization of the Unprotected*. New York: New York University Press, 2012.
Calabrese, John. "Drugs and Counter-drug Policies in Iran: A Brief Historical Excursion." *Middle East Institute*, December 1, 2007. https://www.mei.edu/publications/irans-war-drugs-holding-line#sdfootnote66sym.
Carroll, Dennis. "International Society of Criminology." *British Journal of Delinquency* 2, no. 2 (October 1951): 162–64.
Center for Human Rights in Iran. "Iran Moving Women Political Prisoners to Jails with Common Criminals." October 23, 2020. https://iranhumanrights.org/2020/10/iran-moving-women-political-prisoners-to-jails-with-common-criminals.

Chaqueri, Cosroe. "The Iranian Left in the Twentieth Century: A Critical Appraisal of Its Historiography." *Revolutionary History* 10, no. 3 (2011): 318 f29.

———. *The Soviet Socialist Republic of Iran 1920–1921: Birth of the Trauma*. Pittsburgh: University of Pittsburgh Press, 1995.

Chardin, Sir John. *Travels in Persia 1673–77*. New York: Dover, 1988.

Chelkowski, Peter, and Hamid Dabashi. *Staging a Revolution: The Art of Persuasion in the Islamic Republic of Iran*. New York: NYU Press, 1999.

Cherikha-ye Fadai-ye Khalq [The People's Fadai Guerrillas]. "Zendanha-ye rezhim va zendanian-e siyasi" [The regime's prisons and political prisoners]. *'Asr-e 'amal*, no. 4 (1973).

Chorgroup Munich. *Solh va danesh*. Confederation of Iranian Students, National Union 1354, n.d., 7" EP.

Chorgroup 1973 CISNU. *Long Live the Antiimperialistic Solidarity of the Nations of the World*. Confederation of Iranian Students, National Union 1506, 1973, LP.

CNN International Investigative Unit. "How Iran Used a Network of Secret Torture Centers To Crush An Uprising." *CNN*, February 21, 2023, www.cnn.com/interactive/2023/02/middleeast/iran-torture-jails-black-sites-mahsa-amini-protests-cmd-intl/.

Cockburn, Alexander, James Ridgeway, and Jan Albert. "The Beautiful Butchers: The Shah Serves Up Caviar and Torture." *Village Voice*, November 14, 1977.

Cody, Edward. "Bani-Sadr Says Abuse Continues under Mullahs: Iranian Leader Assails Clergy for Abuses Reminiscent of Shah." *Washington Post*, November 20, 1980.

———. "Iranian Officials Shun the Diplomacy of U.N.'s Pin-striped World." *Washington Post*, October 21, 1980.

Colacello, Bob. *Holy Terror: Andy Warhol Up Close*. New York: Vintage, 2014.

Committee for Human Rights in Iran. *Letters from the Great Prison: An Eyewitness Account of Human and Social Conditions in Iran*. Washington, DC: CHRI, 1978.

Committee of Human Rights Reporters. "Gozaresh-e tekan dahandeh az barkhord-ha-ye surat gerefteh ba motahamin ba onvan-e 'arazel va owbash.'" Mordad 9, 1386/July 31, 2007, https://web.archive.org/web/20100612073006/http://schrr.net/spip.php?article302.

Confederation of Iranian Students, National Union. *Dar barayeh SAVAK* [About SAVAK]. N.p.: Confederation of Iranian Students, National Union, n.d.

———. *Documents on the Pahlavi Reign of Terror: Eyewitness Reports and Newspaper Articles*. Frankfurt: Documentation Centre of Confederation of Iranian Students, National Union, n.d.

———. *Kampf der Tätigkeit des SAVAK in der BRD: Dokumentation: Wie die Bundesregierung die Tätigkeit der Mörderbande des Faschistischen Schah-Regimes SAVAK* in der BRD und Westberlin Duldet und Unterstützt. Darmstadt: Föderation Iranischer Studenten, 1977.

———. *The Legacy of a Revolutionary: Targol.* Frankfurt: CISNU, 1974.

Confederation of Iranian Students, National Union; Indian People's Association of North America; the Committee of Democratic Kampuchean Patriots in Canada; the Third-World People's Anti-Imperialist Committee; the Organization to Fight for the Rights of Immigrants; the Canadian Communist League. *Long Live International Solidarity!–Vive la solidarité internationale!* CF 002, 1979, LP.

Correia, David, and Tyler Wall. *Police: A Field Guide.* New York: Verso, 2018.

Cottam, Richard W. "Human Rights in Iran under the Shah." *Case Western Reserve Journal of International Law*, no. 121 (1980): 121–36.

Creach, Xavier, and Jack Redde. "Iraqi Refugees Heed Call of Home over Comforts of Camp." United Nations Refugee Agency, May 2003. https://www.unhcr.org/en-us/news/latest/2003/5/3ec7532a2/iraqi-refugees-heed-call-home-comforts-camp-iran.html.

Cronin, Stephanie. "Deserters, Convicts, Cossacks, and Revolutionaries: Russians in Iranian Military Service, 1800–1920." In *Iranian-Russian Encounters: Empires and Revolutions Since 1800*, edited by Stephanie Cronin, 143–86. New York: Routledge, 2013.

———. *The Making of Modern Iran: State and Society under Riza Shah, 1921–1941.* New York: Routledge, 2007.

———. *Reformers and Revolutionaries in Modern Iran: New Perspectives on the Iranian Left.* New York: Routledge, 2004.

Curzon, George N. *Persia and the Persian Question*, vol. 1. London: Longmans, Green, 1892.

Dabashi, Hamid. *Close Up: Iranian Cinema, Past, Present, and Future.* New York: Verso Press, 2001.

———. *In Search of Lost Causes: Fragmented Allegories of an Iranian Revolution.* Asheville, NC: Black Mountain Press, 2014.

———. *Iran: A People Interrupted.* New York: New Press, 2007.

———. *The Last Muslim Intellectual: The Life and Legacy of Jalal Al-e Ahmad.* Edinburgh: Edinburgh University Press, 2022.

———. *Masters and Masterpieces of Iranian Cinema.* Washington, DC: Mage, 2007.

———. *Shi'ism: A Religion of Protest.* Cambridge: Harvard University Press, 2011.

———. *Theology of Discontent: The Ideological Foundation of the Islamic Revolution in Iran.* 2nd ed. Edison, NJ: Transaction, 2005.

Dailami, Pezhmann. "The First Congress of Peoples of the East and the Iranian Soviet Republic of Iran." In Cronin, *Reformers and Revolutionaries*, 85–117.

Danesh, Taj Zaman. *Kefarshinasi va elm-e zendanha.* Tehran: Entesharat-e Daneshgah-e Polis, Shumareh 21 [Police Academy Publishing, Number 21], n.d.

———. *Keyfarshenasi va huquq-e zendanha* [Criminology and prison law]. Tehran: University of Tehran, 1352/1973.

———. *Usul-e elm-e zendanha* [The fundamentals of prison science]. Tehran: University of Tehran Press, 1353/1973.

Daniel, Victor, Bijan Shafei, and Sohrab Soroushiani. *Nikolai Markov: Architecture of Changing Times in Iran.* Tehran: Did, 2004.

Dashti, Ali. *Ayyam-e mahbas* [Prison days]. Essen: Nashr-e Nima, 2003.

Davari, Arash. "Indeterminate Governmentality: Neoliberal Politics in Revolutionary Iran, 1968–1979." PhD diss., UCLA, 2016.

Davari, Arash, Naveed Mansoori, Golnar Nikpour, and Omid Tofighian. "Is Abolition Global? Iran, Iranians, and Prison Politics (Part I)." *Jadaliyya*, September 2, 2020. https://www.jadaliyya.com/Details/41658.

Davis, Angela. *Abolition Democracy: Beyond Empire, Prisons, and Torture.* New York: Seven Stories Press, 2005.

———. *Are Prisons Obsolete?* New York: Seven Stories Press, 2003.

———. Foreword to Mohajer, *Voices of a Massacre*, xiv–xviii.

———. *Freedom Is a Constant Struggle: Ferguson, Palestine, and the Foundations of a Movement.* Chicago: Haymarket Books, 2016.

De Camara, Robert C. "The Shah as Tyrant: A Look at the Record." *Washington Post*, March 23, 1980.

Dehqani, Ashraf. "Farar az zendan" [Escape from prison]. *Tehran-e Musavar*, no. 5 (1978): 54–57.

———. *Hamaseh-ye moqavemat* [Epic of resistance]. Tehran: Nashr-e Mardom, 1353/1974. Translated by unknown translator as *Torture and Resistance in Iran: Memoirs of the Woman Guerrilla Ashraf Dehqani.* N.p.: The Iran Committee, 1978. Translated by unknown translator as *Camarade, n'oublie pas le vol, l'oiseau est mortel: Souvenirs d'une révolutionnaire évadée de la prison du chah d'Iran.* N.p.: Commission Conjointe des Peuples Iraniens et Palestinien, n.d.

———. Introduction to *Khaterat-e yek cherik dar zendan: Neveshteh-e az cherik-e fadai-ye khalq*, by Yusef Zarkari, 9–27. 2nd ed. London: Cherikha-ye Fadai-ye Khalq Iran, 1391/2013.

Democracy Now. "Angela Davis on Prison Abolition, the War on Drugs and Why Social Movements Shouldn't Wait on Obama." *Democracy Now*, March 6, 2011. https://www.democracynow.org/2014/3/6/angela_davis_on_prison_abolition_the.

Detroit Free Press. "The Land of the Lion and the Sun: Curios Types and Customs of Persia." August 17, 1902.

Dikötter, Frank. *Crime, Prison, and Punishment in Modern China*. New York: Columbia University Press, 2001.

Doctorow, E. L. Introduction to *The Crowned Cannibals: Writing on Repression in Iran* by Reza Baraheni. New York: Random House, 1977.

Elling, Rasmus Christian. " 'In a Forest of Humans': The Urban Cartographies of Theory and Action in 1970s Iranian Revolutionary Socialism. In Keshavarzian and Mirsepassi, *Global 1979*, 141–77.

Emsley, Clive. *Crime, Police, and Penal Policy: European Experiences 1750–1940*. New York: Oxford University Press, 2006.

Emsley, Clive, and Louis A. Knafla, eds. *Crime Histories and Histories of Crime: Studies in the Historiography of Crime and Criminal Justice in Modern History*. Westport, CT: Greenwood Press, 1996.

Enayat, Hadi. *Law, State, and Society in Modern Iran: Constitutionalism, Autocracy, and Legal Reform, 1906–1941*. New York: Palgrave Macmillan, 2013.

Engelbrecht, Cora, and Farnaz Fassihi. "Protests Intensify in Iran over Woman Who Died in Custody." *New York Times*, September 21, 2023. https://www.nytimes.com/2022/09/21/world/middleeast/iran-protests-mahsa-amini.html.

Esfandiari, Golnaz. " 'Hands Are Stained with Blood': Iranians Outraged after Shah-Era Secret-Police Official Attends U.S. Rally." *Radio Free Europe/Radio Liberty*, February 15, 2023. https://www.rferl.org/a/iran-sabeti-us-protest-savak/32271395.html.

———. " 'Radical Change Will Come': Iranians Propose New Political System after Months of Anti-regime Protests." *Radio Free Europe/Radio Liberty*, February 17, 2023. https://www.rferl.org/a/iran-new-political-system/32276451.html.

Esfandiari, Golnaz, and Mohammad Zarghami. "In Iran, Trials That Are Just for Show." *The Atlantic*, February 27, 2013. https://www.theatlantic.com/international/archive/2013/02/in-iran-trials-that-are-just-for-show/273570.

Esfandiari, Haleh. *My Prison, My Home: One Woman's Story of Captivity in Iran*. New York: Harper Collins, 2009.

Esmeir, Samera. *Juridical Humanity: A Colonial History*. Stanford: Stanford University Press, 2012.

E'temad Online. "Ghabl az enqelab 16 hezar zendani dashteh-im ama aknun 240 hezar zendani darim" [Before the revolution we had 16 thousand prisoners but now we have 240 thousand prisoners]. *E'temad Online*, accessed July 10, 2023, https://etemadonline.com/content/516808/ایم-داشته-زندانی-هزار--16انقلاب-از-قبل-بوروکرا-است-باری-اسف-وضعیت-که-داریم-زندانی-هزار--240اکنون-اما-.

Ettela'at. "Maktub-e Sheikh 'Ali ghatel az zendan" [Sheikh Ali the Murderer's writings from prison]. *Ettela'at*, 8 Mordad 1309/July 30, 1930.

Faghihi, Rohollah. "Enough Is Enough: Iranians Frustrated over Police Drive to Enforce Hijab-Wearing in Cars." *Middle East Eye*, October 25, 2020. https://www.middleeasteye.net/news/iran-morality-police-enforce-hijab-cars.

Fan Group of the Organization of People's Fadai Guerrillas [Goruh-e havadar-e sazman-e cherikha-ye fadai khalq]. *Matn-e defa'iyeh-e mobarez shahid houshang taregol goruh-e javed-e Arman-e Khalq*. N.p., 1357/1978.

Faroughy, Ahmad. "Repression and Iran." *Index on Censorship* 3, no. 4 (Winter 1974): 9–18.

Fars News Agency. "Zendan mahal-e tarbiyat va parvaresh-e akhlaq ast." Esfand 21, 1399/March 11, 2021, https://www-farsnews-ir.translate.goog/kordestan/news/13991221000156/زندان-محل-تربیت-و-پرورش-اخلاق-است.

Fassihi, Farnaz, and Marjorie Olster. "Iran Executes Wrestler Accused of Murder after He Took Part in 2018 Protests." *New York Times*, September 12, 2020. https://www.nytimes.com/2020/09/12/world/middleeast/iran-wrestler-navid-afkari.html.

Fathi, Nazila, and Robert F. Worth. "Strong Words from Iran's Opposition." *New York Times*, July 27, 2009. https://www.nytimes.com/2009/07/28/world/middleeast/28iran.html.

Feldman, Ilana. *Life Lived in Relief: Humanitarian Predicaments and Palestinian Refugee Politics*. Oakland: University of California Press, 2018.

Floor, W. M. "The Police in Qajar Persia." *Zeitschrift der Deutschen Morgenländischen Gesellschaft* 123, no. 2 (1973): 293–315.

Foucault, Michel. *Discipline and Punish: The Birth of the Prison*. 2nd ed. Translated by Alan Sheridan. New York: Vintage Books, 1995. First published 1977 by Pantheon (New York). Page references are to the 1995 edition.

———. *Society Must Be Defended: Lectures at the College de France*. Translated by David Macey. New York: Picador, 2003.

Foucault, Michel, and the Prisons Information Group. *Intolerable: Writings from Michel Foucault and the Prisons Information Group (1970–1980)*. Edited by Kevin Thompson and Perry Zurn. Translated by Perry Zurn and Erik Beranek. Minneapolis: University of Minnesota Press, 2021.

Frankel, Boris. "The 'Gulag Archipelago' and the Left." *Theory and Society* 1, no. 4 (Winter 1974): 477–95.

Gahan, Jairan. "Red-Light Tehran: Prostitution, Intimately Public Islam, and the Rule of the Sovereign, 1910–1980." PhD diss., University of Toronto, 2017.

Gahan, Jairan, and Reyhaneh Javadi. "Sex, Law, and the Archives: A History from Below Using the National Archives of Iran." *Jadaliyya*, August 10, 2021. https://www.jadaliyya.com/Details/43193/Sex,-Law,-and-the-Archives-A-History-from-Below-Using-the-National-Archives-of-Iran.

Gaillard, Xavier. "The Museumification of Prisons in Tehran and Suleymaniyeh: Power, Collective Memory, and Hegemony." PhD diss., Middle East Technical University, 2019.

Getachew, Adom. *Worldmaking after Empire: The Rise and Fall of Self-Determination.* Princeton, NJ: Princeton University Press, 2019.

Ghahramani, Zarah. *My Life as a Traitor: An Iranian Memoir.* New York: Farrar, Straus & Giroux, 2008.

Ghamari, Behrooz. *Remembering Akbar: Inside the Iranian Revolution.* New York: O/R, 2016.

Ghamari-Tabrizi, Behrooz. *Foucault in Iran: Islamic Revolution after the Enlightenment.* Minneapolis: University of Minnesota Press, 2016.

———. *Islam and Dissent in Postrevolutionary Iran: Abdolkarim Soroush, Religious Politics, and Democratic Reform.* New York: I.B. Taurus, 2008.

Ghiabi, Maziyar. "Drugs and Revolution in Iran: Islamic Devotion, Revolutionary Zeal and Republican Means." *Iranian Studies* 48, no. 2 (2015): 139–63. https://doi.org/10.1080/00210862.2013.830877.

———. *Drugs Politics: Managing Disorder in the Islamic Republic of Iran.* New York: Cambridge University Press, 2019.

Ghiasian, Sa'id, ed. *Khaterat-e zendan: Gazideh az nagofteha-ye zendanian-e siyasi-ye rezhim-e shah* [Prison memoirs: A selection of untold stories by the political prisoners of the shah's regime]. Tehran: Sureh Mehr, 1390/2011.

Ghods, Reza M. "The Iranian Communist Movement under Reza Shah." *Middle Eastern Studies* 26, no. 4 (October 1990): 506–13.

Gibson, Mary. "Global Perspectives on the Birth of the Prison." *American Historical Review* 116, no. 4 (2011): 1040–63. http://www.jstor.org/stable/23307878.

Gilmore, Ruth Wilson. *Abolition Geography: Essays towards Liberation.* New York: Verso Books, 2022.

———. *Golden Gulag: Prisons, Surplus, Crisis, and Opposition in Globalizing California.* Berkeley: University of California Press, 2007.

Gilmour, John. *Report on an Investigation into the Sanitary Conditions in Persia Undertaken on Behalf of the Health Committee of the League of Nations at the Request of the Persian Government.* Geneva: League of Nations Health Organisation, 1925.

Globe, The. "Penalties in Persia: Cruel but Effectual Modes of Dealing with Criminals." August 24, 1885.

Golkar, Saeid. "The Evolution of Iran's Police Force and Social Control in the Islamic Republic." *Brandeis University Crown Center for Middle East Studies Middle East Brief*, no. 120 (July 2018): 1–9.

Golsorkhi, Khosrow. "Defa'iat-e Khosrow Golsorkhi" [The defense of Khosrow Golsorkhi]. Reprinted in *Nazm-e novin*, no. 7 (Shahrivar 1364/August–September 1985).

Gorman, Anthony. *Prison, Punishment and Society in the Middle East, 1800–1950*. Edinburgh: Edinburgh University Press, 2023.

Gottlieb Gmelin, Samuel. *Travels through Northern Persia, 1770–1774*. Translated by Willem Floor. Washington, DC: Mage, 2007.

Gramsci, Antonio. *Selections from the Prison Notebooks*. New York: International Publishers, 1971.

Gulf Committee. *Political Prisoners in the Oil States: Bahrain, Iran, Oman, Saudi Arabia* London: Gulf Committee, 1974.

Haghdoost, Ali Akbar, Mohammad Mahdi Gouya, Ali Mirzazadeh, Abbas Sedaghat, and Mostafa Shokoohi. "HIV Trend among Iranian Prisoners in 1990s and 2000s: Analysis of Aggregated Data from HIV Sentinel Sero-Surveys." *Harm Reduction Journal* 10, no. 32 (2013): 1–2.

Hajebi Tabrizi, Vida. *Dad va bidad: Nakhostin zendan-e zanan-e siasi*. Tehran: Entesharat-e Baztabnegar, 2004.

———. *Yadha*. Koln: Forough Books, 1389/2010.

Hakam, Mahmoud. "Iran: Who is Hedayat Farzadi?" *Iran News Update*, February 11, 2022. https://irannewsupdate.com/news/human-rights/iran-who-is-hedayat-farzadi.

Hakim-Elahi, Hedayatollah. *Ba man beh zendan biyaid* [Come with me to prison]. Tehran: Sherkat-e Sehami, 1325/1946.

Hall, Stuart. *Essential Essays*. 2 vols. Durham, NC: Duke University Press, 2018.

Hallaq, Wael. *An Introduction to Islamic Law*. Cambridge: Cambridge University Press, 2009.

Halliburton, Richard. *The Flying Carpet: America's Most Dashing 1920s Adventurer Conquers the Air*. N.p.: The Long Rider's Guild Press, 2002.

Hamshahri Online. "Paband-e elektronik jaygozin-e habs mishavad" [Electronic ankle monitors to be used instead of imprisonment]. *Hamshahri Online*, 4 Farvardin 1400/March 24, 2021. https://www.hamshahrionline.ir/news/591756/پابند-الکترونیکی-جایگزین-حبس-می-شود.

Hanioğlu, M. Şükrü. *A Brief History of the Late Ottoman Empire*. Princeton, NJ: Princeton University Press, 2010.

Harrison, Ann. "A Birthday in Evin Prison: An Opportunity to Remember Iran's Prisoners." Amnesty International, June 10, 2010. https://www.amnestyusa.org/a-birthday-in-evin-prison-an-opportunity-to-remember-irans-prisoners.

Helbig, Elahe. "Performing Violence, Displaying Evidence: Photographs of Criminals and Political Inmates in Qajar Iran (1860s–1910s)." *History of Photography* 45, no. 3-4 (2021): 264–77.

Hiro, Dilip. *Iran under the Ayatollahs*. New York: Routledge, 1987.

———. "Montazeri, Longtime Khomeini Ally, Seen as Successor." *Washington Post*, February 13, 1986. https://www.washingtonpost.com/archive/politics/1986/02/13/montazeri-longtime-khomeini-ally-seen-likely-successor/65c6d881-eb36-4b04-a824-9c678e833007.

Hooman, Ahmad. "Bimari ha-ye ravani dar dadgah ha-yeh keyfari-ye Iran" [Psychological disorders in Iran's criminal courts]. *Kanun-e vokala*, no. 95, Ordibehesht 1344/April 1965): 18–24.

———. *Zendan va zendanian* [Prisons and prisoners]. Tehran: Chapkhaneh Daneshgah, 1339/1960.

Horton, Scott. "Six Questions for Darius Rejali." *Harper's Magazine*, February 2008.

Hosseini, Maryam. "Zendan va zendani dar Iran" [Prisons and imprisonment in Iran]. *Ganjineh* 1, no. 3–4: 44–57.

Hosseinkhah, Maryam. *Zanan-e faramush shodeh: Gheseh-ye zendanian-e band-e nesvan*. Montreal: Asoo Publishers, 1397/2018.

Human Rights Activists News Agency. "A Brief Report about Diesel Abad Prison of Kermanshah." May 8, 2016. https://www.en-hrana.org/brief-report-diesel-abad-prison-kermanshah.

———. "Rais-e sazman-e zendanha: Afzayesh-e zendanian va kahesh sen-e anha beh amalkard hameh dastgah-ha baz migardad." Tir 22, 1394/July 15, 2015, https://www.hra-news.org/2015/hranews/a-861/.

Hussein, Murtaza. "Hawkish Israel Is Pulling U.S. into War with Iran." *The Intercept*, March 1, 2023. https://theintercept.com/2023/03/01/us-israel-iran-war/.

Hussein, Murtaza, and Matthew Cole. "Defectors Tell of Torture and Forced Sterilization in Militant Iranian Cult." *The Intercept*, March 22, 2020. https://theintercept.com/2020/03/22/mek-mojahedin-e-khalq-iran/.

Hussein, Murtaza, and Akela Lacy. "Amid Ongoing Protests, Congress Boosts Cultish MEK Exile Group." *The Intercept*, February 11, 2023. https://theintercept.com/2023/02/11/iran-protests-mek-congress-maryam-rajavi/.

Index on Censorship. *The Iranian Bulletins: The News Bulletins of the Committee for the Defence of Political Prisoners in Iran*. London: Index on Censorship, 1979.

International Solidarity Front for the Defense of the Iranian People's Democratic Rights (ISF-IRAN). *The Crimes of Khomeini's Regime*. N.p., 1982.

Irandefence. *Irandefence: News Bulletin of the Organisation for the Defence of Human Rights in Iran* 6, no. 1 (1976): 8.

Iran Human Rights Documentation Center. *Imprisonment for Debt*. Accessed August 14, 2021, https://tbinternet.ohchr.org/Treaties/CCPR/Shared%20Documents/IRN/INT_CCPR_ICS_IRN_42314_E.pdf.

———. *Rights Disregarded: Prisons in the Islamic Republic of Iran*. New Haven, CT: IHRDC, 2015.

Iran Human Rights Monitor. " 'Ebrat' Ward, Medieval Torture Chamber in Adelabad Prison of Shiraz." September 22, 2020. https://iran-hrm.com/2020/09/22/ebrat-ward-adelabad-prison-of-shiraz.

———. "A Glimpse of Evin Prison, Iran's Most Notorious Jail." October 28, 2018. https://iran-hrm.com/index.php/2018/10/28/iran-evin-prison-irans-most-notorious-jail.

Iranian Students Association. *Defend the 41.* ISAUS, 1973.

———. *Paknejad: Text of Defence Speech of S. Paknejad, a Member of the 'Palestine Group' in Military Tribunal No. 3 of Tehran Dec. 1970.* Houston, TX: ISAUS, 1976.

———. "The Shah of Iran Visits His U.S. Imperialist Bosses!" *Daneshju* [The collegian] (October 1969): 1–3.

Iran International. "Chairman of Prisons Organization Hopes to Prevent Death under Torture in Prisons." November 25, 2019. https://iranintl.com/en/iran/chairman-prisons-organization-hopes-prevent-death-under-torture-prisons.

Iran Prison Atlas. "Zendan-e Kermanshah." Accessed July 9, 2023, https://ipa.united4iran.org/fa/prison/21.

Iran Tribune. "Human Rights Exhibition Opens at Iran Bastan Museum." *Iran Tribune* 1, no. 1 (1968): 32.

———. "Tribune Tattler." *Iran Tribune* 1, no. 1 (1968): 24.

IRIB News Agency. Interview with Asghar Jahangir. "Bedun-e Taarof." October 2019, https://www.youtube.com/watch?v=Hh3iOaRRfo4.

Iriye, Akira, Petra Goedde, and William I. Hitchcock, eds. *The Human Rights Revolution: An International History.* New York: Oxford University Press, 2012.

IRNA. "Ayatollah Gharavian: Mozu' harim khosusi dakhel-e khodroha barresi bishtar darad," 19 Tir 1396/July 10, 2017. www.irna.ir/news/82593185/ آیت‌الله-غرویان-موضوع-حریم-خصوصی-داخل-خودروها-نیاز-به-بررسی-بیشتر.

———. "Zendan-haye zionisti: Makhuf va makhfi" [Zionist prisons: Horrific and secretive]. 11 Farvardin 1392/March 31, 2013. irna.ir/news/80597859/-زندان‌های-صهیونیستی-مخوف-و-مخفی.

ISNA. "Asghar Jahangir: 211 hezar zendani dar keshvar darim," Khordad 24, 1399/June 13, 2020, https://www.isna.ir/news/99032414685/ اصغر-جهانگیر-۲۱۱-هزار-زندانی-در-کشور-داریم.

———. "Haj Mohammadi: Baraye tabdil-e zendan beh amuzeshgah-e nikiha, niazmand-e amuzgaran-e tarbiati hastim," 26 Farvardin 1400/April 15, 2021. www.isna.ir/news/1400012615147/حاج-محمدی-برای-تبدیل-زندان-به-آموزشگاه-نیکی-ها-نیازمند-آموزگاران.

———. "Modir-e tarahi-ye bagh, muzeh-ye zendan-e Qasr," 9 Tir 1385/June 30, 2006. www.isna.ir/news/8504-03527/مدیر-طراحی-باغ-موزه-ی-زندان-قصر-پلان-اصلی-باغ-تاریخی-مبنای.

Jacobs, Jody. "Party Trimmings Fit for a Princess." *Los Angeles Times*, November 10, 1974.

Jahanbegloo, Ramin. *Time Will Say Nothing: A Philosopher Survives an Iranian Prison*. Saskatchewan: University of Regina Press, 2014.

Jakaitis, John M. "Two Versions of an Unfinished War: 'Dispatches' and 'Going after Cacciato.'" In "American Representations of Vietnam," special issue, *Cultural Critique*, no. 3 (Spring 1986): 191–210.

Javadi, Ali Asghar. *Nameh-ha* [Letters]. Tehran: Tandur, 1357/1978.

Javad Moradiniya, Mohammad. *Hekayat-e Qasr: Az Qajar ta pahlavi*. Tehran: Entesharat-e Negah, 1397/2018.

Jazani, Bizhan. *Tarh-e jama'eh shenasi va mabani-ye esteratezhi-ye jonbesh-e enqelabi-ye Iran*. Tehran: Maziyar Press, 1979.

Joint United Nations Programme on HIV/AIDS. *Country Progress Report: Iran*. Joint United Nations Programme on HIV/AIDS, 2020.

Kaba, Mariame. *We Do This 'Til We Free Us*. Chicago: Haymarket Books, 2021.

Kadivar, M. Ali, and Peyman Jafari. "Labor Organizing on the Rise among Iranian Oil Workers." MERIP, August 25, 2021. https://merip.org/2021/08/labor-organizing-on-the-rise-among-iranian-oil-workers.

Kanani, Nasser. *SAVAK: Der Iranische Geheimdienst Eine Dokumentation*. Münster: Periferia Verlag, 1979.

Karadsheh, Jomana, and Tamara Qiblawi. "A Barrier of Fear Has Been Broken in Iran." *CNN World*, October 5, 2022. https://www.cnn.com/2022/10/05/middleeast/iran-protests-regime-intl.

Kashani-Sabet, Firoozeh. *Conceiving Citizens: Women and the Politics of Motherhood in Iran*. New York: Oxford University Press, 2011.

———. *Frontier Fictions: Shaping the Iranian Nation, 1804–1946*. Princeton, NJ: Princeton University Press, 1999.

Kasravi, Ahmad. *Tarikh-e mashruteh-ye Iran* [The history of the Constitutional Revolution in Iran]. Tehran: Amir Kabir, 1930/1951.

Keddie, Nikki. *Modern Iran: Roots and Results of Revolution*. New Haven, CT: Yale University Press, 2003.

———. *Qajar Iran and the Rise of Reza Khan, 1796–1925*. Costa Mesa, CA: Mazda, 2012.

Kermani, Nazem al-Islam. *Tarikh-e bidari-ye Iranian: Jeld-e aval* [The history of the awakening of the Iranians: Volume 1]. Tehran: Amir Kabir, 1384/2005.

Keshavarzian, Arang, and Ali Mirsepassi, eds. *Global 1979: Geographies and Histories of the Iranian Revolution*. Cambridge: Cambridge University Press, 2021.

Keys, Barbara. *Reclaiming American Virtue: The Human Rights Revolution of the 1970s*. Cambridge, MA: Harvard University Press, 2014.

Khabar Online. "Zendan bozorg Tehran pazirai-ye 15 hezar nafar mi shavad." 12 Or dibehesht 1395/May 1, 2016. www.khabaronline.ir/news/148249/زندان-بزرگ-تهران-پذیرای15--هزار-زندانی-می-شود

Khalili, Laleh, and Jill Schwedler. *Policing and Prisons in the Middle East: Formations of Coercion.* New York: Columbia University Press, 2010.

Khalkhali, Sadeq. "All Those Who Oppose the Revolution Must Die." *MERIP Reports,* no. 104 (March–April 1982): 31.

———. *Khaterat-e Ayatollah Sadeq Khalkhali* [The memoirs of Ayatollah Sadeq Khalkhali]. Tehran: Nashr-e Sayeh, 1379/2000.

Khamenei.ir. "Moruri bar khaterat-e Ayatollah Khamenei dar zendanha-ye setam-shahi" [A review of Ayatollah Khamenei's memoirs from the prisons of the oppressive shah]. Bahman 21, 2017/February 9, 2017. https://farsi.khamenei.ir/memory-content?id=35645.

Khaza'i, Ya'qub. *Farayand-e sakhtyabi-ye nehad-e zendan: Az mashruteh ta payan-e pahlavi-ye aval.* Tehran: Agah, 1395/2016.

Khomeini, Ruhollah. *Islam and Revolution: Writings and Declarations of Imam Khomeini.* Translated by Hamid Algar. Berkeley, CA: Mizan Press, 1981.

———. *The Little Green Book: Selected Fatawah and Sayings.* Translated by Harold Salemson. New York: Bantam Books, 1985.

———. *Sahife-ye imam: Majmu'eh asar-e Imam Khomeini, jeld-e shishom.* Tehran: Moassaseh-ye Tanzim Va Nashr-e Asar-e Imam Khomeini, 1379/2000.

Khosnood, Kaveh, Aresh Alaei, Kamiar Alaei, Robert Newman, and Joanne Csete. "In Iran, a New Fight against AIDS" Transcript of panel discussion. Asia Society, New York, October 3, 2003. https://asiasociety.org/iran-new-fight-against-aids.

Kihss, Peter. "Obituary: Mohammad Ali Rajai, Iran's President." *New York Times,* September 1, 1981. https://www.nytimes.com/1981/09/01/obituaries/mohammad-ali-rajai-iran-s-president.html.

Kinney, Katherine. "American Exceptionalism and Empire in Tim O'Brien's *Going after Cacciato.*" *American Literary History* 7, no. 4 (Winter 1995): 633–53.

Knanishu, Joseph. *About Persia and Its People.* Rock Island, IL: Lutheran Augustana Book Concern Printers, 1899.

Kolakowski, Leszek. *Main Currents of Marxism: Its Rise, Growth, and Dissolution.* Vol. 1, *The Founders.* Translated by P. S. Falla. New York: Oxford University Press, 1981.

Kondo, Nobuaki. *Islamic Law and Society in Iran: A Social History of Qajar Tehran.* New York: Routledge, 2017.

Kurzman, Charles. *The Unthinkable Revolution in Iran.* Cambridge, MA: Harvard University Press, 2005.

Lajavardi, Habib, ed. *The Memoirs of Lieutenant General Mohsen Mobasser, National Chief of Police (1343–1349).* Tehran: Safhe-ye Sefid, 1390/2011.

Lewis, Paul. "Iran Agrees to Allow Visit by U.N. Rights Inspector." *New York Times*, December 3, 1989. https://www.nytimes.com/1989/12/03/world/iran-agrees-to-allow-visit-by-un-rights-inspector.html.

Liberator. "Mr. Perkins, Missionary to Persia." April 7, 1837, 58.

Los Angeles Times. "Sister of Shah Hits Race Bias." March 26, 1970.

Lusinchi, Victor A., and Eric Pace. "Torture and Denials of Rights Laid to Iran by Jurists' Group." *New York Times*, May 29, 1976.

Mahallati, Muhammad Ali Sayyah. *Khaterat-e Hajj Sayyah: Dowreh-ye khawf va vahshat*. Tehran: Amir Kabir, 1977.

Mahdi, Ali Akbar, and Abdolali Lahsaeizadeh, *Sociology in Iran*. Bethesda, MD: Jahan, 1992.

Mahmood, Saba. *The Politics of Piety: The Islamic Revival and the Feminist Subject*. Princeton, NJ: Princeton University Press, 2005.

Mahnameh-ye Shahrbani. "Qezel Hesar." *Mahnameh-ye shahrbani* [Monthly police journal], no. 407 (July–August 1969).

Majles-e Shura-ye Melli. *Qanun-e bujeh-ye sal-e 1345 kol-e keshvar* [The budget laws for 1345]. Tehran: Majles-e Shura-ye Melli, 1345/1961.

———. *Qanun-e bujeh-ye sal-e 1346 kul-e keshvar* [The budget laws for 1346]. Tehran: Majles-e Shura-ye Melli, 1346/1962.

Mamdani, Mahmood. *Good Muslim, Bad Muslim: America, the Cold War, and the Roots of Terror*. New York: Random House, 2005.

Mansoori, Davood, Kamiar Alaei, and Arash Alaei. "Prevalence of Clinical Tuberculosis in HIV Infected Patients from Kermanshah Province, Iran." *Tanaffos* 1, no. 2 (2002): 27–33.

———. "The Response to Hepatitis Virus Vaccine in HIV-Infected Patients." *Archives of Iranian Medicine* 6, no. 4 (October 2003): 269–72.

Marashi, Afshin. *Nationalizing Iran: Culture, Power, and the State, 1870–1940*. Seattle: University of Washington Press, 2008.

Markaz-e Amuzesh Va Pajuheshi-ye Sazman-e Zendanha. *Shenakht-e vizhegiha-ye atfal-e bazahkar*. Tehran: Markaz-e Amuzesh Va Pajuheshi-ye Sazman-e Zendanha, 1374/1995.

Marx, Karl. *Capital*. Vol 1, *A Critique of Political Economy*. Translated by Ben Fowkes. New York: Penguin, 1992.

———. *The Grundrisse: Foundations of the Critique of Political Economy*. Translated by Martin Nicolaus. New York: Penguin, 1993.

Mashreq News. "Bakhshnameh-ye samandehi zendanian va kahesh jam'iat-e keyfari-ye zendanha sader shod." 27 Shahrivar, 1395/September 17, 2016. https://www.mashreghnews.ir/news/632044/بخشنامه-ساماندهی-زندانیان-و-کاهش-جمعیت-کیفری-زندانها-صادر-شد.

Matin-Asgari, Afshin. *Both Eastern and Western: An Intellectual History of Iranian Modernity.* New York: Cambridge University Press, 2018.

———. *Iranian Student Opposition to the Shah.* Costa Mesa, CA: Mazda, 2002.

———. "Twentieth Century Iran's Political Prisoners." *Middle Eastern Studies* 42, no. 5 (September 2006): 689–707.

Matn-e defa'iyeh-e mojahid shahid Naser Sadeq [The text of the defense of martyred mojahed Naser Sadeq]. N.p., n.d.

Matn-e kamel-e nameh-ye tute'eh amiz "Tehrani" dazhkhim va shekanjehgar-e SAVAK [The complete text of conspiratorial letter of Tehrani, executioner and torturer of SAVAK]. N.p., 1979.

Medvedev, Roy. "On Solzhenitsyn's 'Gulag Archipelago.'" *Index on Censorship* 3, no. 2 (1974). https://doi.org/10.1080/03064227408S323.

Meyer, Matt, ed. *Let Freedom Ring: A Collection of Documents from the Movements to Free U.S. Political Prisoners.* Oakland, CA: PM Press, 2008.

Middle East Eye Correspondent. "Iran: A Detained PM Issues a Plan to 'Save' the Country and Gains New Prominence." *Middle East Eye*, February 26, 2023. https://www.middleeasteye.net/news/iran-detained-ex-pm-plan-save-new-prominence.

Milani, Abbas ed., *A Window into Modern Iran: The Ardeshir Zahedi Papers at the Hoover Institution Library and Archives.* Stanford, CA: Hoover Institution Press, 2019.

Millett, Kate. *Going to Iran.* New York: Coward, McCann & Geoghegan, 1982.

Mirsepassi, Ali. *The Discovery of Iran: Taghi Arani, A Radical Cosmopolitan.* Stanford, CA: Stanford University Press, 2021.

———. *Political Islam, Iran, and the Enlightenment: Philosophies of Hope and Despair.* New York: Cambridge University Press, 2010.

———. "The Tragedy of the Iranian Left." In Cronin, *Reformers and Revolutionaries*, 229–49.

Mobasser, Mohsen. "Excerpts From Speech of Major General Mohsen Mobasser." *International Police Academy Review* 1, no. 2, (April 1967): 10–11.

———. "National Police of Iran." *International Police Academy Review* 2, no. 1, January 1968: 1–4, 12–13.

Mohammadi, Annabelle Sreberny, and Ali Mohammadi. *Small Media, Big Revolution: Communication, Culture, and the Iranian Revolution.* Minneapolis: University of Minnesota, 1994.

Mohammadi, Narges. *White Torture: Interviews with Iranian Women Prisoners.* Translated by Amir Rezanezhad. New York: Oneworld, 2022.

"Mohemtarin khabarha-ye keshvar va jahan" [The most important news from the country and the world]. *Khandaniha* 9, no. 212 (1946): 213–14.

Mojaher, Nasser. *Voices of a Massacre: Untold Stories of Life and Death in Iran, 1988.* With a foreword by Angela Davis. New York: Oneworld, 2020.

Moradian, Manijeh. *This Flame Within: Iranian Revolutionaries in the United States.* Durham, NC: Duke University Press, 2022.

Moslem Students Society (U.S.A). *The Defenses of Martyred Mojahed Mehdi Rezai.* Washington DC: International Relations Bureau of Moslem Students Society (U.S.A), 1980.

Motamedi, Maziar. "Iran's Khamenei Blames Israel, US in First Comments on Protests." *Al-Jazeera*, October 3, 2022. https://www.aljazeera.com/news/2022/10/3/irans-khamenei-blames-israel-us-in-first-comments-on-protests.

Mottahadeh, Roy. *The Mantle of the Prophet: Religion and Politics in Iran.* New York: Oneworld, 1985.

Mottahedeh, Negar. *#iranelection: Hashtag Solidarity and the Transformation of Online Life.* Stanford, CA: Stanford University Press, 2015.

———. *Whisper Tapes: Kate Millett in Iran.* Stanford, CA: Stanford University Press, 2019.

Moyn, Samuel. *The Last Utopia: Human Rights in History.* Cambridge, MA: Harvard University Press, 2010.

Murakawa, Naomi. *The First Civil Right: How Liberals Built Prison America.* New York: Oxford University Press, 2014.

Mushar, Khanbaba, ed. *Fehrest-e ketabha-ye chapi-e farsi.* Tehran: University of Tehran Press, 1958.

Naficy, Hamid. *A Social History of Iranian Cinema.* Vol. 2, *The Industrializing Years, 1941–1978.* Durham, NC: Duke University Press, 2011.

Nahid, Mozaffari, ed. *Strange Times, My Dear: The PEN Anthology of Contemporary Iranian Literature.* New York: Arcade, 2005.

Najmabadi, Afsaneh. *Land Reform and Social Change in Iran.* Salt Lake City: University of Utah Press, 1988.

———. *Women with Mustaches and Men without Beards: Gender and Sexual Anxieties of Iranian Modernity.* Los Angeles: University of California Press, 2005.

Napazir, Shekast [pseud.]. *Yaddashtha az Zendan-e Evin* [Notes from Evin Prison]. Springfield, MO: Nehzat-e Azadi-ye Iran (Kharej az Keshvar), 1355/1976.

Naraqi, Ehsan. *From Palace to Prison: Inside the Iranian Revolution.* Chicago: Ivan R. Dee, 1993.

National Democratic Front of Iran. *Daftar haye azadi: Beh yad-e Shokrollah Paknejad* [Freedom notebooks: In memory of Shokrollah Paknejad]. Paris: NDFI, 1985.

National Front. *Pareh-i az asrar-e sazman-e "amniyat" (SAVAK).* N.p.: Jebheh-ye Melli (Kharej az Keshvar), 1350/1971.

Navasky, Victor S. "Boycott: The Moral Question, the Political Question, the Practical Question." *New York Times*, August 15, 1976.

Nayeri, Kamran. "Vida Hadjebi Tabrizi: Her Life and Times." *Our Place in the World, a Journal of Ecosocialism*, March 25, 2017, http://forhumanliberation.blogspot.com/2017/03/2585-vida-hadjebi-tabrizi-her-life-and.html.

Nemat, Marina. *Prisoner of Tehran: A Memoir*. New York: Simon & Schuster, 2008.

New York Times. "Around the World: Iran Confirms Executing an Opposition Leader." January 16, 1982.

———. "Iranian Judge Quits in Torture Scandal." December 8, 1980.

———. "Khomeini Is Reported to Put Ban on Consumption of Drugs in Iran." June 27, 1979. https://www.nytimes.com/1979/06/27/archives/khomeini-is-reported-to-put-ban-on-consumption-of-drugs-in-iran.html.

———. "Qotbzadeh, Ex-Foreign Minister, Executed in Iran." September 16, 1982.

———. "The Shah on Israel, Corruption, Torture, and . . ." October 22, 1976. https://www.nytimes.com/1976/10/22/archives/the-shah-on-israel-corruption-torture-and.html.

———. "Shah Reportedly Bitter at Carter in Interview." November 18, 1979.

Nikpour, Golnar. "All Prisoners Are Political Prisoners: Rethinking the Campaign to #FreeThemAll beyond Borders and beyond COVID-19." *Jadaliyya*, March 25, 2020. https://www.jadaliyya.com/Details/40865

———. "Claiming Human Rights: Iranian Political Prisoners and the Making of a Transnational Movement, 1963–1979." *Humanity: An International Journal of Human Rights, Humanitarianism, and Development* 9, no. 3 (Winter 2018): 363–88.

———. "The Criminal is the Patient, the Prison Will Be the Cure: Building the Carceral Imaginary in Modern Iran." In Keshavarzian and Mirsepassi, *Global 1979*, 297–327.

———. "Drugs and Drug Policy in the Islamic Republic of Iran." *Brandeis University Crown Center for Middle East Studies Middle East Brief*, no. 119 (June 2018): 1–7.

Nosrat al-Dowleh, Firuz. *Majmuah-e makatibat asnad khaterat va asar-e firzu mirza Firuz (Nosrat al-Dowleh)*. Tehran: Nashr-e Tarikh-e Iran, 1990.

O'Brien, Tim. *Going after Cacciato*. 1978. Reprint, New York: Broadway Books, 1999.

Organization of Iranian People's Fadai Guerrillas (OIPFG). *Beh aftabkaran: ghazal-sorudeha az band* [To the sunplanters: The songs of the cell]. Tehran, n.d.

———. *Daftarha-ye she'r-e zendan* [Prison poetry notebooks]. N.p.: Entesharat-e Rafiq Hassan Zia Zarifi Dar Khedmat-e Cherikha-ye Fadai-ye Khalq-e Iran, n.d.

———. "A Prisoner's Report from Evin Prison." *Kar*, no. 14 (October 1984): 24.

Organization of Prisons and National Security Measures. *Familiarity with Research and Educational Centre of Prisons Organization*. Tehran: Islamic Republic of Iran Publishing, 1999.

Pahlavi, Ashraf. *Faces in a Mirror: Memoirs from Exile.* Englewood Cliffs, NJ: Prentice Hall, 1980.

Pahlavi, Farah. *An Enduring Love.* New York: Hyperion, 2004.

Pahlavi, Mohammad Reza. *Answer to History.* Translated by Michael Joseph. New York: Stein and Day, 1980.

Paidar, Parvin. *Women and the Political Process in Twentieth-Century Iran.* New York: Cambridge University Press, 1995.

Paik, A. Naomi. *Rightlessness: Testimony and Redress in U.S. Prison Camps since World War II.* Chapel Hill: University of North Carolina Press, 2016.

Pakizegi, Nasrim. "The Shah and His Great University with a Little Help from His Friends." *Harvard Crimson*, May 25, 1976.

Pakravan, Fatemeh. *Khaterat-e Fatemeh Pakravan* [The memoirs of Fatemeh Pakravan]. Tehran: Mehrandish, 1378/1999.

Parent, Deepa, and Ghoncheh Habibzadeh. "They Used Our Hijabs to Gag Us: Iran Protesters Tell of Rapes, Beatings, and Torture by the Police." *The Guardian*, February 6, 2023. https://www.theguardian.com/global-development/2023/feb/06/iran-protesters-police-rapes-beatings-and-torture

Parsa, Misagh. *Social Origins of the Iranian Revolution.* New Brunswick, NJ: Rutgers University Press, 1989.

Parsipur, Shahrnush. *Khaterat-e zendan* [Prison memoir]. Stockholm: Baran Press, 2000.

———. *Kissing the Sword: A Prison Memoir.* Translated by Sara Khalili. New York: The Feminist Press, 2013.

Perkins, Justin. *Residence of Eight Years in Persia among Nestorian Christians: With the Notices of the Muhammedans.* Andover, MA: Allen, Morrill, and Wardwell, 1843.

Peters, Rudolph. *Crime and Punishment in Islamic Law: Theory and Practice from the Sixteenth to the Twenty-First Century.* Cambridge: Cambridge University Press, 2005.

Phillips, Paul. *Marx and Engels on Law and Laws.* Oxford: Martin Robertson Press, 1980.

Pieris, Anoma. *Hidden Hands and Divided Landscapes: A Penal History of Singapore's Plural Society.* Honolulu: University of Hawaii Press, 2009.

Plan and Budget Organization, Statistical Centre of Iran. *Statistical Yearbook of Iran: 1352 (March, 1973–March 1974).* Tehran: Plan and Budget Organization, 1976.

Pontia. "A Palace Turned Prison: A Look inside Tehran's Qasr Prison Museum." *My Persian Corner*, July 21, 2018. https://www.mypersiancorner.com/qasr-prison-museum-tehran.

Power, Jonathan. *Like Water on Stone: The Story of Amnesty International.* Boston, MA: Northeastern University, 2001.

Prison Insider. "Iran: 333% Increase of Prison Populace in 30 Years." *Prison Insider,* May 25, 2017. https://www.prison-insider.com/en/articles/iran-333-increase-of-prison-populace-in-30-years.

Qahremani, Mahmud. "Barresi-ye qavanin-e Iran: Masuliyat az lehaz-e ravan-pezeshki" [A study of Iranian laws: Responsibility from the perspective of psychoanalysis]. PhD diss., University of Tehran, 1338/1959.

Radio Farda. "Exclusive: Leaked Documents from Iran's Notorious Evin Prison Reveal Plight of Inmates." *Radio Free Europe/Radio Liberty,* November 3, 2021. https://www.rferl.org/a/iran-evin-prison-leaked-documents/31544336.html.

———. "Iran's Overcrowded Prisons Hold a Quarter of a Million People, Says Chief Warden." May 12, 2018. https://en.radiofarda.com/a/iran-s-overcrowded-prisons-hold-a-quarter-of-a-million-people-says-chief-warden-/29222716.html.

———. "No Political Prisoners in Iran, Claims Judiciary Chief." February 5, 2019. https://en.radiofarda.com/a/iran-judiciary-claims-no-political-prisoners-in-iran/29753080.html.

———. "Sotangu-ye setad-e amr be ma'ruf: Gasht-e amniyat-e akhlaqi tamam shod; dar charchub-e novintar erae'h mishavad." 15 Azar 1401/December 6, 2022. https://www.radiofarda.com/a/iran-s-propagation-of-virtue-and-the-prevention-of-vice-spokesperson-on-morality-police/32162978.html.

Radio Zamaneh. "Dadkhahi goruhi az zendanian-e siyasi-ye doran-e shah; parviz sabeti ghatel ast; bayad dar barabar dadgah gharar girad." 26 Bahman 1401/February 15, 2023. https://www.radiozamaneh.com/753513/.

———. "Gohardasht Prison or Rajaishahr Prison." March 28, 2022. https://en.radiozamaneh.com/31996.

Radji, Parviz C. *In the Service of the Peacock Throne: The Diaries of the Shah's Last Ambassador to London.* London: Hamish Hamilton, 1983.

Raffat, Donne. *The Prison Papers of Bozorg Alavi.* Syracuse, NY: Syracuse University Press, 1985.

Rafi', Jalal. *Az daneshgah-e Tehran ta shekanjehgah-e Savak: Goftegu ba Jalal Rafi'* [From the University of Tehran to SAVAK's torture chambers]. Tehran: 'Ebrat Museum, 1382/2003.

Rafizadeh, Mansur. *Witness: From the Shah to the Secret Arms Deal, An Insider's Account of U.S. Involvement in Iran.* New York: William Morrow & Co., 1987.

Rahmani, Anahita. "Summer 1988." In Mohajer, *Voices of a Massacre,* 33–41.

Rahmani, Rebin. "Witness Statement of Rebin Rahmani: A Kurdish Activist." By Iran Human Rights Documentation Center Staff. Iran Human Rights Documentation

Center, January 16, 2012. https://iranhrdc.org/witness-statement-of-rebin-rah mani-a-kurdish-activist.

Rahnema, Ali. *Call to Arms: Iran's Marxist Revolutionaries—Formation and Evolution of the Fada'is, 1964–1976.* London: Oneworld Press, 2021.

———. *An Islamic Utopian: A Political Biography of Ali Shari'ati.* New York: I.B. Taurus, 1999.

Rahraw Khuajah, Ahmad, and Nasser Rubay'i. *Tarikh-e zendan dar 'asr-e Qajar va Pahlavi* [The history of prison in the Qajar and Pahlavi eras]. Tehran: Entesh arat-e Qoqnus, 1390/2011.

Randjbar-Daemi, Siavush. *The Quest for Authority in Iran: A History of the Presidency from Revolution to Rouhani.* New York: I.B. Taurus, 2017.

———. "The Tudeh Party of Iran and the Land Reform Initiatives of the Pahlavi State, 1958–1964." *Middle Eastern Studies* 58, no. 4 (2022): 617–35. https://doi.org/10.1080/00263206.2021.1976157

Rao, Anupama, and Stephen Pierce. *Discipline and the Other Body: Correction, Corporeality, Colonialism.* Durham, NC: Duke University Press, 2006.

Razwy, S. A. A. "Khomeini Upheld the Ideals and Values of Islam." *New York Times*, June 8, 1989.

Razzaghi, Emran M., Afarin Rahimi, Mehdi Hosseni, Saeid Madani, and Anindya Chatterjee. "Rapid Assessment (RSA) of Drug Abuse in Iran (1998–1999)." United Nations International Drug Control Programme, the Ministry of Health, Islamic Republic of Iran, and the Prevention Department, State Welfare Department, Islamic Republic of Iran, 1999. https://www.unodc.org/documents/islamicrepub licofiran/publications/RSA2000SUMMARY.pdf.

Reeves, Minou. *Behind the Peacock Throne.* London: Sidgwick & Jackson, 1986.

Rejali, Darius. *Torture and Democracy.* Princeton, NJ: Princeton University Press, 2007.

———. *Torture and Modernity: Self, Society, and State in Modern Iran.* Boulder, CO: Westview Press, 1994.

Resistance. "Mr. Human Rights Meets King Torture." *Resistance* 5, no. 1 (December 1977).

Reuters. "Amnesty Urges Iran to Allow Observers into Trials." August 12, 2009. https://www.reuters.com/article/us-iran-amnesty/amnesty-urges-iran-to-allow-observers-into-trials-idUSTRE57B28L20090812.

———. "Iranian Rial Slides to New Low as Coronavirus, Sanctions Weigh." July 4, 2020. https://www.reuters.com/article/us-iran-economy-rial/iran-rial-slides-to-new-low-as-coronavirus-sanctions-weigh-idUSKBN2450NL.

———. "Iran Reformer Says He Wants to Present Rape Evidence." August 19, 2009. https://www.reuters.com/article/Iran/idUSDAH93169320090819.

———. "U.S. Imposes Visa Restrictions on 14 Iranians over Human Rights Violations." August 21, 2020. https://www.reuters.com/article/us-usa-iran-designations/u-s-imposes-visa-restrictions-on-14-iranians-over-human-rights-violations-idUSKBN25H2AL.

Rezaian, Jason. *Prisoner: My 544 in an Iranian Prison*. Ecco: New York, 2018.

Rezvian, Mahmud, ed. *Naghmihha va ashʿar-e zendanian dar band-e SAVAK* [Prison songs and poetry from SAVAK's cells]. Tehran: ʿEbrat Museum, 1388/2009.

Richards, Stephen C., ed. *The Marion Experiment: Long-Term Solitary Confinement and the Supermax Movement*. Carbondale: Southern Illinois University Press, 2015.

———. "USP Marion: The First Federal Supermax." *Prison Journal* 88, no. 1 (March 2008): 6–22.

Roush, Sandra. "Chapter 19: Enhancing Surveillance." In *Manual for the Surveillance of Vaccine-Preventable Diseases*, edited by Sandra W. Roush, Linda M. Baldy, Mary Ann Kirkconnell Hall. National Center for Immunization and Respiratory Diseases, Center for Disease Control, last reviewed November 17, 2017. https://www.cdc.gov/vaccines/pubs/surv-manual/chpt19-enhancing-surv.html.

Ruggles-Brise, Evelyn. *Prison Reform at Home and Abroad: A Short History of the International Movement since the London Conference, 1872*. London: Macmillan, 1924.

Russell, Bertrand. "Inside the Shah's Prisons." Iranian Students Association of the United States, 1973.

Sadeghi-Boroujerdi, Eskandar. "Gharbzadegi, Colonial Capitalism, and the Racial State in Iran." *Postcolonial Studies* 24 (2020): 173–94.

———. "Iran's Uprisings for Women, Life, Freedom: Overdetermination, Crisis, and the Lineages of Revolt." *Politics* (forthcoming). Published ahead of print, March 23, 2023. https://doi.org/10.1177/02633957231159351.

———. "The Origins of Communist Unity: Anti-colonialism and Revolution in Iran's Tri-continental Moment." *British Journal of Middle Eastern Studies* 45, no. 5 (2018): 796–822.

Sadeghi-Boroujerdi, Eskandar, and Siavush Randjbar-Daemi. "Serving the Leviathan." *Jacobin*, January 18, 2017. https://www.jacobinmag.com/2017/01/iran-rafsanjani-ahmadinejad-khamenei-reform.

Saffari, Siavash. "Taqi Erani, Bizhan Jazani, and a Marxian Framework for the Critique of Religion in Twentieth Century Iranian Political Thought." *Iranian Studies* 54, no. 5–6 (2018): 859–77.

Safi, Ghasim. *Kart postalha-ye tarikhi-ye Irani* [Historical Iranian postcards]. Tehran: Muasaseh-ye Farhangi-ye Gustaresh-e Hunar, 1368/1989.

Sale, Richard T. "Baraheni: An Angry Voice from Iran." *New York Times*, September 4, 1977.

———. "SAVAK: A Feared and Pervasive Force." *Washington Post*, May 9, 1977. https://www.washingtonpost.com/archive/politics/1977/05/09/savak-a-feared-and-pervasive-force/ad609959-d47b-4b7f-8c8d-b388116df90c.

Samakar, Abbas. *Man yek shureshi hastam: Khaterat-e zendan va yadbud-e Khosrow Golsorkhi va Kermat Daneshian* [I am a rebel: Prison memoirs and reminiscences of Khosrow Golsorkhi and Kermat Daneshian]. Los Angeles: Ketab, 2001.

Samdipur, Saʿid. *Shekanjeh dar rezhim-e shah* [Torture in the shah's regime]. Tehran: Markaz-e Asnad-e Enghelab-e Eslami [Center for the Documentation of the Islamic Revolution], 1386/2007.

Saney, Parviz. "Iran." In *International Developments in Criminology*. Vol. 2, edited by E. H. Johnson, 357–69. Westport, CT: Greenwood, 1983.

Savin, Richard. *Vakil Abad Iran: A Survivor's Story*. Edinburgh: Canongate, 1979.

Sazman-e Mojahedin-e Khalq. *Hushyari-ye enqelabi: Vazifeh-ye yek mobarez asir dar zendan* [Revolutionary consciousness: Responsibilities of an imprisoned militant in prison]. Tehran: Sazman-e Mojahedin-e Khalq, 1972.

———. *Sazmandahi va taktikha*. Aden, Yemen: PMOI, 1353/1974.

Schaverian, Anna. "Trial Is Postponed of British-Iranian Woman Held in Iran." *New York Times*, September 13, 2020. https://www.nytimes.com/2020/09/13/world/middleeast/nazanin-zaghari-ratcliffe-iran-delay.html.

Schayegh, Cyrus. *Who Is Knowledgeable Is Strong: Science, Class, and the Formation of Modern Iranian Society*. Berkeley: University of California Press, 2009.

Schenwar, Maya, and Victoria Law. *Prison by Any Other Name: The Harmful Consequences of Popular Reforms*. New York: The New Press, 2020.

Schirazi, Asghar. *The Constitution of Iran: Politics and the State in the Islamic Republic*. Translated by John O'Kane. New York: I.B. Tauris, 1997.

Schneider, Irene. "Imprisonment in Pre-classical and Classical Islamic Law." *Islamic Law and Society* 2, no. 2 (1995): 157–73.

Schrader, Stuart. *Badges without Borders: How Global Counterinsurgency Transformed American Policing*. Berkeley, CA: University of California Press, 2018.

Schull, Kent. *Prisons in the Late Ottoman Empire: Microcosms of Modernity*. Edinburgh: Edinburgh University Press, 2014.

Sepehri Far, Tara. "Why Nasrin Sotoudeh Is on Hunger Strike to Protest Iran's Dire Prison Conditions." *Human Rights Watch*, September 10, 2020. https://www.hrw.org/news/2020/09/10/why-nasrin-sotoudeh-hunger-strike-protest-irans-dire-prison-conditions.

Serena, Carla. *Hommes et choses en Perse*. Paris: Charpentier, 1883.

Seyedalinaghi, SeyedAhmad, Leila Taj, Elham Mazaheri-Tehrani, Sara Ahsani-Nasab, Negin Abedinzadeh, Willi McFarland, Minoo Mohraz, and Ali Mirzazadeh. "HIV in Iran: Onset, Responses, and Future Directions." *AIDS* 35, no. 4 (March 15, 2021): 529–42.

Shahbazi, Mohammad, Marzieh Farnia, Khaled Rahmani, and Ghobad Moradi. "Trend of HIV/AIDS Prevalence and Related Interventions Administered in Prisons of Iran—13 Years' Experience." *Iran Journal of Public Health* 43, no. 4 (April 2014), 471–79.

Shahnavaz, Shahbaz. *Britain and South-West Persia 1880–1914: A Study in Imperialism and Economic Dependence.* New York: Routledge, 2005.

Shahri, Ja'far. *Tehran-e qadim* [Old Tehran]. Tehran: Entesharat-e Mo'in, 1369/1997.

Shahrokni, Nazanin. *Women in Place: The Politics of Gender Segregation in Iran.* Los Angeles: University of California Press, 2020.

Shamlu, Ahmad. "Farhang-e Zendan" [Prison dictionary]. *Ketab-e jom'eh*, 11 Murdad 1358/August 2, 1979, 159–61.

Shannon, Michael K. " 'Contacts with the Opposition': American Foreign Relations, the Iranian Student Movement, and the Global Sixties." *The Sixties: A Journal of History, Politics, and Culture* 4, no. 1 (2011).

———. *Losing Hearts and Minds: American-Iranian Relations and International Education during the Cold War.* Ithaca, NY: Cornell University Press, 2017.

Sharif, Solmaz. "Trying to Conjugate Displacement." *Kenyon Review*, December 30, 2013. www.kenyonreview.org/2013/12/trying-conjugate-displacement.

Sheikholeslami, Reza A. *The Structure of Central Authority in Qajar Iran, 1871–1896.* Costa Mesa, CA: Mazda, 1996.

Shirdel, Kamran, dir. *Women's Penitentiary.* 1965. Film.

Siavoshi, Sussan. *Montazeri: The Life and Thought of Iran's Revolutionary Ayatollah.* Cambridge: Cambridge University Press, 2017.

Siegel, Micol. *Violence Work: State Power and the Limits of Policing.* Durham, NC: Duke University Press, 2018.

Slobodian, Quinn. *Foreign Front: Third World Politics in 1960s West Germany.* Durham, NC: Duke University Press, 2012.

Smelka, Sara. "In or Out of Prison, Iranian Doctors Find a Way to Help." AIDS Foundation Chicago, November 16, 2012. https://www.aidschicago.org/page/news/inside-story/in-or-out-of-prison-iranian-doctors-find-way-to-help.

Sohrabi, Naghmeh. "In Search of Iran's Revolutionary Archives." *Jadaliyya*, October 4, 2021. https://www.jadaliyya.com/Details/43281/In-Search-of-Iran%E2%80%99s-Revolutionary-Archives.

———. "The 'Problem Space' of the Historiography of the 1979 Iranian Revolution." *History Compass* 16, no. 11 (2018): e12500.

———. "Remembering the Palestine Group: Global Activism, Friendship, and the

Iranian Revolution." *International Journal of Middle East Studies* 51, no. 2 (May 2019): 281–300.

Stack, Edward. *Six Months in Persia*. London: S. Low, Marston, Searle & Rivington, 1882.

Steulke, Patricia., *The Ruse of Repair: US Neoliberal Empire and the Turn from Critique*. Durham, NC: Duke University Press, 2021.

Sykes, Ella Constance. *Persia and Its People*. New York: The Macmillan Company, 1910.

Tafreshi, Morteza Sayfi Fami. *Polis-e khofiyeh-ye Iran 1299–1320: Mururi bar rukhdadha-ye siyasi va tarikhchih-ye shahrbani*. Tehran: Entesharat-e Qoqnus, 1367/1988.

Tait, Robert. "Iran's Parliament Exposes Abuse of Opposition Prisoners at Tehran Jail." *The Guardian*, January 10, 2010. https://www.theguardian.com/world/2010/jan/10/iran-prisoners-abuse-jail.

Talebi, Shahla. *Ghosts of Revolution: Rekindled Memories of Imprisonment in Iran*. Stanford: Stanford University Press, 2011.

Talley, Ian. "U.S. Sanctions Iran's Evin Prison, Broadcasting Chief, and Others, Alleging Human Rights Abuses." *Wall Street Journal*, May 30, 2018. https://www.wsj.com/articles/u-s-sanctions-irans-evin-prison-broadcasting-chief-and-others-alleging-human-rights-abuses-1527705343#comments_sector.

Taregol, Houshang. *Sepideh dar hal-e damidan ast: Akharin defa-ye taregol az goruh-e javed-e Arman-e Khalq dar dadgah-e nezami*. Rome: Sazman-e Enqelabi-ye Hezb-e Tudeh-ye Iran Dar Kharej az Keshvar, 1973.

Tasnim News Agency. "Bish az 14 milliard toman baraye sakht-e zendan-e jadid-e Aligodarz lehaz shod" [More than 14 billion toman necessary for building a new prison in Aligodarz]. Khordad 28, 1398/June 18, 2019, https://www.tasnimnews.com/fa/news/1398/03/28/2035130/بیش-از-14-میلیارد-تومان-برای-ساخت-زندان-لرستان-جدید-الیگودرز-لحاظ-شد.-جدید-الیگودرز-لحاظ-شد.

———. "Iran: Police Using Facial Recognition Cameras against Illegal Currency Dealers." *Eurasia Review*, June 26, 2019. https://www.eurasiareview.com/26062019-iran-police-using-facial-recognition-cameras-against-illegal-currency-dealers.

———. "Kanal 'dadsara-ye ershad' baraye daryaft gozareshhaye henjarshekani rah andazi shod." 15 Tir 1398/July 6, 2019. www.tasnimnews.com/fa/news/1398/04/15/2047454/کانال-دادسرای-ارشاد-برای-دریافت-گزارش-های-هنجارشکنی-راه-اندازی-شد.

———. "Khak-e Sefid: 15 sal bad." Mehr 27, 1395/October 18, 2016, https://www.tasnimnews.com/fa/news/1395/07/27/1215482/خاک-سفید-۱۵-سال-بعد.

———. "Taqaza-ye 2 hezar pasdar bara-ye zendanha-ye keshvar." 25 Dey 1392/January 15, 2014. https://www.tasnimnews.com/fa/news/1392/10/20/245032/تقاضای-2-هزار-پاسیار-برای-زندان-های-کشور.

Taylor, Flint. *The Torture Machine: Racism and Police Violence in Chicago*. Chicago: Haymarket Books, 2019.

Teeters, Negley. *Deliberations of the International Penal and Penitentiary Congresses, Questions and Answers, 1872–1935*. Philadelphia: Temple University Bookstore, 1949.

Tehran Times. "Iranian Inmates to Wear Ankle Monitors and Go Free." June 15, 2017. tehrantimes.com/news/414288/Iranian-inmates-to-wear-ankle-monitors-and-go-free.

Televizion-e Rah-e Kargar Dar YouTube. "Azadi zendanian-e siasi beh dast-e mardom." February 9, 2013. YouTube video, 1:58, https://www.youtube.com/watch?v=1uAQhJN2RYI.

Teltsch, Kathleen. "She May Be a Princess, but the Shah's Twin Is More Interested in Equal Rights." *New York Times*, March 22, 1970.

———. "U.N. Opens Year on Human Rights." *New York Times*, January 1, 1968.

Temko, Ned. "Bani-Sadr Strives to Rein in Iran's Revolutionary Guard." *Christian Science Monitor*, June 20, 1980, 4.

Time. "Human Rights: Torture and Policy: The Network of Evil." August 16, 1976.

———. "Iran: The Unknown Ayatullah Khomeini." July 16, 1979.

Times, The. "From Our Correspondent: Confessions Alleged over Iran Plot." January 3, 1969.

———. "Persia: An Execution in Teheran." January 28, 1910, 5.

Tortoise Media. "Evin Prison." Compiled and edited by Xavier Greenwood and Basia Cummings. September 7, 2020. https://members.tortoisemedia.com/2020/09/07/evin-prison-iran-interactivemap/content.html.

Tudeh Party. *SAVAK: Police secrète du chah*. Paris: Comité Central du Parti Toudeh d'Iran, 1976.

Unite! Bookstore. "Support the Iran Revolution, Expose Carter's 'Human Rights' Policy!" Flyer for event with ISAUS and the International Association for Filipino Patriots. Oakland, CA, n.d.

UNODC. *The Opium Economy in Afghanistan: An International Problem*. New York: United Nations, 2003.

Vahabzadeh, Peyman. *A Guerrilla Odyssey: Modernization, Secularism, Democracy, and the Fadai Period of National Liberation in Iran, 1971–1979*. Syracuse, NY: Syracuse University Press, 2010.

———. *A Rebel's Journey: Mostafa Sho'aiyan and Revolutionary Theory in Iran*. London: Oneworld, 2019.

Vergès, Françoise, *A Feminist Theory of Violence: A Decolonial Perspective*. London:

Pluto Press, 2022.

Vitale, Alex. *The End of Policing.* New York: Verso, 2018.

Walsmsley, Roy. *World Prison Population List.* 11th ed. Institute for Criminal Policy Research, 2015. www.prisonstudies.org/sites/default/files/resources/downloads/world_prison_population_list_11th_edition_0.pdf.

Wang, Jackie. *Carceral Capitalism.* South Pasadena, CA: Semiotext(e), 2018.

Wege, Carl Anthony. "Iranian Counterintelligence." *International Journal of Intelligence and Counterintelligence* 32, no. 2 (2019): 272–94.

Williams, E. Crawshay. *Across Persia.* London: E. Arnold, 1907.

Wills, C. J. *Persia as It Is.* London: S. Low, Marston, Searle & Rivington, 1886.

Wilson, S. G. *Persian Life and Customs: With Scenes and Incidents of Residence and Travel in the Land of the Lion and the Sun.* New York: Fleming H. Revel, 1895.

Women's Organization of Iran. *Vali Hazrat Shahdokht Ashraf Pahlavi dar barayeh huquq-e zanan* [Her Royal Majesty Princess Ashraf Pahlavi on women's rights]. Tehran: Women's Organization of Iran, 1354/1975.

World Health Organization (WHO), Regional Office for the Eastern Mediterranean. *Best Practice in HIV/AIDS Prevention and Care for Injecting Drug Abusers: The Triangular Clinic in Kermanshah, Islamic Republic of Iran.* Cairo: World Health Organization, 2004. https://www.who.int/hiv/pub/idu/idu_emro_iran_2004.pdf.

Yang, Anand. *Crime and Criminality in British India.* Tucson, AZ: University of Arizona Press, 1985.

Yari, Ziba. "Behind Prison Walls: Inmates on Execution Wednesdays at Rajaei Shahr Prison." *Iran Wire*, August 19, 2022. https://iranwire.com/en/prisoners/106767-behind-prison-walls-iranian-inmates-on-execution-wednesdays-at-rajaei-shahr-prison.

Young Journalists Club (YJC), Islamic Republic. "Kahesh jam'iat-e keyfari avaliyat-e sazman-e zendanha ast." Young Journalists Club, 13 Dey 1393/January 3, 2015. https://www.yjc.ir/fa/news/5089166/کاهش-جمعیت-کیفری-اولویت-سازمان-زندان-ها-استضرورت-استفاده-از-ظرفیت-های-قانون-مجازات-اسلامی.

Zarinebaf, Fariba. *Crime and Punishment in Istanbul: 1700–1800.* Berkeley: University of California Press, 2011.

Zarkari, Yusef. *Khaterat-e yek cherik dar zendan: Neveshteh-e az cherik-e fadai-ye khalq.* N.p.: Sazmanha-ye Jebheh-ye Melli-ye Iran dar Kharej az Keshvar (Bakhsh-e Khavar Miyaneh), 1352/1973. 2nd ed. with introduction by Ashraf Dehqani. London: Cherikha-ye Fadai-ye Khalq Iran, 1391/2013. Page references are to the 2013 edition.

Zinoman, Peter. *The Colonial Bastille: A History of Imprisonment in Vietnam, 1862–1940.* Berkeley: University of California Press, 2001.

Index

60 Minutes, 129

Abadan prison, 106, 108
Abbasid Empire, 66
Abdi, Abbas, 170
abolitionism, 22, 285n17
Abrahamian, Ervand, 17, 28, 38–39, 45, 102, 181, 186
abrogation of capitulations, 62, 70
absolutism, 36–38, 127
Abu-Jamal, Mumia, 20
activism, 17, 21–22, 130–32, 147, 148, 158, 178, 195, 210; global, 138–40, 164; human rights, 145–46, 163; Iranian, 2, 149, 165, 221; political, 8, 13, 32, 115, 200; prison, 19, 31, 214; revolutionary, 116, 118; student, 100–101, 107, 125, 207. *See also* protestors
Adulyadej, Bhumibol, 135
Afghanistan, 57, 159, 203
Afghan people, 57, 90, 108, 172
Afkari, Navid, 1, 176

Africa, 27; North, 132. *See also* Pan-Africanism
African Americans, 162
aftabkaran-e jangal. *See* Organization of Iranian People's Fadai Guerillas (Fadaian, or OIPFG)
Agency for International Development, 84
Aghasi Khan, 44
Ahmadinejad, Mahmoud, 204–6, 208–9
Ahmad Shah, 57
Ahmadzadeh, Masoud, 97, 127
Ahvaz, 34
Alaei, Arash, 200–201, 203–4
Alaei, Kamiar, 200–201, 203–4
al-Afghani, Jamal al-Din, 50–51
Alam, Asadollah, 149, 257n1
Alavi, Bozorg, 8, 14, 49, 157
Albert, Jan, 160
Al-e Ahmad, Jalal, 155; *Westoxification*, 157
Algeria, 12, 116, 262n68

319

Ali (first Shi'a Imam), 105
Allied invasion (1941), 10
American empire, 158
Amini, Jina Mahsa, 11–12, 219, 223
Amir-Entezam, Abbas, 182
Amir Kabir, 54
amnesties, 48–49, 197, 269n8
Amnesty International (AI), 16, 18, 131, 142, 146–51, 161, 165, 174, 181, 210
amuzeshgah-e nikiha. *See* virtue training schools
Anbar-e Shahi, 49–50, 53, 222
Ancient Iran Museum. *See* Iran-e Bastan Museum
Andrejevic, Mark, 216
Anglophone world, 22
Anglo-Russian agreement (1907), 58
Anjoman-e hemayat-e zendanian. *See* Organization for the Protection of Prisoners (OPP)
Ansari, Hojjat-ol-Eslam Majid, 170, 184, 192
anticolonialism, 15, 35, 50. *See also* colonialism
Arani, Taqi, 85; "The Materialist Concept of History," 86
archival research, 20; of the "minor archive," 97
archive-in-opposition, 100
Arman-e Khalq. *See* People's Ideal, The
Ashraf, Hamid, 95–96
Asia, 27. *See also* Southeast Asia
Assembly of Experts, 192, 277n25
Atatürk, Mustafa Kemal, 140
Atlantic world, 22
Austria, 54, 234n75; Vienna, 55
authoritarianism, 11, 23, 132, 140–41, 220
autocracy, 50, 98–99, 131, 140, 142, 202, 224

Avanessian, Ardeshir, 12, 64
Ayrom, Mohammad Hossein, 68
Azerbaijan (Iranian province), 110, 126
Azeri Turkish language, 47, 122

Babism, 46, 51
bad criminal, figure of, 9. *See also* good citizen, figure of
Bahrami, Fazlollah, 70
Bahrami, Mirza Abdollah, 67
Bajoghli, Narges, 206
Bakhtiar, Teymour, 86, 107
Bamdad (newspaper), 186
Bandar Abbas Prison, 106
Bani-Sadr, Abolhassan, 187–88
Baradaran, Monira, 191–92, 225n4
Baraghani, Fatemeh Zarrin-Taj, 46
Baraheni, Reza, 152–55, 264–65n97, 264n95; *Crowned Cannibals, The*, 156–58
bastinado. *See* falak
Battle of Karbala, 105
Bazargan, Mehdi, 162, 182–84, 267n129
Bazdashtdgah-e Kahrizak. *See* Kahrizak Detention Center
Beccaria, Cesare, 24, 77–78
Becket, James, 146
Beh aftabkaran: Ghazalsorudeha az band (pamphlet), 115
Behpur, Abolhasan: "Prisons and Prisoners" (doctoral dissertation), 77–79
Behrangi, Samad, 126, 155
Behrouzan, Orkideh, 199–200
Belgium, 47
Benjamin, S. G. W., 48
Bentham, Jeremy, 24, 234n75
Bentley, Eric, 152
Bertrand Russell Peace Foundation, 138

INDEX 321

Black internationalism, 99
Black liberation movements, 21–22
Black Panther Party, 20, 142, 261n36
Black Power Movement, 139
Bolshevik Revolution, 83
Bolshevism, 68
Bongah-e taʿavun va Sanaʿi-e zendanian. *See* Institute for the Cooperation and Industry of Prisoners (ICIP)
Braunschweig, Jean Michel, 148–49
Brazil, 25, 116, 254n78
brigandage, 17, 56
British Empire, 30
British Labour Party, 143–52
British Parliament, 32, 130, 143–45
Bush, George H. W., 199
Butcher of Evin. *See* Lajaverdi, Asadollah
Butler, William J., 150–51, 163

Cacho, Lisa, 93
Café Saqi. *See* Qezel Qalʿeh Prison
Cage, John, 152
California: Oakland, 142–43
Cambodia, 118, 159
Campaign for the Abolition of Torture, 147
Canadian Sociological Association, 147
capitalism, 23, 27, 99, 140, 157, 267n114
capital punishment. *See* death penalty
carceral centralization, 7–8, 37–38
carcerality, 16, 99, 105, 205–17, 221; modern, 10, 24, 27, 37, 106, 222–23
carceral politics, 12–13
carceral reforms, 7, 25, 54–60, 86–87, 206, 214
carceral state, 3, 7, 16, 19, 22, 106, 169, 215, 217, 221–24; Iran, 30, 32–33; shrinking of, 206, 214

carceral system, 21, 26, 63, 79, 98, 107–8, 196, 217; modern, 6–7, 10, 23, 31, 60, 65, 139, 175; post-1979, 15, 169, 172
carceral utopianism, 15, 189–90
carceral violence, 2, 16, 32, 138, 165, 168–70, 177–78, 188, 219, 221
Carter, James Earl, Jr., 133–34, 142–43, 151
Caspian Sea, 95–96
Central Intelligence Agency (CIA), 15, 82, 85–87, 151, 156, 176, 247n116
centralization, 10, 38, 63, 172, 183–84; carceral, 7–8, 37–38; legal, 3, 31, 39, 63–67, 70, 73. *See also* carceral centralization
Central Kermanshah Prison. *See* Dizel Abad Prison
Central Police Prison, 59, 71–72, 107
Central Provisional Committee, 183
Central Shiraz Prison, 176
chador, 74, 192
child criminality, 75–76
Childs, J. Rives, 70
Chile, 143
China, 23–25, 27, 50, 269n17
Chinese Revolution, 101
circle of justice, theory of, 39, 78
citizenship, 7–8, 71, 73–74, 79, 131, 167, 176, 178, 182–83, 221–22; "good," 9, 91, 94; Iranian, 81, 93; Islamic, 10, 193, 197, 210; productive, 4, 10, 25–26, 31, 76; US, 50, 70. *See also* good citizen, figure of
civilized nation, notion of, 4, 10, 83
clerical prisoners, 3, 109
clerical revolutionaries, 111, 129–30
clerics, 38, 95–96, 110, 148, 164, 178–79, 183, 204, 224
Cockburn, Alexander, 160

Cold War, 129, 143, 146, 153
colonialism, 4, 22, 25, 27, 30, 52, 115, 267n23. *See also* anticolonialism; neocolonialism; semicolonialism
Committee for Artistic and Intellectual Freedom in Iran (CAIFI), 155
Committee for Human Rights in Iran, 163
common-law prisoners. *See* ordinary prisoners
communism, 76, 84–86, 96, 102, 148, 258n3; anti, 83, 265n101; international, 150, 160; Tudeh Party, 8, 111, 139, 176
Confederation of Iranian Students, National Union (CISNU), 117–18, 139–40, 143–45, 150, 251n20, 261n40
constitutionalists, 50–52, 61, 115. *See also* Constitutional Revolution (1905-1911)
Constitutional Revolution (1905-1911), 30, 35, 38, 50–53, 56–59, 61–63, 202
corruption, 17, 37, 62, 69, 131, 162–63, 186, 190, 202
Cottam, Richard, 151
counterrevolutionaries, 15, 169, 178–79, 186, 190
coup d'état (1921), 10, 30–31, 62
coup d'état (1953), 10, 15, 30–31, 82, 84, 86, 94–95, 107, 116, 156
COVID-19, 195, 212, 215
criminality, 26, 57, 71, 75, 77, 89, 93–94, 170, 180, 195; explosion of, 8, 30, 35
criminal psychology, 68, 77
criminal reform, 4, 10, 24, 78, 210
criminology, 4, 8, 24–25, 31–32, 67, 89–90, 193, 195, 210; European, 68, 88; Iranian, 76–81; Marxist, 233–34n75

critical prison studies, 10, 21–23
Cronin, Stephanie, 57
Cuba, 96, 116
Cuban Revolution, 101
Cunningham, Merce, 152
Curzon, George, 47–48

Dabashi, Hamid, 105
Danesh, Taj Zaman, 80–81
Daneshgah-e ulum-e ghazai va khadmat-e edari. *See* University of Judicial Sciences and Administrative Services
Daneshian, Kermat, 104–5, 109, 155
D'Arcy oil concession (1901), 34
Dargahi, Mohammad, 69–70, 72–73
Dashti, Ali, 64
Davar, Ali Akbar, 63–64, 69, 80
Davis, Angela, 12–13, 21–22, 285n17
death penalty, 15, 46, 55, 213, 220
Dehqani, Ashraf: *Hamaseh-ye moqavemat* (*Epic of Resistance*), 121, 126–28
democracy, 38, 58, 73, 98, 115, 153, 202, 209, 219, 221
despotism, 4, 37, 50, 52, 103, 115, 156, 167, 223
detention, 3, 50, 104, 149, 213; camps, 172, 207; centers, 10, 46, 136, 157, 171, 175, 208–9, 211–12, 219
Detroit Free Press, 43
Deuxième Bureau, 84
dialectical materialism, 83
dialectics, 83, 86, 247n106
diaspora, 20, 33, 222, 227n9, 250n6; Iranian, 2, 100, 139, 220
digital prison mapping, 8
Dikötter, Frank, 23–25
discipline, 14, 23, 100, 104, 109, 120, 159, 211; and Foucault, 26–28; and reform,

80–81; state, 94, 96–98; and Zarkari, 122, 126
diyat, 39, 173. *See also* hudud; ta'zir
Dizel Abad Prison, 199–201, 204, 278n36
Doctorow, E. L., 153–58, 160
Donya (journal), 85
Drug Control Headquarters, 189, 202
drugs, 15, 17, 29, 186–90, 195, 213; charges, 111, 170, 211; and HIV/AIDS, 198–205; use of, 18–19, 72–73, 81, 87, 90, 93, 108, 172, 207, 222. *See also* methadone maintenance therapy; opioids; opium
dungeons, 37, 47, 49, 53, 55, 78, 175
Durkheim, Émile, 67, 241n26

Eastern Europe, 27
'Ebrat (magazine), 176
'Ebrat Museum, 175–77
education, 19, 38, 72, 75, 191, 210–11, 219; in prisons, 76, 82, 100, 110, 173, 192; revolutionary, 104, 118–22. *See also* schools
Egypt, 27, 133, 179
Elling, Rasmus, 115
elm-e zendan. *See* prison sciences
Emsley, Clive, 24–25
Enayat, Hadi, 37–38, 40, 62
England, 24, 30, 35, 144; London, 36, 48, 58, 67–68, 70, 144, 149, 151–52
English language, 1–2, 8, 98, 137, 141–42
English people, 24, 35–36, 45, 48, 56–57
Ennals, Martin, 131
ephemera, 97, 100, 112–13, 115, 185
escalation, 12, 15–16, 175, 189, 205, 210, 214
Esmaili, Gholamhosseim, 211–12
Ettela'at (newspaper), 102, 104, 144

Europe, 40, 42, 49, 67–68, 76, 117, 143, 152; and activism, 129–31, 138–39, 145, 147–48, 164; and colonialism, 30, 61–62, 99; influence from, 4, 12, 47–48, 51, 54–56, 58–60, 80, 86, 89; penal reform influence from, 24–25, 27, 36–37. *See also* Eastern Europe; police, European style
European colonialism, 30, 37, 61–62, 99
Evin Prison, 13, 64, 111, 152, 167–75, 185–86, 191–92, 208, 211–12, 222; interrogation centers, 118, 124, 126; solitary confinement, 107–8, 204
Evin University. *See* Evin Prison
executions, 128, 133, 145, 149, 162, 206; extrajudicial, 109, 132, 148, 163, 221; of guerrillas, 101–5; under the Islamic Republic, 178–79, 181, 184–89, 200, 209, 226n4, 275n104; of Navid Afkari, 1, 176; of political prisoners, 108, 192; prison, 22, 196–97; public, 26, 205, 267n119; Qajar era, 45–46, 48, 54–59
expatriates, 2, 103, 117, 130, 132, 138–39, 141–42, 164
Expediency Council, 202

Fadaian-e Islam party, 8, 243n41
failure, 23–24, 73, 88, 98–99, 101
falak, 40, 42–44, 50, 58, 108
falakeh (nickname of Anbar-e Shahi). *See* Anbar-e Shahi
Farhangestan-e Zaban-e Iran. *See* Persian Language Academy
Fars, 88
fascism, 14, 140, 156
Fashafouyeh. *See* Greater Tehran Central Prison
Fath 'Ali Khan, 43–44

Fazli, Abdolreza Rahmani, 210
Fellah, Mohammad, 202
female prisoners, 45–46, 59, 72–75, 82, 91, 106, 200–201, 263n68
feminism, 21, 135, 147, 156, 220
Firuz Nosrat al-Dowleh, 72
Ford, Gerald, 135
Foucault, Michel, 19, 101, 235n83; *Discipline and Punish*, 26–28. *See also* Groupe d'information sur les prisons (GIP)
France, 19, 25–27, 67, 79, 81, 84, 135, 148–49, 159; Neauphle-le-Château, 180; Paris, 76–77
Franco, Francisco, 135
Frankfurt School, 83
Fraser, Donald, 150
freedom, 9, 72–73, 90, 141, 149, 155, 159, 161–63, 224; movements for, 23, 96, 122, 220, 260–61n36; postrevolutionary, 3, 222
Freedom to Write Committee, 153. *See also* International PEN

Gahan, Jairan, 71
Gaillard, Xavier, 177
gendarmerie, 57–58, 88, 107, 175, 248n120
gender, 31, 91, 156, 186, 216, 220, 222
Georgia (country): Tbilisi, 68
Germany, 40, 140; Frankfurt, 139; Munich, 220, 284n13
Gest, Michel, 148–49
Getachew, Adom, 99
Ghamari-Tabrizi, Behrooz, 99, 167
Gharavian, Mohsen, 215–16
Ghiabi, Maziyar, 61, 87, 187, 202, 208
Gibson, Mary, 27

Gilan, 115
Gilmore, Ruth Wilson, 21
global south, 9, 24, 27, 83, 234n78
Globe, 48
Gohar Dasht Prison, 173
Golrou, Mahdieh, 221
Golsorkhi, Khosrow, 104–6, 109
good citizen, figure of, 9, 90, 94. *See also* bad criminal, figure of
Gramsci, Antonio, 30
Grant, Ulysses S., 50
Great Britain, 1, 31–37, 47, 52, 55–57, 67, 130, 137, 144, 163; and the liberal left, 143–52. *See also* British Empire; British Labour Party; British Parliament; England
Greater Tehran Central Prison, 171, 211
Greece, 140; Athens, 138
Green Movement, 205–6, 209, 219
Groupe d'information sur les prisons (GIP), 19
Group of 53, 85, 141
Group of Twelve, 104, 106, 109
group therapy, 11, 93
guerrilla movement, 8, 31, 95–105, 108–29, 139–41, 161, 164, 166, 175, 222; Fadaian, 148, 187. *See also* Organization of Iranian People's Fadai Guerillas (Fadaian, or OIPFG); People's Mojahedin Organization of Iran (PMOI)

habsiyeh, 66. *See also* prison poetry
Hajebi Tabrizi, Vida, 147, 167, 262–63n68
Hajj Sayyah. *See* Mahallati, Mirza Mohammad-'Ali
Haj Mohammadi, Mohammad Mehdi, 24–25, 216

hakem-e shar', 185, 187
Hakim-Elahi, Hedayatollah, 71–76, *91*, 243n44
Hall, Stuart, 21
Halliburton, Richard, 70
Hamadan, 173
harm reduction programs, 200, 203–5, 208, 213, 217
health of prisoners, 78
Hegel, Georg, 83
Helbig, Elahe, 58
Heldmann, Hans, 148–49
Heller, Joseph, 155, 158
hepatitis B, 201, 204
Her Britannic Majesty's Consul (Iran), 35
hijab, 12, 195, 215–16
Hijazi, Muhammad Baqir, 71
historiography, 16–17, 21, 27, 32, 53, 97, 116, 228n17, 249–50n6
HIV/AIDS, 33, 195–205
Hooman, Ahmad, 4, 55, 72, 79–80, 107
Hosseini, Maryam Alsadat, 65
Hosseinkhah, Maryam, 201
Hotel Saqi. *See* Qezel Qal'eh Prison
Hoveyda, Amir Abbas, 13, 134, 149, 185
Hoveyda, Fereydoun, 134
Hudson, Rock, 199
hudud, 39, 173. *See also* diyat; ta'zir
humanitarianism, 24, 26, 71, 83, 174, 234n75
Human Rights Commission, 135
human rights industry, 130, 132
human rights movements, 12, 19, 32, 130, 132, 139, 158
human rights organizations, 2, 18, 130, 132, 142, 174, 181, 184, 213. *See also individual human rights organizations*

human rights revolution, 32, 131
Hungary, 12
hunger strikes, 1, 181, 231n48

Illinois: Marion, 11, 92
imagination, 10, 18, 27; political, 99, 101, 116, 159, 207, 219; revolutionary, 105, 113
Imperial Guard, 166
Imperial Iranian Gendarmerie, 87
imperialism, 11, 30, 37, 103, 140, 156, 161, 187–88, 221; anti-, 143, 164; Euro-American, 11; European, 99; Pahlavi, 142; US, 13. *See also* American empire; British Empire; Russian Empire
Imperial Russian Army, 68
India, 30, 47, 50, 56, 118, 159, 269n17
Institute for Social Science and Research (ISSR), 76. *See also* University of Tehran
Institute for the Cooperation and Industry of Prisoners (ICIP), 82, 89, 92–94
International Association for Filipino Patriots, 143
International Association of Democratic Lawyers, 148
International Commission of Jurists (ICJ), 129, 150–51, 163
International Conference on Human Rights (1968), 136–37
International Congress of Criminology, 77
International Herald Tribune, 183
"International Human Rights Year" (1968), 135
International PEN, 152–61, 264n94

International Penal and Penitentiary Conference (1925), 67
International Police Academy (IPA), 84, 87
International Police Academy Review, 87–88
International Prison Commission (IPC), 67–68, 79. *See also* International Penal and Penitentiary Conference (1925)
International Women's Day, 183
interrogation centers, 2–3, 33, 118, 129, 151, 158–60, 189, 219; SAVAK, 103, 106–8, 136, 166. *See also* Komiteh-ye Moshtarek-e Zedd-e Kharabkar
intravenous drug use, 198–99, 201–2, 205
Iran-e Bastan Museum, 137
Iran Human Rights Documentation Center, 18
Iranian Americans, 50
Iranian Army, 84, 87
Iranian Association of Jurists, 162
Iranian Bar Association, 4, 72
Iranian Bureau of Prisons, 88
Iranian cabinet, 82
Iranian Committee for the Defense of Freedom and Human Rights (ICDFHR), 162–63, 267n129, 268n137
Iranian Communist Party, 12, 64, 84, 86
Iranian Cossack Brigade, 68
Iranian Ministry of Defense, 68
Iranian Ministry of Finance, 68
Iranian Ministry of Justice, 68, 184
Iranian National Police Bureau of Identification, 81
Iranian Parliament, 144–45
Iranian Revolution. *See* Islamic Revolution of 1979

Iran-Iraq war, 20, 32, 189, 196, 217
Iran National Bank, 92
Iran Radio, 185
Iran Tribune, 137
Iron Curtain, 152
Isfahan, 59, 122, 173, 184
Isfahan University, 76
Islamic Azad University, 192
Islamic leftists, 178, 181
Islamic liberals, 178, 180–82, 185
Islamic Republic News Agency (IRNA), 199
Islamic Republic of Iran, 2, 11, 19, 24, 32, 130, 169, 172–73, 223, 228n17
Islamic Republic's Organization of Prisons and National Security Measures. *See* Prisons Organization
Islamic Revolutionary Guard Corps (IRGC), 171, 176, 202, 207–8
Islamic Revolution of 1979, 2, 30, 32, 59, 113–14, 186
Islamists, 8, 116, 139, 153, 157, 165, 176, 190, 261n40; carceral, 223; clerical, 109; intellectuals, 97; left, 250n6; Marxist, 98, 100, 101; militant, 182; organizations, 181; prisoner, 3, 12, 111, 115, 148; revolutionary, 110, 178
Israel, 3, 11, 15, 93, 220, 247n116
Israeli Institute for Intelligence and Special Operations (Mossad), 15
Italian Committee for the Defense of Political Prisoners, 148
Italy, 30, 54, 77, 148

Jafari, Peyman, 220
Jahangir, Asghar, 7, 25, 212–14
Jangal movement (1915-1921), 115
Japan, 25, 50, 68

Javadi, Ali Asghar, 162–63
Javadifar, Amir, 208
Jazani, Bizhan, 8, 97, 101, 127, 148
Joint Anti-Sabotage Committee. *See* Komiteh-ye Moshtarek-e Zedd-e Kharabkar
Joint UN Programme on HIV/AIDS, 203
journalists, 71, 104, 129–30, 133, 156, 170, 219
Judicial Organization of the Military of the Islamic Republic, 163
juridical system, 11, 40, 42
jurists, 63, 178, 182–83, 196, 222, 276n17, 277n25
justice, 7, 19, 41, 48, 51, 59, 73, 77, 99, 141; circle of, 39, 78; criminal, 79–80, 93; Iranian, 61–62; Islamic, 32, 173–74, 179–80, 188–89; revolutionary, 128, 186

Kaba, Mariame, 21, 214
Kahrizak Detention Center, 207–9
Kalantari, Mokhtar, 202
Kamrani, Mohammad, 208
Karaj, 92
Karimi, Ehsan, 220
Karroubi, Mehdi, 206, 208
Karun River, 34
Kashani-Sabet, Firoozeh, 37
Kasravi, Ahmad, 53–54
Kayhan (newspaper), 89, 202
Kayhan (publishing company), 137
Kermani, Mirza Reza, 51
Kermani, Nazem al-Islam, 53
Kermanshah, 173, 199–201
Ketab-e Hafteh (journal), 111
Keys, Barabara, 131, 146
Khalkhali, Sadeq, 106, 179, 185–88, 202

Khamenei, Ali, 3, 162, 176, 178, 195–96, 198, 201–2, 206, 208–14, 277n25
Khandaniha (journal), 74
Khatami, Mohammad, 201–2, 204, 206, 219–20
Khoi Prison, 110
Khomeini, Ayatollah Ruhollah, 19, 103, 112, 130–33, 161–62, 164, 198, 276n18; and 1963 protests, 84, 117, 138; death of, 32, 170, 177, 196–97, 217; and revolutionary Iran, 166, 168, 173–75, 178–84, 186–87, 189
Khosrow, Nasser, 111
Khuzestan, 88
Kianuri, Noureddin, 189
Kissinger, Henry, 160
Knanishu, Joseph, 42–43, 45
Komiteh-ye defaʿ az huquq-e bashar dar Iran. *See* Committee for Human Rights in Iran
Komiteh-ye Enqelab, 180–81, 184, 188, 202, 216, 276n13
Komiteh-ye Moshtarek-e Zedd-e Kharabkar, 107, 175, 266n113
Komiteh-ye Towhid. *See* Oneness of God Committee
Kosiński, Jerzy, 155, 158, 265n105
Kun, Béla, 12
kundeh, 51–53, 59
Kurdish people, 12, 199–200, 219
Kurdish people's movement, 178

Labor Party, 149
Lahidji, Abdol-Karim, 162–63
Lajaverdi, Asadollah, 191–92, 275nn2–3
Larijani, Ali, 208
Larijani, Ayatollah Sadeq Amoli, 18, 208, 213, 231n50

Latin America, 27, 133, 143, 249n4
Law, Victoria, 214
law enforcement, 12, 24, 36, 58, 71, 87–89, 179–81, 185, 195, 207–8; changes in, 54, 60; and heroin trafficking, 203–4; Iranian, 214–16; officials, 4, 56, 63; Pahlavi, 68, 81, 83–84, 90. *See also* gendarmerie
Law of the Principles of Criminal Trials (1912), 62
Lawrence, T. E., 70
Lawrence of Arabia. *See* Lawrence, T. E.
League of Nations, 58
Le Bon, Gustave, 64
leftists, 12, 14, 49, 83, 126, 176–78, 181, 185, 189, 250n6; British liberal, 143–52; guerillas, 8, 111–13, 125; international, 102, 116, 130; Iranian, 85–86, 95, 109–10, 141, 155; Islamic, 98, 105, 119
legal code, 3, 63
legal fetishism, 37
legality, 37, 57, 62–63, 72, 141, 150, 174, 182
legal reforms, 7, 37, 52, 54–55, 61–63, 77, 163
Lenin, Vladimir, 83, 111. *See also* Marxism-Leninism
letter-writing campaigns, 2, 144, 227n9
Levasseur, Georges, 150
liberalism, 12, 27–28, 130–33, 139, 141–52, 155, 162–64, 215, 223; Islamic, 178, 180–82, 184–85, 250n6; and reforms, 26, 213. *See also* neoliberalism
liberation, 8, 21–22, 118, 176
Long Live International Solidarity (album), 118
Los Angeles Times, 135
Lynch and Company, 34–35

Macdonald, Dwight, 155
Mahallati, Mirza Mohammad-'Ali, 50–51, 54
Mahdavi Kani, Mohammad Reza, 183
Mahmood, Saba, 126
Majles, 192, 209
Mandela, Nelson, 18, 231n51
Mansoori, Davood, 201
Maoism, 83, 130, 139, 145, 178, 261n40
Maoist Revolutionary Organization, 143
mapping, 8, 96, 99–100, 117–18, 255n84. *See also* digital prison mapping
Marighella, Carlos, 254n78
Marion Penitentiary, 11, 92–93. *See also* USP Marion
Markaz-e amuzesh va pajuheshi-ye sazman-e zendanha. *See* Prisons Organization Research and Education Center
Markaz-e mobarezah ba mavad-e mokhadar. *See* Drug Control Headquarters
Markov, Nikolai, 68–69
Marshall, Leon, Weill, and Mahoney (legal team), 153
martyrdom, 3, 103–4, 115, 120, 123, 196
Marx, Karl, 26, 37, 83, 233–34n75
Marxism, 26–27, 30, 109, 111, 148, 155–56, 176, 190, 261n40, 265n101; Fadaian, 115, 122, 187, 249n4; guerrilla, 95, 97, 103; Iranian, 83–86, 127 (*See also* Iranian Marxism); Islamist, 98, 157; revolutionary, 100–102, 105, 140, 143, 147, 257n3, 262n68
Marxism-Leninism, 12, 83, 98, 105, 114, 130, 142, 165, 178, 266n106
Marxist-Islamists, 98, 101, 157
Masculine History, theory of, 156–57
Mashhad, 11, 50, 90, 108, 173, 182

Mashhad University, 76
mass arrests, 15, 33, 178, 188, 194, 205, 221
mass criminalization, 7, 10, 222
mass incarceration, 7, 9, 14, 178, 185, 214
mass movements, 96, 112, 120, 131. *See also* Tudeh Party
masters of wrath. *See* mir ghazab
material cultures, 97, 112–18
Matin-Asgari, Afshin, 86
maximum-security prisons, 11, 92, 106
Mecca, 50
mental health, 19, 79–80, 90, 191, 193
Metaxas, Ioannis, 140
methadone maintenance therapy, 203–5
methodology of possibility, 99. *See also* Moradian, Manijeh
methodology of the book, 3–4, 6–33. *See also* archival research; critical prison studies; historiography
Mewbold, Greg, 93
Mexico, 269n17; Mexico City, 133
Middle East, 132
migrant camps, 172, 271n32
military tribunals, 101–2, 105, 118, 141, 145, 185
Millett, Kate, 147
Minelli, Liza, 160
minimum-security prisons, 92
Ministry of Health, 202, 204
Ministry of Intelligence and Security, 171, 175
mir ghazab, 45
Mirza Kuchek Khan, 115
Mirza Nasrollah Khan Mushir od-Dowleh, 57
missionaries, 40, 42
Mobasser, Mohsen, 82–90

modernity, 4, 8, 10, 23, 94; carceral, 14, 16, 27, 57, 94
modern prison system, 3, 6, 8, 14, 64–65
Moghaddam, Nasser, 185
Mohajer, Nasser, 22
Mohammad Reza Shah Pahlavi, 95–96, 106, 129, 131–38, 146, 150–51, 160, 166, 179, 220; prisons under, 2, 63–64, 82–84, 90, 93, 108, 112–*14*, 163, 177. *See also* Pahlavi era
Moinian, Nosratollah, 162
Mojahedin-e Khalq Organization. *See* People's Mojahedin Organization of Iran (PMOI)
Monaqah, Amir Nosrat, 107
Montazeri, Ayatollah Hossein-Ali, 110+11, 130, 148, 196–97, 276n18
Monteforte, Conte di, 54–55, 78
Moradian, Manijeh, 99
Morad Mirza Qajar Hessam ol-Saltaneh, 48
Mortazevi, Saeed, 209
Mossad. *See* Israeli Institute for Intelligence and Special Operations (Mossad)
Mossadeq, Mohammad, 15, 82, 139
Mothers of Khavaran, 221
Mousavi, Mir Hossein, 206, 208, 219
Movement of Catholic Intellectuals, Pax Romana, 148
murder, 17, 34–36, 39–42, 74, 76, 89, 133, 174, 186, 221
museums, 3–6, 70, 81, 175–77, 242n30
Muslims, 50, 95, 107, 110, 114, 139, 178, 186, 199, 210
My Prison, My Home, 2

Naderpour, Bahram, 185–86
Naraqi, Ehsan, 76

330 INDEX

Nasser al-Din Shah, 30, 34, 38, 46, 51, 54–55, 235n1
Nasseri Period, 44, 46, 49, 54
Nassiri, Nematollah, 151, 185–86
National AIDS Prevention Committee, 199
National Front, 139
National Intelligence and Security Organization. *See* SAVAK
nationalism, 9, 12, 23–25, 37, 58, 61–62, 99, 139, 195, 258n3; anticolonial, 15; Iranian, 40, 51–53, 55, 66, 74; Pahlavi, 4, 89; secular, 178; state, 10, 102, 137. *See also* patriotic motherhood
National Police Force, 75–76, 84–85, 87–88, 175
National Research Institute of Tuberculosis and Lung Disease, 201
National University of Iran, 76
nazmiyeh, 54, 58, 64
Nedamatgah-e mardan va zanan. *See* Penitentiary for Men and Women
Negahdar, Farrokh, 148
neocolonialism, 132
neoconservativism, 13
neoliberalism, 132
Newens, Stan, 143–44
newspapers, 8, 48, 148, 150; Iranian, 70–71, 73, 89, 102, 104, 144, 185–86, 189
Newsweek (magazine), 111
New York City, 135, 160, 184, 203; Manhattan, 20, 135
New York Times, 135, 146, 150, 155–56
New Zealand, 11, 93, 182
NGOs, 132
Nikkhah, Parviz, 145
nonpolitical prisoners. *See* ordinary prisoners

North Africa, 132
North America, 23
Nowruz, 48–49

O'Brien, Tim: *Going after Cacciato*, 158, 160
Oneness of God Committee Prison, 75, 175–76,
opioids, 203–4
opioid substitution therapy. *See* methadone maintenance therapy
opium, 61, 187, 202–3
opposition literature, 142, 156
opposition movements, 130, 151, 172, 174–75, 180–81, 189, 192; abroad, 143, 145, 149, 160–64; Iranian, 63, 84, 94–95, 127, 132, 135–40, 146; political cartoons by, 112
ordinary prisoners, 16, 20, 29, 189, 222–23; common-law prisoners, 17–18, 106, 108, 169, 171, 173, 200, 213, 231n49
'orf (customary) law, 39–40
Organisation for the Defence of Human Rights in Iran, 137–38
Organization for Islamic Propaganda, 3, 227n10
Organization for the Protection of Prisoners (OPP), 82
Organization of Iranian People's Fadai Guerillas (Fadaian, or OIPFG), 101, 103, 115–16, 121–22, 125, 148, 187, 250n9, 256n111
Organization of Tehran University Students (OSUS), 139
Orientalism, 11, 27, 47, 156, 223
Ottoman Empire, 38–40, 61
Oxford University, 71

Pace, Eric, 150
Pahlavi, Ashraf, 74–75, 134–35, 142, 157
Pahlavi, Farah, 90, 134
Pahlavi, Reza, 220, 227n9
Pahlavi era, 38, 42, 52, 68, 80, 93, 115–16, 193, 200, 224; government, 10, 24–25, 66–67, 96, 100–103, 112, 122, 149, 168–77, 189–90; and human rights, 130–38, 144–45, 147, 150–52, 157–64, 222; monarchy, 2–4, 15, 130, 146, 218; policing, 7, 30–31, 54–55, 58–63, 81–84, 86–87; prisons, 64, 70–78, 88–92, 94, 97–99, 105–11, 118, 121, 129; security, 123–24, 128, 148; torture, 13, 17, 28, 32, 139–40, 142–43, 179–80, 185–86. *See also* Mohammad Reza Shah Pahlavi; Reza Shah Pahlavi
Pahlavi University, 76
Paik, A. Naomi, 27
Paknejad, Shokrollah, 103, 118, 141–42
Pakravan, Hassan, 185
Palestine, 12, 96
Palestine Group, 103, 118, 141
Pan-Africanism, 99
Paremoremo prison, 93
Pars news agency, 167
Partisan Review, 155
patriotic motherhood, 74. *See also* nationalism
Peacock Throne, 82
Peake, Charles Maclean, 87–88
penal code, 3, 55, 78
Penal Code (1917), 62; Article 131, 78
penal reform, 9, 24, 63, 67
PEN International. *See* International PEN
penitentiaries, model of, 9, 24
Penitentiary for Men and Women, 9. *See also* Central Prison for Men and Women
Pennsylvania: Philadelphia, 20–21
penology, 8, 77
People's Ideal, The, 103
People's Mojahedin Organization of Iran (PMOI), 101–3
Perkins, Justin, 42
Persian-British treaty (1836), 40
Persian Language Academy, 66
Peru, 27
Philippines, 143
philosophy, 17, 24, 83, 130, 133
Place of Counsel (Andarzgah), use of term, 9
Pohl, Reynaldo Gallindo, 197
Poland, 155
police, European style, 51, 54–55, 58
policing, 6–10, 15, 26–27, 30–31, 33, 36–38, 86, 179, 207–8, 222–24; modern, 71, 81, 214; morality, 12, 217; Pahlavi, 124, 128; in Tehran, 54–55; US context of, 20–22; US influence on, 63, 84, 87
policymakers, 130, 132–33, 145, 150
political belonging, 7, 221
political cartoons, 97, 112–14
political incarceration, 3, 13, 18–19, 32, 51
political legibility, 22–23
political prisoners, 15, 64, 101, 106, 118, 152, 191. *See also* security prisoners
political prisons, 100, 111
political violence, 46, 97, 101–2, 127–28, 139, 146, 155–56, 158, 160
Pompeo, Mike, 13
positivism, 24, 26, 77
postcolonialism, 99
postmodernists, 27

prerevolutionary prisons, 2–3, 97, 163, 173
prison (zendan), use of word, 9
Prisoner of Conscience Week, 147
Prisoner of Tehran, 2
prisoners of conscience, 16–18, 147
prisoner-workers, 91–92. *See also* prison factories; prison labor
prison expansion, 9, 63–67, 83, 169–77, 195, 211–13, 217
prison factories, 9, 76, 82, 139. *See also* prisoner-workers; prison labor
prison industrial complex, 13
prison labor, 48, 55, 82, 90, 92. *See also* prisoner-workers
prison massacre of 1988, 17, 22, 92, 170, 178, 193, 196, 206, 221
prison memoirs, 2, 8, 14, 71, 121–26, 176
Prison Number One, 64
Prison Number Two, 64
prison poetry, 66, 97, 152
prison reform, 25, 68, 73, 77, 81–94, 223
prisons. *See individual prisons*
prisons, repurposing of, 3, 175
prisons as proof of legitimacy, 2, 67
prisons as rehabilitative, 9, 89, 211
prison sciences, 77
prison slang, 29
Prisons Organization, 7, 25, 170–72, 184, 191–95, 199, 203–4, 210–14
Prisons Organization Research and Education Center, 193
prison system, origins of, 3–6
Problems of Communism (journal), 176
productive citizens, 4, 9–10, 24, 31
Progressive Lawyers Group, 162
progressiveness, 4, 9, 13–14, 49, 67, 78, 82, 96; and prisons, 23–24, 31, 93–94, 98, 139, 223

protestors, 1, 5, 7, 116, 161, 205–10, 219, 221, 223. *See also* activism
Provisional Central Committee of The Communist Party of Iran, 86
Psychiatry Institute of Tehran, 191
public confessions, 102, 182
public executions, 26, 46, 58–59, 205–6, 267n119
public health, 19, 25, 56, 200, 204
public life, 28, 31–32, 97–98, 168, 175, 221–22; of guerrillas, 101–5; and prisons, 6–10, 130–33, 158, 207
punishment, 13–14, 18, 20–21, 30–33, 67, 94, 106, 111, 210, 224; contemporary, 212–14, 217; extrajudicial, 143, 150; history of, 77–79; modern, 4, 6–8, 11, 71, 101; during Pahlavi era, 83, 87–89, 140; painful, 124–25, 152, 158; penitentiary model of, 24; public, 26–28, 59; of Qajar era, 36–48, 50–54; as rehabilitation, 192; in revolutionary Iran, 173–74, 178–79, 182; and SAVAK, 108. *See also* death penalty

Qahremani, Mahmud, 79–80
Qajar era, 4, 18, 30, 34–54, 56–59, 61–64, 67, 106, 115, 222–23
Qajar palace, 68–69
Qalibaf, Mohammad Baqer, 207
Qasr Prison, 14, 84, 91, 106, 114–15, 118, 121, 126–27, 136, 172, 231n48; history of, 4–6, 68–73; and Tudeh Party, 8, 108–11
Qasr Prison Museum, 176, 242n30
Qazvin, 67, 185
Qezel-e Sorkh. *See* Qezel Qalʻeh Prison
Qezel Hesar Prison, 92, 173
Qezel Qalʻeh Prison, 107–8, 125, 136

Qoddusi, Ali, 182
Qom, 219
Qom Seminary, 215
Qotbzadeh, Sadeq, 186–87, 189
Qur'an, 110

racism, 13, 19–21; anti-Black, 22–23
Radji, Parviz, 144, 151
Rafsanjani, Ali Akbar Hashemi, 148, 198–99, 277n25
Rahmani, Rebin, 200, 278n36
Raisi, Ebrahim, 206, 221
Raja'i, Mohammad 'Ali, 184–85
Rajaishahr Prison. *See* Gohar Dasht Prison
Rastakhiz Party, 163
Reagan, Ronald, 19
Red Castle. *See* Qezel Qal'eh Prison
Red Cross, 112, 151
Refah School, 179
refugees, 18, 172, 271n32
regicide, 143, 148
Regional Office for the Eastern Mediterranean of the World Health Organization (WHO/EMRO), 199–200
Regulatory Code Governing Prisons and Affiliated Industrial and Agricultural Institutes, 91
rehabilitation, 9, 23, 67, 79, 89, 192–93, 211, 222, 224
Rejali, Darius, 28
reparative justice, 19
repression, 23, 54, 134, 138, 152–53, 156, 221, 224; global forms of, 21, 96; Pahlavi, 98–100, 109, 118, 121, 145, 162; state, 30, 95
Resurrection Party. *See* Rastakhiz Party
retaliation, 39, 173–74

Reuter concession (1872), 34
Revolutionary Committees. *See* Komiteh-ye Enqelab
Rezai, Hossein, 149–50
Rezai, Mohsen, 208
Reza Khan. *See* Reza Shah Pahlavi
Reza Shah Pahlavi, 4, 31, 38, 78, 84–85, 141, 183, 228n17; prisons under, 7–10, 49, 60–70, 106. *See also* Pahlavi era
Ridgeway, James, 160
riot control, 15, 88
Rokn-e dovvom. *See* Second Bureau
Rouholamini, Abdolhossein, 208–9
Rouholamini, Mohsen, 208–9
Ruggles-Brise, Evelyn, 67–68
Russell, Bertrand, 12, 32, 137–38, 142, 145
Russia, 25, 30, 52, 56, 269n17. *See also* Soviet Union
Russian Empire, 36, 61

Sabeti, Parviz, 150, 220–21
Sadat, Anwar, 179
Sadeghi-Boroujerdi, Eskandar, 198
Sadeq, Naser, 103, 251n19
Saduk (attempted murderer of Tanfield), 34–35. *See also* Tanfield (victim of Saduk's attack)
Safabi, Navab, 8
Saffari, Siavash, 85
Saif, Abdollah Khan, 67
Sale, Richard, 156
Salehabad Prison, 171
Samakar, Abbas, 106, 109, 231n48
Sanandaj, 173
sanctions, 13, 32, 99, 137, 170, 215
Sartre, Jean-Paul, 12, 32
SAVAK, 15, 96, 102–3, 105–8, 144–45, 148, 150–52, 166–68, 174–76, 220–21; and interrogation, 122–23, 136; targeting

SAVAK (cont.)
of, 178, 185–87; and torture, 112, 120, 127–30, 134, 139–42, 158–60; US involvement with, 15, 85–86; violence by, 118, 125
Sazman-e ettela'at va amniyat-e keshvar. See SAVAK
Sazman-e qaza'i-e artesh-e jomhuri-ye eslami. See Judicial Organization of the Military of the Islamic Republic
Sazman-e tabliqat-e eslami. See Organization for Islamic Propaganda
Sazman-e zendanha va eghdamat-e ta'mini va tarbiyati-e keshvar. See Prisons Organization
Schayegh, Cyrus, 76–77
Schenwar, Maya, 214
schools, 26, 68, 75, 77, 176; prisons as, 8–9, 76. See also education; virtue training schools
Schreiber, Marc, 136
scientific socialism, 86
Second Bureau, 84–86
security prisoners, 17–18. See also political prisoners
semicolonialism, 24, 99
Serena, Carla, 47
sexually transmitted infections, 200, 203. See also HIV/AIDS
sex work, 17, 190, 220
Shah, the. See Mohammad Reza Shah Pahlavi
Shahid Beheshti University of Medical Sciences, 201
Shahrbani-ye kol-e keshvar. See National Police Force
Shahr-e Kord, 211
Shahri, Ja'far, 44–45
Shahrokni, Nazanin, 197
Shahshahani, Abolfazl, 180
Shakarami, Nika, 209
Shamlu, Ahmad, 109, 235n84; *Book of the Street*, 29–30
Shannon, Matthew K., 150, 258n8
sharia (Islamic law), 11, 39–41, 61, 63, 173–74, 179, 185, 236n17
Shari'ati, Ali, 97, 110
Shariatmadari, Ayatollah Mohammad Kazem, 182
Shi'ism, 40, 116
Shiraz, 11, 76, 92, 151, 173
Shiraz Arts Festival, 152
Shirdel, Kamran, 78, 244n62; *Women's Penitentiary*, 73–74
Shooshtari, Ayatollah Mohammad Esmail, 204
Siahkal uprising, 95–96, 101–3, 109–11, 115–16, 118, 121–22, 124
Siam. See Thailand
Siavoshi, Sussan, 111
Sistan, 56
slavery, 22
social deviance, 9, 31, 222
socialism, 85–86. See also scientific socialism
social work, prison expansion as, 9, 92
social worlds, 3, 8–9, 28–29, 100, 139
sociology, 24, 67, 76, 79, 89, 111, 147, 170, 197, 241–42n26
solitary confinement, 11, 28, 93, 107–8, 110, 200, 204, 269n12
Solzhenitsyn, Aleksandr, 157; *Gulag Archipelago*, 153–55, 265n101
Sotoudeh, Nasrin, 1, 231n49

INDEX   335

Southeast Asia, 143
sovereignty, 4, 10, 26, 28, 30, 37, 40, 45, 58, 62
Soviet Union, 83, 154–55, 176. *See also* Russia
Spain, 135
Stalin, Joseph, 83
Stalinism, 83, 176, 266n106
state power, 27, 30, 97–98, 100, 102, 132
state violence, 94, 96–97, 140, 143, 154, 165
State Welfare Organization, 202
stocks. *See* kundeh
Strange Times, My Dear (anthology), 153
student activists, 101, 107, 125, 207. *See also* Confederation of Iranian Students, National Union (CISNU); Organization of Tehran University Students (OSUS); United States Iranian Students Association (USISA)
Sunnism, 40
Supreme Judicial Council, 171
surveillance, 6–12, 26, 81, 110, 167, 172, 203–5, 210, 213–17, 222–24; and SAVAK, 85–87, 150; surveillance state, 20, 125; techniques of, 14, 33, 58, 195, 212
Susskind, David, 153
Sweden, 51, 57–59, 64, 81
Switzerland: Geneva, 76, 140, 150

Tabatabai-Qomi, Ayatollah Taqi, 182
Tabriz, 83, 173
Tabriz University, 76
Tahereh Qurrat al-'Ayn. *See* Baraghani, Fatemeh Zarrin-Taj
Talebi, Shahla, 125, 152, 176

Taleghani, Ayatollah Mahmoud, 130, 148
Tanfield (victim of Saduk's attack), 34–35. *See also* Saduk (attempted murderer of Tanfield)
Tanzimat reforms, 38
Taqut nameh (pamphlet), 113–14
Tarde, Gabriel, 24, 67, 79, 242n26
Taregol, Houshang, 103–4
Tasnim News Agency, 215
Taylor, Elizabeth, 160–61
ta'zir, 39, 173. *See also* diyat; hudud
technocracy, 31–32, 77, 93, 96, 190, 192, 195–205
Tehran, 4; Citadel Square (Maydan-e arg), 49; Khak-e Sefid neighborhood, 207; Tupkhaneh Square (Maydan-e tupkhaneh), 58
Tehran Film Festival, 152
Tehrani. *See* Naderpour, Bahram
Tehran Morality Police, 11–12, 217, 219
Tehran Police Academy, 81
Ten Days of Dawn, 166
Thailand, 68, 135, 269n17
Third Worldism, 99, 115, 126, 130, 139, 143, 165, 258n3, 259n24, 260n31
Time (magazine), 111
Times (newspaper), 144
tobacco revolt (1890s), 34–35, 52
Tofighian, Omid, 172
Towhid Committee. *See* Oneness of God Committee
transnationalism, 11–16, 21, 23, 33, 130
Treaty of Turkmenchay (1828), 40
Trotskyism, 155, 266n106
Tudeh Party, 8, 84–86, 96, 139, 157, 189, 262n51; incarcerated members of, 107, 109, 111, 143, 176
Turkey, 140, 159

ulama, 54, 98, 110–11, 138, 176, 180–81, 184, 188, 192; Shiʿa, 39–40, 148
UNESCO, 76
Unite! (bookstore), 142
United Nations (UN), 76, 131, 134–38, 141, 144–46, 157, 162, 197, 203, 262n65
United Nations Security Council, 184–85
United States, 4, 19–20, 27, 129, 144, 160, 162, 164, 169, 199; and drugs, 188, 203; Iranians in the, 99, 138–39; prisons in, 11, 92; and SAVAK, 15, 150, 247n116
United States Iranian Students Association (USISA), 139
Universal Declaration of Human Rights (1948), 136, 141, 145–46, 161, 259n24
University of Geneva, 63
University of Judicial Sciences and Administrative Services, 25
University of St. Petersburg, 68
University of Tehran, 76–77, 79, 81, 125, 162
UN Office on Drugs and Crime (UNODC), 203
UN Security Council Resolution 598, 196
US Congress, 32, 130, 150, 152, 156
US Department of State, 18, 84, 87–88, 246n97, 264n81
US Department of the Treasury, 13
US Federal Bureau of Narcotics, 87
US federal supermax system, 11
US government, 2, 129–30
US House Subcommittee on International Organizations, 150
US Marxist-Leninist Communist Party, 142–43
US military, 13, 15, 63, 86–88, 146, 159
US Office of Public Safety, 84

USP Marion, 11, 92–93. *See also* Marion Penitentiary
US policymakers, 130, 132–33, 145, 150
utopian terror, 177–90

Vahabzadeh, Peyman, 121
Vakil Abad Prison, 90, 108
Vartan, Melik, 43
Vazifeh (newspaper), 71
vernacular language, 29, 235n84
Vietnam, 12, 96; Saigon, 138
Vietnam War, 146, 158–60
Village Voice, 160
virtue training schools, 9

Wallace, Mike, 129, 150, 177, 257n1
Ward 209, 222. *See also* Evin Prison
Warhol, Andy, 160–61
war on narcotics, 15, 87
Washington, DC, 84, 153
Washington Post, 185
Westdahl, Gunnar, 58, 60
"Westoxification," concept of, 157. *See also* Al-e Ahmad, Jalal
White Revolution, 82, 84, 86, 112, 138, 145, 187, 246n103, 252n37
white torture, 28
Whyte, J. F., 35
Williams, E. C., 56
Williams, Garland, 87
Wills, C. J., 45, 47–48
Wilson, William, 149
Woman, Life, Freedom uprising, 1, 205, 210, 217, 219
women's rights, 134–35
World Health Organization (WHO), 200, 203
worldmaking, 96, 99

Yazd, 36
Yazdi, Ebrahim, 162, 185
"Year of the Woman," 135
Yushij, Nima, 66

Zaghari-Ratcliffe, Nazanin, 1
Zahedi, Ardeshir, 144, 152–53, 160–61, 257n1
Zanjan, 44
Zanjani, Ayatollah Mousa Shobiri, 215
zanjirkhaneh, 46–47

Zarinebaf, Fariba, 39
Zarkari, Yusef: *Khater-at-e yek cherik dar zenan* (*Memoir of a Guerilla in Prison*), 121–28
zendan, use of, 9, 66
Zendan-e markazi-ye mardan va zanan. *See* Central Prison for Men and Women
zendani-ye 'adi. *See* ordinary prisoners
zendani-ye amniyati. *See* security prisoners

Stanford Studies in Middle Eastern and
Islamic Societies and Cultures

Laleh Khalili and Sherene Seikaly, editors
Joel Beinin, founding editor

Elastic Empire: Refashioning War Through Aid in Palestine   2023
    LISA BHUNGALIA

Colonizing Palestine: The Zionist Left and the Making of the Palestinian Nakba   2023
    AREEJ SABBAGH-KHOURY

On Salafism: Concepts and Contexts   2023
    AZMI BISHARA

Revolutions Aesthetic: A Cultural History of Ba'thist Syria   2022
    MAX WEISS

Street-Level Governing: Negotiating the State in Urban Turkey   2022
    ELISE MASSICARD

Protesting Jordan: Geographies of Power and Dissent   2022
    JILLIAN SCHWEDLER

Media of the Masses: Cassette Culture in Modern Egypt   2022
    ANDREW SIMON

States of Subsistence: The Politics of Bread in Contemporary Jordan   2022
    JOSÉ CIRO MARTÍNEZ

Between Dreams and Ghosts: Indian Migration and Middle Eastern Oil   2021
    ANDREA WRIGHT

Bread and Freedom: Egypt's Revolutionary Situation   2021
    MONA EL-GHOBASHY

Paradoxes of Care: Children and Global Medical Aid in Egypt   2021
    RANIA KASSAB SWEIS

The Politics of Art: Dissent and Cultural Diplomacy in Lebanon, Palestine, and Jordan 2021
    HANAN TOUKAN

The Paranoid Style in American Diplomacy: Oil and Arab Nationalism in Iraq 2021
    BRANDON WOLFE-HUNNICUTT

Screen Shots: State Violence on Camera in Israel and Palestine 2021
    REBECCA L. STEIN

Dear Palestine: A Social History of the 1948 War 2021
    SHAY HAZKANI

A Critical Political Economy of the Middle East and North Africa 2020
    JOEL BEININ, BASSAM HADDAD, AND SHERENE SEIKALY, EDITORS

Showpiece City: How Architecture Made Dubai 2020
    TODD REISZ

Archive Wars: The Politics of History in Saudi Arabia 2020
    ROSIE BSHEER

Between Muslims: Religious Difference in Iraqi Kurdistan 2020
    J. ANDREW BUSH

The Optimist: A Social Biography of Tawfiq Zayyad 2020
    TAMIR SOREK

Graveyard of Clerics: Everyday Activism in Saudi Arabia 2020
    PASCAL MENORET

Cleft Capitalism: The Social Origins of Failed Market Making in Egypt 2020
    AMR ADLY

The Universal Enemy: Jihad, Empire, and the Challenge of Solidarity 2019
    DARRYL LI

Waste Siege: The Life of Infrastructure in Palestine 2019
    SOPHIA STAMATOPOULOU-ROBBINS

Heritage and the Cultural Struggle for Palestine 2019
    CHIARA DE CESARI

For a complete listing of titles in this series, visit the Stanford University Press website, www.sup.org.

The authorized representative in the EU for product safety and compliance is:
Mare Nostrum Group
B.V Doelen 72
4831 GR Breda
The Netherlands

www.ingramcontent.com/pod-product-compliance
Lightning Source LLC
Chambersburg PA
CBHW031754220426
43662CB00007B/397